DATE DUE

WITHDRAWN

See,
I Told
You So

Also by Rush Limbaugh

The Way Things Ought to Be

RUSH
H. LIMBAUGH, III

See, I Told You So

POCKET BOOKS
New York London Toronto Sydney Tokyo Singapore

POCKET BOOKS, a division of Simon & Schuster Inc.
1230 Avenue of the Americas, New York, NY 10020

Library of Congress Cataloging-in-Publication Number: 93-86342

ISBN: 0-671-88807-2

First Pocket Books Special Edition printing November 1993

10 9 8 7 6 5 4 3 2 1

POCKET and colophon are registered trademarks of
Simon & Schuster Inc.

Printed in the U.S.A.

To my grandfather, Rush H. Limbaugh,
who celebrated his 102nd birthday on September 27, 1993.
Thank you, Pop, for your guidance,
your sterling example, and most of all your love.
You are the Limbaugh America should know.

ACKNOWLEDGMENTS

SPECIAL THANKS TO JOSEPH FARAH, A DEDICATED CONSERVATIVE soul brother from Sacramento, California, who devoted several months to this project. His precise recommendations regarding the structure of the book and advice on how to build upon *The Way Things Ought to Be* provided the guiding force behind the effort and are deeply appreciated.

My brother, David Limbaugh, as with the first book, edited with the touch of a true artist. Thank you so much.

Diana Schneider, editor extraordinaire of my newsletter, *The Limbaugh Letter*, provided expert finishing touches and made herself available on a moment's notice despite the overwhelming demands on her time. Ditto Denise Mei, graphics editor of *The Limbaugh Letter*, who assembled the charts and tables.

My very good friend and economics adviser Thomas W. Hazlett of the University of California at Davis provided invaluable expertise, knowledge, and painstaking research for the chapter on the Fairness Doctrine. This chapter was a late addition, and Tom, a noted national expert on the Federal Communications Commission and telecommunications, went into high gear to make deadline. I can't thank him enough.

I also extend deep gratitude to my friend Roger Ailes, who offered his crack research specialist, Zack Van Amberg of Ailes Communications in New York, to assist in the research required to assemble this massive work.

ACKNOWLEDGMENTS

Once again, I express my heartfelt gratitude and appreciation for the encouragement, advice, and sheer perseverance of my editor, Judith Regan, who, in addition to suggesting spicy augmentations and surgical erasures, defended the project against attack from the customary leftist quarters. We are learning together the price of being politically incorrect in the world of New York publishing

Thanks are also in order for the meticulous work and thoughtful assistance of Jonathon Brodman and Dr. Jeffrey Schwartz.

And let me here acknowledge the appreciation I have for my staff, Kit "H. R." Carson, James Golden, and Kathy Dellacava, for their understanding, patience, and just plain great work.

Finally, I thank my wonderful audience, without whom none of this would be possible. Your loyalty and support mean so much.

CONTENTS

Introduction xiii

1 I Answered My Phone 1

2 The Power of You: You Make
   It Work 11

3 America Is Not Over 23

4 New Democrats: Yeah, Yeah 34

5 Punishing Achievement 53

6 Dead White Guys
       Or
   What Your History Books
   Never Told You 66

7 Are Values Obsolete?
       Or
   How to Win the Culture War 78

CONTENTS

8   Dan Quayle Is Right
     Or
     Our Poverty of Values 90

9   Dan's Bake Sale 101

10   Eight Years of Reagan:
     The Eighties Was Not a
     Decade of Greed 110

11   The Decade of Fraud and Deceit 127

12   To Your Health, Hillary
     Or
     Understanding the Politics
     of Meaning 142

13   *Algore:* Technology Czar 158

14   The O! Zone—An Environmental
     Update 171

15   The Dumbing-Down of America 185

16   The Latest from the Feminist
     "Front" 200

17   Words Mean Things 214

18   Political Correctness and the
     Coming of the Thought Police 227

19   Conservatism and Race 239

CONTENTS

20 America Is Still Worth Fighting For 249

21 The Case for Less Government 262

22 The Many Purposes of Culture 274

23 Lies Are Facts; Facts Are Lies 286

24 There They Go Again 295

25 The Politically Correct Liberal
   Lexicon 309

26 "The Hush Rush Law" 323

27 A Summary and Prescription
   for the Future 341

   Index 355

INTRODUCTION

YOU HOLD IN YOUR HOT LITTLE HANDS, MY FRIENDS, AMERICA'S NEXT great publishing milestone. Soon, *See, I Told You So* will eclipse all publishing records known in the English-speaking world—most of which, by the way, were set by my first tome, *The Way Things Ought to Be*.

But this book was never supposed to be. In fact, the conventional wisdom was that after the 1992 election, I was just going to fade away into obscurity—a relic of a Republican era of greed and selfishness. They said there would be no room for me in the Age of Compassion that would assuredly be dawning come January 20, 1993.

Well, once again, the "experts" were wrong. Dead wrong. Not only did the Rush Limbaugh radio program soar to new, previously uncharted heights in the annals of Marconi's invention, but my television show also became the nation's hottest new late-night program. *The Limbaugh Letter*, my stellar journal of opinion, became what is arguably the most successful start-up publication in history. And, of course, we all know about the first book—which is still setting records in hardcover sales as this follow-up goes to press.

Let's see now: I've conquered radio, television, the newsletter business, and the book world. How is this possible? How could this be? Why have I been so successful in areas where so many others have tried and failed? What accounts for the unprecedented popularity of my words—whether broadcast or in print? How do I defy all the odds, again and again? It's actually quite simple.

"Finally! Here is someone saying what I think" is the most often-heard reaction people have when they are exposed to my ruminations. People respond to what I say because it is right. My wit and wisdom are like a lifeline of reason tossed to a culture nearly drowning in confusion and murkiness. No wonder more people are clinging to my hopeful and incisive words every day.

That's why I decided to write *See, I Told You So.* I wanted to accomplish several things at once. First, so many important developments have occurred since *The Way Things Ought to Be* was published—from the election of Bill Clinton to Dan's Bake Sale—that there was a lot of ground to cover. Second, there were issues and topics I didn't get a chance to address in the first book—sacred cows that were, until now, never skewered (or gored, as the case might be). But, most important, I realized early on just how right I have been about so much.

And that's the theme of this book. But don't mistake this as an exercise in self-aggrandizement. I don't need any more ego gratification. Like everything I touch, this book is on the cutting edge of societal evolution. It is loaded with insight, brimming with profoundity. It explodes the hypocrisy, fraud, and deceit of the liberalism that is holding this nation hostage. It shatters the lies of the Clinton administration that are routinely covered up by the dominant media. It sets the agenda for conservative thought through the remainder of what historians will someday refer to as the Era of Limbaugh.

But I should interject a word of caution here. Not all of you about to plunge into this wellspring of undiluted truth are conservatives. No doubt hundreds of thousands of liberals are picking up this book out of curiosity, perhaps, or maybe in the desperate pursuit of opposition research. For those of you who fit this description, I want you to prepare yourself. Make certain you are in familiar surroundings, sitting down, wearing comfortable clothing, and have not inhaled any illicit substances for at least the last thirty minutes. Should shortness of breath occur as you immerse yourself in the following pages, be sure to seek the assistance of an experienced conservative counselor. You may well need someone to talk you through this.

As you read this book, you will encounter a great number of themes interwoven throughout its pages. Some points will resurface in various chapters of the book because, although each chapter stands on its own, this is an integrated work. It is important for you to understand that my purpose is not to trash liberals or liberalism, but merely to elucidate the many political and economic issues and events of our times. In illuminating these issues for you, I admittedly speak from a decidedly conservative worldview. In the process, an inevitable discussion of the liberal worldview ensues. And though I believe liberalism to be a misguided, destructive political and cultural philosophy, I do not endeavor to personally indict, impugn, or castigate all of its purveyors. I've said this a hundred times: This is not personal and it is not about personalities. It's about the future of this country. Though I denounce liberalism's effect on our body politic, our culture, and our society, I deliberately eschew alarmism and fatalism. I reject the pessimistic notion that our nation is so infected with cultural poisons that it has one foot in the grave. Why should right-thinking people capitulate just because Bill Clinton and a liberal Democratic Congress are in office? This gives us the golden opportunity to demonstrate the failure of their ideas. They are now in control and will not be able to escape accountability. Mr. Clinton and his Ivy League colleagues are now relatively free to use this country as their grand laboratory experiment. All of their theorems will be tested, with America and all Americans (not just the wealthy) as their guinea pigs. But don't despair. They don't have enough savvy to ruin this country in four years, even if they try. America is much more resilient than that. The only thing we must guard against once the inevitable failure of their programs manifests itself is the rhetorical spin Mr. Clinton and his propagandists will immediately place on it. Later in the book I forecast for you some of the excuses they will offer when their programs fail, so I won't spoil it for you by telling you here. Just keep a sharp eye out and be prepared to combat their propaganda, sophistry, and history revision with the truth. For, as I have told you, you must have the courage to believe the truth. And always, be of good cheer and remember how to smile. This will always distinguish you from your liberal friends. Pour yourselves a Snapple, prop your feet up, and enjoy.

You are, my friends, about to be exposed to the kind of bristling, cogent analysis available nowhere else. Because of this, your initial reaction may be shock and disbelief. But this, too, shall pass. It is merely the normal, reflexive reaction to unbridled truth. Don't fight it. Don't even try. Surrender yourself.

In time—in fact, before you finish digesting this sage guidebook —you will come to the inevitable conclusion that I am right, have been right, and will likely continue to be right in the future. You will find that the information is accurate, the explication sound, the analysis penetrating, and the format profound. I predict you will, before too long, even begin to enjoy this. Don't be afraid. It's okay. Really.

Meanwhile, prepare your mind to be challenged as it has never been challenged before. Don't be surprised if your brain is stimulated to the point that genuine human thought takes place. This is normal for non-liberals. You are making progress.

One more thing. Since this book is largely devoted to recording and documenting my many searing insights and successful prognostications, let me reiterate and affirm one more. The conventional wisdom, once again, is betting against me. It seems there's something of a sophomore jinx in publishing. Second books, it is said, never sell as well as first efforts. Well, that, ladies and gentlemen, is simply because, until now, I had never written a second book. I just hope those publishing experts are smart enough to get out of the way of the stampedes this book will inevitably incite at retail outlets all over the fruited plain. Here it comes. *See, I told you so!*

"Our wretched species is so made that those who walk on the well-trodden path always throw stones at those who are showing a new road."

—*Voltaire*

"If one advances confidently in the direction of his dreams, and endeavors to live the life which he has imagined, he will meet with a success unexpected in common hours."

—*Henry David Thoreau*

"It has been said that though God cannot alter the past, historians can."

—*Samuel Butler*

"The fundamental idea of modern capitalism is not the right of the individual to possess and enjoy what he has earned, but the thesis that the exercise of this right redounds to the general good."

—*Ralph Barton Perry*

"Society in every state is a blessing, but Government, even in its best state, is but a necessary evil; in its worst state, an intolerable one."

—*Thomas Paine*

"The office of government is not to confer happiness, but to give men opportunity to work out happiness for themselves."

—*William Ellery Channing*

"They can conquer who believe they can."

—*Virgil*

"Isn't it amazing that these guys knew all this . . . without having to listen to me?"

—*Rush Limbaugh, October 10, 1993*

1

I ANSWERED MY PHONE

"SO, MR. LIMBAUGH . . . WHEN DO YOU HOPE TO CONQUER AMERICA? And after you do, Mr. Limbaugh, just how oppressive will you be?"

No matter how many times I hear this misguided line of questioning from the media, it still surprises me. Why? Because I'm a nice guy—a harmless little fuzzball with a strong live-and-let-live credo. The furthest thing from my mind is to carry out some devious master plan to "take over the airwaves" and impose my views on anyone.

As I've said many times before, but it bears repeating, I work in the media. My job—whether on radio, TV, or in the publishing field—is to attract as large an audience as possible and maintain it as long as I can. That's not to say that I don't believe passionately in the ideas I espouse. I do. In fact, I hold to my convictions with every bit as much fervor as any other commentator or talk-show host. Maybe more.

"But what are your goals, Mr. Limbaugh? You are, after all, everywhere—on radio, TV, in bookstores. Do you really expect us to believe, sir, that this is not part of a cunning strategy to further your agenda and foist your opinions on the rest of us?"

If these journalists were really doing their jobs, they would be directing these questions at Ross Perot rather than at me, don't you think? What have I done to warrant this baseless charge of nefarious plotting? Or, looked at another way, how did I become this beacon of virtue, morality, and clear-headed thinking in such troubled times of murkiness, gloom, and despair? The truth, ladies and gentlemen, is that I didn't seek out this position of national mentorship to which I have now been elevated; I didn't solicit any volunteers; I simply answered my phone. Let me explain.

My radio show has grown from 56 stations to more than 600 in under five years. The phone rang. Reporters asked questions. I answered them. I was written up, talked about—mostly reviled—and the phone kept on ringing. I was invited to appear on television: "Nightline," "60 Minutes," "Good Morning America," "Today," "Meet the Press," and yes, my friends, even "A Current Affair." I was asked to write a book. That book, the record-setting *The Way Things Ought to Be*, became the fastest-selling hardcover non-fiction book in the history of its publisher, Simon & Schuster Inc. Sales totaled 2.5 million copies in less than a year. I was asked to host my own television show. And, within months, despite the unanimous prediction of failure, the program was outdrawing both David Letterman's and Arsenio Hall's shows. I answered the phone and was asked to pen tome No. 2—which you, esteemed and discerning readers, are now highly privileged to possess.

Again, I did not seek out any of this. It is simply that my achievements—and they are considerable—have generated new opportunities. Success begets further success—kind of an internal trickle-up. My liberal critics would never acknowledge that pursuing excellence requires prodigious energy and commitment, and that the overwhelming majority of successful people have earned what they have. That's one of the many reasons achievers should not be punished. When you punish people for engaging in certain behavior, that behavior is deterred. So to punish the successful, for example, with confiscatory taxes is to take aim at hard work and productivity. And if you deter productivity, whose pockets will the liberals have left to pick in order to fund their redistributionist programs? Liberals, you see, believe that opportunities are created by government, not by individual achievement. So, if doors are opening to me, they assume it must be the result of some unfair advantage available to me at the expense of the "more deserving." An enticing thought, but the fact is, the short, preceding paragraph summarizes years of enormous effort.

Some people seem to think that at a certain level of success, everything becomes a breeze. Nothing could be further from the truth. Actually, I have to prove myself every day—live, impromptu, extemporaneously, without the benefit of TelePrompTers, or cue cards, before millions of viewers and listeners. All creative endeavors demand acute focus and intense concentration. And my incomparable level of performance, and the preparation it requires, is hard work—as is staying knowledgeable, motivated, passionate; and ready, willing, and able to articulate my core beliefs.

Before sitting down to compose this second bestseller, I toyed with the idea of writing an editorial for my newsletter entitled "What It's Like to Be Me." The angle was to show what a day in the life of Rush is really like. Then I scratched the concept. Why? Because as wonderful, incomparable, satisfying, and fun as it is to be me, I realized that a typical day in my life is, ultimately, about work. A chronicle of someone's work schedule may not make for such interesting reading, but it is my work, for the most part, which dictates my schedule and activities. I am just so fortunate that to me it doesn't seem like work, because I am doing what I love.

As host, I need to be informed. So I read voraciously—nine newspapers a day, to be exact, in addition to the countless magazines and books I devour relentlessly. I swim in faxes sent to me by my audience, whose collective contributions represent the best clipping service in America today. I receive at least fifteen serious speaking offers every month, though I must turn down more than 99 percent. Monday through Friday, I do three live hours of the most sophisticated, spontaneous, entertaining, and informative talk radio in the universe. Every day I host a thirty-minute television program that has already become one of the highest-rated late-night shows. I write best-selling books. I publish the fastest-growing non-financial monthly newsletter in the country. Frankly, folks, there is little time for anything else.

This is what it is like to be me. It's hard work. But I wouldn't trade it for anything. After all, this is what I have sought. Despite the suspicions of critics and pundits, my goal is not to conquer America for conservatism (although that eventually will happen). My goal is, has been, and always will be the pursuit of excellence. (In addition to making fun of Secretary of Health and Human Services Donna Shalala and Secretary of Labor Robert B. Reich*hhhh*—but that's just gravy.)

Still, there's something very significant about the cynicism implicit in the attacks by my critics. Their recurring questions about my supposedly sinister motives reveal something disturbing about the way our society has changed in recent years. We no longer think about success the way we once did. Liberals, as well as an increasing number of average apolitical citizens, have no idea how America works; what success is; how it happens; what it means; and just how common and accessible it still is in this country . . . without government help! In addition, more and more people have been propagandized to believe that anyone who is successful has somehow stolen his success, is selfish, greedy, cruel, criminal, or worse. (What's worse than being criminal? Being a conservative, of course.) These misconceptions are extremely dangerous to the health and well-being of our country. And, unfortunately, like some dreadful disease, they are infecting the minds of the general population.

Let me give you an example. An Illinois woman once called in to my radio show to tell me how pitiful her family's economic plight was. I asked her to imagine what it would take to get her out of this hole. It turns out that the best thing she could think of to get her life back on track was to receive a little tax refund from the federal government.

As politely as I could, I tried to tell her she was simply hoping for the wrong thing. She, too, was trapped into that dependency mind-set. It is wrong to expect some kind of payment from the government as a reward for being an honest, hard-working, taxpaying citizen. The government—local, state, and federal—is already taking too much of our money through taxes. Any little bit it returns to us after income-tax time should not be considered a gift, because it has already taken too much from our paychecks to begin with.

The government has succeeded in convincing most people to overpay their taxes. Some people actually arrange to have more of their salaries withheld in order to get bigger refund checks later on. This pattern of forced savings breeds a distorted notion of the government's role as provider and caretaker. Why let the government get far more than it requires just so you can get some of it back with no interest? See how easy it is to fool some people? Just because they receive a refund check (of money that was due them in the first place) that allows them to go out and buy something, people get the false impression that they have outsmarted the IRS.

Meanwhile, as the government is picking our pockets, the liberal media establishment is constantly beating the drum for even higher taxes to fund more do-good, social-welfare programs and "get even" with the so-called rich. The press loves to exaggerate the magnitude of their pet problems/causes by labeling them "crises." A crisis, you see, virtually demands, then assures, government intervention—the liberals' perpetual panacea. Never mind that the government's track record for solving social problems is abysmal. And don't wait for the liberal media to point this out.

But when was the last time you saw your local newspaper (at least if you are on either the East or Left coasts) profile a successful entrepreneur who pulled himself up by the bootstraps and built a business that has created jobs for people throughout the community? I'll bet you can't remember, right? Why? Is this not happening anymore in America? Of course it is. It's just not fashionable anymore to call attention to it. And I think that is tragic.

This cynicism about private-sector success and achievement is harmful to our society, but it's even more destructive to the individuals who harbor it. It breeds contempt for the ethic of self-reliance and, ultimately, fosters dependency. I remember a terrible scene after the Los Angeles riots, when block after block of South Central L.A. had been reduced to smoldering rubble. There, in the aftermath, television news reports showed lines of people forming in front of piles of brick and glass shards where the U.S. Post Office had once stood. People were gathering as usual, lining up, on the day they would ordinarily receive and cash their welfare checks. As the camera panned the faces in the crowd—and I'll never forget this scene—so many of these people had tears streaming down their cheeks.

It was a wrenching image for me, because I saw the hopelessness

5

of these folks who had never been encouraged to consider an alternative to this way of life. There would be no checks cashed that day: Rioters had burned and destroyed most of the locations that cashed their checks. And the limited experience of those in line caused them to be so totally oriented toward dependence on government that when it was temporarily unavailable, they were utterly lost. This, my friends, is an illustration of the heartbreaking, dignity-robbing, heinous effects of liberalism.

To liberals, compassion means expanding the dependency cycle and spreading the misery among that ever-growing dependency class. What's worse, another class of people—those who make a living in the massive welfare bureaucracies—has been empowered by what can only be characterized as institutionalized oppression. Ever wonder why no welfare bureaucracy has ever solved a problem and disbanded? Because those who work in them depend on them for their livelihood. They literally have a vested interest in ensuring that conditions never really improve. In fact, if conditions deteriorate, the welfare bureaucracy expands. This is yet another reason that the problems of our inner cities have become progressively worse, even though the federal government has poured more than $3.5 trillion into social programs since the Great Society programs of the 1960s.

The only government bureaucracy that is shrinking in size is the one that was successful in, not to mention essential to, the preservation of our liberty—the military. The military's job was to maintain the readiness and to perform at a level of excellence sufficient to enable us to win the Cold War. It did. Mission accomplished. And what is the military's reward? Massive budget cuts, base closings, and attempts by civilians and anti-military politicians to conduct silly little social experiments on the remaining ranks. But with the exception of the military, I defy you to name one government program that has worked and alleviated the problem it was created to solve. Hhhmmmmmmm? I'm waiting. . . . Time's up.

I remember another lady who called in to my radio show to complain that life was just not treating her fairly. She told me she had been out of work for more than a year. She had been on many job interviews, but was not being offered employment in her chosen career as a secretary. What were the potential employers telling her? That she needed more training, particularly in the area of dictation. Did she take the hint and get the additional training? No. She was complaining that employers lacked compassion and understanding, and therefore thought the government should be concerned enough about it to retrain her. This is how we have been programmed. Too many people are waiting for the government to solve their problems instead of taking the initiative themselves.

So how do we break this growing cycle of government dependency? Simply, people need to be re-oriented and re-educated. (Have no fear, my liberal friends, this will not require special camps. We merely need to penetrate the film of confusion created by liberal psychobabble with the piercing power of undiluted logic and common sense.) People simply need to be shown what made this country great and how to access opportunity. We need to emphasize excellence—not equality, sameness, or fairness. The Founding Fathers, who liberals fraudulently identify as their soul mates, incorporated into the Constitution the principle of equality of opportunity, not equality of result. Like the Founding Fathers, we must understand that individual and national excellence can be achieved only if we reward rather than punish achievement and success.

My hysterical critics often accuse me of "threatening democracy." To the contrary, ladies and gentlemen, it would be more accurate to describe me as Rush Limbaugh, D.D.—Doctor of Democracy. We don't need national health insurance and socialized medicine, Hillary. I have the cure for what ails us. Here's my prescription: Self-reliance. Morality. Personal responsibility. Optimism and good cheer. Confidence in the irrepressibility of the human spirit. Dependence not on the government, but on the universal yearning for freedom and the desire to make life better for oneself and one's family. These are the underpinnings of the free market, and we need free-market solutions, not government remedies. That's my specialty, and I do make house calls.

Because I articulate these old-fashioned values, I am cursed and condemned—by the "sensitive" and "tolerant" among us. You must never underestimate just how threatening this message of self-reliance is to liberals. Why? Because they truly don't believe people can take care of themselves. Moreover, they don't want them to. If there are fewer people in need, there is less demand for the expansive role of government, and thus, a declining need for liberals. So for liberals, you might say, it's self-preservation, a survival mentality. Only they—the educated, "compassionate," and self-proclaimed enlightened ones—are capable of steering the benighted population toward correct paths, decisions, and attitudes. All for a price, of course.

But there isn't a conviction I hold that makes liberals livid more quickly than this one: America is the greatest country on Earth and in history, still abounding with untapped opportunity for ordinary citizens. No other nation on the planet presents its citizens with such a gift—the promise that they can pursue whatever dream they have, with whatever talents they have, with all the effort and savvy they can marshal. And their reward will be the possibility of the dream realized. This is a social contract unique in history, and like a magnet, it has drawn those with dreams from every other continent. Liberalism is indeed a massive tax on those very dreams.

More than anything else, I want to counter the ceaseless avalanche of lies about America and the wacky notion that there is no future left here. Despite what you've been told, this country is still a place of nearly infinite opportunities. I am absolutely confident in my view that what I have accomplished, though unique, is illustrative of what is possible in this country—for you! So many of you are better than you think you are and capable of reaching higher in life than you think you can.

Liberals become defensive and hostile when I speak this way. But despite their accusations, I am not interested in forcing my views on anyone. Yes, I want a strong country. But I believe that this country's strength is a product of the strength of its individual citizens. This vision of rugged individualism has been the hallmark of America throughout most of her history.

No, I am not about to break into a canned motivational essay here; this heartfelt conviction that everyone can accomplish more comes directly from my own experience. Don't listen to those who say that only some privileged few in this country can seek or attain success. The so-called greed decade of the eighties saw more upward class mobility than any other time in recent history. So, don't listen to those who characterize individual achievement as bad, coldhearted, greedy, selfish, and deserving of punishment.

Anyone who tells you that has been reading too many *New York Times* Anthony Lewis columns or Democratic National Committee platforms—or, worse yet, buying into Bill Clinton's demagogic theme of class warfare. The consequences of that lie are hideous. Spreading these falsehoods leads to divisiveness and the erection of insidious psychological barriers among people—barriers that impair the vision and short-circuit the dreams of millions of Americans. I am tired of being told by politicians and the media that middle-class America is not giving enough money to take care of our country's problems. I am tired of being told how rotten everything is. I am fed up with the fact that individualism and self-reliance are now equated with greed. I am fed up with the fact that certain self-evident truths—the ideals American citizens have embraced for generations and that have launched this nation to the pinnacle of human history—are constantly denounced as attitudes that are going to destroy the country. I want only the best for everyone—not, by the way, as defined by me, but as people define it for themselves.

Yes, I am fortunate that I have the opportunity to do what I love. But nobody handed it to me on a silver platter. I had to work at it and prove myself every step of the way. My story is nothing more than an example of the Original American Ethic: hard work, overcoming obstacles, triumphing over enormous odds, the pioneer spirit. These things, my friends—not such vacuous symbolic gestures as wearing ribbons on lapels or government intrusion into every aspect of our lives—are what built this country.

But don't think I am some kind of Pollyanna. I have seen tough times as well. I've been on every rung of the socioeconomic ladder. I've been fired six times. I've been broke twice. I've been hopelessly in debt. I've gone through periods in which I made very little money. I've also been near the top. I've seen life from all sides.

Because of this, my own experience is particularly instructive. It is my heartfelt belief that, no matter what your status in life, you can learn about what's possible for you in this country by studying me. And if you attain even a fraction of my level of excellence, you will have arrived.

So let the lesson begin. Get out your yellow marker and highlight the next chapter. All of it.

2

THE POWER OF YOU: YOU MAKE IT WORK

I WAS FLYING TO CHICAGO WITH THE PHOENIX SUNS AFTER THEY HAD lost the first two home games of the 1993 National Basketball Association championship series to Michael Jordan's Bulls. Naturally, the team was a little down—and more than a little puzzled about their predicament. I was sitting with veteran guard Danny Ainge, no stranger to championship play as a longtime member of the Boston Celtics.

To put things in perspective, Ainge is one of only five NBA players to play for three different championship teams. He has also played in a total of six championship series. (The great basketball player Larry Bird, by comparison, made it to only five.) This is no coincidence. It's not a matter of luck. Ainge is a hard-nosed competitor who understands the dynamics of winning. He is one of the very few people to have made it to the major leagues in two sports—baseball and basketball. Anyway, during that flight, Ainge said something that may seem obvious, but it's also so profound and insightful that it hit me right between the eyes.

"There's a huge difference between showing up, playing, having

11

fun and doing well, and really playing to win," he said. "It's an entirely different mind-set. It's not a physical thing. It has nothing to do with athletics. It has to do with attitude."

He's so right. Part of Ainge's success stems from his willingness to get the ball in any situation—to take a risk, and yes, even to face failure. This principle applies in any field of endeavor, not just sports. As the popularity of the Excellence in Broadcasting Network soars to new heights, reporters frequently approach me and ask, "Did you ever expect to rise to the top the way you have?"

My answer is always the same: "Yes, of course. I was striving for it. I didn't move to New York just to be in the top five. My eye was always on Number One." The fact of the matter is that I've always been that way, ever since I was a little kid. I was never intimidated by the prospect of failure. I knew that if I missed the mark, I could live with myself. What I couldn't live with, however, was the prospect of not having taken my best shot at the brass ring.

I believed in myself. I knew that I lived in a country that rewarded hard work and excellence. I never doubted that the American Dream really worked. Some people are beginning to wonder about that today, and I think that is tragic. Too many people think that achievers have lost touch with what America is about. They act as if you can be a true American only if you're mired in mediocrity, misery, and unhappiness.

As someone who wants America to be a great nation and wants everyone to live up to their dreams, I find this attitude frustrating. I take it personally when people tell me the American Dream is a thing of the past. What does that attitude say about anyone in this era who succeeds? Somehow, they must have cheated. They must have "benefited unfairly," the Clinton administration would say.

This anti-competitive, anti-achievement attitude is terribly destructive. And it is infecting virtually every aspect of our lives. For instance, every year in New York, the Van Cliburn Competition seeks to find the best pianists. Even Hollywood apparently never before found this offensive, as it produced a movie about that event, called *The Competition*, starring Richard Dreyfuss and Amy Irving. But, how things have changed. In 1993, the director of the program told *The New York Times:* "We must stamp out the concept of 'better.'" Now, we all know that some people play the piano better than others. Why would we want to pretend otherwise? Why wouldn't we want to acknowledge the best? Why wouldn't we want to celebrate it?

But, as I've noted, *competition* has become a dirty word among liberals in our society. These moves toward equality of outcome and sameness permeate our educational system and every other aspect of our lives. They are even beginning to make inroads in professional sports. The National Football League, for some reason, is constantly striving for parity. The league apparently would love to ensure that every team finishes the season with an 8–8 record. Whenever a team becomes dominant in the NFL, the league changes the rules to mitigate some of the prowess of that particular team.

For the life of me, I can't understand this kind of thinking. During game three of the Phoenix–Chicago NBA Championship Series, NBC Sports reporterette extraordinaire Hannah Storm did a quick interview with me. She asked if I had given the Suns any advice. Yes, I said. I told them to run every play from the right. At that point, play-by-play guy Marv Albert made this comment: "You know if Rush Limbaugh owned or ran a basketball team, you'd get five years in jail for a traveling violation." Then he chortled at his wit.

This is just an example of what it's like to be me, folks. I have to get used to people, usually in the media, totally mischaracterizing my point of view. Like Bill Clinton's stab at humor at the Washington press corps dinner, Marv Albert's joke lacked the one element crucial to successful satire—a basis in truth. I am a guy who believes in following the rules. If I ran the NBA, when someone traveled it would result in a turnover—nothing more, nothing less. Someone who committed a personal foul would get one shot or two, according to the situation. I would simply enforce the rules.

Likewise, in our society, I would like to see our laws enforced. I wouldn't make up new rules on the spot. I wouldn't attempt to impose stricter penalties than the law allows. However, I would like to see justice served. Is that too much to ask?

But what if guys like Marv Albert and other liberals ran the NBA?

Let's imagine what the game might be like. How would they handle personal fouls? Each violation would be examined in light of the background of the person who committed it. The impact of the foul on his psyche would be analyzed. Could he deal with being called for a foul? They would also examine the interpersonal relationships between the fouler and his teammates. How would it affect their self-esteem? Then they would have to stop the game to study the root causes behind the foul. Why did he do it? It isn't his fault. He didn't mean to do it. There must be a societal reason. Perhaps there was something in his childhood that caused him to hack that guy's arm. So the game would be stopped and a study, funded by the government, would be conducted. Then they would take into account the race of the two parties involved in the violation. There would be bias-related fouls. You would have hate fouls. Is the official politically incorrect? Has he ever been guilty of sexual harassment? Then you would have to do a community-impact study to determine how the fans feel about it. Maybe the victim of the foul is a homophobe, in which case it's okay. You can do anything to a homophobe. The fouler, in this case, would be celebrated.

People wonder why I use so many sports analogies. Simple. There's a lot to learn from sports. People who play to win have a different attitude. They get into "the zone." This is something we need to teach to our young people. It can help in every facet of life. This is a frequent theme for me, but not an overused one: We need to motivate people to be the best they can be—to pursue excellence.

Most people have no idea how good they are—even people who are excellent at what they do. Do you know why? Because most people allow themselves to be shackled or constrained in some way. It might be the result of a self-imposed limitation or the restrictions of their job or the responsibilities they've accepted.

Admittedly, I had an advantage over some because I had parents who always told me I was special. That's an important first step.

The idea of pursuing excellence and being the best you can be at whatever you do always works. Every time you try it, you do better than you otherwise would have done. Often when we assume that people are not very good, we decide that they're not going to reach their potential and be successful without special help. The assumption is that underachievers need to be coddled, taken care of, felt sorry for, pitied, and patronized.

That's a precarious situation for any individual to be in. And if too many people in a given society find themselves in that predicament, the country is literally at risk. The relentless pursuit of equality, of sameness in the name of fairness, gets us nowhere. Those are goals that are hard to define and impossible to achieve. That's why liberalism embraces them. The lifeblood of liberalism is the pursuit of perpetually unattainable objectives.

Let's go back to Desert Storm as an illustration. Can you imagine if the number-one objective of Norman Schwarzkopf, commander-in-chief of allied forces, was equality or fairness? Imagine this conversation on the front line:

"You mean our unit has to go get the republican guard, and these other guys only have to drive the fuel-supply vehicles?"

"Right."

"That isn't fair!"

"Well, okay. Any of you guys who don't want to go get the republican guard, fall out!"

But that's a conversation that would never occur in a properly run, disciplined military setting. Everybody does what he is ordered to do because that is the nature of the military. And in Desert Storm, everyone performed to the best of his ability. Would you have wanted it any other way?

There is a myriad of examples of people successfully pursuing the American Dream. Yet there are still skeptics. A man from Alabama recently wrote me a computer letter accusing me of being too upbeat and optimistic. He said that by listening to me, one would get the idea that there is no hurting or suffering going on in the world and that everything is working out for the best. Wrong. I realize that there are failures and suffering. I just happen to believe that there would be a great deal more of them if everyone had that writer's pessimistic, defeatist attitude. We can feel compassion all day for "the Suffering," but what do we do the next day? Feel sorry for them again? No. What "the Suffering" need is steady doses of confidence-building optimism.

This needs to be discussed in a psychological sense. Today, so much of America is under assault that achievers are under assault. The Democratic Party has so successfully exploited class envy that people hold the wealthy and successful in contempt. The Democrats are breeding resentment. They have many people believing that anybody who is doing well is a cheater, a crook, selfish, and/or doing something unfair and unjust.

I am now enjoying success in my life. That doesn't mean I don't remember what it was like to struggle. I'm also sensitive and sympathetic toward the troubles other people experience. But it would serve no constructive purpose for me to sit around and wring my hands every day over the disadvantaged, the poor, the homeless, the middle class, and others. That would be the liberal thing to do. I would rather show, by example, that it is still possible to succeed, that hard work still pays off, that the American Dream can still be a reality.

We have to remember there will never be a time when everyone is doing well. (Not even when Bill Clinton is gone.) But, should we, therefore, for the rest of our days, stop enjoying life because there are some who do not?

America needs a cheerleader—someone who can make us feel good about ourselves and give us the confidence to be ourselves again. That is exactly what Ronald Reagan did. One of the keys to Reagan's enormous success and popularity was that he made us feel good about America. He made us proud. He made us feel there were infinite possibilities in this country. Most of us instinctively understood this and responded favorably to the message. But the liberals, once again, were threatened by the idea of people taking charge of their own lives, and they attacked Reagan mercilessly as a media charmer, soft on substance.

Don't kid yourself. I am fully aware of the very real problems our nation faces. But I would rather suggest answers and solutions and encourage people to take responsibility than to sit around and whine about how unfair the world is. That accomplishes nothing.

I believe in my heart, based on my own experiences and on those of my friends, that it is possible and preferable to elevate most people to new heights rather than to equalize society by taking away from those who have succeeded.

Sometimes it seems as if you wake up every morning, turn on the radio or TV, and are bombarded with doom and gloom. You come home from work, watch the evening news or pick up the newspaper, and it is more doom and gloom. I, for one, am tired of all the negativism. And I suspect this is one of the secrets of the success of the Rush Limbaugh programs.

New York culture critic David Hinckley wrote a column recently in which he stated: "The thing with Rush Limbaugh's fans is that they don't know he's kidding." I suspect that like so many other liberals, he just can't believe that my message is sincere. This is another example of how most of the press has a problem admitting that there are intelligent people and opinion leaders such as myself who have heartfelt and rationally considered conservative convictions. But Mr. Hinckley's comment also betrays a contemptuous attitude toward my audience—whom he obviously believes are mentally incapable of distinguishing my rapier-like wit from my scintillating wisdom. Oh, how mistaken he is!

This contempt for me and my audience has backfired. It has only served to coalesce and strengthen us. I don't mind being dismissed, disparaged, castigated, maligned, and reviled for my views, my achievements, or my continued audacity to breathe. I have thick skin—and the satisfaction of knowing that I am right. That's why I remain full of good cheer, confident in the success of my endeavors, despite the naysayers. Nevertheless, I am growing weary of the critics of my show who feel it is obligatory to impugn *you*, the audience.

You are called "followers," right-wing zealots, reactionaries, bigots. You are described as my "minions," easily provoked dimwits on the fringes of society whom I can whip into a frenzy at my whim.

These are the same critics, however, who have been profoundly wrong about my program at every turn—its prospects, its appeal, its listeners. When I launched the EIB Network in 1988, we had fifty-six stations and an audience of 250,000 people. Everybody who was anybody said it would fail. It was "impossible" to get a daytime national show on serious radio stations; only local issues, local calls, and local hosts were wanted. It was "impossible" to have a show without guests. "You can't do three hours all by yourself—who's going to listen to that?"

After it was up and running, the critics said, "It isn't going to last. This guy's a flash in the pan. He won't be here a year from now. Besides, the show is so controversial it's not going to get advertisers. It's going to die."

When it became the most listened-to, long-form talk program on commercial radio, with the largest audience for a program of its type since television was invented, the objections, fears, and predictions of doom and gloom were repeated for my television show. "You're not going to have guests? Up against Whoopi Goldberg? Who do you think you are? You're too controversial, you're too conservative, you're too fat. It isn't going to work on TV. And if it does work, it's not going to last. Anyway, you're not going to get advertising."

I'm convinced that twenty years from now, when I have a combined audience of 90 million people in radio and on television, critics are still going to say, "This guy's a flash in the pan. It isn't going to work."

They have missed every call when it comes to my accomplishments, but their abysmal track record concerning me does not bother them in the least. They haven't the slightest embarrassment about being so mistaken for so long and about so much. It certainly doesn't prevent them from making inane assertions about you—you, the so-called "rednecks" and "social misfits" whom they believe comprise my audience. In fact, one of the most consistent threads in their erroneous analysis is misjudging, misunderstanding, and underestimating you.

But clearly, your numbers do bother them. "How do you explain it, Limbaugh?" I am often asked. "How do you account for the millions listening to you, watching you, buying your books?"

I usually reply that I haven't spent a lot of time thinking about why so many people listen. It is no mystery to me. Of course, we have statistics and studies and surveys of my audience. We know it is upscale and educated. The EIB audience research shows that more than 60 percent of the audience has gone to college for at least two years, and the show has its largest following in the twenty-five-year-old to fifty-four-year-old age group. (Scarier still for the liberals, however, is the fact that there are 4.6 million listeners at any given moment, and 20 million per week.) It is simply the largest audience in the history of talk radio.

I communicate with thousands of you—by phone, fax, electronic mail, and in my travels. I am very interested in your opinions and ideas. But, as I have stated countless times, my show is not about what my audience thinks, or what my callers think, or what my readers think. It is about what I think.

Nevertheless, one of my many enormous advantages over my critics is that I know who you are—and I am constantly grateful, never wanting to take you for granted. The point is this: My understanding of my audience grows directly from my faith in the character of those who make this country work.

So let me set the record straight. You are the ones trying to hold the society together in the face of a full-frontal assault on your values. You are the ones who obey the law, pay the taxes, raise your children to be moral and productive citizens. You are the community volunteers, the entrepreneurs, the risk-takers, the achievers. You are saving to send your kids to college, start a new enterprise, trying to scrape enough money together to make a down payment on a house. You are the parents, the churchgoers, the PTA members, the scout leaders, the small-business owners. And you are doing it all with the help of God and your family, never once whining about the lack of federal funding or burning down your neighborhood because the government is "neglecting" you.

And what has been your reward? You are called selfish and greedy. Your desire to live a moral life and teach your children virtue is laughed at, sneered at, scorned. And the worst of it is, you are the ones who have to pick up the pieces and pay more taxes for yet another program when the liberal social experiments fail once again.

So don't take any of this unwarranted criticism to heart, my friends. My show has been on the air for more than five years and has done nothing but experience phenomenal growth. This cannot be done with phoniness, disingenuousness, insincerity, or shtick. The major media analysts continue to miss the real story of my program's success. My show works because people are tired of being insulted elsewhere on the radio or TV dial. They enjoy listening to someone who respects their intelligence, who shares their values.

"I sometimes worry that talk-show America is going to dominate the dialogue, and that we are all going to be pushed into positions that we may find harmful to the country," said NBC's John Chancellor recently at Columbia University. "Problems that face America today are very complicated . . . I think you need a better way of running this country and electing people than just turning it all over to the people."

Here you have it in a nutshell, my friends. The smug assumption that people who listen to my show are just too stupid to tackle America's complicated problems and that the country has to be protected from people like you is sheer arrogance.

But there is something else, too. In this comment and others like it is a genuine fear of your power. Lurking behind Chancellor's condescending words is another message: Oh, no—could it be? What if the majority of the country really is conservative? Uh-oh. . . . What if Limbaugh's audience is actually America's political center?

And there is plenty of evidence on the current political scene that liberals do recognize the nation's basic conservatism—though they adopt it only cynically. All you have to do is watch a liberal run for office as a "New Democrat," or listen to a liberal presidential candidate panic while refuting that characterization and instead insisting that he is a progressive while riding around in a tank wearing a helmet eighteen sizes too big for his mush-brained head. Liberals lose ideologically based elections—unless they can convince voters that they aren't liberal.

Here is precisely what my audience finds upon tuning in to my show, which is communicated with passion and conviction, good humor, and, of course, brilliance: the celebration of individual achievement, excellence, and the universal yearning to prosper; recognition of the power and greatness of ordinary people; belief that most folks are better than they realize and are capable of much more than they know; honoring the fruits of freedom, human capital unleashed, the unparalleled achievements of the United States of America.

Where else are these things celebrated? Where, in all of the culture—in movies, on television, in books—are such values championed?

Everywhere else, *you* are the people who are impugned, blamed for every problem. And as you look around, the accusations simply go against your own experience and common sense; what you see, primarily, is a country to be proud of, not the vast wasteland of misery and despair portrayed in the media.

Yet liberals constantly ask, "Limbaugh doesn't really believe all that stuff, does he?" The question reveals their fundamental misunderstanding of their fellow citizens, most of whom believe "that stuff" from their core, in their hearts and souls.

And the appeal of the message is huge. Enormous. And growing. For too long the liberal conventional wisdom has held sway in the media, on college campuses, in the vocal culture. I challenge it, and debunk it—with logical analysis and irreverent humor. Liberals' angry, bitter reaction to me and to you simply reveals them as intolerant and small-minded; it is high time their sacred cows were skewered and their many hypocrisies exposed.

So, who listens to me? In my audience are strong women who are tired of militant feminists claiming to speak for them; animal lovers who are sick of militant animal-rights activists bullying the medical-research profession and the beef industry; conservationists who are embarrassed by the loony antics of the environmental wackos; law-abiding citizens tired of seeing crime go unpunished and even be justified; productive members of society tired of being burdened by bureaucratic regulators whose only business experience is running seminars or communes.

In my audience, also, are many people who disagree with me. Those who appreciate a good debate, being challenged, being forced to re-examine their assumptions and defend a case on its intellectual merits. In time, of course, they will agree with me . . . as will the entire country. But for some of you, this process can take months. In the meantime, you know that the challenge is intellectually honest and enjoyable—not, as critics claim, "full of hate."

Who listens to me? The answer is obvious: All across the fruited plain, ordinary Americans of every walk of life listen. You know who you are—you are the ones who have the courage to face and believe the truth. You are the people who make the country work.

3

AMERICA IS NOT OVER

"RUSH, YOU'RE OUT OF TOUCH. AMERICA IS FULL OF RECESSION, unemployment, despair, decline. Sure, things look rosy for you, but you're successful. So you have no idea what America is really like."

Tell me something, friends. If you wanted to become a major-league baseball player, whose advice would you value more—baseball star George Brett's, or Donna Shalala's? If you wanted to become a teacher, would you listen to Jaime Escalante, who successfully taught advanced calculus to disadvantaged Hispanic kids in East L.A.; or some pointy-headed college professor, ensconced in the political-correctness milieu of academia and familiar with all the latest educational theories? If you simply wanted to achieve success in the career of your choosing, would you solicit the counsel of someone who has already achieved success in the real world, or someone who is counting on the government to raise his standard of living?

Dear reader, I hope the answers to these rhetorical questions are self-evident. But we do live in an upside-down world, so I will take nothing for granted. After all, to whom do we as a society turn these days for expert advice on how to avoid getting AIDS? Answer:

23

Magic Johnson. When we want to create jobs, to whom do we listen? If the last presidential election is any indication, we listen to people who have never worked in the private sector—professional politicians whose idyllic view of government causes them to believe that job creation and allocation are a proper function of the "invisible foot" of government, rather than economist Adam Smith's invisible hand.*

When we wanted to determine whether homosexuals should be permitted to serve in the armed forces or whether women should be allowed to fight in combat, did we call on the wisdom and experience of General Colin Powell, then chairman of the Joint Chiefs of Staff? Thankfully, yes, although the solution, the infamous "don't ask, don't tell" policy that survived, was the best we could get against the open-door demands of the likes of Representative Pat Schroeder (D-Colorado), Representative Ronald V. "Red" Dellums (D-California), and a former draft dodger.

If you wish, you may simply ignore the advice I am about to impart to you. You can choose to believe that because of my own phenomenal career success I am out of touch with the everyday realities of modern Americans. But believe me, folks, my memory is not that short. I firmly believe that, whatever your pursuit in life, success—not failure—should be your model.

Furthermore, despite what you have been told by the current occupants of the White House and the denizens of the dominant media culture, the United States of America is still a place of enormous opportunity. America is not over. Not by a long shot.

I believe what I believe about America and the opportunity for individual initiative and achievement because I've lived it. Unlike Robert B. Reich*hhhh*, Laura D'Andrea Tyson, the Clinton administration's chair of the Council of Economic Advisers, and other members of Bill Clinton's inner circle, I am not a theoretician. I have

---

*Adam Smith said that people, in the process of pursuing their own best interests, create opportunities and jobs for others. He said that it was as if an invisible hand were creating these jobs, even though they were really created by people pursuing the most advantageous use of their own resources.

A few years ago, Representative Dick Armey (R-Texas) coined the phrase "invisible foot," a humorous play on Smith's use of invisible hand, to describe the fact that when government gets involved, things invariably get more complicated and the results are never what's promised.

not written term papers about self-improvement. I have not written a doctoral thesis about free enterprise. Humbly speaking, as the Doctor of Democracy, I *am* free enterprise. And I operate in the real world, not in the insulated atmosphere of the ivory-tower academy.

From firsthand experience, I have learned that it is still possible to succeed, not by relying on government handouts and affirmative-action programs, but through self-reliance, risk-taking, hard work, and the courage to believe in yourself.

I wasn't planning on telling the story I am about to tell in this chapter. Everyone is aware of my aversion to self-promotion and braggadocio. All must surely realize by now how it pains me to talk about my own personal accomplishments. Plus, I was planning on saving it all for a future best-selling autobiography. But I now feel compelled to share—excuse me, *discuss*—at least some of this material with you because of the diabolical efforts of the Clinton regime to mischaracterize America as rotten, corrupt, and unjust— as it lays its foundation to "change the face of America," a shorthand euphemism for exponential government expansion.

Simply put, the message "the man from Hope" offers the American people is a far cry from the one he was delivering as "Candidate Clinton" when he deceitfully described himself as a "New Democrat." No, this New Democrat is actually an unreconstructed New Dealer, whose political energies are fueled by the hackneyed liberal notion that we are incapable of taking care of ourselves and our families and that we need the government to help us. In *Billary*'s paternalistic utopia, there will be family-leave bills, minimum-wage legislation, comparable-worth laws, affirmative-action plans, and, most important, in order to protect American children from their greatest enemy—their own parents—child-protection/parent-emasculation laws.

Today, when someone loses a job in this country, the "compassionate," knee-jerk response is extended unemployment benefits and government retraining programs. And lest you think I am overstating the point, I recently observed Clinton's labor secretary and economic mentor, Robert Reich*hhhh*, pontificating on the responsibilities of employers. He actually said that in the near future he envisioned a system, mandated by legislation, that would guarantee employment for employees even beyond the closing of the employer's business. Under this scenario, government funds would be available to subsidize the employer in retraining employees for new employment. Now, Mr. Reich*hhhh*, where is that government money going to come from? That's right, from tax revenues, the lion's share of which will have been paid by other small-business owners, whom you propose to punish for making the right economic decisions.

As someone who, during the course of his life, has been involuntarily relieved of his professional duties six times, I often wonder what would have become of me had Bill Clinton been around during those tough periods. What if I had waited around for the government to help me rather than learn from my experiences and take charge of my own destiny? I can tell you this unequivocally: If I had been so inclined, i.e., to become a ward of the government rather than a productive member of society, I would not be where I am today. And believe me, I would be much worse off in every way—and incidentally, so would you because you wouldn't have me to enlighten you.

Had I been inclined to believe the government would provide for me, what might I be doing today? Building a water slide in Puerto Rico? Digging a hole for a community swimming pool in Midland, Texas? Doing graffiti abatement in Highland, California? Awaiting the never-ending extension on my unemployment benefits? One thing is certain. Had I left my future up to government policies, I would be mired in misery, wandering aimlessly, still searching for what would make me happy and productive.

Instead, I took stock of myself. I took some risks. I relied on my own resources, skills, talents, and hard work. And today, instead of collecting unemployment, I am employing others. Think of it. We have helped resurrect AM talk radio, which, before I blitzkrieged the medium, was on its last leg. Robert Reich*hhhh*'s solution to re-energize AM would not have been Rush Limbaugh. He would have proposed a government takeover of the entire industry, guaranteeing employment for everyone, regardless of performance and irrespective of ratings. If the ratings became too low, he might have offered tax subsidies to taxpayers who would tune in to AM so as to boost the ratings. I don't need to tell you what the results of such a strategy would have been. But, to the industry's eternal gratification, Robert Reich*hhhh* was not yet around to bail it out. Instead, it was EIB, Excellence in Broadcasting, that revived floundering AM radio stations around the country. It was Rush Limbaugh who sold millions of books and provided huge economic boosts to countless broadcast sponsors.

This, my friends, is how real, meaningful, permanent, worthwhile jobs are created, by the application of Adam Smith's invisible hand, not through government make-work programs. Let's go back and retrace how it all began—and how easily it all could have been short-circuited by the liberal inclination to exempt individuals from the responsibility of supporting themselves and imposing that responsibility on the state.

I grew up in a great home with a great family in Cape Girardeau, Missouri. My parents inculcated me with good values. I was encouraged to achieve, but school never interested me. In high school, however, I did like football. And some of the lessons I learned on the gridiron have served me well throughout my life.

I was an offensive tackle. Every day after practice we were required to run wind sprints. I hated wind sprints. At some point during these laps, someone from the coaching staff would yell, "First three tackles through for the day!" That meant that if you finished first, second, or third in the next sprint, you could hit the showers. The others would continue running. It didn't take me long to realize that if I paced myself during the early sprints, I would have some gas left to finish in the top three and get out of any further running for the day. At first, it worked like a charm. But after three days of this, assistant coach Norm Dockins called me over.

"Mr. Limbaugh, I notice that you're usually in the middle of the pack during wind sprints until we call out 'first three tackles,'" he observed astutely. "Then you seem to finish near the top. Why is that?"

"I'm pacing myself, Coach," I explained.

"Well, son, in football we don't pace ourselves," the coach explained. "We go all out all the time. You'd be wise to do that your whole life, son. If I see you doing that again, you're going to run ten extra sprints. Is that clear?"

Well, I sure didn't want to run ten extra sprints. So, after that I ran as hard as I could all the time and I usually didn't finish in the top three. But it was a valuable lesson to me. And today I'm still going all out all of the time.

Why is it today that we seem to be afraid of urging kids on to excellence and achievement? Our society is more inclined to let kids develop at their own pace—not to push them too hard. We have a whole new concept in teaching—"Outcome-Based Education"—which holds that the old A-through-F system of grading is antiquated and injurious to students' self-esteem. Instead of failing a kid, its practitioners come up with new euphemisms that make it difficult to understand just how the pupil is performing. I am not one given to conspiracy theories, but I feel I must point out that there is a common thread that runs through this aversion to healthy competition and the pursuit of excellence and the pressure toward equalizing everyone at the lowest common denominator. I'm referring to the themes of anti-capitalism and pro-socialism, which hold that self-distinction and personal achievement are inherently immoral. Only if everyone's piece of the pie—whether it be an economic pie, a school-grade pie, or an athletic-event pie—is identical will we achieve a moral society. They call it egalitarianism. I call it sapping individuals of their lifeblood, depriving them of their human spirit, and, in the name of helping some, relegating everyone to mediocrity or worse.

I remember running into this young lady one day at the house of Roger Ailes, CNBC president and my television producer. In the course of an innocuous conversation, she began uttering certain feel-good liberal platitudes. On the surface, her opinions seemed innocent enough and were certainly made with good intentions. They were the kind of things that people often say these days without even considering the real meaning of the words.

Her feeling was that we should not push kids so hard, but should seek to understand them and cut them some slack to let them develop at their own pace. And by no means should we ever drive them to compete.

Most people might simply choose to shrug off a statement like that. But I called her on it. I told her it was nonsense. Kids are the ones who don't understand. They don't know enough. That's what being a kid is all about. We need to push kids—for their own good. That's what being parents is all about. Think back. Who were your best teachers or coaches? Weren't they the ones, like Jaime Escalante or Norm Dockins, who demanded more of you and got more out of you than you thought you had? And it didn't hurt you one bit, did it? We've got to get over this ludicrous notion that kids are so fragile that they can't handle disappointment. It's exactly the opposite. If you shelter them from real-world situations with real-world consequences today in the interest of sparing their feelings, you are going to cause them irreparable damage in the long run. Because it is only through dealing with life's ups and downs, the struggles of everyday living, and, yes, even a bit of adversity that they will mature into adults capable of taking care of themselves and their dependents and becoming productive members of society.

Kids have to be shown early on that striving for excellence will yield them benefits. Today, as liberalism has been re-empowered, it's fashionable again to punish achievement—at all levels. We punish people who put their money at risk. We punish entrepreneurs, not just in their pocketbooks; they are actually vilified as parasites by the Clinton administration and the dominant media culture. We punish people who have been successful and who, through their own achievement, have provided opportunities for others.

It's a sad thing. Liberals want to equalize everybody. But redistribution of wealth has never given anybody dignity or self-respect. It goes against the grain of human nature. It has never worked in the history of the world—ever. And it never will. The rest of the world is rapidly coming to that realization. Under Clinton's stewardship, we are regressing.

I have always known this—instinctively. I have also always believed that someday I would be very successful. I wasn't always sure what it was that I would be doing, but I never had any doubt that it would be fun and important. In one sense, I am now getting paid to do what I've been doing all my life. I have always cared passionately about issues and ideas. I have always enjoyed discussing the news of the day. But I didn't always have the discipline and maturity required for success.

I had no patience with schooling and formal education. I dropped out of college in my freshman year and became a full-time disc jockey. I had always loved radio and I was convinced I could be successful without a diploma. But this development caused my father great anguish. He was convinced I would never amount to anything without that sheepskin.

When I went to work for the Kansas City Royals, my dad was relieved. At least I was with a good company. My future was more secure. That was not my attitude, however. I was the same person then as I am today. I enjoyed debating and grappling with the hot topics of the day. But, naturally, this was of no interest to the Royals. It simply didn't help them sell tickets. And that's what I was employed to do.

I was twenty-eight years old when I joined the organization and was paid $12,000 a year. To put this in perspective, I was making $15,000 a year working in radio at the age of twenty. I was literally on a downward financial spiral from the age of twenty-one to the time I turned thirty-two. Each year I earned less money than the year before. To say the least, I was not distinguishing myself professionally. But I was trying—desperately—to find my niche.

It wasn't until those years with the Royals that I even began to be conscious of money. Being around people with money—lots of money—can have that effect. Because I didn't have any, I couldn't do many of the things my friends were doing. Because of my financial status, I began to think I was worthless and could never be attractive to anybody. But I also had an incentive to improve my lot in life. I had something to strive for.

After five years of being unsatisfied professionally, economically, and socially, I took a chance. I wasn't going to play it safe anymore. I decided to do what I did best. I went to a Kansas City radio station and told the people who ran it that they simply had to hire me. It wasn't Excellence in Broadcasting, folks, but I was back in radio, where I knew I belonged. Before my experience in Sacramento in 1984, I was never given the chance to be myself—to develop a unique radio program and a style of my own. But I was able to experiment in talk radio.

I had always wanted to do talk radio. To me, that was the ultimate form of being in control in radio. As a disc jockey, I never liked the fact that records and contests were part of the reason people were listening. Even then I wanted them to listen to *me*.

I remember one of my early experiences at an FM music station in Kansas City. The station management realized it was not doing enough community-service broadcasting to fulfill the requirements of the Federal Communications Commission. Suddenly, the managers got a brainstorm.

"Why don't you take questions on community topics between records?" they asked me. Because I wanted to do talk and to develop a radio personality, I agreed. But there was a catch. The station management said it wanted me to be controversial, to insult people. There was already an insult jock in town at that time and he was experiencing some success, so the managers thought this would be a good idea.

Well, I found out something about myself during that experience, something that was quite disturbing. I found out I was really, really good at insulting people. For example, the topic one day was "When you die, how do you want to go?"

"I want to go the cheapest and most natural way I can," one nice lady caller from Independence, Missouri, said.

My response was: "Easy. Have your husband throw you in a trash bag and then in the Missouri River with the rest of the garbage."

When I went home after a day of this, I didn't like myself. After all, these people's feelings were being hurt when I did this. And what was the point?

Realizing that I was allowing my talents to be exploited toward destructive ends, I decided to change course. I resolved to make a detailed study of the media—especially the personalities, like Johnny Carson, who had longevity in show business. I discovered something important: None of them insulted people. They didn't mistreat the people who were invited to participate in their show. There are some people who have done it, but they have lasted only a year or two—people like Joe Pyne and Morton Downey. (Don Rickles is the only insult performer who has enjoyed sustained success, but when his show is over he apologizes and everyone understands that it was all in fun.)

This study was an eye-opener for me. And it gave me something to think about. When my big break came in 1984 and I was hired by radio station KFBK in Sacramento, I was ready for the challenge. I finally knew who I was. And I had a clear idea of what I wanted to do.

Ironically, I was hired to replace the infamous Morton Downey. KFBK didn't want another Downey. But the management still wanted controversy. They just didn't want me to make anything up. That was okay with me. My idea was to stir controversy in discussing substantive issues rather than with shock, rudeness, and insult. I was not going to go on the air just to be outrageous. I wanted credibility. I knew that was the key to having longevity—or "legs," as members of the media refer to it—*and* to securing sponsors.

I made a conscious decision (from which I have never retreated) that the controversy I generated would never be from the way I treated people on the phone. And to this day I give people who disagree with me more time than those who agree. I don't hang up on them. I am never rude. I practice the same standard of civility that I live in my personal life. I still do parody and satire and I love to mix it up with people on substantive issues, but I try never to be cruel—especially to my listeners and callers.

I also knew from the start that I did not want guests on my show. Again, I wanted to be the focal point of the show. Why should I interview the same guests who were appearing on every other talk show in the country? How would that distinguish me from the pack?

From the very start, however, everybody agreed that this kind of show would not work. It couldn't be done. Nevertheless, I remained persistently dedicated to my vision. And, needless to say, it worked.

Then when we first planned to develop the nationally syndicated program, the naysayers were even more vociferous. The industry flat-out told me that what we wanted to do was impossible. So we literally redefined radio—the way the programming was done, the way time was sold; the whole enchilada.

Because of all this, folks, if anybody knows that the American Dream is worthwhile, possible, justified, accessible, and attainable, it is I. I do know America. I don't think Bill Clinton knows America. I don't think liberals know America. I have confidence in my success. I am not simply riding the crest of a wave. I'm in control of this wave. I'm the one who dictates how long I'm going to be on top. I am defining my audience and developing an audience based on what I am. It has been a studied effort, based on almost twenty years of experience, both of mediocrity and, more important, of success.

I am a recent convert to the power of an optimistic, self-reliant outlook. I've heard all the motivational speakers and for many years I thought they were a bunch of kooks or simply charlatans out to make a buck. It may sound clichéd to say, "There's no such word as *can't*." But there's an important element of truth in this kind of thinking.

Admittedly, I have some gifts—a good memory, a nice voice. But they are hardly unique. Look what I have done with them. Look what America has allowed me to do. Could this kind of success have been achieved anywhere else? Does any other nation give people such opportunities?

I believe that if others learned from my experience and applied these same basic principles to their own lives, their chances for success would be greatly improved. No guarantees, mind you. Only liberals dare to give guarantees about life. They seek to create a safe, risk-free world of equality, sameness, and mediocrity. I, on the other hand, champion excellence and achievement.

Don't believe the doomsayers. Don't believe the negativity-mongers. Don't believe the America-bashers—even if one of them is the president of the United States. Don't buy into the lie that punishing high achievers will bring you happiness. Your own success—born of your own ingenuity and industry—is what will make you happy.

This is still America. And America is not over.

4

NEW DEMOCRATS:
YEAH, YEAH . . .

HERE'S ANOTHER ORIGINAL RUSH MAXIM FOR YOU TO PONDER AND cherish. Graduates of the Limbaugh Institute for Advanced Conservative Studies should be required to commit this to memory. And anyone who wishes to dazzle his friends with my wit and wisdom would be well advised to do the same.

Any time you see the adjective "new" employed—be it in politics, religion, or commerce—assume that the label is mere smoke and mirrors, calculated to obscure the fact that there is nothing "new" about what is being described. Rather, it is the same old stuff simply repackaged.

Think about it. What was new, for example, about the so-called "New Left" of the 1960s? It was simply the tired old left dressed up in tie-dyed shirts, sandals, and granny glasses. What's new about the "New Age"? In spite of what Shirley MacLaine and *Algore* might tell you, it's nothing more than recycled paganism. And when Madison Avenue calls laundry detergent "new and improved," how many of you blindly accept the label at face value?

Why, then, did so many believe it when Bill Clinton professed to be a "New Democrat"? Moreover, why did so many believe there was any such thing as a "New Democrat"?

As the days pass, it is becoming increasingly clear that there is nothing new about Bill Clinton's Democratic Party. He sought to change that image with the appointment of David Gergen as Communications Director, and with his decision to pull the nomination of Lani Guinier for Assistant Attorney General for Civil Rights, but only time will tell. But the point is that, as a candidate, Clinton did hold himself out as a "New Democrat" during the campaign. He and his handlers understood that if he was perceived as a "liberal," he would lose. So he ran a stealth campaign. He portrayed himself as a "moderate" and a "New Democrat." In other words, he lied.

He knew that his best chance of winning the election, if nominated, would be to create the perception that he was conservative. Indeed, during the campaign he co-opted the traditionally conservative issues from George Bush, who couldn't seem to get out of the starting block. He promised a middle-class tax cut, deficit reduction, welfare reform, federal spending cuts, and a massive Reaganesque slashing of the bureaucracy. Bill Clinton said anything he had to say to get a vote. He proved to be the ultimate politician. But can you blame him? After all, he was and remains unencumbered by the constraints of conscience and, aside from me, there was no one around to hold him accountable. The big, powerful, liberal media, eager to recapture the White House and place it back in their ideological domain, helped him perpetuate the greatest electoral hoax in recent memory.

Well, we all know how the election turned out. But get this: It was not a repudiation of conservatism. Why do I say that? Well, despite a magnificent performance by Clinton, who may lie more convincingly than any politician in our country's history, all he managed to do was to hold on to the roughly 43 percent of the hard-core Democratic vote that went to Carter, Mondale, and Dukakis. The rest of the vote was split between President Bush and that little hand grenade with a crewcut, H. Ross Perot. Perot represented the real difference in the race, breaking up the Reagan coalition that represented about 57 percent of the electorate that had given the

Republicans huge wins in 1980, in 1984, and, to a lesser extent, in 1988. So, Bill Clinton achieved a 43 percent plurality by preaching conservative themes. Though George Bush alienated many of the Reagan coalition because of his abandonment of conservative principles, his 38 percent nevertheless consisted mostly of conservatives who were confident he would govern more conservatively than Clinton. Ross Perot's 19 percent included many conservatives who were attracted to certain themes historically owned by conservatives, such as government reform and deficit reduction. Admittedly, not all of his followers were conservative—especially those who favored his proposals for astronomical tax increases. But the point is, a good many of Perot's supporters were conservative.

So the fact that Bill Clinton won the election and turned out to be a liberal (as I warned incessantly before the election) does not mean the country has shifted to the left. He is finding this out with every leftward move he makes and trial balloon he flies—from his proposal to allow gays to serve in the military to his Indian-giving appointment of Lani Guinier.

Since taking office and revealing himself to be *extremely* liberal, Bill Clinton has proposed a so-called "jobs stimulus package," ostensibly to create make-work government jobs, but in reality to pay off his special-interest constituencies with barrels of pork. Within weeks of taking office he offered the largest tax increase/ wealth distribution in the history of the world. But despite his protestations to the contrary, this will mean higher taxes for everyone, not just the rich. Get ready, folks, for the biggest confiscation of your money ever by government. Franklin Delano Roosevelt and Lyndon Johnson look like pikers compared to this guy. Clinton's highly touted "Putting People First" plan is, in actuality, putting government first. After all, that's where his heart is. But Clinton's radical agenda is hardly limited to the economy. Before Chelsea was even enrolled in her exclusive private religious school, Bill and Hillary had unveiled their extreme leftist blueprint for the rest of us—gays in the military, women in combat, federally subsidized abortion, fetal experimentation, universal health care, and, always, more and more government dependency and control in every facet of our lives.

Make no mistake. There's nothing moderate about this program. The New Democrat is the same old social engineer. There were plenty of clues along the way, if only people had been willing to pay attention to anything besides Ross Perot's charts and Bill Clinton's manipulation of words and symbols.

Even the godfather of modern liberalism, George McGovern, publicly forewarned us about Clinton's true colors early in the campaign by calling the Democratic ticket "a Trojan horse." He explained: "I have a hunch that they're much more liberal underneath and will prove it when they're elected."

My friends, this was a historic prediction in more ways than one. It may represent the first time George McGovern was ever right about anything. You see, this was the man through whom the Democratic Party's character was profoundly changed in 1972. Let's take a brief excursion through recent American political history to ascertain how the Democratic Party was hijacked by extremists and what this means to us today.

Remember 1968? That was the year Tom Hayden, Abbie Hoffman, Jerry Rubin, and the rest of the gang disrupted the Democratic National Convention in Chicago because the radical left was angry at the way President Lyndon Johnson was escalating the war in Vietnam. There were riots in the streets and mayhem on the convention floor. But the result was that a traditional liberal Democrat, then–Vice-President Hubert H. Humphrey, was nominated as the presidential candidate, much to the chagrin of the radicals. Humphrey was to be the last of his kind ever to be nominated by the Democratic Party.

What do I mean by that? Humphrey was a liberal, all right. But not as we define that term today. He was anti-communist. He was pro-American. Yes, he, like Johnson, tended to favor big-government solutions to problems in the tradition of Roosevelt. But one could never question Humphrey's patriotism, nor his support for traditional American values.

After the debacle of the 1968 Democratic convention, the radicals took control of the party apparatus and the rules governing primary elections. They made it not only possible for a fringe candidate to capture the nomination; they very nearly made it impossible for a traditional, mainstream Democrat to win it without catering to a long list of special-interest groups—feminists, Naderites, labor unions, anti-nukers, unilateral disarmers, environmentalist wackos, etc. The result four years later was the nomination of George McGovern and the biggest landslide defeat the Democrats had ever faced up until that time. (It would get worse later.) McGovern's mistake was that he didn't try to hide his liberalism. Naïvely, but in fairness, to the credit of his character, he wore it like a badge of honor.

Then in 1976, on the heels of the Watergate scandal and the unpopular pardoning of Richard Nixon, Jimmy Carter promised to restore honesty in government and a moderate, born-again populism and managed to squeak through a tough election fight with President Gerald Ford. He would never lie to us, he pledged. He might have been the first "Trojan horse" candidate the Democrats put forward in the post-McGovern era. Or he may simply have "grown" in the job, as Washington's liberal establishment likes to say about anyone who allows it to swallow him up after a few months in office. In any case, once the American people got a taste of Carter's liberal policies and the untold havoc they produced (Does anybody remember gas lines and simultaneous double-digit unemployment, interest rates, and inflation?), they couldn't wait to get rid of him.

Then there were two more honest liberal nominees: Walter Mondale and Michael Dukakis. Remember Mondale's running mate? Remember Dukakis boasting that he was "a card-carrying member" of the American Civil Liberties Union? Both were quickly and enthusiastically dispatched to political retirement by the U.S. electorate. It was beginning to look as if the Democrats would never again be able to win the White House.

Then along came Bill Clinton. Like Carter, he was a Southern Baptist governor who talked like a good-old boy. He promised to break with the past. Remember the Democratic Leadership Council? This was to be the breeding ground for New Democrats. And Bill Clinton, in his characteristically calculating style, positioned himself as the leader of the pack. It was all a smoke-screen.

I tried to warn you, folks. Day after day, I told millions of Americans that Clinton was pulling a scam of monumental proportions. Where else, for instance, would you have heard about the background of Derek Shearer, the principal architect of Clinton's Rebuild America economic program?

And just in case you had the misfortune of missing my program that day, Shearer is the former Tom Hayden–Jane Fonda ally who invented the term "economic democracy" as a pseudonym for socialism. Shearer and his wife, Ruth Goldway, were active in the transformation of what was once a quiet and lovely California beach town into what is now commonly referred to as the "People's Republic of Santa Monica." Goldway had served as mayor from the time when the town blazed the trails of political correctness on such issues as rent control, homeless rights, and domestic partnerships. But it is in the field of economics that Shearer has made his mark.

"I particularly like the phrase 'economic democracy,'" Shearer was quoted as saying in the October 12, 1981, edition of *Barron's*. "Even Bernie [Sanders, now Vermont's socialist member of Congress], I think, doesn't object to this because it has been referred to by some of my friends as the 'great euphemism.' And while we can't use the 's' word [socialism] too effectively in American politics, we have found that in the greatest tradition of American advertising, the word 'economic democracy' sells. You can take it door to door like Fuller brushes, and the doors will not be slammed in your face. So I commend it to you, for those who are willing to compromise on the 's' word."

Shearer, you should know, along with Labor Secretary Robert Reich*hhhhhh* and socialized-medicine czar Ira Magaziner, has been a longtime Bill Clinton confidant, going back to their days together at Oxford in the late 1960s. He began his work with the Clinton administration as deputy undersecretary for economic affairs at the Commerce Department, where he was in charge of the economics staff. He has since retired, presumably to work at the grass-roots level.

There are many left-wing extremists now running the executive branch of the federal government. There's Health and Human Services Secretary Donna Shalala, the queen of political correctness; Chairwoman of the Council of Economic Advisers Laura D'Andrea Tyson, who marvels at the wonders of Eastern European–style central planning and collectivism; and Environmental Protection Agency Administrator Carol Browner, whose *Algorean* chants to Mother Earth make her a favorite among the tree-hugging set.

Make no mistake: This is not a group of centrists that Bill Clinton has surrounded himself with. But even more telling than the backgrounds of these key advisers is the political history of his closest companion, Hillary Rodham Clinton.

Hillary is well known for her work in the Children's Defense Fund and for championing "children's rights." That sounds great, doesn't it? Children's rights. How can "rights" ever be a bad thing, especially for children? Well, let's examine what is meant by this term. What the Children's Defense Fund supports, in essence, is the legal independence of children after early childhood. That means that kids would no longer be primarily accountable to their parents. So, the next question is: To whom would they be primarily accountable? The answer, of course, is the state. The benevolent state, then, would transcend the Orwellian "Big Brother" role and become surrogate parent. It would grant your children "rights" and be their legal guardian.

That doesn't sound quite as innocuous as "children's rights," does it? Lest you think I am exaggerating, this is precisely what the Children's Defense Fund advocates. For the record, authoritarian and totalitarian regimes—be they fascist or communist in nature—have always sought to destroy the traditional family unit by severing the bonds between parents and their children, thereby increasing the power of the government. Quite simply, Donna Shalala, Hillary Rodham, and other modern statists (actually sixties throwbacks) believe they can raise your children better than you can. That's what they mean by "children's rights"—the rights of children to be liberated from the shackles of their evil parents.

But Hillary's concerns go well beyond children. From 1987 through 1988, she served as director and chairwoman of the board of directors of the New World Foundation, which savored its reputation as one of the most "progressive" organizations in the United States. The group gave grants to radical think tanks like the Institute for Policy Studies, left-wing litigation specialists such as the National Lawyers Guild, and pro-communist propaganda arms like the Committee in Solidarity with the People of El Salvador.

To describe Hillary as a "liberal" would be an understatement of breathtaking proportions. But we didn't even need to look to the future First Lady for clues that Bill Clinton was no "New Democrat." Need I remind you about his draft record? His anti-war activism? Remember that letter in which he talked about how he "loathed the military"? And how about that mysterious vacation to Moscow and Prague in the dead of winter?

Is it any wonder, then, how quickly Bill Clinton shed his "New Democrat" costume upon assuming the highest office in the land? It's just amazing to me how many people were fooled. Some smart people, too. People who should have known better.

In fact, every independent-thinking person should have known better. How could anyone have accepted Clinton's self-appointed centrist label in view of the wildly inconsistent positions he took during the campaign? He tried to be all things to all people. Just look at the dichotomy: He claimed to be pro-business, while being labor's best friend and supporting even greater regulatory burdens on employers; he pandered to the government dependency class, while promising welfare reform; he boasted about his pro-family orientation, while promoting values that undermine the traditional family unit; he promised massive health-care reform (without imposing additional taxes, by the way), yet virtually guaranteed safe haven to the trial lawyers whose excesses and abuses account for much of the health expenditure explosion; he pledged his commitment to implementing an economic proposal with three times as many dollars in spending cuts as in tax cuts, but his

plan, as now passed, arguably includes a startling near-rever-
sal of those ratios; and he professed to be a deficit-
reduction hawk, while slobbering over the prospect of adding
hundreds of billions of dollars in new spending programs. Even
rudimentary calculations revealed the fraud in his economic plan.
The numbers simply didn't add up. When he was already lying
before our eyes during the campaign, how could anyone have
believed he would deliver on even a tiny percentage of the promises
he so glibly made during the campaign? Let's review just some of
the highlights.

On March 27, 1992, he launched a blistering political and
ad hominem (i.e., *personal*, for those of you in Rio Linda, California) attack on President Bush's Haitian policy: "I think President Bush played racial politics with the Haitian refugees. I
wouldn't be shipping those poor people back." Six days before he
even took office, after dozens of Haitians died on the open seas
as a direct result of his previous statements, the president-elect
did a 180-degree turn on the issue: "The practice of returning those
who fled by boat will continue, for the time being, after
I become president. Those who do leave Haiti by boat will
be stopped and directly returned by the United States Coast
Guard."

The precipitousness of this reversal leads to the inescapable
conclusion that he didn't change his mind after he took office and
had time to study the issue. The fact is, he didn't have time to study
the issue in those first six days. It's now obvious that when he
attacked George Bush on moral grounds, he had not yet even
studied the issue—or, worse yet—he had studied it and knew that
Bush was pursuing the appropriate and humane policy. His irresponsible exploitation of the Haitian refugees for sheer political
gain is unconscionable. And he has the gall to tell belea-
guered people that he "feels their pain." Spare us, please, Mr. President.

The most important and relevant flip-flops, of course, were those
from "conservative" or "New Democrat" positions to those we
have come to expect from liberals. On January 19, 1992, candi-

date Clinton stressed the importance of a middle-class tax cut as part of his economic program: "I want to make it very clear that this middle-class tax cut, in my view, is central to any attempt we're going to make to have a short-term economic strategy." The tax cut was also promoted in campaign ads.

But then, once elected, Clinton couldn't figure out why anyone cared about that pledge: "From New Hampshire forward, for reasons that absolutely mystify me, the press thought the most important issue in the race was the middle-class tax cut. I never did meet any voter who thought that." How facilely he rationalizes his breaches of the public trust. And that, my friends, is the most frightening thing about Mr. Clinton.

In the "Putting People First" plan, Clinton pledged to "attack violent crime by putting another 100,000 police officers on the street." When the president's budget was unveiled in April 1993, it included $50 million for community policing grants—enough to hire 3,000 new police officers over the next two years, or, as even the liberal *Washington Post* observed, "a mere 3 percent of the president's goal." In the actual crime bill he introduced in the summer of 1993, he called for 50,000 additional officers. His figures change so quickly it is hard to keep up with them. At any rate, it is clear that he had not the slightest intention of even proposing 100,000 additional officers. Why? Because he couldn't afford to, given the grandiose public-works schemes he was drooling over.

But perhaps the most egregious example of how deceitful, cunning, and disingenuous this president can be is illustrated by his response to Bush-Quayle campaign ads that proved that in order to accomplish all he promised by way of simultaneous new spending and massive deficit reduction, he would have to raise taxes on every family earning more than $36,000 a year. And that was assuming there was a static economy, one in which people's economic behavior is unaffected by fiscal policy. In the real world, we know that economies contract when people's earnings are overburdened with marginal income-tax rate increases. Factoring in this dynamic reality, Clinton's figures are shown to be that much more ludicrous.

But Clinton's response to the Bush ad: "It is blatantly false," he retorted. "It is a disgrace to the American people that the president of the United States would make a claim that is so baseless, that is so without foundation, so shameless in its attempt to get votes under false pretenses."

Of course, just weeks after he took office, it became clear that the only thing false about the Bush-Quayle campaign ad was that it underestimated Clinton's tax-and-spend propensity. Today we realize that Americans who earn as little as $20,000 a year will be subject to higher gas taxes. And, in fact, almost all Americans—no matter what they earn—will be paying significantly higher taxes of other kinds. And the other shoe (health-care reform) has yet to drop as of this writing.

When confronted with this contradiction after taking office, Clinton coolly and unctuously blamed his actions on the $346 billion budget deficit, which he claimed was $50 billion higher than he expected. But in July 1992, he told *Business Week* magazine that he expected the deficit would approach $400 billion. The Congressional Budget Office (CBO) had projected such a total and Clinton was relying on it. Folks, I'm not making this stuff up. Go check it out for yourself. If anything, Clinton should be relieved that the deficit he inherited was not as high as the Democrat-controlled CBO said it would be.

This may sound harsh, ladies and gentlemen, but there is no other plausible explanation for this phenomenon. There is a pattern here. Bill Clinton lies brazenly. Then he lies brazenly to cover his brazen lies. Then he lies brazenly to cover his brazen cover. Then, I'm sure, he asks Hillary what to do!

What's clear even from these few examples is that Bill Clinton ran as a different kind of Democrat—a no-nonsense, tax-cutting, law-and-order candidate. Now we know he is none of those things.

I ask you in all humility: Who warned you about all this? Who told you that once Clinton was elected, he would quickly resort to the old tax-and-spend formula of the modern liberal? Who was that lonely voice crying out in the media wilderness? *Hhhhmm-mmmm?*

I get no satisfaction out of saying, once again, See, I Told You So. Truly, I don't. But I'm going to say it anyway, if for no other reason than it happens to be the title of this book: See, I Told You So.

LIES, LIES

The Limbaugh Institute for Advanced Conservative Studies, in an effort to amply demonstrate the disingenuousness of the Clinton administration, has cataloged this avalanche of falsehoods. This list first appeared in The Limbaugh Letter *and is reprinted here by popular demand.*

- "We need to provide a tax credit of up to $800 per child to ease the burden on working families."
  —BILL CLINTON, MARCH 1992

- "We will lower the tax burden on middle-class Americans. Middle-class taxpayers will have a choice between a children's tax credit or a significant reduction in their income tax rate."
  —BILL CLINTON, "PUTTING PEOPLE FIRST"

- "We should cut middle-class taxes immediately by 10 percent."
  —BILL CLINTON, CAMPAIGN DOCUMENT, SEPTEMBER 1992

- "We want to give modest middle-class tax relief to restore some fairness, especially to middle-class people with families with incomes of under $60,000 per year."
  —BILL CLINTON, FIRST PRESIDENTIAL DEBATE, OCTOBER 1992

- "I've offered a comprehensive plan to get our economy moving again. It starts with a tax cut for the middle class."
  —BILL CLINTON, FIRST CAMPAIGN AD, JANUARY 1992

- "I want to make it very clear that this middle-class tax cut, in my view, is central to any attempt we're going to make to have a short-term economic strategy."
  —BILL CLINTON, JANUARY 19, 1992

"From New Hampshire forward, for reasons that absolutely mystified me, the press thought the most important issue in the race was the middle-class tax cut. I never did meet any voter who thought that."
— BILL CLINTON, PRESS CONFERENCE, JANUARY 14, 1993

- "I will slash boondoggle projects."
— BILL CLINTON, "PUTTING PEOPLE FIRST"

- "We're slashing subsidies and canceling wasteful projects. Many of these programs were justified in their time and a lot of them were difficult for me personally . . . We're going to have no sacred cows."
— BILL CLINTON, STATE OF THE UNION, FEBRUARY 18, 1993

"The Clinton team's search for programs 'that don't work or are no longer needed' found only eleven."
— THE WALL STREET JOURNAL, MARCH 23, 1993

- "I will not raise taxes on the middle class."
— BILL CLINTON, JUNE 21, 1992

- "I'm not going to raise taxes on the middle class."
— BILL CLINTON, JULY 13, 1992

- "The middle class has paid through the nose for a decade. We have to be somewhat wary of making a problem of inadequate income even worse by taxing people whose incomes are going down. That's my premise."
— BILL CLINTON, QUOTED IN *TIME*, JULY 20, 1992

"I had hoped to invest in your future without asking more of you. And I've worked harder than I've ever worked in my life to meet that goal. But I can't."
— BILL CLINTON, OVAL OFFICE ADDRESS, FEBRUARY 15, 1993, ANNOUNCING
MIDDLE-CLASS TAX INCREASE AFTER BEING IN OFFICE LESS THAN ONE MONTH

- "I can tell you this. I'm not going to raise taxes on middle-income Americans to pay for the programs I've recommended. If the money does not come in to pay for these programs, we will cut other government spending or we will slow down the phase-in of these programs."

—Bill Clinton, last presidential debate,
October 19, 1992

$178 billion: cost of Clinton's proposed new spending.
$173 billion: revenues raised under Clinton plan from Social Security, income, energy, and gas taxes.
— Bill Clinton's budget document, "A Vision of Change for America,"
February 1993

- "The only people who will pay more income taxes are the wealthiest 2 percent, those living in households making over $200,000 a year."

—Bill Clinton, September 8, 1992

- "It is a disgrace to the American people that the president of the United States would make a claim that is so baseless, that is so without foundation, so shameless in its attempt to get votes under false pretenses."

—Bill Clinton, October 1, 1992, in response to a Bush-Quayle ad that people with incomes of as little as $36,000 would pay more taxes under the Clinton plan

"There are [tax] increases for every family making more than $20,000 a year."

—New York Times *analysis of Clinton's budget*

- "When I began the campaign, the projected deficit was $250 billion. Now it's up to $400 billion."

—Bill Clinton, quoted in *Business Week*, July 6, 1992

- "When I started in New Hampshire working with those numbers, we felt the deficit was going to be around $250 billion a year, not $400 billion."

—Bill Clinton, quoted in *Time*, July 20, 1992

"The deficit of this country is about $50 billion a year bigger than I was told it was going to be before the election."
— Bill Clinton, February 10, 1993, after "discovering" that the deficit was $290 billion, $110 billion less than he had claimed in July

48

- "My plan will cut the deficit in four years and assure that the deficit continues to fall each year after that."
  —BILL CLINTON, JUNE 20, 1992

- "My economic package will cut $500 billion from the deficit in five years."
  —BILL CLINTON, PRESS CONFERENCE, MARCH 23, 1993

Deficit in 1998 with Clinton budget: $234 billion.
Deficit in 2001 with Clinton budget: $401 billion.
— *BILL CLINTON'S BUDGET DOCUMENT, "A VISION OF CHANGE FOR AMERICA,"*
FEBRUARY 1993

- "I don't like to use the word *sacrifice*."
  —BILL CLINTON, MAY 1992

"It will not be easy. It will require sacrifice."
— *BILL CLINTON, JANUARY 1993*

- "My plan is basically 50–50, spending cuts and revenues the first four years."
  —BILL CLINTON, FEBRUARY 1993

- "If the Senate will adopt a budget resolution like the House did, the American people will know we are not going to raise taxes until we cut spending, and we are going to create jobs."
  —BILL CLINTON, PRESS CONFERENCE, MARCH 23, 1993

Net new taxes: $267 billion—Net new spending cuts: $55 billion—
83 percent taxes, 17 percent spending cuts
— *CONGRESSIONAL BUDGET OFFICE ANALYSIS OF CLINTON*
BUDGET, MARCH 1993

- "He [Bush] hasn't fought a real war on crime and drugs. I will."
  —BILL CLINTON, DEMOCRATIC NATIONAL CONVENTION, JULY 16, 1992

121 positions at the Office of National Drug Control Policy elimi-
nated. Policy of random drug testing for White House staff revoked.
— *WHITE HOUSE ANNOUNCEMENT, FEBRUARY 9, 1993*

- "I think President Bush played racial politics with the Haitian refugees. I wouldn't be shipping those poor people back."
  —BILL CLINTON, MARCH 27, 1992

- "The practice of returning those who fled by boat will continue, for the time being, after I become president. Those who do leave Haiti by boat will be stopped and directly returned by the United States Coast Guard."
  —BILL CLINTON, JANUARY 14, 1993

- "My Haiti policy is not the same as the Bush policy."
  —BILL CLINTON, JANUARY 14, 1993

"Administration to Defend Bush Haitian Policy in Court"
  —THE WASHINGTON POST, *MARCH 1, 1993*

- "If [Mr. Hussein] wants a different relationship with the United States, all he has to do is change his behavior."
  —BILL CLINTON, QUOTED IN *THE NEW YORK TIMES*, JANUARY 13, 1993

- "Everybody who heard those conversations was astonished that such a conclusion could be drawn. Nobody asked me about normalization."
  —BILL CLINTON, JANUARY 14, 1993, DENYING THAT HE MADE CONCILIATORY REMARKS REGARDING SADDAM HUSSEIN

"The president inadvertently forgot that he was asked and he regrets denying that it was asked."
  — *GEORGE STEPHANOPOULOS, JANUARY 15, 1993, AFTER* NEW YORK TIMES *TRANSCRIPTS REVEALED THAT CLINTON HAD BEEN SPECIFICALLY ASKED ABOUT "NORMAL RELATIONS" AND "NORMALIZATION," NOT ONCE, BUT FIVE TIMES*

- "We call for an immediate repeal of the ban on gays and lesbians serving in United States Armed Forces."
  —BILL CLINTON, CAMPAIGN DOCUMENT, OCTOBER 1992

- "I was frankly appalled that we spent so much time in the first week on gays in the military."
  —BILL CLINTON, FEBRUARY 10, 1993

- "Senators in the other party wanted it dealt with now. I actually spent very little time on the issue myself."
  —BILL CLINTON, FEBRUARY 10, 1993, A FEW MINUTES LATER

- "I'm going to ask them [Congress] to cut spending in a broad range of areas."
—BILL CLINTON, FEBRUARY 10, 1993, REFERRING TO BUDGET THAT CUTS SPEND-
ING PRIMARILY IN ONE AREA: THE MILITARY

"As long as I am president, I will do everything I can do to make sure that the men and women who serve under the American flag will remain the best trained, the best prepared, the best equipped fighting force in the world."
— *BILL CLINTON, JOINT SESSION OF CONGRESS,*
FEBRUARY 17, 1993

- "I will save the country $700 billion by the turn of the century under my proposals to cap health care costs."
—BILL CLINTON, SEPTEMBER 24, 1992

- "This plan is not play or pay. It will require no new taxes."
—BILL CLINTON, SEPTEMBER 24, 1992, IN A SPEECH ON HIS HEALTH-CARE
PLAN TO EMPLOYEES OF MERCK PHARMACEUTICALS IN RAHWAY, NEW JERSEY

"Clinton Health Plan to Cost $100 Billion a Year"
—WASHINGTON TIMES, *APRIL 23, 1993*

- "The health-care task force has just met."
—BILL CLINTON, ANNOUNCING THE FORMATION OF THE TASK FORCE OF 526
MEMBERS UNDER HILLARY CLINTON, JANUARY 25, 1992

"The health-care task force has never met."
— *ARGUMENT MADE BY WHITE HOUSE LAWYERS BEFORE FEDERAL JUDGE*
ROYCE LAMBERTH ON THE LEGALITY OF THE CLOSED TASK FORCE MEETINGS,
MARCH 1993

- "I did not mean to float a trial balloon about a national sales tax. It's not under consideration at this time. Ten to 15 years away."
—BILL CLINTON, FEBRUARY 19, 1993

- "We have to reject tax-and-spend economics."
—BILL CLINTON, NATIONAL LEAGUE OF CITIES CONFERENCE,
MARCH 8, 1993

"Certainly, we're looking at a VAT tax."
— *DONNA SHALALA, SECRETARY OF HEALTH AND HUMAN SERVICES,*
APRIL 15, 1993

- "The problem of the structural deficit is rooted in the early 1980s when we cut income taxes and increased defense spending." —Bill Clinton, "Putting People First"

Individual income taxes 1980: $244 billion.
Individual income taxes 1992: $476 billion.
National defense spending 1980: 5.1 percent of GDP.
National defense spending 1992: 5.0 percent of GDP.
  —U.S. Budget Office, January 1993

- "I'm sure—after almost five weeks in office—that there are more [budget] cuts coming."
  —Bill Clinton, U.S. Chamber of Commerce, February 1993

"The president had no specific cuts in mind and no schedule for making them."
  —George Stephanopoulos, the next day

- "We don't need to tamper with Social Security."
  —Bill Clinton, September 1992

"The budget plan does ask older Americans with higher incomes who do not rely solely on Social Security to get by to contribute more."
  —Bill Clinton, State of the Union, January 1993

- "I have confirmed that I intend to present to the leadership in Congress a plan of action for the first hundred days of the next presidency."
  —Bill Clinton, June 6, 1992

- "If I'm elected, I'll have the bills ready the day after I'm inaugurated. I'll send them to Congress and we'll have a hundred-day period."
  —Bill Clinton, "Good Morning America," June 23, 1992

- "My first one hundred days will be the most productive in modern history."
  —Bill Clinton, June 1992

"People of the press are expecting to have some 100–day program. We never ever had one."
  —Dee Dee Myers, January 12, 1993

Source: House Republican Conference and press reports.

5

PUNISHING ACHIEVEMENT

"GREED IS GOOD," EVIL CAPITALIST GORDON GEKKO TELLS AN AUDI-
ence in director Oliver Stone's movie *Wall Street.* "Greed works."
This may surprise some of my detractors, but I don't believe that
greed is good. Frankly, I don't know how any thinking person
could. But let me paraphrase Gordon Gekko. Let me rewrite his
mini-monologue in a way that should be instructive to those who
unhappily have bought into Bill Clinton's and Hollywood's propagandized version of the eighties:

Profits are good; profits work.

To some, this statement may seem to be the moral equivalent of
Gordon Gekko's. I assure you, it is not. Greed and profits are not
the same. Neither are greed and the pursuit of profits. They have,
however, been intentionally confused by certain opportunistic
politicians in our society.

Similarly, the phrase "trickle-down economics" was bandied
about with calculated frequency during the presidential campaign.
The relentless use of the phrase by the Clinton-Gore team and their
effort to equate profits with greed were part of their shameless
exploitation of the politics of class envy.

So impressive was the Reagan record that liberals knew they had to take drastic action if they were to have any hope of recapturing the hearts and minds of the voters. How do you attack seven years of unbridled economic growth? It is axiomatic that with less governmental burdens, most economic classes of people will do well. Even many of those in need who depend on transfer payments are able to improve themselves in a free-market environment. Not surprisingly, the Democrats reverted to their age-old theme of class envy. It is a political strategy that dates back at least to the days of Karl Marx. Like so many other political tactics, it pits one group against another.

Since the empirical evidence of the eighties was unassailable, the Democrats decided to shift the debate to a question of fairness. The idea was to play to people's baser emotions of envy, jealousy, and distrust. Convince the lower and middle classes that they were worse off after fifty-nine consecutive months of record-setting post-war growth, even though they were doing demonstrably better—because the wealthy also did better. The meaning was clear: Achievement must be vilified; the rich must be punished. Instead of holding up successful people as role models and promoting the American Dream that it is still possible to be successful through hard work, the Clinton message was, and still is, to demonize that segment of the population that is allegedly "benefiting" unfairly. By using these themes, the Democrats hope to lay the emotional groundwork for wealth redistribution, which is ultimately their ticket to power.

Bill Clinton may be the most effective practitioner of class warfare since Lenin. Just keep this in mind: Today it's the pharmaceutical manufacturers, the cable-TV industry, insurance companies, physicians, and chief executive officers of major corporations he's targeting. Tomorrow it could be you.

In analyzing this issue, here are the key questions to ponder: When do profits become unfair and excessive? And who should make that determination? Almost everyone—from former communists to Bill Clinton—pays lip service to free enterprise, market economics, and capitalism these days. But for too many, mere lip service is where it stops. Often, they do not appreciate how the system works. They seem to be uncomfortable about the philosophical underpinnings of capitalism and adverse to the great American spirit of rugged individualism and competition. Unwittingly, in many cases they are actually egalitarians: those who believe that the U.S. Constitution does—or, if not, at least should—guarantee equality of outcomes rather than equality of opportunity. This concept is also known by other names, such as "economic justice," a favorite of the Rev. Jesse Jackson and Representative Maxine Waters (D-California). They simply don't believe that market forces, unfettered by government, can possibly effectuate an equitable allocation of resources. According to them, competition and the profit motive, the twin evils of avarice-based American capitalism, simply bring out the baser side of human nature. As such, they advocate Draconian governmental intervention in the economy.

What every liberal politician in America—Bill Clinton included—ought to be forced to do is to sit through an Economics 101 course taught by a non-Marxist university professor. Knowing how unlikely that is, given the current PC climate in academia, Professor Limbaugh, the Doctor of Democracy and Chancellor of the Limbaugh Institute for Advanced Conservative Studies, will endeavor to offer that curriculum in this chapter.

The fundamental flaw in socialist theory is that we live in a zero-sum world—that when someone wins or achieves something, someone else is, by necessity, losing. Or, stated another way, the productivity and income pies are finite—when one person earns an extra dollar, he must be taking it from someone else. This is a demonstrably false assumption. Liberals seem unable to comprehend the concept of wealth creation: that our economy is not a zero-sum game; that one person's achievement is not necessarily the other person's loss; that burdensome taxes have a deterrent effect on the production of income and wealth and jobs. You can see real-life applications of this as the Senate Finance Committee is employing simple mathematics to determine what combinations of tax and spending programs must be proposed to yield a certain amount of deficit reduction. The committee's attempt to make these revenue calculations in a vacuum, totally ignoring the critical variable of human behavior, would be comical if it were not so destructive to the nation. Specifically, having scrapped the BTU tax proposal (estimated to generate $72 billion in revenues) in favor of a

4.3 cent transportation tax increase (expected to yield much less in revenues), they are agonizing over what other spending cuts (such as $19 billion more in Medicare) or tax increases (such as increasing the corporate income tax rate from 34 percent to 35 percent) will make up the difference. They never pause for a millisecond to consider the revenue-retarding effects of their gargantuan tax and tax-rate increases, despite decades of history to guide them. It must take effort to ignore such a well-established truth. Instead, Democratic Senate leaders George J. Mitchell of Maine and Daniel Patrick Moynihan of New York focus on the "progressive" nature of the bill. Ironically, by "progressive" they mean anything but "progress." They mean that the tax burden is progressively higher on those with higher levels of income.

Let me use my own experience to demonstrate how one person's gain is not necessarily someone else's loss.

In July 1988, I started a nationally syndicated radio program. The experts said it couldn't be done. But I took a risk and tried. Others placed their money at risk and invested in my effort. The experts were wrong. It worked. Big-time. My partners and I realized considerable earnings. Bluntly stated, we made money, we did not receive benefits. So did many of those who were wise enough to advertise on my program. And we all continue to.

The relevant question is: Who lost money? The answer: Nobody. "But wait," some of you skeptics may be asking. "How about the other radio shows—your competitors? Didn't they lose out?"

Good question, but the answer is an emphatic "no!" If you read the broadcasting trade publications, you will learn that the Rush Limbaugh program is actually being hailed in some quarters as "saving AM radio." Now, in the interest of preserving my image of humility I will not go that far. But I must tell you that another group did benefit tremendously from the success of the radio program—the stations that carry it. In some cases, the program has literally lifted radio stations out of the ratings doldrums or worse and into prosperity.

What those stations find is that not only are more people listening to my program, they are also listening to radio more. So even more people are benefiting indirectly from the success of the show. There are simply no losers in this game—except, my dear friends, those who are not listening. And the same principle applies to my other areas of success—television and publishing. Nobody loses except those who don't participate.

"But, Professor Limbaugh," some of you may be asking, "isn't your success story unique? Aren't there losers in more traditional industries? Don't we need to protect the citizenry from unreasonable profiteering?"

This is where many people in our society—liberals as well as normal folk—go astray and get confused. They simply don't understand the nature of profits and the positive role they play in a free-market economy. This is where the real beauty of the marketplace enters the picture.

The pursuit of profits provides the incentive that encourages entrepreneurs and developers to experiment—to do market research, to innovate, create, and invent, let us say—all at private expense. The important role profits play in an economy is to signal to investors—risk-takers—where to send more resources and where to send less. Take IBM, for instance. Here's a gigantic computer company that invested billions of dollars in certain kinds of products, and recently many of them failed to make it in the marketplace. Even a major corporation like IBM can't dictate to the marketplace. The marketplace rules, but not arbitrarily, as the government does in its capacity of allocating resources. And that is the critical distinction. When the market is the final arbiter, consumers' needs will be satisfied, because consumers, collectively, are the market. So even though IBM's risk in developing certain products failed to pay off, consumers still got the kind they wanted. Such occurrences are incomprehensible to liberals because they believe that in almost all situations the evil corporate giants will prevail to the detriment of consumers.

"Yes, but Professor Limbaugh," others of you may be questioning, "weren't tens of thousands of people thrown out of work by those miscalculations? What about those poor people?"

Yes, it is true that there was serious economic dislocation for people in the case of the IBM cutbacks. Bad things do happen to people—even good people, innocent people. There are risks in life.

If a venture doesn't succeed, then a company doesn't turn a profit. It stops doing what it is doing. Not even the most zealous capitalist would tell you that the free market is a panacea. The Bible assures us that we are never going to eradicate poverty completely. Utopia is not achievable on this Earth, but capitalism is the best system available to provide the most wealth for the most people. The alternative is to employ Robert Reich*hhhh*'s plan and force IBM, with the supplement of government subsidies, to continue to employ those who, unfortunately, are no longer needed, at a much larger expense to the overall economy and the consumer.

Regardless, don't believe any politician who tries to exploit the misfortunes of others for political gain. And that, my friends, is what Bill Clinton and his band of class warriors are all about. No one—no matter what they may tell you—has developed a better system than the market for determining what gets produced and what doesn't.

Command economies and central planning have simply never worked. The world has been an excellent laboratory for experiments in government control of the economy. It didn't work in the Soviet Union. It didn't work in any of the Eastern European countries that tried it. It hasn't worked in China. It is not working in Cuba. And the more we experiment with it here in the United States, the more misery we inflict on our people, all in the name of "fairness."

The new brand of smooth-talking, Ivy League–educated, Armani-clad class warriors, led by our commander-in-chief, would have you believe that exceptionally high profits should be taxed at an exceptionally high rate. They say things that sound good, like: "We cannot have profits at the expense of our children." At first glance, such a non sequitur rings true with most good people. That's right, people think: I don't want profits at the expense of my children. But what does this mean? What is their solution? It's always the same, folks: Give them the reins. They're more humane. They'll do what's right for you. "Give us the power—we'll protect you," they say.

And, unfortunately, the electorate complied. Bill Clinton managed to get 43 percent of the vote precisely because enough people liked the idea of punishing achievement—soaking the rich. Even if there wasn't going to be anything in it for them, they liked the idea of inflicting a little pain on the wealthy.

I've got news for you, folks. The wealthy aren't the only ones affected. Economic hardships trickle down, as well. It's ordinary working people who bear the brunt of such misguided policies.

Let me give you an example. This is one the Democratic congressmen hope we forget. Remember a few years ago, during another administration, Congress got the bright idea to impose a luxury tax on us. Most middle-class and poor people didn't object. After all, they thought: We don't buy diamonds and airplanes and yachts. Only the rich do, and they can afford to pay more. This was the vapid logic behind the luxury tax.

And what happened? Almost everyone now agrees that it was a rotten idea. Why? Because it didn't raise revenues for the government and it inflicted great suffering—not on the rich, but on working people. How? The wealthy simply postponed buying as many luxury items as they might have purchased under normal circumstances. And the manufacturers of those items—especially boats—cut back on their production and laid off workers. So not only did unemployment increase, but government lost revenues because fewer luxury items were bought and sold. And you want to know a dirty little secret? This luxury tax on yachts, jewelry, boats, and airplanes was rescinded in the 1993 deficit reduction bill, a quiet (Shh! Don't tell this to anyone!) admission that raising tax rates on the activities of the rich had a negative result on middle-class people. So highlight this example, folks. A tax increase yielded negative revenues! But if you're a liberal, the highlighter won't rescue you from your incredulity. You simply don't have the capacity to comprehend such concepts. If you did, we wouldn't have to continue to be bludgeoned with class-warfare rhetoric and America could return to its historical path of productivity and growth.

There's a valuable supply-side lesson here for those who would raise just about any tax. In the 1980s, the federal treasury saw a massive increase in tax revenues after a tax-rate cut. Despite what the revisionists tell you, revenues nearly doubled. Because, as I've told you, people's economic behavior is affected by changes in marginal tax rates. In the case of the eighties, lower marginal tax rates provided the incentive to produce, which created more jobs and more taxpayers. Mr. Jack Kemp was right. A rising tide lifts all boats. A luxury tax sinks them.

So remember these things the next time you are confronted by a guilt-peddling liberal railing against "trickle-down" and preaching the zero-sum myth. In a free-market environment, or one even approaching it, wealth is constantly being created, and usually it is without victimization, without pain.

But you must understand that the creation of wealth and prosperity does not serve the interests of the class warriors. The key to power for them is in scapegoating achievers.

Think of it. Working people today are more frustrated than ever because they seem to have less buying power. Why do they have less buying power? Because they are being taxed into serfdom. Americans now work an average of 123 days (and the figure is rising) simply to pay their tax bills at the federal, state, and local levels. That means that you, dear readers, work exclusively for the government in January, February, March, and April. Sometime in early May you actually begin working for yourself and your family. That's not free enterprise, my friends. That's slavery. And what does this beneficent government do for most of you? Beyond providing a national defense, not much, I daresay.

But because the class warriors don't want you to realize it is they who are picking your pockets, they blame others. For example, they beat the drum about the high cost of medical care and blame, in part, the pharmaceutical industry for profiteering. President Clinton excoriated the drug companies because their profits were "rising at four times the rate of the average Fortune 500 company." So what? Isn't that good? Maybe they should be held up as a model of achievement rather than be singled out for punishment. Wouldn't we all be better off if other American companies were experiencing as much success as the pharmaceutical industry? Wouldn't there be more jobs, more investment, and more new consumer products available in the marketplace? Wouldn't that be a bonanza for our country? Shouldn't that be our goal?

But there's also another side of this story that you won't hear from the major media or from the administration.

What they don't tell you is that these same profiteering companies are investing an unprecedented amount of their profits back into research and development. That translates into medical break-throughs for you and your family—a longer life, perhaps, and certainly better health for all of us. Do we really want to discourage this? Well, you'd better get used to it, because many drug compa-nies are now scaling back on life-saving research because of onerous taxes and regulations and the promise of even more.

The Clintons' solution is to nationalize health-care policy. Let them decide who earns what and how much medical attention your family needs and deserves. Oh, sure, they refer to it euphemistically as "managed competition" (an oxymoron if I've ever heard one), in which major groups will consolidate their forces and become grandiose purchasing agents. Would you rather take your chances in the marketplace, or wait in a government line for rationed care?

But some people still don't get it. They don't understand the choices they face. I remember attending the wedding of my good friend George Brett, the future baseball Hall of Famer who plays for the Kansas City Royals. A young woman attending the ceremony—someone who obviously did not know much about baseball—commented, "It doesn't seem fair that he makes so much money."

This woman could not understand why a superstar major-league baseball player like George Brett can make $3 million, while a schoolteacher earns only about $29,000 a year. She suggested we ought somehow stop paying the multimillion-dollar salaries in professional athletics. This presumably would make schoolteachers feel better about their own self-worth.

I disagree. Just as I radically disagree with Clinton's pernicious proposal to eliminate income tax deductions for corporate executive salaries that are in excess of $1 million. Let the market decide. There are only about 650 people at any one time qualified to play major-league baseball in America. Those are the people we pay to see or turn on the television to watch. If they don't play, fans don't watch. It's market economics at work. Regardless, it's none of government's business to tell people how much they can earn. It's hard to believe that the governing elite have such a learning disability concerning world history. In trying to equalize incomes, they'll help no one and ultimately enslave everyone.

But in terms of the economic realities of modern professional sports, the reason athletes' salaries have escalated so dramatically in recent years (other than the obvious effects of inflation) is the impact of television. During the days Babe Ruth played, the revenues generated by a team were largely limited to its ticket sales and sales of concessions during games. So Babe Ruth, even though he was the greatest player of his time, never got paid much more than the low six figures. Even as late as the 1960s, before the profit potential of television could be fully exploited by sports franchises, the great players—like Mickey Mantle—still made only in the $100,000 range.

All that began to change in the 1970s. As the potential for profits grew, salaries grew, too. This is *the way things ought to be*, to coin a phrase. Like it or not, the Chicago Bulls are sold out every year, largely because of Michael Jordan.

How does all this relate to teachers' salaries and other alleged inequities? It's easy to sit on the sidelines and make a value judgment that a teacher is more important to society than someone who can hit home runs or win twenty games. But in a free-market economy, there is nothing out of kilter. Without denigrating the teaching profession or teachers, for whom I have untold respect, the fact of the matter is that only a small percentage of people play professional baseball. There are millions of people involved in education. Special skills—especially those in areas where potential profit is great and those skills can be parlayed into the creation of wealth—are rewarded.

Nobody is forced to become a schoolteacher. There is no teacher shortage. It is an occupation that is vitally important, but many people possess the basic skills and competence to become teachers. If salaries were so low that people no longer wanted to become teachers, the magic of the marketplace would cause salaries to rise. That's the way the market works (to the extent it's allowed to) in education and every other field. It's called supply and demand.

Liberals would love to get their hands on the controls—on the levers of the marketplace. They would love to set wages and prices, not because they really care about inequities, but because it would empower them as the moral arbiters of how much each person should make. Whenever this has been tried, it has failed— miserably. Do you remember when President Richard Nixon briefly and regrettably imposed wage and price controls? It was a completely un-American thing to do, especially for a Republican. And, for those of us old enough to remember, it was an unmitigated and thankfully short-lived disaster.

Big government has not been able to solve any of this country's social problems. None. So why should we be looking to grant big government any more responsibility over our lives? But beware, the current crop of class warriors intends to extort more money from the productive sector of the economy and to steer even more people into government dependency.

Under the guise of compassion, liberalism is actually empowered by dependency. Liberals love it when people like the ponytail guy in Richmond, Virginia, get up at presidential debates and plead for help from government, because, "We're your children." Oh, please! American citizens do not want to be treated like children by their government. They do not want to become wards of the state.

Now, back to the issue of high salaries for athletes and CEOs. Even if you assume they are unfair, which assumption I wholly reject, what is the liberals' solution for it? Nothing sophisticated. They simply want to cut the high salaries. Not one of them proposes ways to raise the salaries of the average worker. Liberals, you see, don't know how to do that. They continue to sponsor minimum-wage legislation when it is known to increase unemployment for the very group it purports to assist. But in the liberals' world, symbolism prevails over substance. They are content, once again, to punish achievement—even at the expense of many on the lower end of the economic spectrum—rather than help productive people become more productive.

You, as a worker and as an employee, must realize that punishing CEOs and athletes will not improve your life at all. But it seems that those who talk about fairness today actually mean retribution. It seems they want to exact revenge on achievers to make themselves feel better on some level.

So what is my solution? It's certainly nothing unique or anything I came up with myself. I've said it before and I'll say it again and again and again. We need to teach self-reliance. We need to re-establish the American work ethic. It's a fact of life that when something is *given* to someone, he values it far less than when he *earns* it through his own sweat. Government handouts with no strings attached ultimately rob individuals of their dignity. But in the liberal welfare state, who needs dignity when they've got Big Brother to take care of everything?

We are not doing nearly enough to teach and to help people seize the opportunity that already exists in this country. Instead, we are too busy making victims out of people and blaming others for their plight. In the process, we have created a class of people fully capable of producing who are merely surviving and taking—a parasitic class.

The tragic result of this class warfare—this politics of envy—will not be the brave new world Bill Clinton and company envision. Instead, it will be something closer to economic Darwinism. The best, the brightest, the fittest, and the most successful will, out of necessity, become even more productive. And those for whom Bill Clinton's big government is the messiah will degenerate into a hopeless, dependent underclass. These policies will simply foster even greater rugged individualism in those who already have it.

The entire economic program of the class warriors is based on confiscating more and more money from those who have earned it, produced it, and saved it, and transferring it to a political and bureaucratic class in Washington to spend as they see fit. People should be encouraged to work hard, strive for excellence, and take prudent risks. Instead, liberals continue enacting policies that spread the misery by shrinking the productive sector of the economy and then proclaiming that the result is fairness.

The big-government crowd probably salivates in anticipation of the day when 51 percent of the people in this country rely on government for their survival. That way, they figure, they will be perpetually empowered. They will win every election simply by promising to keep feeding those who are already eating at the public trough. Alexis de Tocqueville, the nineteenth-century French political philosopher, in observing America, warned that once the people realized they could vote themselves money from the public trough, this great democracy would be in peril.

The sad reality is that by making those promises for more and more government help and intervention in our lives, liberals are doing even their own pathetic constituency a great disservice. Causing people to rely more on government and less on themselves is the worst thing any government can do to its own people. It's not compassion. It's exploitation. America's economic renaissance requires less government and the unleashing of the entrepreneurial spirit. That is the direction in which this country should be headed as we approach the twenty-first century.

6

DEAD WHITE GUYS
OR
WHAT YOUR HISTORY BOOKS
NEVER TOLD YOU

OUR COUNTRY IS INHERENTLY EVIL. THE WHOLE IDEA OF AMERICA IS corrupt. The history of this nation is strewn with examples of oppression and genocide. The story of the United States is cultural imperialism—how a bunch of repressed white men imposed their will and values on peaceful indigenous people, black slaves from Africa, and women.

No, don't worry. Rush has not become a commie-lib. The paragraph above, though, does summarize what is being taught today about American history on the average college or university campus. Why? What makes the education establishment so hostile to America? Because, in the last twenty-five years, a relatively small, angry group of anti-American radicals have bullied their way into power positions in academia. And while they preach about the evils of "cultural imperialism," they themselves are, ironically, the ultimate practitioners of it.

The indoctrination taking place today in American academia is disingenuously disguised as "multiculturalism" by its academic purveyors. A more accurate description would be "politically motivated historical and cultural distortion." It is a primitive type of historical revisionism.

Because unexpurgated history has been so cruel in its judgment of liberalism and socialism, it seems the only recourse left for their adherents is to rewrite history. Even the history of the 1980s—a decade most of us lived through and should remember—is being rewritten before our very eyes by people who want to deny it was a decade of great prosperity and success. It was, they keep telling us, "a decade of greed." Think about it. If events of the last decade can be so badly distorted right in front of people who experienced them and should know better (more on that later), imagine the spin that politically inspired revisionists would put on early American history, with there being virtually no counter-voices to refute it.

Obviously, history is not being taught well enough in schools or I wouldn't have to do this chapter to set the record straight. There's a massive amount of deception to overcome, both in the "facts" and the underlying themes being presented. But, as usual, I am more than up to the challenge. What you are about to read was once routinely learned by every schoolchild in America. Today, as a hapless student of our public school system, you probably wouldn't hear most of this stuff even if you pursued a post-graduate degree in American history (unless, of course, that degree was from the Limbaugh Institute for Advanced Conservative Studies).

Let's start at the beginning with America's first important dead white male—Christopher Columbus. The politically correct view of old Chris today is that the Italian explorer did not actually discover America, because people were already living here. And, more important, he brought nothing to the peaceful New World "paradise" but oppression, disease, brutality, and genocide.

First of all, let me state something unequivocally: **Columbus really did discover America.** By making that claim, I am obviously not suggesting that no human being had set foot on the continent before 1492. But there can be no denying that Columbus was the person who brought America to the attention of the technologically advanced, civilized world and paved the way for the expansion of Western civilization (what a horrifying thought). True, if *Algore* had discovered the New World, we would still be living in the jungle exchanging wampum for milo. If you long for that scenario, please discontinue reading at this point.

What kind of a world did Columbus discover? Did he find blissful natives living in perfect harmony with one another and communing with nature, as today's liberals would have us believe? Hardly.

What he found was a land sparsely inhabited by nomadic hunting tribes. Many were constantly on the verge of starvation. They had not yet discovered the wheel and had no written language. Tribe against tribe—they lived a violent and brutal existence. Of those Caribbean Indians Columbus came into contact with, the Arawaks attacked and enslaved the Siboney. The Caribs feasted (literally) on members of both tribes.

Here's a scene one of Columbus's search parties discovered on Guadeloupe: "They found large cuts and joints of human flesh . . . caponized Arawak boy captives who were being fattened for the griddle, and girl captives who were mainly used to produce babies, which the Caribs regarded as a particularly toothsome morsel."

Today, it is fashionable to romanticize Indian life. But even a cursory examination of the historical record shows that life was far from utopian for these people—long before Columbus. In fact, while there were certainly atrocities against Indians by white people, there were just as many—and probably to a greater degree of savagery—committed by other Indians. Also, there are more American Indians alive today than there were when Columbus arrived or at any other time in history. Does that sound like a record of genocide?

Know this: When you hear people bashing Christopher Columbus, as they did incessantly during the five-hundredth anniversary celebrations in 1992, Columbus himself is merely a symbol, a vehicle, a retrospective scapegoat; their real target is America and Western civilization. The Indians were wonderful, they say. The dead white men were the oppressors. It's all so black and white to the revisionists. These *Columbashers* harbor an irrebuttable (in their own minds) presumption of prejudice against Western culture. Historical facts and evidence at variance with their predisposition, if ever even considered, are summarily rejected. At the core of this anti-Western view is a not-so-subtle racism so insidious and pervasive as to be almost unspeakable.

But I will speak about it. Let me translate multiculture-speak for you and put it into more direct language we all can understand: *Indians are good. White Europeans are bad. Blacks are good. Asians, we're not too sure about.* Regardless of how they camouflage it, this is the essence of multiculturalism and the kind of psychobabble being disseminated in our institutions of higher learning today. The corollary themes are that character and identity are primarily shaped by ethnicity. The pattern is easy enough to follow. First, they ascribe fictitious misdeeds to people not alive to defend themselves; then they categorically indict the entire race for the fabricated atrocities attributed to some. Is this not overt racism emanating from self-described ethnically and racially sensitive people? If we have learned anything in this country in the last thirty years, isn't it that we should judge people by the content of their character rather than the color of their skin? Isn't that what Dr. Martin Luther King, Jr., taught us? Why, then, are liberals allowed to get away with this stuff?

Well, folks, let's allow our real, undoctored-American-history lesson to unfold further. If our schools and the media have twisted the historical record when it comes to Columbus, they have obliterated the contributions of America's earliest permanent settlers—the Pilgrims. Why? Because they were a people inspired by profound religious beliefs to overcome incredible odds.

Today, public schools are simply not teaching how important the religious dimension was in shaping our history and our nation's character. Whether teachers are just uncomfortable with this material, or whether there has been a concerted effort to cover up the truth, the result is the same. Kids are no longer learning enough to understand and appreciate how and why America was created.

The story of the Pilgrims begins in the early part of the seventeenth century (that's the 1600s for those of you in Rio Linda, California). The Church of England under King James I was persecuting anyone and everyone who did not recognize its absolute civil and spiritual authority. Those who challenged ecclesiastical authority and those who believed strongly in freedom of worship were hunted down, imprisoned, and sometimes executed for their beliefs.

A group of separatists first fled to Holland and established a community. After eleven years, about forty of them agreed to make a perilous journey to the New World, where they would certainly face hardships, but could live and worship God according to the dictates of their own consciences.

On August 1, 1620, the *Mayflower* set sail. It carried a total of 102 passengers, including forty Pilgrims led by William Bradford. On the journey, Bradford set up an agreement, a contract, that established just and equal laws for all members of their new community, irrespective of their religious beliefs. Where did the revolutionary ideas expressed in the Mayflower Compact come from? From the Bible. The Pilgrims were a people completely steeped in the lessons of the Old and New Testaments. They looked to the ancient Israelites for their example. And, because of the biblical precedents set forth in Scripture, they never doubted that their experiment would work.

But this was no pleasure cruise, friends. The journey to the New World was a long and arduous one. And when the Pilgrims landed in New England in November, they found, according to Bradford's detailed journal, a cold, barren, desolate wilderness. There were no friends to greet them, he wrote. There were no houses to shelter them. There were no inns where they could refresh themselves.

And the sacrifice they had made for freedom was just beginning. During the first winter, half the Pilgrims—including Bradford's wife—died of either starvation, sickness, or exposure. When spring finally came, Indians taught the settlers how to plant corn, fish for cod, and skin beavers for coats. Life improved for the Pilgrims, but they did not yet prosper! This is important to understand because this is where modern American history lessons often end. Thanksgiving is actually explained in some textbooks as a holiday for which the Pilgrims gave thanks to the Indians for saving their lives, rather than as a devout expression of gratitude grounded in the tradition of both the Old and New Testaments.

Here is the part that has been omitted: The original contract the Pilgrims had entered into with their merchant-sponsors in London called for everything they produced to go into a common store, and each member of the community was entitled to one common share. All of the land they cleared and the houses they built belonged to the community as well.

Bradford, who had become the new governor of the colony, recognized that this form of collectivism was as costly and destructive to the Pilgrims as that first harsh winter, which had taken so many lives. He decided to take bold action. Bradford assigned a plot of land to each family to work and manage, thus turning loose the power of the marketplace.

That's right, long before Karl Marx was even born, the Pilgrims had discovered and experimented with what could only be described as socialism. And what happened? It didn't work! Surprise, surprise, huh? What Bradford and his community found was that the most creative and industrious people had no incentive to work any harder than anyone else, unless they could utilize the power of personal motivation!

But while most of the rest of the world has been experimenting with socialism for well over a hundred years—trying to refine it, perfect it, and re-invent it—the Pilgrims decided early on to scrap it permanently. What Bradford wrote about this social experiment should be in every schoolchild's history lesson. If it were, we might prevent much needless suffering in the future.

"The experience that was had in this common course and condition, tried sundry years . . . that by taking away property, and bringing community into a common wealth, would make them happy and flourishing—as if they were wiser than God," Bradford wrote. "For this community [so far as it was] was found to breed much confusion and discontent, and retard much employment that would have been to their benefit and comfort. For young men that were most able and fit for labor and service did repine that they should spend their time and strength to work for other men's wives and children without any recompense . . . that was thought injustice."

Do you hear what he was saying, ladies and gentlemen? The Pilgrims found that people could not be expected to do their best work without incentive. So what did Bradford's community try next? They unharnessed the power of good old free enterprise by invoking the undergirding capitalistic principle of private property. Every family was assigned its own plot of land to work and permitted to market its own crops and products. And what was the result?

"This had very good success," wrote Bradford, "for it made all hands industrious, so as much more corn was planted than otherwise would have been." Bradford doesn't sound like much of a Clintonite, does he? Is it possible that supply-side economics could have existed before the 1980s? Yes. Read the story of Joseph and Pharaoh in Genesis 41. Following Joseph's suggestion (Gen. 41:34), Pharaoh reduced the tax on Egyptians to 20 percent during the "seven years of plenty" and the "Earth brought forth in heaps." (Gen. 41:47).

In no time, the Pilgrims found they had more food than they could eat themselves. So they set up trading posts and exchanged goods with the Indians. The profits allowed them to pay off their debts to the merchants in London. And the success and prosperity of the Plymouth settlement attracted more Europeans and began what came to be known as the "Great Puritan Migration."

Now, let me ask you: Have you read this history before? Is this lesson being taught to your children today? If not, why not? Can you think of a more important lesson one could derive from the Pilgrim experience? If Bill Clinton had been exposed to these lessons of history as a schoolboy in Hope, Arkansas, maybe we would all be a lot better off today.

But guess what? There's even more that is being deliberately withheld from our modern textbooks. For example, one of those attracted to the New World by the success of Plymouth was Thomas Hooker, who established his own community in Connecticut—the first full-fledged constitutional community and perhaps the most free society the world had ever known. Hooker's community was governed by the Fundamental Orders of Connecticut, which established strict limits on the powers of government. So revolutionary and successful was this idea that Massachusetts was inspired to adopt its Body of Liberties, which included ninety-eight separate protections of individual rights, including: "no taxation without representation," "due process of law," "trial by a jury of peers," and prohibitions against "cruel and unusual punishment."

Does all that sound familiar? It should. These are ideas and concepts that led directly to the U.S. Constitution and Bill of Rights. Nevertheless, the Pilgrims and Puritans of early New England are often vilified today as witch-burners and portrayed as simpletons. To the contrary, it was their commitment to pluralism and free worship that led to these ideals being incorporated into American life. Our history books purposely conceal the fact that these notions were developed by communities of devout Christians who studied the Bible and found it prescribes limited, representative government and free enterprise as the best political and economic systems.

There's only one word for this, folks: censorship. There was a time when every schoolchild learned these basic lessons of the American culture. Now these truths are being systematically expunged from the history books in favor of liberal social-studies claptrap.

This brings us to our Founding Fathers—the geniuses who crafted the Declaration of Independence and the U.S. Constitution. These were men who shook up the entire world by proclaiming the idea that people had certain God-given freedoms and rights and that the government's only raison d'être was to protect those freedoms and rights from both internal and external forces. That simple yet brilliant insight has been all but lost today in liberalism's relentless march toward bigger, more powerful, more intrusive government.

Don't believe the conventional wisdom of our day that claims these men were anything but orthodox, Bible-believing Christians. They were. And they were quite adamant in stating that the Constitution—as brilliant a document as it is—would work only in the context of a moral society.

"Our Constitution was made for a moral and religious people," stated second president John Adams. "It is wholly inadequate for the governance of any other."

George Washington, the father of our country, was of like mind. He said: "Of all the dispositions and habits that lead to political prosperity, religion and morality are indispensable supports."

James Madison, primary author of the Constitution, agreed: "We have staked the whole future of the American civilization, not upon the power of government, far from it. We have staked the future . . . upon the capacity of each and all of us to govern ourselves, to control ourselves, to sustain ourselves, according to the Ten Commandments of God."

The eighteenth-century Irish statesman and orator Edmund Burke, some of whose precepts formed the core of conservatism, eloquently stated in his 1791 "A Letter to a Member of the National Assembly":

Men are qualified for civil liberty, in exact proportion to their disposition to put moral chains upon their own appetites; in proportion as their love to justice is above their rapacity; in proportion as their soundness and sobriety of understanding is above their vanity and presumption; in proportion as they are more disposed to listen to the counsels of the wise and good, in preference to the flattery of knaves. Society cannot exist unless a controlling power upon will and appetite be placed some-where, and the less of it there is within, the more there must be without. It is ordained in the eternal constitution of things, that men of intemperate minds cannot be free. Their passions forge their fetters.

Many Americans look to government for their salvation today. It dominates so many aspects of our lives. And for too many liberals, government has become their religion. And there are many oppor-tunistic politicians who would encourage such dependency. It empowers them. Our Founding Fathers understood this threat and warned about it.

What most Americans don't seem to understand is how fleeting and rare freedom actually has been throughout history. Nothing lasts forever in this world. We have become spoiled by 200 years of liberty. Particularly, the post–World War II generations have no concept of sacrifice and the incalculable cost of freedom. This ignorance, born of complacency, is dangerous, folks, for all of us. Because too many Americans are ready to trade in their freedom for security—even a false security!!

If that choice is made, it will be made out of ignorance. Because Americans simply don't know their own history, much less that of the rest of the world. And, as American philosopher and writer George Santayana said, those who don't learn from the past are doomed to repeat it. Americans today seem ready and eager to trade in everything for which their forefathers fought and died for an autocracy that far surpasses anything King George III ever dreamed of.

Why are we so oblivious to what is going on? Though I am not given to conspiracy theories, some have suggested the degradation of our educational system is so profound that it could only be a deliberate attempt to deny America's young people their cultural and political heritage.

"From the new textbooks, the children of the American republic will never gain knowledge of, or the slightest incentive to participate in, public affairs," wrote Walter Karp in *Harper's* in 1980 in an article about the sad state of U.S. textbooks. "No reader of these degraded texts will ever learn from them how to 'judge for themselves what will secure or endanger their freedom.' The new textbooks have snuffed out the very idea of human freedom, for that freedom at bottom is precisely the human capacity for action that political history records and that the textbooks are at such pains to conceal. . . . What the political history of the textbooks reveals is that a powerful few, gaining control of public education, have been depriving the American republic of citizens, and popular government of a people to defend it. And the American history textbook, so innocent-seeming and inconsequential, has been their well-chosen instrument."

Unless we know where we have been as a nation, it is impossible to know where we are going. Our public educational system is so bereft of this country's seminal priorities and values that our kids are being hopelessly shortchanged and deprived of that essential background.

Think about this: At the time of the drafting of the Declaration of Independence—before we were even a nation—the quality of education in America was high. As Alexis de Tocqueville wrote at the time of our Constitution's fiftieth anniversary in his master-piece, *Democracy in America*:

In New England every citizen receives the elementary notion of human knowledge; he is taught, moreover, the

75

doctrines and the evidences of his religion, the history of his country, and the leading features of its Constitution. In the states of Connecticut and Massachusetts, it is extremely rare to find a man imperfectly acquainted with all these things, and a person wholly ignorant of them is a sort of phenomenon.

How could this be? Why, there wasn't even a Department of Education established. There were no public schools. There was no National Education Association. Why were people better educated before the American Revolution with no public funding than in 1993, when we are spending in excess of $100,000 per classroom?

You can't fully appreciate how screwed up modern liberalism is without contrasting its vision (or lack thereof) with the broad view of our nation's founders. Americans throughout history—from the earliest settlers to the generation that fought World War II—have always understood and accepted sacrifice. They intuitively knew there were things worth dying for.

The early pioneers tamed a wilderness. Nothing was handed to them. And they sought only freedom and a better life for their children. Today, government is taking away our freedom and mortgaging with debt the future lives of our children. But not to worry. Government is more than willing to provide you with food stamps, welfare payments, unemployment benefits, day care, socialized medicine, free condoms, subsidized abortions—you name it. Can't you see how the vision has been turned upside down?

The founders knew they were bestowing upon us only an ingenious political system of checks and balances, limited government, and a legacy of human and civil rights. It would be up to future generations to make it all work. But it would only work, they warned (reread the quotes from Adams, Washington, and Madison on page 73), if the society was girded on a bedrock of solid values and Judeo-Christian principles.

Where and how did we lose our moorings? With such a great start, why did we allow liberalism, moral relativism, and secular humanism to poison our nation's soul? And what can we do to recapture the original American spirit of freedom and individualism?

For answers to these questions I refer you to the next chapter. There we will examine the origins and depths of this ongoing assault on our culture and consider what we can do to defend it. Don't lose heart, my friends. As we return to our founding principles, the best for this country is yet to come.

7

ARE VALUES OBSOLETE?
OR
HOW TO WIN THE CULTURE WAR

MANY YEARS AGO, I COMPILED SOME OF THE MOST LUCID OBSERVATIONS the world has ever known in the form of "The Thirty-five Undeniable Truths of Life." Every one of those insights has withstood the test of time. I could literally sit here and say, "See, I Told You So," about every single one of those verities. But over the years my utterances of profound truths have not been limited to those thirty-five. Another truism that I've often proclaimed is: "Liberalism poisons the soul."

When I originally made that observation, even *I* didn't realize how profound it was. I don't pretend to be a prophet (just a humble sage, with talent on loan from God), yet this statement is much more relevant now than it was when I first made it.

Originally, it may have sounded harsh to some, trite to others; scintillating to the politically astute. Today, I am convinced it is more on the mark than ever. Here's what it really means to me: Modern-day liberalism is like a disease or an addiction that literally has the power to destroy the character of the person who falls under its spell.

Now, before we proceed any further, let me say that I am not indicting or impeaching the character of all liberals. I want to be clear on that. In my mind, the liberal camp can be divided in two. First, there are leaders, activists, and theoreticians. The second group, however, is made up of people who either have not really thought through the major issues of the day, or don't fully comprehend the nature of liberalism. Of this second category, many are truly well meaning; they may not, however, fully understand the ramifications of the social prescriptions of the left.

You've heard the term "knee-jerk liberal." The phrase implies, and probably accurately, that some liberals are simply so conditioned into the mind-set that they respond reflexively in a leftward direction to various stimuli. For example, the cure for: a) the budget deficit = more taxes; b) unemployment = more taxes; c) recession = more taxes; d) environmental problems = more taxes; e) illiteracy = more taxes; f) L.A. riots = more taxes. It doesn't matter what the nature of the problem is. The liberal answer is always the same—bigger and more powerful government and higher taxes.

We almost need to come up with another term for these people whose liberalism can be traced exclusively to the Pavlovian conditioning we are all exposed to in the media and our educational institutions. For instance, I devised the term "femi-Nazi" to distinguish a very small, hard-core group of militants from well-intentioned but misguided people who call themselves "feminists." We need a way to separate the liberal wheat from the liberal chaff, too. Maybe we could call those reflexive liberals "knee jerks." Perhaps "intellectually challenged" would be more sensitive.

How do people allow themselves to be conditioned into liberalism without ever coolly analyzing the rationale? I'll tell you. Liberalism is seductive and insidious. It can take hold of you before you realize it. Do you know why? Because it doesn't take any guts to become a liberal. It's the easiest decision you could ever make in your life. It's the most effortless, gutless thing you could do. All you have to do to be a good liberal is to say yes to everything, except cutting spending and downsizing government. Just say yes. Government should do more to end homelessness. It should spend more on education. It should guarantee health-care benefits to everyone. It should provide day care. You name it; the omnipotent, central government should do it. All you have to do to prove your compassion is to say yes, yes, yes, yes, yes, yes. What could be easier?

Liberals have the additional luxury of rarely being challenged on their beliefs. The establishment media are very kind to liberals— even the most arrogant and hypocritical ones—perhaps because it is fashionable, chic, and presumptively compassionate to be liberal. It surrounds one with an aura of moral superiority and being "hip." Take the Rev. Jesse Jackson, for example. He was typical of the national "civil rights" leaders who refused to condemn unequivocally (some would even say marginally) the rioters and looters responsible for mayhem and murder in the city of Los Angeles in the spring of 1992. We had to understand, he pleaded, that people in certain communities had been oppressed for so long that this was a natural and understandable response. Of course, many liberals, including the occasionally thoughtful Senator George Mitchell, didn't stop there, but warned that the cities would burn during the summer of 1993 unless the administration's "stimulus" package of pork-barrel spending was signed into law.

This is simply liberalism carried to the logical next step. You want what's in that store. Just break the window and take it. As long as you can position yourself as a member of a "victimized" group, your action will be justified and vigorously defended. Just say yes. You see, it's not just in the economic arena where we are witnessing the toxic effects of liberalism. Its toxins are permeating and infecting the moral foundations of our entire culture.

Modern liberalism tends to be nihilistic. It assaults the structural values to which people anchor themselves in order to achieve a modicum of stability in their lives and order in their society. It even contradicts the traditional notions of right and wrong, blaming much criminal and anti-social behavior on economic determinism. What used to be accepted as truisms in our society because they were (and still are) true are now either wholly rejected or turned entirely upside down. You may be saying to yourself that this description fits only the extreme left. Surely, mainstream liberals (another flagrant oxymoron) would not have excused the rioters' behavior, as did Jesse Jackson and Maxine Waters. Oh, no? Then tell me why none of the liberal leadership had the moral fortitude to condemn those irresponsible pre- and post-riot statements. Their uniform silence was deafening. In fact, their silence in short order turned to promises for more money to the cities, the lesson being that if you want more money, burn your cities. The amount of $3.5 trillion since the "War on Poverty" began in the 1960s has not been enough greenback compassion. Over the years I have become convinced that this is a deliberate effort—at least by the extreme liberal elite. Attacking traditional standards of all kinds, and imposing their own set of arbitrary rules and regulations, represents another way that liberalism empowers itself.

When you hear about "the Culture War," ladies and gentlemen, know that this is what it's all about. It's a war of competing ideas and worldviews. On one side, you have people who believe in living by a set of divinely inspired moral absolutes—or, at the very least, they believe that following such a moral code represents the best way to avoid chaos and instability. On the other side, you have people who insist that morality is simply a personal decision. Any attempt to enforce it is viewed as oppression. Quite simply, many liberals believe that efforts to adhere to and enforce behavioral rights and wrongs is simply the powerful in society attempting to force their views and judgments on the "victims" of society, rather than what it is: an attempt to maintain the standards that have evolved and survived throughout human civilization and which produce a quality life.

Let's set the record straight. Morality is not defined by individual choice. Long before anyone was talking about "the Culture War," I had made that point in "The Thirty-five Undeniable Truths of Life." It's Number Twenty-two, to be exact.

To understand what that means, let's examine a real-life example of one little skirmish in the ongoing Culture War. Singer Ice T records an album with one song clearly condoning, if not advocating, the killing of cops, and another glorifying the violent sexual abuse of women. When other artists, music executives, and media wizards see nothing wrong with that, alarm bells go off. The average person recognizes a problem. But anyone who dares to criticize the record or suggest that standards should be imposed is ridiculed and called an intolerant bigot.

Let's face it, there are things in life that every decent person with common sense knows are wrong. There are other things almost everybody understands are right. Most people have been raised and are imbued with a sense of right and wrong. Some choose to reject those standards. Others simply never learn them early in life. But at some level, almost everyone, with the exception by definition of the criminally insane, recognizes right from wrong.

When liberals hurl epithets at you because you have pointed out the obvious error of their ways, just know that you have hit a nerve. If you criticize their behavior and they call you a pig, a bigot, or a fascist, their consciences must be giving them problems; or else they acquired their liberal values by rote and without comprehension. They claim to have a monopoly on the market of open-mindedness and tolerance, but in truth are often extremely closed-minded and intolerant.

Remember 2 Live Crew? That was a rap group that produced an album that included a song called "Me So Horny." In frighteningly vivid detail, the song described the destruction of a female vagina. Its defenders call it art. But only a total breakdown of artistic standards could allow anyone to make such an assessment. But, of course, the breakdown of standards of any kind is the liberals' forte.

In case you didn't understand what I meant earlier when I said that liberals sometimes knock down standards because to do so empowers them, I'll give you an example. Take the case of Leonard Jeffries, the chairman of City College of New York's black-studies department. For years Mr. Jeffries served in this job while he launched outrageous attacks against Jews and other groups of white people. He did it both in the classroom and outside the university setting. He became such an embarrassment to City College that when part of a racist, anti-Semitic speech made by him was reprinted in the *New York Post*, school officials fired him.

Though Mr. Jeffries successfully sued the college for his wrongful termination, a more important question remains: How did he get *hired* in the first place? And how did he survive in his position for about twenty years? The reason we have hate-mongers like Jeffries in key positions is because of declining standards. Did anybody care about Jeffries's level of scholarship when he was hired or during the time he served as chairman of a department? No. School officials were happy to let him teach his half-baked theories about how all the world's civilizations stole their cultural achievements from sub–Saharan Africa. They were content to let him ramble on about a conspiracy between world Jewry and the Mafia until it became a public embarrassment to them.

One of the reasons you abolish standards is so you can never say someone is doing a bad job. Without a standard by which to measure one's performance, one cannot under-perform. This is a way to build a powerful teachers' union and liberal political power base on campus or in a government agency or in some other institution. Lots of people like Jeffries were hired after the 1960s simply to appease the mob mentality that was demanding more minority control over institutions of higher learning.

Why are these issues so important? Why are they worth fighting for? Because if there are no ultimate standards of behavior that descend from God, and if morality is merely an individual choice, then life itself has lost its greater meaning. It's no big deal for you to take a gun to school and shoot some kid over a dispute about a leather jacket or a pair of sneakers. That is precisely what an overly permissive, excessively tolerant, nothing-is-wrong attitude leads to. Of course, liberals will argue that these actions can be laid at the foot of socioeconomic inequities, or poverty. However, the Great Depression caused a level of poverty unknown to exist in America today, and yet I have been unable to find any accounts of crime waves sweeping our large cities. In fact, I can't find reliable information that even documents a noticeable increase in crime, period, during the Great Depression. Let the liberals (perhaps they would prefer to be called economic determinists?) chew on that.

Regardless of what you call them, they don't see the connection —or pretend they don't. So anyone who publicly expresses concern for decency in our society invites assault. Any expression of concern for solid values is mocked and ridiculed. The thought that there should be standards of behavior and accountability in all walks of life is portrayed as absurd.

Why do they react that way? They take the offensive because deep down they know they're wrong. They know they're engaging in activity that is base. In many cases, they are simply hedonists. They won't accept any limits on personal behavior whatsoever. That's what freedom means to them: no responsibility, no consequences for anything. It's whatever feels good. That is the underlying dimension of most of the aberrant behavior going on in America today.

Liberalism is the political ideology that adds legitimacy and credence to these aberrant behaviors. It says: "People have been victimized and oppressed in America and they are forced to act this way." Liberals excuse bad behavior. They rationalize it. And they act as the unholy choir to denounce as religious extremists decent people who call attention to it.

The things that once offended us don't anymore. The things that we used to find repugnant are now accepted. My friend William Bennett, who served under both the Reagan and Bush administrations, likes to point out that in the 1950s the biggest problems teachers had with students were talking in class, tardiness, and gum-chewing. Today, teachers consider the worst problems to be drugs, weapons possession, pregnancy, and assault. And I might point out that poverty and economic disparities between the lower and upper classes were greater during the former period. The difference is that back then the nuclear family was still overwhelmingly dominant and instilled values in our children.

We're reluctant as a society now to teach that certain things are wrong. We think the highest ideal is simply to teach people how to love one another and get along. That may have a nice ring to it, but what that means in practice is teaching kids about anal sex and using a textbook called *Heather Has Two Mommies*. Today, in our increasingly secular world, loving one another doesn't just mean "loving." It means being forced to accept as normal those behaviors and lifestyles that are absolutely abnormal. It's not enough to live and let live. You must chant their mantra as well; you must repent, renounce your own values, and pronounce those of the radical left as superior and adopt them. However, some things are strictly forbidden in this brave new educational world. For instance, we can't teach the Ten Commandments. In fact, we can't even post them in the classroom. Why? Because their origin is religious, and that (God forbid!) might offend.

Well, let me ask you: What's wrong with stealing? What can we tell young people about the looting we all saw on television during the Los Angeles riots? Let's say, for the sake of argument, that they knew they could get away with it. Why shouldn't they throw a brick through the window and steal that stereo? Sure, it's against the law. They might get caught and go to jail. But suppose there was no chance they would get caught. What would you tell them then?

The reason kids shouldn't steal is because it's wrong. Period. It's right there in the Ten Commandments, which, as commentator Ted Koppel brilliantly reminds us, are not the Ten Suggestions. All of our laws descend originally from those stone tablets handed down by Moses. If you visit the U.S. Supreme Court building, you will see the Ten Commandments emblazoned on the wall right above the likenesses of the past justices. Yet, we can't publicly tell kids in our society to obey these laws because they have a religious origin. We dare not suggest to them that there is a higher morality than our state and national laws. We can't introduce the idea that someday they might have to answer to God for their behavior.

Let me tell you, folks, you don't want to live in a society in which the great majority of the people do not believe that ultimately they are accountable to an authority higher than the state. That is a recipe for national disaster.

How many times have you heard the hackneyed slogan "You can't legislate morality"? Liberals have twisted the intended meaning of this phrase to suit their purposes. It has been misused so often that the incorrect meaning is now accepted as the norm. The phrase was initially adopted by conservatives of the sixties, such as Barry Goldwater, to describe the reality that people's attitudes, prejudices, character, and integrity cannot be altered by well-meaning legislation. For example, this society can and did outlaw discrimination based on race, etc., with the civil-rights laws of the sixties—and fortified those laws with remedial enforcement mechanisms. Although the law did and does prevent acts of discrimination (and this is good law), it does not change the hearts of people. Though we have less racial discrimination, we don't have one less racist as a result of these laws.

The feel-good generation of me-first liberals co-opted the phrase and use it as a credo to legitimize their advocacy of unlimited freedom without responsibility. Thus, when arguing in favor of abortion on demand, for instance, they chant reflexively, "You can't legislate morality."

Mere superficial analysis reveals the folly of their reasoning. Of course, society can, and indeed it is morally imperative that it does, legislate morality—if by that it is meant that the law proscribes certain immoral behavior. In fact, that's what our entire system of criminal law is—the codification of societal restrictions on human behavior that is accepted as being immoral. Our traditional criminal laws prohibiting murder, and other violent acts against persons or property, for example, are laws prohibiting certain acts coupled with criminal intent. These laws do not seek to change the personal morality of those who violate them; rather, they seek to prevent the proscribed acts and to punish the actors for their wrongs. Interestingly, it has only been liberals through the years who have sought to use the criminal justice system for the purpose of rehabilitating the wrongdoers. So don't fall for this notion that society cannot enforce moral codes because of the misunderstood slogan "You can't legislate morality."

When did we begin descending down this slippery slope of relativism? Some suggest it was in the late 1960s. That was a time when, for some, any action taken to oppose the war in Vietnam was considered not only acceptable but commendable. It started with the riots at the Democratic National Convention in 1968 and it deteriorated into the bombing of the U.S. Capitol in 1971.

But all along the way, the agents of "change" excused and rationalized each and every act of defiance—no matter how violent, no matter how unlawful. Every illegal act was glorified under the high-minded ideal of "civil disobedience." The nineteenth-century American writer Henry David Thoreau and the Indian nationalist and spiritual leader Mahatma Gandhi became the spiritual icons. (But demonstrators conveniently forgot that these men advocated facing the consequences of acts of civil disobedience.) Campus buildings were taken over, students were denied the right to attend classes, public officials were denied the right to speak. Anything went, as long as the cause was right. The end justified the means. We're still reaping a bitter harvest from the seeds that were planted by the sixties kids. And now they're running things.

No, I don't just mean Bill Clinton in the White House. The sixties gang is even more firmly entrenched in all of the key cultural institutions that are so influential in setting the agenda and establishing the rules of debate in a free society.

I mean, isn't it ironic that as America is celebrating its victory in the Cold War over communism, those same, tired, oppressive ideas are still winning the hearts and minds of millions of Americans? As Russia staggers desperately toward a system of free-market capitalism, we're moving more quickly than ever toward socialism and statism. Why? Because we have lost control of our major cultural institutions. Liberalism long ago captured the arts, the press, the entertainment industry, the universities, the schools, the libraries, the foundations, etc. This was no accident.

In the early 1900s, an obscure Italian communist by the name of Antonio Gramsci theorized that it would take a "long march through the institutions" before socialism and relativism would be victorious. Up until then, most of the radical left still believed that they would take power only when they convinced enough people in the working class to take up arms in their cause. But Gramsci theorized that by capturing these key institutions and using their power, cultural values would be changed, traditional morals would be broken down, and the stage would be set for the political and economic power of the West to fall.

The key, according to Gramsci, was to change the way the whole society thinks about its problems. For starters, he wrote, you have to subvert and undermine the belief in God. Chip away at the assumption that there are a set of divinely inspired moral absolutes, and everything more or less begins to fall into place for the socialists, relativists, and materialists.

Now, the name Gramsci is certainly not a household name, even among the most enlightened people on Earth—my readers. But trust me when I tell you that his name and theories are well known and understood throughout intellectual leftist circles. Leftist think tanks worship at Gramsci's altar.

Gramsci succeeded in defining a strategy for waging cultural warfare—a tactic that has been adopted by the modern left, and which remains the last great hope for chronic America-bashers. It is simply not possible to refocus this nation's public-policy debate through electoral politics alone. As we saw during the 1980s, we can elect good people to high office and still lose ground in this Culture War. And, as we saw in 1992, the more ground we lose in the Culture War, the harder it is to win electoral victories. What we need to do is fight to reclaim and redeem our cultural institutions with all the intensity and enthusiasm that we use to fight to redeem our political institutions.

The left has been very successful because it understands the importance of the culture—of framing the debate and influencing the way people think about problems. But the Culture War is a bilateral conflict, my friends. There's no reason on earth we should be content to sit back and watch our values and our cultural heritage slip away. Why don't we simply get in the game and start competing for control of those key cultural institutions? In other words, why not fight back?

And that, my friends, is exactly what sets me apart from the so-called "conservative movement." Believe it or not, I don't have a personal political agenda. By that, I mean I don't have some political goal for my radio program or my TV show or my books or my newsletter. I'm not trying to change the world, but I do want to open people's minds to the events that are taking place and encourage them to be confident in themselves and the principles and values they have always held sacred.

I'm just one voice in a virtual cacophony of media ultra-liberalism, but look at the result! We are making a difference. We can win this battle. Liberalism is a paper tiger, to coin a phrase of its old friend Mao Tse-tung. Its support is a mile wide but only an inch deep. The lesson of Rush Limbaugh's success is that if you stand up confidently for your beliefs, people will respect you.

I get letters all the time from people wondering what to do in the face of adversity. I got one recently from a seventeen-year-old who said his teacher thinks he's a nut because of his conservative views. What do I advise? Don't be daunted and intimidated by the thought police. Despite what they'd have you believe, you are not a criminal. Stick to your principles; don't be afraid to unapologetically admit your belief in those corny old traditional values. Ultimately, this will get you respect. Once you have respect, then you will have the ability to persuade. That's the way to reclaim our culture. Live your life the way you think it should be lived. Influence the people around you. But don't do it with rancor, bitterness, or hatred. Be of good cheer. Be a living example of that which you advocate. No matter where you are or in what walk of life, that lesson applies. If you follow that principle, you will be a beacon of truth and righteousness among those with whom you associate.

8

DAN QUAYLE IS RIGHT
OR
OUR POVERTY OF VALUES

To a great extent, this book is about setting the record straight. Not just because I enjoy saying, "See, I Told You So," but because it's important to dispel widespread misconceptions. After all, it's impossible to understand where you really are or where you're going if you don't know where you've been.

I've been saying it for a long time. It's undeniable, folks. Liberalism has left our social fabric in tatters. Things are so bad that even liberals are beginning to notice. What they don't understand or won't admit is that they and their philosophy are, to a great extent, the culprits.

Remember former Vice-President Dan Quayle's much-maligned "Murphy Brown" speech? Did you ever read the entire text in any major newspaper? Was it ever extensively excerpted in your local newspaper? Did you ever hear more than two sentences of it quoted verbatim on the radio or television? What most Americans heard about that speech is wrong. Just plain wrong. We have been told by the media and the cultural elite that Quayle was attacking single mothers, when he was attacking no one. Neither his message, nor his tone, was mean-spirited. He was simply lamenting our society's departure from the traditional values that once defined and shaped it. In fact, the speech delivered to the Commonwealth Club of California in San Francisco on May 19, 1992, was actually one of the most thoughtful articulations of our society's battle over values by a major American political figure. In effect, it was a formal Declaration of the Culture War.

The substance of the seven-page speech was mostly lost in the media furor over Quayle's one-sentence criticism of a TV show's glamorization of unwed motherhood. That's a shame. For what Quayle said about values, poverty, morality, and media responsibility is something that desperately needs to be said and heard, over and over and over again. And although Quayle's views still represent the mainstream of this country, too few in public life have had the insight and courage to express them because of the vociferous and intimidating outcries of bigotry on the part of the media and the left.

Let's recap: In offering an explanation of the widespread rioting, killing, and looting in Los Angeles, Quayle said the "lawless social anarchy which we saw is directly related to the breakdown of family structure, personal responsibility, and social order in too many areas of our society."

In illustrating the problems of our cities, Quayle cited some revealing statistics:

• In 1967, 68 percent of black families were headed by married couples. In 1991, only 48 percent of black families were headed by both a husband and wife.

• In 1965, the illegitimacy rate among black families was 28 percent. In 1989, 65 percent—two-thirds—of all black children were born to never-married mothers.

• In 1951, 9.2 percent of black youths between the ages of sixteen and nineteen were unemployed. In 1965, it was 23 percent. In 1980, it was 35 percent. By 1989, the number had declined slightly for the first time (during the evil decade, you may note), but it was still 32 percent.

• The leading cause of death of young black males today is homicide.

"The intergenerational poverty that troubles us so much today is predominantly a poverty of values," Quayle explained. "Our inner cities are filled with children having children; with people who have not been able to take advantage of educational opportunities; with people who are dependent on drugs or the narcotic of welfare. To be sure, many people in the ghettos struggle very hard against these tides—and sometimes win. But too many feel they have no hope and nothing to lose."

The biggest obstacle to climbing out of that hole of poverty and hopelessness, Quayle said, is the breakdown of the two-parent family. As proof, he pointed out that since 1967, the median income of black two-parent families has actually risen by 60 percent in real terms. Marriage, he showed (despite federal tax policies discriminating against it, I might add), "is probably the best anti-poverty program of all."

"For the government, transforming underclass culture means that our policies and programs must create a different incentive system," he said. "Our policies must be premised on, and must reinforce, values such as: family, hard work, integrity, and personal responsibility."

Based on these principles, Quayle outlined a host of what he called "empowerment programs" (not empowerment of the government, but of the individual), such as home ownership for public-housing dwellers, tax cuts for investment in blighted urban areas, more educational choice, and welfare reform that removes penalties for marriage and creates incentives for saving. But Quayle made it clear that government mandates and programs alone can't solve all the problems.

"When families fail," he said, "society fails. The anarchy and the lack of structure in our inner cities are testament to how quickly civilization falls apart when the family foundation cracks. Children need love and discipline. They need mothers and fathers. A welfare check is not a husband. The state is not a father. It is from parents that children learn how to behave in society; it is from parents above all that children come to understand values and themselves as men and women, mothers and fathers."

Again, emphasizing the economic side of the equation, among families headed by married couples today, there is a poverty rate of 5.7 percent. But for families headed by a single mother the rate is 33.4 percent.

Now, listeners to the Rush Limbaugh radio show and viewers of my TV show know about these things. But these eye-opening statistics and their profound implications have been buried by the media and Quayle's political adversaries. Quayle, already the left's favorite whipping boy, was made the butt of countless jokes because of the "Murphy Brown" throwaway line. Why? Because his message repudiates the long-held beliefs of the elitists that redistribution of wealth is all that's needed to cure our social ills. Our real problems reside at a much more fundamental level and do not lend themselves to quick-fix solutions, such as massive redistributions of wealth. Quayle correctly observed that it is the unraveling of our society's moral fabric that is responsible for most of our social problems. He deserves accolades for inaugurating the public debate on these issues and for having the courage to champion unapologetically moral absolutes in today's censorial climate of political correctness.

"Even though our cultural leaders in Hollywood, network TV, and the national newspapers routinely jeer at [the idea], I think that most of us in this room know that some things are good, and other things are wrong," he told the Commonwealth Club of San Francisco. "Now it's time to make the discussion public. It's time to talk again about family, hard work, integrity, and personal responsibility. We cannot be embarrassed out of our belief that two parents, married to each other, are better in most cases for children than one; that honest work is better than handouts—or crime; that we are our brothers' keepers; that it's worth making an effort, even when the rewards aren't immediate."

In conclusion, Quayle said: "So I think the time has come to renew our public commitment to our Judeo-Christian values—in our churches and synagogues, our civic organizations and our schools. We are, as our children recite each morning, 'one nation under God.' That's a useful framework for acknowledging a duty and an authority higher than our own pleasures and personal ambitions."

Interestingly, when the presidential elections were safely over, suddenly "family values" became a legitimate story again and a subject suitable for civil discourse. The most remarkable of several follow-ups to the "Murphy Brown" flap was published in *The*

Atlantic Monthly in April 1993. The cover said simply: "Dan Quayle Was Right."

The Atlantic Monthly is not, by the way, a magazine known for its tendency to lean toward the right, especially in matters domestic and social. But I offered only one correction to this thoroughly researched report on the importance of traditional families. Rather than "Dan Quayle Was Right," the headline should have read "Dan Quayle *Is* Right."

The central thesis of the article was this: "After decades of public dispute about so-called family diversity, the evidence from social-science research is coming in: The dissolution of two-parent families, though it may benefit the adults involved, is harmful to many children, and dramatically undermines our society."

My question: Why do we need scientific research to tell us the obvious? Why do we need a survey to show us things that most people understand instinctively or through common sense? Why is it necessary to spend millions of dollars studying an issue that anybody with the IQ of a pencil eraser already knows? I may have just come up with a functional use for a liberal's head.

I'll tell you why. The reason is that the very values that help define our common-sense view of the world are under assault. People have taken to the extreme this spurious notion of freedom without responsibility. There are no more moral guardrails in our world. The people who live on the medians and on the shoulders of our society are told by the dominant media culture that they are right in the middle of the road. No judgments are permitted to be made about anybody's behavior or conduct. Nothing is wrong anymore (except, of course, conservative thoughts and expressions).

But, clearly, things are not right. So when people like me point out what's wrong, it's not with the intent to humiliate. It's for the purpose of enlightening.

Fact: Single-parent families are not the best way to raise children. While there are many wonderful, qualified, and loving individuals who function admirably as single parents, single parenthood is simply not the optimal way to head a family. Those of you who are in single-parent families should understand that this is not an attack on you, the position you find yourself in, or the job you are doing. It *is* an attack, however, on those who have promoted this lifestyle to the detriment of the two-parent family and the health and well-being of children. It is yet another example of the erosion of traditional distinctions: Single-parent families are at parity with two-parent families. It also betrays the true liberal mind-set. It is not enough to live and let live. We must do more than acquire acceptability. We must achieve superiority. It's analogous to the extreme gay-rights advocacy. They don't simply want the same civil rights afforded to all other Americans. They already have them! They want special, preferential treatment accorded by law.

There is nothing mysterious about Quayle's message. All he said was that glorifying single-parent families, romanticizing them, celebrating them, and promoting them was unhealthy for our society as a whole. Single-parenting should not be held up as a model because the evidence is irrefutable that, as a general rule with few exceptions, the two-parent family is a superior environment for the raising of children. Moreover, the Murphy Brown character is far from the norm. She's got plenty of money to hire a nanny (even though house painter Elden serves admirably in that role). She has a nontraditional and glamorous job.

The dissolution of intact, two-parent families is harmful to large numbers of children, Barbara Dafoe Whitehead wrote in the *Atlantic* article. Family diversity, in the form of more single-parent and stepparent families, does not strengthen the social fabric, but, rather, dramatically weakens and undermines our culture. Divorce and out-of-wedlock births are transforming the lives of real American children—and not for the better.

This theory is nothing new. We've been talking about this for a long time. My friend Bill Bennett did an admirable job of illustrating the high cost of immorality with his "Index of Leading Cultural Indicators." But as far back as the 1960s, Daniel Patrick Moynihan was trying to bring this problem to the forefront for discussion. As assistant secretary of labor for President Lyndon Johnson, Moynihan wrote a controversial study predicting that family breakdown among black Americans would lead to social disaster. At that time, about one-fifth of black babies were born out of wedlock. The rate for whites then was one in forty. Today, less than thirty years later, one-fifth of white babies are born to unmarried mothers, and, as earlier noted, the rate has reached two-thirds for blacks!

Sometimes I think people have become so desensitized to the outrageousness and extremism of the left that they have forgotten how dramatic the cultural degeneration of this society has been. To put this in perspective I played on my radio show segments of a speech delivered by Minnesota senator Hubert Humphrey on these issues of family and cultural values. The speech was delivered by Humphrey to a gathering at the Smithsonian Institution in Washington in 1968. Now, anyone who is old enough to remember, or who has a sense of recent history, will readily acknowledge that Hubert Humphrey was considered to be a liberal Democrat for his day. Yet the words of his address that day bear a striking resemblance to those of Dan Quayle's "Murphy Brown" speech. Yesterday's liberals would scarcely be recognized as such today, because they were firm believers in traditional values. True, the liberals of that day have common roots with those of today in that both favor an ever-increasing governmental role in society. But the liberal wing of the Democratic Party has set a new standard for extremism when it comes to cultural issues. Indeed, they embrace ideas that are so far afield that they would shock the likes of Hubert Humphrey.

But when you try to make this point and explain how destructive this trend is for our culture, many in the media and politics will scoff at you and ridicule you for wanting to return to the days of dominance of the nuclear family. May I ask a question? Just what is wrong with that desire? If the answer to that question is that it is impossible for the nuclear family to again triumph in our society, then the point is made: Our society has surrendered to the creeping debasement of our culture.

In an *American Scholar* article (Winter 1993), Senator Moynihan made an interesting point. The 1929 St. Valentine's Day Massacre merits two entries in the *World Book Encyclopedia*. It resulted in the Constitution being changed and Prohibition being ended. Why? Seven gangsters were killed by four rival gunmen in Chicago. At the time, that was considered so appalling, so heinous, that it became the standard against which to measure horrible crimes for decades to come. Today, however, that sort of thing happens with such frequency in this country that on most occasions it doesn't even make the news.

Moynihan calls this "defining deviancy down." We are, he points out, getting used to behavior that is not good for us. "We keep the level of punishment more or less constant in our society by redefining deviancy," he writes.

In other words, we are applying different grades of punishment to certain types of behavior than we used to. Across the board, the punishment meted out is less severe in relation to the criminal behavior involved. So, although the level of punishment remains fairly constant, the gravity of the offenses to which that punishment corresponds becomes increasingly more severe. In short, we have lowered our standards, on the faulty assumption that we can't stop the decline anyway: "People are going to do what they are going to do," say those who rationalize the problem away.

Don't you love the way some people appeal to the Catholic Church (and other churches, for that matter): You've got to bend with the times. You've got to change Church doctrine, so that what we're doing isn't defined as sin anymore. "You've got to get with the nineties, Catholic Church."

And the Church rightly responds: "We are the standard. We are not going to water down our teachings, our beliefs, or our doctrine so that you can feel better about your sin."

The Catholic Church stands firm, but we in society are bending. And look at the price we are paying for it.

We must learn to discipline ourselves again. Discipline is a virtue that has been lost and forgotten in our society. Self-restraint and patience have also been consciously discarded in the all-out pursuit of "freedom" and hedonism. The result—at least as far as the American family is concerned—has been out-of-wedlock births, single-parent child-rearing, poverty, and an increasingly dysfunctional society. Here are some staggering statistics to ponder (all from *The Atlantic Monthly*'s "Dan Quayle Was Right" article):

• After World War II, more than 80 percent of children grew up in a family with two biological parents who were married to each other. By 1980, however, only 50 percent could expect to spend their whole childhood in an intact family.

• According to social and scientific evidence, children in families disrupted by divorce and out-of-wedlock birth do considerably worse academically, socially, and economically than children with intact families.

• Children of single parents are six times as likely to be poor and will usually stay poor longer.

• These kids are two to three times as likely to have emotional and behavioral problems. They are more likely to drop out of school, to get pregnant as teenagers, to abuse drugs, and to get in trouble with the law.

• Children who grow up in these environments tend to be less successful as adults—particularly in love relationships and in the workplace.

These are tragedies we're talking about here, dear readers, *avoidable* tragedies. No intellectually honest person can deny that the breakdown of the nuclear family leads to adverse social consequences. Every single one of these broken homes represents personal heartbreak as well as greater potential for societal decay. I want to throw out a word here for you to consider. I think it is relevant and helps to explain so much of the discord seen in our crumbling family structure. The word is *selfishness.*

At some point in the 1960s, increasing numbers of Americans began to change their minds about the meaning and importance of divorce and single parenthood. Prior to that point, these things had always been discouraged because people knew they were bad for children. They didn't need a doctoral thesis or a think-tank report to figure it out. They simply understood that the best interests of children dictate that they be raised in two-parent, traditional families. But in the late 1960s and early 1970s, the best interests of children began to be subordinated in importance to the happiness of adults.

We all know model families. There are many homes I look toward with admiration and respect—including my own. One constant in all of them is the way the parents give of themselves totally in the upbringing of their children. Instilling good values is always paramount—teaching right from wrong. And they are always willing to sacrifice their own fun, frivolity, and pleasure whenever it is necessary for their children's well-being.

Think about it. Today we're told by the experts that kids are going to have sex as young teenagers and there's nothing we can do about it. That's just the way it is. But I know many families that sent their kids to school during a period of time when drugs and alcohol and fast cars were the rage. Somehow, many of those kids resisted the temptation and the peer pressure. Usually, those kids came from homes in which their parents took the time to make them feel loved. They knew they didn't need those things for happiness. They didn't need those things for self-esteem. They didn't need those things for a high or a good time because they were getting love at home. Their parents made them feel special.

That's a tough challenge for parents. It wasn't easy in the past and it's exceedingly more difficult today with the constant barrage of sexually explicit messages being hurled at children via MTV and the like. It takes sacrifice and hard work. It's imperative that successful parents not be selfish when it comes to their kids. Kids are and should be dependent, and parents must give selflessly of themselves to their children.

Today, it seems, the happiness of the parents has become the most important issue in many families. In the 1950s, most Americans believed that parents should stay in an unhappy family for the sake of the children. By the 1970s, a majority believed that divorce wasn't the worst option in an unhappy marriage. In fact, the new view became that divorce was inevitable. We can't stop it. We can't be an Ozzie-and-Harriet nation anymore. It's another example of defining deviancy down.

So relaxed have we become that we not only don't discourage aberrant behavior, but we encourage it by devising new forms of public and private support for it. The government sponsors all kinds of subsidies for dysfunctional families and the popular culture reinforces this destructive pattern of propping them up—even going so far as to celebrate divorce and unwed motherhood.

No matter how clear the evidence is that single-parent families have severe disadvantages, they are still promoted and encouraged by government, the press, Hollywood, pop psychologists, and the art world. At the same time, these institutions portray the traditional nuclear family as the home of incest, rape, abuse, the imprisonment of women, and other assorted ills.

Regularly now we're seeing hideous, inexplicable crimes committed by children. Many times, we've asked ourselves why. Why
would two seventeen-year-old kids break into a home in San Jose,
California, for the purpose of stealing $100 and end up torturing,
mutilating, and killing the only occupant—a ten-year-old boy?
Why do these things happen? Why are little kids being shot in
school with increasing frequency? Why was the Central Park jogger
victimized and brutalized the way she was? Who would do such a
thing? I've said it before and I'll say it again: America is being
stripped of its soul.

How do we fight back? Well, we've got to begin by having an
honest and open debate about the problem—without name-calling
and *ad hominem* attacks. We've got to stop pretending that
everything's okay and stop lying to ourselves by saying that there's
nothing that can be done to change people's behavior. It's time to
start championing old-fashioned virtues like fidelity, chastity,
sobriety, self-restraint, self-discipline and self-reliance, and responsibility. Is that so unthinkable? Is that too much to ask?

9

DAN'S BAKE SALE

"THE SPECTACLE WAS ENOUGH TO DRIVE A STAKE THROUGH THE HEART of liberalism."

Now, for the record, folks, that's not how I, Rush Limbaugh, described Dan's Bake Sale. That's how the event was depicted on a CBS News report on May 23, 1993, after some 65,000 people flocked to Fort Collins, Colorado, for what was billed variously as "Rushstock '93," or a "right-wing love-in."

Think about that. CBS News, in effect, not only declared liberalism dead with that report, it actually drew an analogy between liberalism and a vampire! Who else but I could prompt a network newscast to make such an assertion? Who says we're not winning? How can anyone say we're not making progress?

When I was first struck with the inspiration for Dan's Bake Sale, I had no inkling that it would develop into the kind of phenomenon the world was to witness on that stormy spring day in the Rockies. It all started innocently with a call from Dan Kay, a former flea-market employee, despairing that his wife would not allow him to spend $29.95 for a subscription to the hottest publication in

America, *The Limbaugh Letter.* It culminated, the Associated Press would report, in "a sort of fund-raising, patriotic Woodstock."

Now, I could have taken the easy way out. When Dan Kay told me that a friend was photocopying the newsletter and sending it to him because he lacked the funds to subscribe, I could have taken the liberal approach and given away a subscription. If you listen to my radio show regularly, you know I am a generous person and have, in appropriate circumstances, not only made gifts of newsletter subscriptions, but more valuable merchandise as well.

But I wanted to send a message not only to Dan Kay, but to all my listeners. If we have learned anything from liberalism by now, it is that giveaway programs don't work. Welfare and other "entitlements" victimize not only the person whose wealth is being confiscated to pay for them, but also the self-worth of most of the people receiving the so-called "assistance."

I was not about to emulate on my own radio show the shameful example of the last thirty years of liberalism. After all, would I not be a hypocrite if I talked about self-reliance and free enterprise but didn't practice it on my program and encourage it among my own listeners?

Also, I wanted to contrast this sharply with other bake sales that had been organized around the country to attack the deficit problem. It struck me as absurd and nothing more than meaningless symbolism and pseudo-consciousness-raising to encourage schoolchildren to throw their hard-earned money away on a problem created by irresponsible government spending. So our bake sale came on the heels of those that encouraged third-graders to have Saturday-afternoon bake sales, raise $150, and send the money to Washington to reduce the national debt. And our president showed how much class he had when he accepted these donations. He even sent the schoolchildren faxes praising their efforts.

What a terrible lesson! These kids were misled into believing that they had done something meaningful. What they were taught is that a symbolic gesture founded only in caring and concern actually makes a difference. What they should have been taught was what actually causes budget deficits: spending more money than you have. In usual liberal fashion, they were taught to treat the

symptoms rather than the causes. So these deficit-bake-sale orga-
nizers and the president were clearly sending children the wrong
message: that government should be excused, then rewarded, for
spending profligately and irresponsibly.

But, to keep things in perspective, I could see that a bake sale
would be a fine way—an entrepreneurial way—to raise enough
money to pay for something so eminently affordable as a newsletter subscription. This, I decided, would be in the true spirit of
capitalism. It would also, as I love to do, demonstrate absurdity by
being absurd. Buy a cookie for conservatism. What a concept!

I didn't mind giving Dan Kay a little promotional help with this
event. I figured a plug here and there on my radio show could turn
this into a successful event that would help raise far more than the
$29.95 needed by Dan—maybe even enough to help pay off his
student loan.

Well, as they say, the event began to take on a life of its own.
Within the first couple of days, Jack Jolly of Root Outdoor Advertising called and offered to design and display fifteen billboards
throughout Colorado to help promote the bake sale in Fort Collins.
Other vendors inquired about setting up booths. A baker from
Guam announced he intended to bring 200 pounds of macadamia-
nut cookies. A world-class, five-star establishment in New Orleans
(and one of my personal favorites), Brennan's, decided to dispatch
its top chefs to serve up some 8,000 portions of bananas Foster, all
for charity. Of course, the pièce de résistance came when I
announced on my show that, yes, I, Rush Limbaugh, would be
attending Dan's Bake Sale.

All the weeks leading up to Dan's Bake Sale, I had a vision of
what the event would be like—I should say, what I *hoped* it would
be like. Because, keep in mind, hope is all I had. I did not
orchestrate this event. In a way, it just sort of happened. Don't get
me wrong. Many people worked their hearts out to make it a
success. But mostly we all just let the bake sale evolve and take
shape by itself. We didn't structure it. We didn't try to turn it into a
show or a carnival. We just set the wheels in motion and let it
happen. I allowed this unique confab to unfold on its own because I
have supreme confidence in you people—my readers, my listeners,
my audience. You are good people, decent people, and I knew you

were fully capable of maintaining civility and order in your own community. I knew my audience was optimistic and upbeat and would not let this gala deteriorate into the kind of ugliness we have seen at so many leftist gatherings over the years.

But, **never,** folks, in my wildest dreams could I have imagined just how exhilarating, fun, and emotionally rewarding this experience would be. If you bake it, they will come. And they did—by plane, by train, by automobile, by bus, by RV, by caravan. Even the liberal media seemed a bit stunned by the magnitude of it all.

We can argue about how many people were there. No one will ever know for sure because the event was unprecedented in the annals of Old Town Square in Fort Collins. The local authorities estimated that at least 35,000 showed up. The media reports generally guessed at between 25,000 and 45,000.

Let me tell you a few reasons why I know there were considerably more—probably at least 65,000. First of all, my staff took 25,000 copies of *The Limbaugh Letter* and gave all of them away. Many people there didn't get one, so you know there had to have been considerably more than 25,000 in attendance. Second, it was an eight-hour event, which means that people came and went throughout the day. Though some traveled great distances to get there, others lived nearby and could afford to stop in for a few hours and leave. Yet, throughout the day the size of the crowd did not diminish. Last, I know many people never even got to the site because traffic was so backed up for miles in all directions. When *EIB One* flew over I-25, we saw traffic backed up for twenty-five miles. It was the kind of traffic jam one would expect to see in New York or Los Angeles, not in a rural area of northern Colorado.

"This is a bigger party than a Broncos game," observed U.S. Senator Hank Brown (R-Colorado), who addressed the throngs at the sale. For the record, the Broncos stadium holds 78,000. Colorado state senator Bob Schaffer, who represents Fort Collins, said he "personally witnessed eighty thousand people united by common sense and simple decency."

After landing at Fort Collins–Loveland Airport, we traveled by motorcade, surrounded by eight mounted police officers, to the sale. There was a violent storm raging. It was raining and hailing, and I was told that we'd have to wait until it stopped before I could make my appearance.

"I'm not waiting any longer than twenty minutes," I responded.

In twenty minutes the skies opened, the clouds parted, and brilliant rays of sunshine beamed down on the brick streets of Old Town Square. It was a sight to behold. To see all those thousands of people happily jammed together shoulder to shoulder like sardines and literally cuddling in companionship and warmth was something I will never forget. The instant fellowship that took place was truly a moving experience.

And when it was all over, something even more remarkable had taken place. There was no litter, no pollution, no graffiti, and no vandalism. The cleanup crews were finished with their work by 6 P.M. Compare that with the Earth Day events in New York City and Washington, D.C., where the people who come "to save the Earth" always leave a mess of worldwide proportions. Yes, these watermelons (Environmentalist Wackos who are green on the outside but red on the inside), who actually make the biggest messes, have the gall to claim that those who demonstrate the most respect for the world and the property of others are destroying the Earth, simply by living prosperous lives.

Frankly, just about everything the liberals say about us is a lie. They'll tell you, for instance, that I am motivated by hate and bigotry. The truth is that I have profound love and respect for all people. I have great expectations for them. I have confidence in them. I want people to be the best they can be. It's the liberals in our society who, through their words and actions, demonstrate contempt for people and believe they cannot take care of themselves and need the government to run every aspect of their lives.

The people who attended Dan's Bake Sale are the kind of folks the liberal media love to laugh at today. But the joke's on the liberal establishment. Dan's Bake Sale was living proof that responsible people—decent people with good values—can get together in large numbers with no crime, no theft, no problems. The toughest thing the cops of Fort Collins had to do that day was to get me on and off the stage.

The entire event made me proud. It gave me even more confidence in my beliefs and in the values that we share. It confirmed for me not only that America is good, but that it works—just the way it's supposed to. What we saw in Fort Collins was indeed a microcosm of America—a gathering of confident, happy, productive people who weren't complaining, protesting, nervous, or angry; a group of ordinary, mainstream Americans who are self-motivated and self-sufficient and don't rely on others to make things happen for them.

Senator Schaffer said it best in a letter he wrote the day after the event: "The bake sale proved that Americans are still capable of assembling around a deep-rooted love for our country without militant chanting, protesting, or law-breaking. Liberals are baffled. Your visit was unquestionably the largest, most important single event in the history of Fort Collins."

What happened in Fort Collins was simply one of the most positive events held in this country in recent years. But it's only an example of what could be happening all over America. It could be happening right now if we just had the right kind of leadership. Imagine if we had someone in the White House talking about how great people can be. Remember how powerfully that message was delivered and received when Ronald Reagan employed it in the 1980s? He understood that we would all be a lot better off if we motivated good people, successful people, and productive people rather than punishing them. And so he did; he literally re-ignited the entrepreneurial spirit of America with his policies and, just as important, his leadership. To liberals it's corny; to us it's patriotism.

Just think of the economic boost Fort Collins and Colorado realized because of this event. People came from all over the country—Florida, Alaska, California—and from as far away as Guam, the United Kingdom, and Angola. They came to spend money. Yet there wasn't one Washington policy wonk involved in planning it or organizing it. To their great credit, Fort Collins officials from the Conventions and Visitors Bureau, the mayor and her staff, the police department, and the population at large worked tirelessly to plan for and accommodate the overflow crowd in all the essential areas. Bill Clinton and *Algore* certainly didn't have any-

thing to do with it. They might even have had trouble understanding how or why it worked. Just imagine: At least 50,000 people
showed up in Fort Collins and spent an estimated $50 to $100 each
along the way. That, my friends, is "trickle-up-trickle-down-trickle-
all-around economics" at its best.

This was free enterprise on the march. It all began in the pursuit
of $29.95 for a newsletter subscription, and look how it blossomed.
Plus, Dan was not given a handout; that would have been the easier
way out for me. But, instead, he had to earn it and in the process
learned valuable lessons about free enterprise. And for Dan the
learning didn't stop with that day's end. He has used that experience to launch other profitable projects for himself and others. It's
contagious. The entrepreneurial experience feeds on itself. It's not a
miracle, as some said. It's just capitalism. You should look into it,
Mr. President.

Now, what if Bill Clinton had been there instead of me? First
of all, 99 percent of the people who showed up wouldn't have come.
(I mentioned this at the bake sale and someone suggested the
figure was closer to 100 percent.) But, more important, if this had
been an event organized by Clinton and the federal government,
it would have been considered a success only if they were able to
make off with all the money. As I told the assembled multitudes
in Fort Collins: "Instead of you dropping a hundred dollars on
your trip here, Bill Clinton would have left with your hundred
bucks."

Dan's Bake Sale was, thus, a perfect metaphor for why conservative principles—economic as well as social—work so well. It
illustrated how self-reliant people—pure in heart—could assemble
for a common purpose, bring prosperity to one another, enjoy a
great time, and suffer no adverse consequences. All that, mind you,
without one government grant, without federal subsidies, without
environmental impact studies, and without even a task-force report
being filed.

Conservatives believe America works. And Dan's Bake Sale was
an example of how and why it does. In a microcosm, it showed the
value of individual initiative and private enterprise—cornerstones
of the American Dream.

After all, are we just indentured servants to a massive paternalistic federal government whose job it is to watch over us like some misguided nanny from hell? Or is the American Dream about removing the shackles and turning loose individuals to create and produce and enjoy the rewards of their own hard work and investment? Wasn't America founded as a collection of communities and people choosing freely and voluntarily to associate and confederate for mutually beneficial purposes—buying, selling, trading, and providing services to one another? To me, this was the essence of Dan's Bake Sale. Sure, it was a fun and frivolous event, but, at another level, there are important lessons to be learned from this experience.

And, unlike those pitiful liberal excuses for bake sales that generated a few hundred dollars earmarked to reduce the federal deficit, this wasn't pure symbolism. Real money was spent. Real money was earned. Real entrepreneurship was demonstrated. Real wealth was created. During the Clinton administration, no less! This is what happens when you give people an achievable goal and they have the proper incentives and motivations to reach it.

Despite what liberals think, Americans know how to take care of themselves. They know how to solve their own problems in their own communities. They do not sit around waiting for Washington to tell them when to come in from the rain. Dan's Bake Sale was an example of good-old American ingenuity and enterprise. And these types of activities ought to be encouraged. People should be empowered to run their own lives and to determine their own destiny. They should not be shackled by overregulation and the red tape of government intrusion in every aspect of their lives.

Without overstating the case, Dan's Bake Sale showed us the possibilities. It established the potential. On center stage, in front of the whole world, it asserted with dignity and confidence: "This is the way conservatives have fun. This is the way we treat one another. This is the way we solve our problems."

Dan's Bake Sale itself was not exactly the final "stake through the heart of liberalism," but the individual initiative it exemplified surely will be in time. The script for liberalism's demise has already been written. It was authored in the 1980s by Ronald Wilson Reagan. In the next chapter, you will see how liberals are trying to forestall the death of their bloodsucking system by obfuscation and distortion of the historical record during that important and misunderstood period.

10

EIGHT YEARS OF REAGAN: THE EIGHTIES WAS NOT A DECADE OF GREED

IN *THE WAY THINGS OUGHT TO BE,* THE FIRST OF WHAT PROMISES TO BE a long series of bestsellers by me, I predicted that liberalism would stop at nothing to rewrite and revise the history and lessons of the 1980s. To quote myself (page 285 in the hardcover edition): "Beware. Liberals will pursue relentlessly their goal of destroying the legacy and truth of the Reagan presidency." Well, folks, I don't want to be redundant. I hate to keep on saying, "See, I Told You So." So, from now on, within the confines of this tome, let's just shorthand it like this: "SITYS."

Liberals correctly perceive the Reagan record as their most dangerous enemy. Why? Because what happened during the 1980s —prosperity at home (the longest period of peacetime growth in this nation's history: fifty-nine consecutive months), strength abroad—directly contradicts every liberal shibboleth. Liberals know that if they are to have any success they must redefine the public's perception, rewrite the history, and distort the public record of that period.

Bill Clinton and his gang that can't govern straight have been successful at one thing—thoroughly and artfully confusing people about the 1980s and the Reagan legacy. I can still hear, echoing cacophonously in my head, their dissonant chorus of class envy and vexation: "The rich got richer, the poor got poorer. The rich didn't pay their fair share. It's time to target those who benefited unfairly during the 1980s. The Decade of Greed and Selfishness caused the deficit."

I hoped the discordant symphony of despair would end mercifully when the 1992 campaign was over. But, no, the constant drumbeat has been building to a mind-numbing crescendo. Clinton and the Democrats in Congress, in a deliberate attempt to deceive, continue to disparage "the last twelve years," despite the fact that the last three years of "those twelve" were governed by the 1990 budget deal and its disastrous policy changes, which veritably destroyed the legacy of the 1980s and were then renewed in the Omnibus Deficit Reduction Act of 1993! Now, they gleefully proclaim, "Trickle-down [Reaganomics] is dead." Well, Reaganomics died in 1990, and with it, expansive growth of the economy.

Republicans, meanwhile, have failed miserably to offer an effective counterpoint to the inharmonious lies trolled about this crucial decade. So, once again, the job is left to me. But, as always, I am more than up to the challenge. In this chapter I will present factual, documented, undeniable, take-it-to-the-bank proof that the 1980s have been totally and intentionally mischaracterized by slick liberal politicians with the active complicity of the mainstream establishment media.

It's time to set the record straight. If you listen to liberals, you might get the impression that every problem we experience in our society arose during the Reagan and Bush years. Frankly, I am sick and tired of the Democrats pretending that history began in the 1980s. Sometimes it sounds as if they're actually trying to convince people that we had the American Revolution and then came 1980.

Here's the truth: The 1980s could and should serve as a model for our nation's future economic policies for generations to come. And the image of Ronald Reagan, the man responsible for shaping that decade, should be carved into Mount Rushmore, minted into coins, and emblazoned in a place of honor in every schoolchild's history text as a constant reminder of this great man's contributions to world freedom, national pride, and individual prosperity.

That's right. I'm an unabashed, unequivocating, out-of-the-closet, die-hard champion of the 1980s. With my record of enthusiastic eighties cheerleading, some cynics might assume that I'm one of those infamous and selfish people who profited unfairly in what liberals malign as the Decade of Greed. Surprise, folks. The fact of the matter is that I never made less money in my life than in the eighties—especially the first half of that decade. My convictions about the 1980s have nothing to do with my own personal achievements. They have everything, however, to do with our nation's best interests.

I, for one, remember the long gas lines of the 1970s. I remember Jimmy Carter's 21 percent interest rates, 14 percent inflation rate, and massive unemployment. I remember how real income for the average American family fell from 1977 through 1981. I remember the liberal Democratic president blaming Americans for being in a "malaise" and warning of even worse times to come. What an inspiration he was! What a leader!

In 1979, I was working for the Kansas City Royals and we depended on leisure-time dollars. We were trying to draw people from five states—Iowa, Nebraska, Kansas, Missouri, and Colorado. To do that, gasoline had to be affordable and hotels needed to be reasonably priced. Remember those fuel shortages? I'll tell you, we were sweating it out in those days, as were many other businesses.

Those gas lines were a direct result of the foreign oil powers playing tough with us because they didn't fear Jimmy Carter. They didn't respect him. He didn't believe in peace through strength. He believed in peace through good intentions. It didn't work. When we had strong Republican administrations through 1992, we never had those problems, even though our dependence on foreign oil had not decreased. But the real miracle of the eighties—and the one I want to focus on for the purposes of this chapter—was unprecedented economic growth and prosperity. Some 20 million jobs were created—real, long-term jobs in the private sector (and they were not hamburger-flipping jobs), not the kind of public, make-work, short-term taxpayer-rip-off jobs Bill Clinton is promoting. Businesses grew, small companies started up. People were investing their money, taking risks, and, contrary to popular opinion, every segment of society benefited.

From 1982 through 1990, the United States experienced ninety-six continuous months of economic growth—the longest peacetime expansion in history. (Did I already say that? Good. It needs to be repeated and repeated to counter the lies.) Interest rates were brought down from the stratosphere. The stock market nearly tripled in value. And we were able to finance the military buildup that brought the Soviet empire to its knees. America reached full employment while simultaneously nullifying inflation, making obsolete the renowned Phillips Curve of the Keynesian school of economics, which graphically demonstrated that there was a necessary trade-off between unemployment and inflation, i.e., you couldn't attack both problems at the same time. Well, we did, just as Jack Kemp and other supply-siders predicted would happen before the Kemp-Roth across-the-board marginal income-tax-rate reductions were implemented. But outside of this book and some other obscure ones, you won't hear Reagan, Kemp, Jude Wanniski, president of Polyconomics in New Jersey, Robert Bartlett, *Wall Street Journal* editor, and other seminal supply-siders being given the credit for this. So learn it here, folks, and remember it.

Here are some of the nitty-gritty details—some facts and figures —about what really happened in the so-called "Decade of Greed." I advise all resident scholars of the Limbaugh Institute for Advanced Conservative Studies to commit them to memory so you are well armed in your never-ending pursuit of truth:

• Average real family income grew by well over 15 percent from 1982 to 1989, according to the U.S. Bureau of the Census.

• For the poorest fifth of Americans, real income grew almost 12 percent.

• Families earning more than $50,000 (in 1990 dollars) went from less than 25 percent of families in 1980 to 31 percent in 1990.

• The percentage of families earning less than $15,000 dropped.

• According to the U.S. Treasury's Office of Tax Analysis, of those who were in the bottom-fifth income bracket in 1979, 65 percent jumped at least two income brackets during the 1980s. In fact, more made it all the way to the top than stayed in the poorest group.

• Taxpayers were five times more likely to increase their income than have it fall.

• Federal Reserve data show that families with incomes between $10,000 and $50,000 a year experienced a higher percentage of growth in net worth than those in the top-one-fifth income group.

• The top 1 percent paid more than 25 percent of all federal income taxes in 1990, a 40 percent increase over 1980, according to the Congressional Budget Office. The bottom 60 percent paid 11 percent of federal taxes in 1990—20 percent less than in 1980. (Don't do a double take here. You heard me correctly. The rich did pay their fair share in the eighties, and Clinton knows it. More on this in a moment.)

• The black middle class grew rapidly, from 2.6 million households with incomes of $25,000 or more in 1979, to 3.9 million in 1989.

• Between 1983 and 1989, the total population under the poverty line decreased by 3.8 million people, with an unprecedented number of poor entering the work force.

• The proverbial misery index took a nosedive: We experienced sustained economic growth without inflation, low unemployment, and low interest rates. Also, some 20 million new jobs were created, 82 percent of which were in the higher-skilled, higher-paying occupations.

• The poor were not neglected: Federal spending on the poor for income, food, health care, housing, education, training, and social services increased.

• Between 1978 and 1982 the number of poor blacks rose by more than 2 million; between 1982 and 1989 the number of poor blacks fell by 400,000.

• The 1980s was a decade of greatly increased personal and corporate charitable giving.

• Despite the charge that the rich got richer, the poor got poorer, and the middle class was almost decimated during the 1980s, **all income groups from the poorest to the richest experienced real income gains. Yet during the Carter years—when liberalism was flourishing—only the income of the top 1 percent grew. The share of income gains going to the top 1 percent of families was 160 percent higher under Carter than under Reagan.**

Between 1982 and 1989, real after-tax income per person rose by 15.5 percent, and real median income of families, before taxes, went up 12.5 percent.

• Despite the charge that "the rich got richer and pay less tax, the poor got poorer and pay more," **between 1980 and 1992 the wealthy not only paid more income taxes in actual dollars, but they paid a greater share of income taxes as a percentage of their income, compared to other income groups. The income taxes as a percentage of their income of all income groups was reduced, with each of the four lowest quintile groups experiencing greater percentage reductions than those income groups above them. In other words, all income groups paid less taxes as a percentage of their income during the Reagan years, but the poor received the most relief, the middle class the next, and the rich, the least. Further, the rich paid a greater share of all taxes paid in the 1980s than in the Carter years.** (See chart, page 116.)

But Rush, you may ask, isn't it a fact that Reagan cut poverty programs? Didn't he destroy the social "safety net"?

No. That's absolutely false. Federal spending on poverty programs in 1991 dollars increased from $140 billion in 1982 to $180 billion in 1991, an annual growth rate of 3 percent. In other words, the welfare state grew under Reagan—and the liberals are still complaining!

But, you may say, this is all well and good, but during those years the federal deficit skyrocketed. That, my friends, is undeniable; in fact, the deficit did rise to $230 billion in 1985–86; but it was not because of the tax cuts. It was because of unchecked growth in entitlement spending. And don't blame that on Reagan, either. He tried his best to reduce spending, but every one of his budgets was proudly pronounced "dead on arrival" by the Democratic Congress. Plus, if you look at 1987, 1988, and 1989, when the real economic growth reached full steam, the deficit fell to $150 billion, even with the unchecked spending. It fell because of economic growth that created a bigger base of taxpayers and, therefore, more tax revenue. If Congress had made any strides toward curbing skyrocketing spending during this period, there would have been no deficit by the end of the Reagan presidency.

In the interest of illuminating the present discussion about deficit

REDUCTION OF TAX RATES

Income Quintile	Top Income in Bracket	1980 (% of Income Paid As Taxes)	1992 (% of Income Paid As Taxes)	1992 (% of Taxes Cut)
Poorest 20%	$20,300	−0.5%	−3.2%	−540%
2nd lowest 20%	$36,800	4.5%	2.8%	−37.8%
Middle 20%	$64,500	7.9%	6.2%	−21.5%
2nd highest 20%	$82,400	11%	8.7%	−20.9%
Richest 20%	------------	17.2%	15.6%	−9.3%
Richest 1%	------------	23.9%	22%	−7.9%

Source: U.S. Bureau of the Census

reduction, it should be pointed out that even President Reagan begrudgingly agreed to sign on to a couple of "deficit reduction" tax increases, one of which was, at the time, the largest tax increase in the nation's history, which included $2 of spending cuts for every $1 in increased tax revenue. But guess what? In a foreshadowing of its double-cross of George Bush in 1990, the Congress failed to make the budget cuts it had pledged. We are still waiting for them. And you think the promised cuts of 1993 are going to happen? Heh, heh, heh!

So I don't mind telling you that I'm growing weary—in fact, angry—at the duplicitous assertion that the tax cuts caused the deficit to increase. News commentator Sam Donaldson must say it every other week on "This Week with David Brinkley." Syndicated newspaper columnist George Will is even tired of arguing with him about it. In fact, during the Reagan tax-cut era, IRS collections actually nearly doubled. When Ronald Reagan took office in 1981, the top marginal tax rate was at 70 percent. When he left office in 1989, the top marginal rate was down to 28 percent. Liberal logic (an oxymoron if ever there was one) would thus suggest that the government would collect less money in taxes because the rates have been cut. Right? Wrong. Actual revenues nearly doubled, from $550 billion to about $991 billion. How did that happen? If the liberals would stop ridiculing so-called "trickle-down" economics for a while and take an honest look at reality, they would understand.

Cuts in marginal tax rates spur economic growth by providing entrepreneurs an incentive to invest their marginal tax dollars, causing many of them to earn more money and pay more taxes on their earnings, albeit at a lower marginal rate, and create new jobs. Again, this is an application of Adam Smith's "invisible hand." These new jobs result in a bigger employment base and, thus, more taxpayers. More taxpayers translates into higher tax revenues— even at lower marginal rates.

Supply-side economics is nothing new. It's a restatement of the classical economists, from Adam Smith to nineteenth-century economists David Ricardo and Jean-Baptiste Say. Supply-side is an extrapolation of Say's Law: Supply creates its own demand. In very rudimentary terms, if you increase productivity, i.e., supply (through tax incentives), you will cause more dollars to be pumped into the economy (demand), and the economy will grow. Of course, Clinton, at his best, is a demand-sider—a Keynesian who believes that artificially increasing aggregate demand through boosts in government spending will cause real economic growth (witness his "stimulus" package). The truth is, as most credible economists will now confess, government pump-priming only artificially stimulates demand on things such as short-term public-works jobs, and causes inflation and deficit expansion.

But Clinton et al. won't even engage in a discussion about their own economic programs (and they are never put to the test by the self-styled watchdog media). Again, their tactic is simply to divert attention from them by exploiting class-warfare themes. They pejoratively refer to supply-side as trickle-down economics. You've heard it before. Here's how liberals define "trickle-down" economics: "You give tax breaks to the rich with money that really belongs to the middle class and poor. [How that works out is beyond me, but so goes the propaganda.] Then the rich, who are supposedly honest and compassionate, will just hand out this extra money in ways that the middle class and poor get it back."

You see, the liberal problem centers on the notion that what people have they are given, or somehow receive as benefits. When "the rich" selfishly didn't stand around on corners stuffing dollars into the pockets of the starving hoi polloi, our liberal buddies declared the venture a failure. "If you are going to give money away, let us show you how it's done," they demanded, demonstrating their belief that no one legitimately earns what he has—he is given it. So now it is 1993 and they are showing us, aren't they?

Well, that is not what the 1980s were about. Nevertheless, "trickle-down" has negative connotations because the term has been misappropriated by liberals and mercilessly ridiculed. However, let me illustrate for you that there is nothing farfetched about the trickle-down theory and that even liberals sometimes have to acknowledge that it works. For instance, how does Bill Clinton say he won the election? Who does he say he appealed to? He claims his was a grass-roots campaign, right? Think of "trickle-down" as nothing more or less than a system of applying water to the Earth's surface in the expectation that some will soak through the earth and nourish the grass roots. It's really a matter of common sense, isn't it?

How many liberals do you know who dig holes in their lawn so they can apply water directly to the roots of their grass? When you drive through Beverly Hills and look at the homes of people like Harry Thomason and Linda Bloodworth-Thomason, top TV producers and Clinton confidants, how many open trenches do you see on their lawns?

The governor of New York State, Mario Cuomo, is another liberal who, notwithstanding his disclaimers, sometimes believes in "trickle-down" economics. Let me give you an example. Mercedes-Benz has been planning to build a factory in the United States to make four-wheel-drive vehicles to compete with Ford, Chevrolet, and Jeep. Every governor, including Cuomo, wants that plant in his state. What's Mario offering? Tax breaks. Now, correct me if I'm wrong, but Mercedes is a big company. Businesses, according to liberals, are the root of all evil. Why is he offering them tax breaks and other kinds of economic incentives? He's even offering to relax some of New York's harsh environmental restrictions. In other words, he's trying to make it very easy for Mercedes to turn a profit. Why does he want Mercedes? Certainly not because he likes the company. Precisely because the economic activity spurred by its presence in the state will trickle down to others in the state in the form of new jobs, greater spending, increased revenues, and the rest.

Just look at what liberals do when they want new business. They offer incentives. They try to bribe companies. They try to reward them. But then they turn around and punish existing businesses. And, after a while, if Cuomo lures Mercedes, he'll no doubt punish the company by raising its taxes and tightening the regulations. If Mercedes then moves the factory, Cuomo will find some way to blame it on Ronald Reagan.

It's as plain as day for people to see how the world works. This is not theory, it is reality—even the liberals grudgingly acknowledge supply-side or trickle-down economics when it suits their purposes. But once again, their hypocrisies are never exposed, present company excepted.

But we've probably got to stop using the term "trickle-down." It has been corrupted beyond repair by the Clinton gang and the media. Therefore, I am going to suggest we ban further use of it. From now on, let's go back to referring to the kind of free-market, entrepreneurial capitalism we witnessed in the 1980s as "Reaganomics." The beauty of that term is that, like "trickle-down," it was coined by liberals as a term of derision. But once the truth is universally understood, the eighties will have been so effectively vindicated that the term "Reaganomics" will be used only as a term of endearment and respect.

Liberals simply reject the notion that the Reagan tax-rate cuts had anything to do with all the wealth and prosperity that were created. If you listen, for instance, to Laura D'Andrea Tyson, Bill Clinton's chairwoman of the Council of Economic Advisers, taxes have nothing to do with the economy of a nation.

"In direct contradiction to twelve years of Republican ideology [Uh, Ms. Tyson, don't forget about the 1990 budget deal, which slew the Reagan dragon], there is no relationship between the level of taxes a nation pays and its economic performance," she said.

Imagine that! Not only does this statement defy mountains of evidence to the contrary, but it simply defies logic and common sense. Here is President Clinton's top economic adviser telling us that it doesn't matter how much you tax a nation; it won't have any impact on the productive side of the economy. Is it possible she can really believe this? Apparently so; as I've said before, some of these sixties throwbacks still believe the economy is a zero-sum game, with people's economic behavior being wholly unaffected by the level of taxes.

John Fund, a friend of mine and editorial writer for *The Wall Street Journal*, who collaborated with me on *The Way Things Ought to Be*, provided some illuminating insights into the mind-set of the Clinton policy wonks. In a *Journal* column, he explained that "much of the Clinton administration has a quiet love affair with German social democracy." He quotes Christian Tenbrock, U.S. correspondent for the German newspaper *Die Zelt*, as saying: "It's surprising how much of the German economic model Clinton is trying to adopt." Fund notes that this shouldn't be surprising in that "most politicians are captives of the ideas they had in their twenties. They seldom re-evaluate them once in the electoral rat race." Fund added that Germany was the first place on the Continent that Clinton visited during his 1968–69 sojourn in Britain. At that time, according to Fund, Germany was considered a model welfare state whose "structural weaknesses remained hidden for another decade" when Clinton was long gone. He also says that Clinton and his advisers have a fatal attraction for the highly statist policies of Germany and other Western European nations and are trying to emulate them, despite the economic crises all those nations find themselves in. Mr. Fund's research and brilliant analysis may help us understand the incomprehensible: how Clinton could be attracted to socialism when it has failed everywhere it has been tried.

So, the facts are indisputable that as soon as the Kemp-Roth tax cuts kicked in in 1983, the job-creating machine in this country took off and continued unabated until President Bush broke his "no new taxes" pledge in 1990.

Before we leave the subject, let's dissect another liberal-spawned myth associated with the eighties. I've mentioned it before, but it too is worthy of repeating. They call it the "Decade of Greed." Well, my friends, it was in this so-called "Decade of Greed" that Americans became more charitable than ever before. No matter how you measure it—whether it's in absolute terms, in real dollars adjusted for inflation, or in contributions relative to national income—the 1980s were, indeed, the Decade of Giving. According to a report by Richard B. McKenzie, professor at the Graduate School of Management at the University of California, Irvine, the annual rate of growth in total giving in the 1980s was nearly 55 percent higher than in the previous twenty-five years. And this trend continued right through 1992, year twelve of the so-called Reagan-Bush era. Americans gave 2.01 percent of their income to charity in 1992, the highest rate since 1971. Overall, donations totaled $124.31 billion, up 6.4 percent, after inflation. Individuals gave $109.98 billion, representing the greatest percentage of total family income given to charity since 1963.

It's common sense to realize that when people earn more and feel more secure in their positions, they give more. The converse, of course, is also true. When gargantuan portions of people's paychecks are confiscated by the federal, state, and local governments, they will have less discretionary income to donate to charity, or anything else, for that matter.

But you must understand that when liberals refer to the eighties as the Decade of Greed, they mean it in a different sense. They mean that because marginal income-tax rates were lower across the board (of course, they lie and say they were lower only for the rich), people paid less taxes and didn't finance necessary government spending. So, people were greedy for keeping a larger portion of what they earned for themselves, rather than donating it to the government to spend on wasteful, pork-barrel projects. As a result, deficit spending was necessary and we had to rob from our grandchildren—all because we wouldn't finance these *necessary* spending projects. But don't fall for this. Again, people did not neglect their fiscal obligations during the eighties, as demonstrated by the near doubling of revenues. The spending simply outpaced the revenues. Rather, the paradigm of greed during the eighties, as well as the years before and since, was and is the federal government under the stewardship of the socialistic Congress.

When you hear Clinton talk about people getting a free ride during the eighties, who's he talking about? You. Productive working people. When he talks about those who benefited from the eighties, who's he talking about? People like you. People who busted their behinds. People who earned a living. These are the people he is coming after today. Did you get a free lunch during the 1980s? Listen, folks, the only people getting a free lunch are those who are being given money by the federal government. That happens to be Bill Clinton's constituency. And he wants it to grow—at your expense.

So many people have become convinced that government is the only vehicle that can deal with problems. Let me tell you, there are always going to be problems and inequities. What do liberals attempt to do in the process of making life fair? They take from achievers. Under the guise of fairness, they redistribute wealth. Through regulations, taxation, disincentives to invest, they bring people down, lower their financial status, and make them wards of the state. That's what I mean by spreading misery. I'm not going to quit saying it: It's simply repackaged socialism.

Clinton's approach short-circuits the American Dream. It doesn't allow for people who are trying to become wealthy. It discourages them. It maligns their ambitions. Reagan's approach was to allow the miracle of the marketplace to elevate everyone. And it worked!

Government simply cannot be the source of prosperity. No country has ever become great because of tax increases or government spending. Nations become great because people are given the freedom to achieve. By freeing people from the burdens of government intervention in their lives, Ronald Reagan empowered millions of people to reach new heights of excellence.

Everybody agrees now that we need to create jobs. But for the economy to be turned around, wealth needs to be created, too. We have been indoctrinated with the idea that creating wealth is somehow evil. Remember this: The government can't create wealth; it can only destroy it or confiscate and redistribute it.

The greatest thing about the eighties was the incredible upward class mobility—the way poor people became middle-class people, and sometimes even rich people. It would be comical if it weren't so tragic, but Bill Clinton talks about making those people pay now—the ones who had a "free ride" in the 1980s. Funny thing is, so prevalent was upward mobility that he is not talking about the same people. Even Slick Willie can't hit a moving target. Large numbers of the "wealthy" today, as Clinton defines them, were not nearly so well off in the 1980s. They were able to become wealthy because of the robust opportunities made possible by Reaganomics. Clinton plans to dismantle all of that. So despite what he tells us, his tax is not on the wealthy, but on the creation of wealth. This climate of growth, of upward class mobility, is America's greatest promise, and it was never fulfilled better than in the 1980s. This is not something government does for people, it is simply something that government can allow to happen.

When Reagan came along and explained this and showed us by example how it all worked, liberals were shocked and running scared. If the real lesson of the 1980s were allowed to take hold, it would have been the death knell for liberalism. But fortunately for liberalism, George Bush came along and, seeking to get along with the Democrats in the interests of smooth government, changed course—at least economically. He betrayed the most important political promise he ever made and made a huge political sacrifice in the process, and ended up compounding a cyclical recession.

Liberals then brilliantly took the natural cycle of recession and blamed it completely on the 1980s. They had been predicting doom and gloom for ten years and finally had some evidence. Now, I can predict that something is going to happen. And if I say it every day for ten years, eventually there is going to be some evidence that it is actually happening. That's exactly what the liberals did, with the full support and complicity of the media establishment.

This was a conscious, deliberate strategy, too. Clinton adviser Stanley Greenberg exposed the scam when he wrote in the journal *American Prospect:* "Democrats need to create an imagery of Reagan-Bush America that supersedes the Carter years and impeaches the credibility of conservative governance for middle America. The battle to define the Reagan-Bush years is a critical arena where Democrats have the opportunity to disrupt the Republicans' hold on the middle class."

Greenberg also betrayed the Clinton plan to create more dependency on government: "To recreate a rationale for electing Democrats, the party must once again become the party of government." He advised expanding social-welfare programs that cater to the lower and middle classes.

Still, despite all that, look what Bill Clinton had to do to get elected. He had to pretend he was a conservative. He had to convince people that he was a "New Democrat." He talked about welfare reform. He promised a middle-class tax cut. He talked conservatism. People thought they were getting someone from the Democratic Leadership Council. They thought that the moderates were taking the party back from the liberal wing. He fooled a lot of people. He didn't fool me. I predicted exactly what was going to happen. SITYS.

I have predicted that when Bill Clinton serves out his first and only term as president, people will no longer be talking about the twelve years of Reagan-Bush. Instead, they will link the Bush and Clinton years. The era of Reagan will stand alone as clearly one of the most prosperous periods in American history. Just the other day in *The Wall Street Journal,* the lead editorial referred to the Bush-

Clinton era. Economist Milton Friedman, I understand, has also been referring to it that way. I apologize for being so prescient. I can't help it. I have talent on loan from God.

The only reason this isn't obvious right now is the role of the media. Hollywood and the press establishment love to poke fun at what conservatives believe in. They love to ridicule us and impugn our motives. For a long time, people were intimidated by that. Nobody likes to be laughed at. But during the Reagan era, conservative ideals prospered just like the economy, and conservatives became confident. We need to rediscover that confidence, folks.

This is a war that is never going to end. But you have to remain optimistic. Never compromise your beliefs, your integrity, your honesty. Eventually even the liberals will learn to respect you if you stick to your principles. That's when you can persuade them.

I am never going to compromise on Reaganomics. I will never stop promoting economics that empower people. I will never give up talking about the importance of pursuing excellence. I will relentlessly and tirelessly urge people to be the best they can be.

I'm a long-term thinker. I have a passionate concern for people who will live after us. I understand that to return to these principles requires us to change the way people think. It will require educating people—informing them. People need to understand how the world really works, not how we would like it to work or how we wish it would work.

The reason I'm passionate about this is that I love people. I care about people. It disturbs me when young people are told by America's leadership that it doesn't matter what you do because the system is rigged, or that unless you are born to wealth and privilege, you can't succeed, so you might as well be grateful for the crumbs that government will throw your way.

That's not what America is about. As I've said, I want people to be the best they can be. And I want the country to be the best it can be. For that to happen we need strong, self-reliant individuals. We need to reward risk and stop punishing achievement. Let the marketplace work. President Reagan showed the way in the 1980s, President Kennedy in the 1960s. We can return to that kind of prosperity again with the right kind of leadership.

But before we get there, folks, we've got to understand fully those who are calling the shots today. We've got to understand the way their minds work. This is no easy assignment with liberals. But, again, I am up to the challenge. Take a deep breath. Pour yourself a beverage and prepare for the most lucid analysis of the current liberal mind-set ever published.

11

THE DECADE OF FRAUD
AND DECEIT

THE DAY AFTER CLINTON'S STATE OF THE UNION ADDRESS ON FEBRU-
ary 17, 1993, a *Washington Post* reporter came by the EIB studios to
listen to my radio program. She wanted to get an idea of what real
Americans thought about the speech, and what better way than to
eavesdrop on my show? After listening to my first hour, in which I
offered—with flair and aplomb—my usual insightful critique of
the liberals steering our ship of state, she smiled and said, "You
must really love this, huh?"

"Not really," I replied.

"Why?" she wondered.

"There is real pressure on me. It's like an oral final exam," I said.

"What do you mean? I don't understand."

"The president of the United States has an army of researchers, a
battery of staff, a bunch of writers," I explained. "They've worked
on this speech for weeks, they've rehearsed it, tried it out on people.
Then they deliver it. I have only a few hours to prepare my
response. I don't have guest experts in. I don't call a series of people
to find out what they think. I must marshal my knowledge and
opinions on the spot when the clock strikes noon.

"So when I respond it's got to be educated, informed, passionate. My opinions have to be succinct, organized, and properly delivered without TelePrompTers, rehearsals, and rewrites. If I'm going to refute things the president of the United States says, I'd better be right. I go out there feeling more pressure than he feels, because most of his pressure is, at that point, related strictly to performance. He is not worried about the content because that's been dealt with: He's got a written, rehearsed speech on a TelePrompTer. I, on the other hand, have to combine the performance and content into one unrehearsed presentation. I'm doing it cold, ad-libbed with 20 million instructors out there waiting to grade me, based on their expectations, which are high because they have come to expect superior performance and content from me. That's pressure. Admittedly, I respond well to it. I welcome it. But if you asked me on Saturday afternoon, 'Hey, Rush, what do you feel like doing?,' I would not say: 'I want to go answer a Bill Clinton State of the Union Address.' It's hard work." It's not all fun and games, nor recreational.

On the other hand, somebody has to stand up for truth. Someone has to challenge the flagrant dishonesty of this administration. Someone has to set the record straight. This country needs and deserves a potent voice of loyal opposition to the policies of statism and socialism that this president represents. I'm happy to do it. I'm honored. I relish the opportunity, and, yes, as always, I am more than equal to the task.

Just as it is critically important to correct the lies that are being told about the past decade (as we did in the previous chapter), it is equally important to dispense some truth about the 1990s. The 1980s, we now understand, were not the Decade of Greed, as the liberal revisionists would have us believe. In fact, this chapter is devoted to explaining why the 1990s—defined by Bill Clinton–style liberalism—should and will ultimately be remembered as "the Decade of Fraud and Deceit."

But the story doesn't begin with Bill Clinton's election as president. No, the story begins back in the 1960s, "the Age of Aquarius," the decade in which Bill Clinton's values (as they are) and core beliefs were formed. Remember the 1960s? That was the decade in which our president claims he only exhaled. But we know better. This was the period during which he inhaled the intoxicating aromas of burning flags, of mindless radicalism, of freedom without responsibility, and of moral relativism. It was an era that celebrated drug abuse, political alienation, anti-war protests, campus mayhem, flower power, and a self-centeredness and egomania that bordered on the absurd. This was the incubator that nurtured the ideas shaping our lives today: Clintonomics, gays in the military, federal funding of abortion on demand, and God knows what else he still has up his sleeve.

There was truly a feeling among the 1960s crowd—no, a *conviction* would be more accurate—that they had a better understanding of the world and could accomplish more than any other generation. After all, they were at one with the oppressed peoples of the Third World. They were in harmony with nature. And they just knew that if things were left to them, peace would guide the world, and love would steer the stars. The 1960s kids were morally superior and somehow gifted with more compassion and wisdom than their parents and grandparents. They told one another this, and, worse yet, they believed it! How do I know this? I was there, folks.

This was the original Me Generation. And the self-indulgent, humanistic nature of it all quickly deteriorated into a hideous, destructive nihilism and anti-Americanism. One of the shepherds of the 1960s New Left, Paul Goodman, observed that it was a movement defined mostly by a "loss of patriotic feeling."

In the eyes of the 1960s activists, America could do nothing right. The United States was no longer perceived as the greatest experiment in democracy and freedom in the history of the world, but as a center of militarism, imperialism, racism, and economic oppression.

It was in this reality vacuum that Bill Clinton and most of those he has surrounded himself with for counsel and advice were reared. Six weeks after he helped organize a massive anti-war, anti–U.S. protest in England in 1969, he turned up in the Soviet Union—the pre-Gorbachev Evil Empire that was supporting the communists in Vietnam with weapons and advisers. He dodged the draft and talked about how he "loathed" the U.S. military. Bill and Hillary

Clinton are products of the 1960s. No matter how you look at it, their humanistic, socialistic values are unmistakably the values of the anti-American sixties.

Lots of us lived through the 1960s. But only a segment of us allowed ourselves to be defined by it. The Clintons clearly believed the rhetoric of the 1960s that said their generation was different, unique, and had a special rendezvous with destiny. They truly believed that it was the dawning of the Age of Aquarius, that they were the center of the universe, and that their lives would miraculously usher in a higher plane of consciousness for the nation.

"Don't trust anyone over thirty" was one of the popular slogans of the day. Why? Because no one from the previous generation could possibly be as caring and compassionate and as spiritually connected and intellectually enlightened as the sixties kids.

These, my friends, are the twisted roots of the 1990s—the Decade of Fraud. The sixties people are in power for the first time. And they still think they know better than everyone else. The worst of them—including our First Couple—haven't learned any lessons from the 1960s. They don't have any new ideas; just a bunch of tired, old notions that have failed every time they've been tried—socialism, humanism, statism. Why would these old ideas work now? Because they believe that only they can make these ideas work. It is not that the ideas were bad, just that the right people haven't been in charge yet to implement them. What unabashed arrogance!

That's the essence of New Age liberalism. "We care. We're good people. We love people and we have good intentions. We're more compassionate than ordinary mortals. So everything we say and do is right, and everything anyone else says and does is reactionary and wrong." Well, folks, as a 1960s person myself, I can understand how many kids were swallowed up in this utopian idealism. I wasn't. But I certainly knew many who were. More difficult to understand, however, is how these failed ideas and this embarrassing level of immaturity survived intact into the 1990s.

You know, there's an old saying: "Anyone under thirty who isn't a liberal has no heart; anyone over thirty who is a liberal has no brain." That's at least half true. But, seriously, to the young, idealistic, emotional, and immature, the rhetoric of liberalism and socialism is understandably appealing. But when sensible people see—over and over again—how these ideas do not work in the real world, they walk away from them.

The problem with the liberal solutions being tried once again in Washington today has nothing to do with good or bad intentions—the problem with them is that they don't work! They never have, and they never will. Lots of people have realized this along the way, but the true-believing liberals simply can't accept it—or won't.

As I have said many times before, world history shows that no nation has ever taxed itself into prosperity. There is no way that government redistribution of wealth can create wealth. All over the world, in fact, nations are abandoning this idea in favor of market economics. Nations once absolutely committed to the idea of total state control of the economy—from Russia to China to the countries of Eastern Europe and Latin America—are now running from it. Why? Simply because it doesn't work, and for nations that embrace it, it inevitably leads to national economic suicide.

"But, Rush, what about the Great Depression?" you might ask. "Didn't the New Deal bring us out of the worst economic slump in American history?"

The answer is an emphatic "no." The Depression began in 1929. During the worst of it, unemployment reached about 25 percent. In 1939, when the New Deal was fully in force, the unemployment rate was down only to 17 percent. It wasn't the New Deal that ended the Depression, it was World War II. There's so much revision of history going on today. It's not just the liberals who are behind this. The media are either willing accomplices or unwitting dupes. And this nonsense has permeated our universities and other institutions. This is at the root of our misunderstanding of problems and solutions.

But it's not just the liberal economic ideas that are bankrupt. Their social policies always attack phantom problems and symptoms instead of addressing root issues. Take, for example, the problem of crime.

Remember the story about the Japanese exchange student who got lost in New Orleans? He went up to a house and knocked on the door in hopes of getting some help. Instead, tragically, he was gunned down by a resident who thought the victim was trying to break into his house.

Now, how do liberals respond to that? The problem, according to them, is the fact that the gun was there. Now, I don't know where these people live or who they talk to. I know they can't possibly live among the people they claim to represent and understand. They apparently have no concept of the level of fear that the average, law-abiding person feels. They have locks on the doors, bars on their windows, and they're scared to death of a knock on the door.

Crime is out of control in most of our urban areas, and even in many of our suburban and rural communities. Everybody, it seems, is afraid in our society except the criminals. They're not scared. They do not feel intimidated by law enforcement, the judicial system, or our government. The liberal crime policy—as with so many of their programs—is completely upside down.

It's a gut-wrenching thing to have an innocent kid get lost and get shot when he knocks at a door. But where is the root of the problem? The root of the problem is rampant crime, and fear of it. Liberals never get to the root. They will go for the easy answer—the symbolic gesture—every time. It's easier to take guns away from law-abiding citizens than from the criminals, so that's what they will do. What would rigid gun-control measures do toward solving the root problem? Exacerbate it, by eliminating the primary weapon of self-defense still available to the law-abiding homeowner.

Controlling and preserving tranquility in our society is the number-one responsibility of government. If government can't do anything else, this should be its primary mission. Yet, it is usually the first responsibility liberal government abdicates. Whether it's the defense of the nation from foreign adversaries or policing our local communities, liberals have no respect for the aggressive use of force. It is usually the first area of the budget that gets cut. And increasingly, liberal politicians will do everything possible, it seems, to handcuff law enforcement from doing its job. Now that the police have been emasculated, the liberals want to disarm all the law-abiding people based on the theory that doing so increases their safety.

When I spoke to the National Rifle Association in Nashville, its leaders presented me with a couple of rifles. Now, keep in mind, I have never pulled the trigger of a gun—except a BB gun. I didn't even like that. But, because these rifles were gifts, they are meaningful to me. Guess what? I can't get them into my home. Because I live in New York, I've got to register them. To do that, I've got to get fingerprinted. Then I will get turned down because rejections are routine on first applications. Then I will need to do the whole thing over again. In thirty-two weeks I might get my gift, according to associates more experienced in such matters than I am.

Now, we are all aware of the astronomical crime rate in New York. Right? If I wanted a gun for illegal purposes, I could stand in the street in any neighborhood and buy as many illegal guns as I wanted. If I didn't obey the law, I could get anything I wanted. But I'm a law-abiding citizen. I've been given the gift of some rifles. I can't get them registered with ease. The hassle is amazing. But I'm going through with the hassle just because the NRA was so gracious and because there's a principle at stake.

But think about this: If gun control worked, there wouldn't be any violent crime in New York. Liberals think that everyone will be nice if you just don't give them the tools to be mean. They think the gun is what makes you mean.

Then, to top it off, they want the gun-control laws to apply only to everybody else. Remember the incident with columnist Carl Rowan? He was always writing about how we needed to have stricter gun-control laws. He lived in Washington, D.C., which has tough laws on firearms possession. He didn't understand why others thought he was a hypocrite for shooting at someone in his hot tub with an unregistered gun. Liberals think everyone should live by their rules but them.

The rest of us need a paternalistic government telling us what to do and how to behave. But not them. This is the way liberalism works—or doesn't work.

You have to assume that fuzzy-headed academicians, the sandal-clad theoreticians, and the nearsighted pointy-heads in this administration have never held jobs in the real world. (Excuse me, I forgot to acknowledge Robert Rubin and Roger Altman, Wall Street financial gurus who made big bucks in the evil 1980s but still condemn the "wealthy.") What they have done is write term papers and doctoral theses on public-policy subjects. And they are certain their theories will work if given a chance because, after all, they always worked on paper.

Sure, sure, Clinton and his "coterie of the concerned" care more. They're more concerned. They're more compassionate. And this time, these theories are going to work. But their arrogance and condescension do more harm than their good intentions do good, because their demonstrations of "caring" and "concern" are actually founded in a lack of faith in the individual.

The liberals who are running our government right now see the American people as an unintelligent, uninformed, incapable bunch. Liberals like to think that you can't make it without them. You need affirmative action by big government in order to improve your life.

But that's only part of the explanation for what motivates these folks. Some of them—many of them, perhaps—are just plain diabolical and dishonest to the core. There's a growing element within liberalism that knows these policies don't work. But for the sake of their own empowerment, and at the expense of our national interests and individual prosperity, they still promote them.

These people want to create as much government dependency as possible—not because they believe it will improve the quality of lives or is in the best interest of our nation, but because it will empower them. For proof of this theory you need only refer to the fact that whatever liberal legislation these folks impose on our society, they invariably exempt themselves from its rules and effects.

Imagine if we heard about a dictator in some far-off Third World country who announced that all of the nation's very restrictive laws applied to everyone but himself. Americans would be shocked and outraged by such hypocrisy and arrogance. But the fact of the matter is that our own U.S. Congress—the body responsible for creating our laws in the first place—does just that, all the time. And we, as an electorate, continue to tolerate it. We continue re-electing these incumbents and have yet to invoke term limits.

The Imperial Congress, which has been under the domination of Democrats for forty years, routinely makes laws that apply to everyone but its own members. For instance, the newspaper *Roll Call* uncovered a scandal a few years ago in which congressional staffers were being forced to work around the clock, without overtime pay and under threat of dismissal. While the allegations were substantiated, no charges were ever brought against anyone because Congress had exempted itself and its members from the nation's labor laws.

The very people who arrogate to themselves the role of the nation's conscience; the ones who chastise you for not caring enough, for not sacrificing enough, totally exempt themselves from the rules. Want another example? Although she has escaped being classified a liberal, Supreme Court Justice Ruth Bader Ginsburg professes to believe many things that are indeed rooted in liberal orthodoxy. During her confirmation hearings she was asked by Senator Orrin Hatch (R-Utah) if she believed that a business could be guilty of racism if the percentage of minorities on its payroll was less than the percentage of minorities living in the community where the business was located. She emphatically replied that racism could indeed be established by this simple statistical variance, without any proof that racist policies in hiring practices led to the disparity. Senator Hatch then informed her that during her several years in the D.C. Court of Appeals she had hired fifty-seven people in assorted positions and that none of them was black! Justice Ginsburg unwittingly indicated by her answer that she is prepared to rule from the bench that racism can be defined by her own actions. He let her off the hook by then assuring her that he didn't think this fact alone defined her as a racist, because he knew her not to be.

Congress has exempted itself from the provisions of the Civil Rights Act, the Equal Employment and Opportunity Act, the Equal Pay Act, the National Labor Relations Act, the Occupational Safety and Health Act, the Freedom of Information Act, the Privacy Act, the Ethics in Government Act, and a host of other laws. Even the Civil Rights Act of 1964, legislation that is the pride and joy of every liberal worth his or her salt, doesn't apply to Congress. In 1984, the House of Representatives, under pressure to review this kind of indefensible double standard, voted on whether to continue exempting itself from the law that forbids discrimination based on race. The vote wasn't even close, with 277 in favor of continuing the exemption, to 125 opposed.

Now, if such laws are desirable for the people of the nation, why, we might ask, would Congress exempt itself from their effects? If they really believed in these laws, why would they object to living under them?

The answer is simple. They don't really believe in these principles. These laws are passed only to enhance the power of government and to create greater dependency on it.

The Founding Fathers, in their wisdom, warned against this kind of government duplicity and presumptuousness. James Madison wrote in *The Federalist Papers* that Congress must be under the law so as to limit the harm it might do to the nation. Congressmen, he wrote, should "make no law which will not have its full operation on themselves and their friends, as well as on the great mass of society. This has always been deemed one of the strongest bonds by which human policy can connect the rulers and the people together. It creates between them that communion of interests and sympathy of sentiments of which few governments have furnished examples; but without which every government degenerates into tyranny."

How true! The Imperial Congress long ago began its deterioration into tyranny. The liberal U.S. Congress is a living testament to the old adage from the great English historian of liberty, Lord John Acton: "Power corrupts, and absolute power corrupts absolutely."

Poor Madison. The way he saw it, the Congress would never exempt itself from the laws of the land because it would understand the fundamental importance of staying in touch with the will of the people. The way Senator Ted Kennedy (D-Massachusetts), Barney Frank (D-Massachusetts), and company see things, it's a whole lot easier to get legislation passed by a bunch of people for whom that legislation holds no threat. Is it any wonder that the income level where the new confiscatory tax-rate increase begins is just above the congressional salary level? In their own professional lives, at least, all these do-gooder laws are essentially irrelevant and meaningless.

Let me tell you about this patronizing, bleeding-heart attitude on the part of liberals in power. It is the road toward statism. This is the way we could lose our freedom. One of the purposes of this book is to make people aware of this cycle. If Clinton and his liberal friends are successful, the result will be more poor, disaffected, alienated people who are more dependent on government for their every need. Don't forget that political freedoms are inextricably tied to and dependent upon economic freedoms. In other words, our personal liberties are diminished in direct proportion to the erosion of our economic freedoms; and our economic freedoms are eroded in direct proportion to the aggrandizement of government, through its onerous regulations and taxes.

Liberals have succeeded in convincing too many people that America guarantees economic prosperity to all of its citizens. The founders' promise of equality of opportunity is gradually being supplanted by the government's promise of economic entitlement. Whereas all Americans used to be assured that there would be no government impediments allowed to thwart their opportunity to achieve, now they are being told that they are entitled to the fruits of others' achievements. Today, everything is becoming a "right." Not only do we all have the rights delineated in the U.S. Constitution and its Bill of Rights, but, according to liberals, we also have a right to low-cost housing, a right to a public subsidy, a right to low-cost health care, a right to public education, and a right to a job and a right to keep that job even if you don't perform adequately. Most of the federal budget, then, consists of what liberals call "entitlements." These are funds, presumably, not that we bestow on those less fortunate out of a feeling of collective philanthropy, altruism, generosity, or compassion, but because they are "entitled" to them. They have them coming. It's their "right."

"Entitlements" in the federal budget make up between 50 percent and 55 percent of U.S. spending, and they are growing all the time. Annual budget increases for these programs are written into the law. You can change the entitlement increases only by changing the law. And, of course, taking away something that someone believes he is "entitled" to is usually a politically unpopular decision.

Changing the law is tough because so many people are receiving so much money. When you propose cutting those parts of the budget, you are affecting a great many potential votes and, thus, a huge lobbying force. This is, in effect, the liberal constituency. The conservative constituency, on the other hand, is composed mostly of productive, self-reliant, taxpaying people who make all these "entitlements" possible. Perhaps we should call our constituency "the economically oppressed." To realize I am not engaging in hyperbole, just consider for a moment the benefits most hard-working people derive from government compared to what they pay into it. (I refuse to use Clinton's euphemism of "broad-based contributions" to describe taxes.)

We're now at the point where the amount of money spent on entitlements is a secondary issue to the liberals. The real issue, as far as Democrats are concerned, is the number of people receiving something from the government. This is exactly what Franklin Delano Roosevelt had in mind when he created this monster. And Clinton is planning to expand it beyond Roosevelt's wildest dreams. He wants more people receiving whatever meager amount the government can provide in order to create more dependency and a bigger constituency for his party so he can further solidify his power. It's as simple as that. Remember these things when you hear him talk about how compassionate he is and what a big heart he has for the poor and downtrodden and how he feels their pain (in between $200 haircuts, of course).

Occasionally, just occasionally, you'll hear a liberal politician talk about spending cuts other than in the defense budget. Always keep this in mind: To them, a spending cut is not a spending cut. A spending cut is merely a reduction in the amount of the increase they plan to spend. The people who work out budgets for the federal government assume a certain percentage of increases in their spending each year. Let's say they assume a 10 percent increase. If you tell them they are getting only a 5 percent increase, they consider that a 5 percent cut in the budget—even though the budget actually increased 5 percent. Of course, when it comes to Clinton's tax plan, the deception is even more pronounced. In order to claim they are cutting one dollar of spending for every dollar of increased taxes, they characterize taxes on Social Security income as spending reductions, and they count some $102 billion in unspecified and unenforceable spending cuts and $60+ billion in reduced interest on the federal debt (based on the highly questionable assumption that their package will slow the growth of the federal debt). They also double-count some $40 billion of funds that were cut in the 1990 budget deal. It's just a brazen sham. Merely congressional business as usual.

One of the dirtiest little secrets in Washington is the annual budget process. Let's say you run a $20 million business that one year collects only $15 million. You therefore have a $5 million deficit. As you prepare your budget for the next year, you are obligated to cut spending by $5 million. So you lay some people off, close some offices, cut your office supplies and whatever else you can in order to get back in balance. Then you project your next year's income based on the previous year's figures and honest assumptions based on existing market data. Well, this is not how it happens in Washington.

Congress uses what is called the Current Services Baseline to prepare a budget, which basically allows them to ignore spending levels of prior years. This has been the method used since the Budget Reform Act of 1979, which was created primarily for two reasons. Double-digit inflation at the time meant, among other things, that recipients of social spending were losing ground because annual increases were well below the inflation rate, and Congress also was seeking a way to project the consequences of current decisions. Simply put, baseline budgeting allows Congress to increase each budget item by 10 percent to 12 percent each year—period. It looks at current services (spending levels) and automatically assumes it will spend 10 percent to 12 percent additional to stay even. When the budget is completed, Congress may discover it increased a certain budget item by only 8 percent. It then proudly announces a cut in spending, despite the 8 percent increase. This explains how $500 billion in deficit reduction nevertheless results in the national debt growing by $1 trillion, which is exactly what the Clinton budget promises.

Let me illustrate with a consumer example. In September you

decide you are going to buy a fancy new car that costs $50,000. In January you rethink it and decide to buy an ordinary new car that costs only $20,000. You then tell yourself you have saved $30,000 despite the fact you are spending $20,000. Miraculous, isn't it? Well, this is exactly how the entire federal budget is assembled. Actually, shoppers have been doing this for eons. You notice that laundry detergent is being sold at half price at Wal-Mart, so you drive on over in your ordinary new car and buy a six-month supply, using all your disposable cash. Then you applaud yourself for saving tons of money, despite the fact that you spent nearly all the money you had stocked up.

Several reputable economists, including Lawrence Kudlow of Bear Stearns in New York, insist that if we would simply freeze federal spending at current levels, while allowing for growth equal to but not greater than the annual inflation rate, we could balance the budget in five years—with no increase in taxes. In addition, this would strip Congress of much of its power, so it should become a priority.

Only in Washington, then, are spending increases considered spending cuts. Don't be fooled by this rhetoric. It often sounds good. But it is usually dishonest. Take, for example, Clinton's pledge that his Cabinet would "look just like America." He and his fellow Democrats maligned the Cabinets of Reagan and Bush, you might recall, for being millionaires' clubs. Well, guess what, folks? Once again, you have been deceived by empty, insincere rhetoric. While 62 percent of Reagan's Cabinet members were millionaires and 71 percent of Bush's were, guess what percentage of millionaires serve in the Clinton Cabinet. Seventy-seven percent. A similarly high percentage of them are lawyers. Who cares? you ask. Certainly not I. But Clinton's the one talking about it. If you live by the photo-op, you die by it. If you derive your political image from external appearances and bean-counting, you must be held to that standard. See how the truth can get distorted? Perception becomes reality. Thank goodness I'm here to straighten all this out. I'll never cease to be amazed by the fact that there are still people who think the government can take care of their families better than they can—can raise their kids better than they can. That's basically the promise that liberalism holds. "We know what's best for you," say Bill and Hillary. "We did such a bang-up job turning Arkansas around, we want to turn your life around."

So get ready. Next on their agenda is choosing your doctor, and the kind of health care that's best for you. Stay tuned for an inside look at how Hillary plans to improve your life.

12

TO YOUR HEALTH, HILLARY
OR
UNDERSTANDING
THE POLITICS OF MEANING

WHEN YOU THINK BACK IN YOUR LIFE AND REMEMBER THE GOOD TIMES, what comes to mind? Do you know what I recall? The best memories for me are of times when I was really struggling professionally and financially.

Does that surprise anyone? Probably not.

The greatest rewards we experience in life generally come through our relationships with family and friends. I mean, how many people really remember the first time they flew first class? Not too many. It might be important for six months or a year or two. You may want to brag about it for a little while. But you get past that. And then it's no longer any big deal. It's certainly not the kind of thing people recall on their deathbed.

But I'm not telling you anything you don't already know. Most people instinctively realize that happiness and fulfillment are not achieved primarily through materialism. You can't buy love. You can't even buy contentment. And you shouldn't need an Ivy League degree to understand this. It's common sense. It's the kind of universal truth that most everyone takes for granted.

Not Hillary Rodham Clinton. And not the liberal media. Oh, no.

Since her anointment as co-president, Americans have been treated to some of the silliest, most sanctimonious, arrogant, condescending morality lessons to come out of the Oval Office and the Washington press corps in a long time. With her halo aglow, she has fearlessly castigated the pharmaceuticals industry and excoriated the medical profession. Despite her moral pretentiousness, though, Saint Hillary (which she has actually been called by a media disciple in a *New York Times Magazine* article devoted to her) was already in her mid-forties when she told a *Washington Post* Style-section writer that she had recently made some profound discoveries.

"There are things larger than yourself in life," she said. "You can get everything you want and still have a meaningless life."

Oh, really? Welcome to adulthood, Ms. Rodham. To her, what most grown-ups understand intuitively is a profound revelation, a weighty spiritual insight. This is a new truth to Hillary, a personal revelation unknown to anyone else—certainly not to most Americans, who are, after all, a bunch of boobs who actually voted for Ronald Reagan. With evangelical fervor, she is now on a mission to share this important observation with everyone—when, in fact, she's the one late in arriving to the party.

It reminds me of the *Time* magazine cover that I have talked so much about. Somebody at the nation's premier news weekly discovered that men and women are actually born different. This was considered so newsworthy that it became a *Time* cover story. Imagine that! Men and women are actually different.

All over the world, in every culture, this would be considered an article of faith. But the sixties kids were taught that there was no real difference between the sexes, and they believed it. It was supposed to be a cynical generation that questioned authority, but in reality the sixties kids believed everything they were told—including myths about themselves.

They were praised for having the "courage" to protest the war. They were told they were morally superior. They were a messianic generation that would liberate the planet. And they bought it—lock, stock, and barrel!

Some of them—Hillary included—still believe it all. She continues to identify new realities the rest of us have never learned and are probably incapable of ever grasping. After all, she is so much more in touch with her inner self. She is so much smarter, so much more conscious of all that is good, decent, and virtuous in the world. If she didn't share with us, why, we couldn't be enlightened. Only through the good fortune of her being First Lady do we now have an opportunity to learn the truth. And the problem is that this image of Hillary is being reinforced by the media, which have been fascinated with the First Lady since she emerged on the public scene with her dramatic "60 Minutes" appearance defending her husband against Gennifer Flowers's allegations of his adultery. Among the liberal elite, the infatuation intensified when she snidely quipped that she could have stayed home to bake cookies rather than pursuing a career. Other people, likely the majority, were put off by the remark, and realizing this, Hillary abruptly changed her image, hairstyle and all, from harridan to homemaker for the balance of the campaign. Following the campaign, she has reclaimed her true identity, shortened her hair, and proudly resurrected her maiden name. By publicly parading her liberalism and her plans to foist it on the rest of us, she has become a feminist icon. Even when Bill makes noises about moving to the "center," liberals feel secure that Hillary is there to return him to the fold. She has not been bashful about asserting herself.

Do you think I'm exaggerating? Here's Hillary, in *The New York Times Magazine:* "You know, I'm going to start thanking the woman who cleans the restroom in the building that I work in. You know, maybe that sounds kind of stupid, but on the other hand I want to start seeing her as a human being." (This was said only days before President Clinton bombed an Iraqi intelligence building at 2 A.M., when only cleaning people would have been inside. Whatever else the bombing accomplished, we can rest assured that it is now more difficult finding good weekend custodial help in Baghdad.) This is our First Lady! It's as if none of the rest of us has respect for people who do custodial work. Decent people learn this when they're seven years old. She's just now realizing it at forty-six. What an admission!

She told *The Washington Post* that she has "a burning desire to make the world around me—kind of going out in concentric circles—better for everybody." Her goal is the "remaking of the

American way of politics, government, indeed, life." She is convinced that she alone can save America from two of its most vexing problems (both of which are highly exaggerated and distorted): the health-care "crisis" and the country's spiritual malaise. How is she going to do this? What's her game plan?

It's called the Politics of Meaning. How's that for arrogance. Can you imagine the ridicule and derision that someone on the right would be subjected to if he or she had the audacity and presumptuousness to claim originality for ideas that have been around thousands of years, at least since Socrates, Plato, and Aristotle? Hillary groupies in the media are exhibiting their sophistry and embarrassing ignorance when they praise her "politics of meaning" as if it is some profound revelation. (*The New York Times Magazine* went even further in its "Saint Hillary" cover story, calling her New Age philosophy "The Politics of Virtue.")

This is an example: "She has goals," the *Post* article said, "but they appear to be so huge and so far-off—grand and noble things twinkling in the distance—that it's hard to see what she sees" as she "floats comfortably above the fray of day-to-day Washington."

Give me a break. Moral issues have always been a central focus of the great political debate. Proponents of any political or economic system throughout recorded history, even Machiavelli, I daresay, have believed, or at least purported to believe, in the moral superiority of their ideas. If you liberals out there don't believe me, all you need to do to verify this is review the Great Books of the Western World. Thumb through the pages of Plato, Aristotle, Hobbes, Locke, Rousseau, Montesquieu, Marx, Bacon, Adam Smith; you name it. You'll see that all of them defend their particular political and/or economic systems foremost on moral grounds. To pretend that what Hillary is saying is something new is an insult. Liberals can get away with treating us as ignorant fools only if we let them.

But I'm not going to fall into their pattern of behavior. I'm not going to assume liberals are stupid, as they do with conservatives. No, I'll attribute it instead to more fraud and deceit. What all this metaphysical gobbledygook actually amounts to is an attempt to purloin the "values" issue from conservatives and put it to use in the liberals' already formidable propaganda arsenal.

Keep in mind that liberals understand that traditional or family values are very important to mainstream America. That's why James Carville and Clinton's other strategists have resorted to intimidation tactics to keep Republicans from capitalizing on the issue. They know that conservative Republicans are at one with the electorate on the subject of traditional values, so they try to remove this as an issue. Knowing that the issue won't ever go away, the liberals are simply trying to restructure it, as they do with so many other issues. They believe they have to recapture the moral high ground from Republicans in order to perpetuate their inferior economic programs, which cannot pass muster under economic scrutiny.

The architect of the liberals' plan to reclaim the values issue is Michael Lerner, the editor of the leftist Jewish magazine *Tikkun*. He credits the right—and Ronald Reagan, in particular—for recognizing early on that America's traditional values were breaking down and that this was important to people. Lerner and Hillary are said to be tight, or, as they put it, they're "on the same wave length." (What's the frequency? I wonder. Not one the EIB Network broadcasts on, that's for sure!)

Lerner has been described as "a rabbi with a flirtatious bent." However, he admits he is not really a rabbi; he just acts like one. The liberal *New Republic* characterized him as a jargon-spouting Rasputin presiding over the First Lady's "yuppie awakening." Ex-lefties David Horowitz and Peter Collier remember Lerner as "the bloviating leader of the 'Seattle Liberation Front,' who officiated at his own New Left wedding. The bride and groom exchanged rings made out of the fuselage of a U.S. aircraft that the communists had downed in Vietnam and served a wedding cake with the inscription SMASH MONOGAMY on it." (The marriage ended a few years later.) Lerner is the archetypal product of the mindless, chimerical Marxism of the sixties. As reported in the journal *Heterodoxy*, Lerner once said, "Until you've dropped acid, you don't know what anything else is." Don Feder (himself Jewish), of the *Boston Herald*, notes that to find "a Jew to the left of Michael Lerner one would have to exhume the remains of Leon Trotsky." And the *National Review* reports that in 1971, Lerner's group endorsed "a guaranteed minimum income for those who could not or would not work." Today, *NR* says that Mr. Lerner calls for unemployment insurance at levels "equal to the amount the workers were making at the time of their employment or equal to the median income in the society." This is the man who has Hillary under his spell.

Remember the First Lady's famous commencement address at the University of Texas? The speech was pure Lerner. Syndicated newspaper columnist Charles Krauthammer described it as a "cross between Jimmy Carter's malaise speech and a term paper on 'Siddhartha.'" I'm not even going to attempt to top that description.

Some of what Lerner says may sound deep and meaningful to the shallow thinker. He is telling liberals that life is more than feeding, clothing, and housing people. (This is actually news to many of them.) He explains that it's time "to get away from thinking about programs and start thinking about values." That, in itself, sounds encouraging, even refreshing. But don't be fooled. Rather than causing liberals to rethink their commitment to the ever-expanding welfare state, Lerner's philosophy actually calls for greater intrusion by government into every facet of people's lives. That's what Lerner means by "values"; again, you must remember that for extreme liberals, values descend from government.

"The Department of Labor," he suggests, for instance, "should create a program to train a corps of union personnel, worker representatives, and psychotherapists in the relevant skills to assist developing a new spirit of cooperation, mutual caring, and dedication to work."

Huh? Reading between the lines of this psychobabble, it sounds as if he's suggesting that the government should endeavor to teach employees to love their work. It's hard even to imagine how Thomas Jefferson and the founders would have viewed the notion that it was a proper role for the federal government to teach people to like their jobs. But, keep in mind, this guy is on the same wave length as Hillary, and presumably, at least on the same communications band (FM, no doubt) as her husband.

But there's something else important about this philosophy. Later in this book I will deal with one of the pressing crises of liberalism: the fact that none of their existing programs works. At some point, it's only fair that liberal programs be judged on their merits and accomplishments rather than on their stated intentions. Liberals are expert, however, at evading responsibility. They are adept at finding new problems to rationalize why their old solutions didn't work. That's just what Lerner is doing for liberalism. What he is saying, in effect, is that liberal solutions haven't worked so far, in part, because they lacked a spiritual dimension and the context of fundamental values. So naturally, we not only need more time for the old prescriptions, but we need an even bigger dosage of liberalism to heal the patient. And, of course, we also need more money. Especially yours.

The Clintons have been longtime devotees of the Lerner philosophy and "the ethos of caring." Hillary, in particular, is a rabid enthusiast of such ideas. She knows she needs help, because, as she told the *Post*, "It's not going to be easy redefining who we are as human beings in this post-modern age."

"We are on the same path," Lerner told the *San Francisco Chronicle*. "We're partners, friends exchanging ideas. . . . This woman is as sensitive and as morally fine as I am." [What a testament, huh?] "She's as morally high as any person I've ever met." [Now, exhale!]

At the roots of Lernerism is the same kind of anti-capitalist, anti-market, anti-logic zealotry that has been the signature of left-wing liberalism from the get-go. When I first read the quote that appears in the following paragraph, I wished I could place it in the hands of millions of Americans so they could study it and learn what motivates Hillary—the most powerful woman in America. Now, with this book, I get to do just that.

In a revealing *Wall Street Journal* article, Lerner explained his theories about Hillary's newly adopted philosophy, the politics of meaning: "The right ignored the role of the competitive marketplace: the way our daily lives in the world of work lead us to subordinate all values to the struggle for material success. Nor could the right acknowledge that an economy whose bottom-line mentality rewarded those who were most effective at manipulating or controlling others would necessarily produce narcissistic personalities who were unable to sustain loving relationships in family life."

Well, let's analyze these words. They are very important and provide a real insight into the way Hillary Rodham Clinton's mind must work. This is her political and spiritual guru saying that regardless of whether the marketplace works economically, it is not worth the societal price. Our jobs leave us devoid of values, he says. Capitalism rewards not hard work, but manipulators and controllers, he contends. The breakup of the family is caused not by the degeneration of our society's moral and spiritual fabric, but by the free market and the individual struggle for material success, he claims.

It's ironic that Lerner should denounce manipulation and control, because they are the earmarks of liberalism. Lerner obviously still buys into that old liberal canard that anyone who prospers does so at someone else's expense—the finite-pie mentality, the zero-sum myth. He is clearly rejecting the free market, which shouldn't surprise us because he comes from a radical sixties background steeped in socialism . . . and seasoned with various kinds of exotic herbs, no doubt.

It turns out that the politics of meaning is simply a new rationalization for the continuation of failed liberal policies and the introduction of even more radical, left-wing economic restructuring and redistribution. In other words, folks, you have not yet seen the Clintons' final tax bill. Not by a long shot.

In the previous chapter, I discussed how liberalism pretends to offer more "caring" and "compassion" for the less fortunate. Lernerism, or Rodhamism (or, better yet, Rodhamist-Lernerism), understands how important it is to continue this charade. It's amazing how many people fall for this stuff. For instance, polls show that people actually believe liberals care more about homelessness, the environment, the unemployed, and so on, than conservatives do. This is not because liberals have actually done anything tangible about these problems, but because their rhetoric is kinder and gentler. They keep saying they care, and some begin to believe it.

I have put forth this theory before, and I am more convinced than ever that it is true: Most liberals know that their solutions do not work, yet they continue to promote these ideas as their ticket to power. Lerner certainly understands this. He even goes so far as to suggest that liberals might be forgiven for their policy failures if they can just demonstrate enough goodwill through his politics of meaning.

". . . If the Clintons have the courage to persist," he writes in the *Journal*, "their politics of meaning may do what deficit-reduction schemes and policy wonkery cannot—show Americans that the Clintons understand and care about their lives."

In a nutshell, folks, that's all liberalism is about: symbolism over substance. It doesn't matter that the policies don't work. "We care. We're compassionate. We're good people. So keep on voting for us, not those right-wing meanies."

But liberals' rhetoric, as transparent as it might be, is gloriously innocuous when compared with their actions. While Hillary talks about the need to rediscover "individual responsibility" and to create "a system that gets rid of micro-management . . . regulation, and the bureaucracy, and substitutes, instead, human caring, concern, and love," it sounds great, at least in part. She sounds somewhat like the New Democrat her husband was supposed to be. But we know from experience what these high-minded ideals translate into in the real world: huge new bureaucracies, hundreds of billions in tax increases, price controls, rationing of health care, and expansive new federal regulations over all our lives. Folks, here we have exposed the real fundamental fallacy of liberalism: that human caring, concern, and love emanate from government. Wrong. They emanate from the individual. The only way liberals have to implement their involuntary "compassion" schemes of wealth redistribution is through "micro-management . . . regulation, and the bureaucracy," and Hillary knows it. So when she, Lerner, or any other liberal starts talking about reducing or eliminating the role of government, you must know that it's a ruse; to do so is fundamentally incompatible with their big-government philosophy/religion.

The fact of the matter is that Rodhamist-Lernerism, as is so often the case with liberalism, misanalyzes the problem: They speak of an American spiritual void. First, what they mean by "spiritual" is a far cry from what I or mainstream America means by it. To them, spirituality is a secular, New Age concept. I'm not saying that the Clintons are not religious or God-fearing people; I don't know and won't presume to guess. But listen to what they say. They don't speak as if morality descends from God, but from man. Theirs appears to be a humanistic perspective.

Second, in my opinion, though there has been an all-out assault on American's spiritual and religious heritage (primarily by liberalism), the assault has not been successful in creating a spiritual "void." America is much healthier spiritually than Ms. Rodham and Mr. Lerner would ever imagine. America is still a God-fearing nation. America is a truly compassionate country built on a firm Judeo-Christian orthodoxy. Americans, therefore, do not respond well to New Age mumbo-jumbo and liberal psychobabble. Americans seek meaning in their lives not through government, but through their families, their friends, and their churches and synagogues. In misanalyzing the problem, it's inevitable that they misidentify the solution. Ironically, the very things that Lerner and Hillary see as the solution are what most Americans see as the problem: erosion of individual responsibility, collective economic solutions, governmental largesse, situational ethics, affirmative action, confiscatory taxation and wealth redistribution, and the entire gamut of liberal prescriptions for society.

That brings us to the other phony crisis Hillary is attempting to solve—health care. Yes, we've got a problem, but it is not a crisis, and its solution should not be concocted in a crisis atmosphere. It's the usual liberal modus operandi. They overstate a problem and work society into a frenzied state in order to justify their invariable, big-government solution. They do this all the time with environmental issues (more on this in the next chapter). But when Americans figure out what Hillary has done to them with respect to health care, she's going to need all the help she can get from her soothsaying friends. What she and Bill are about to do is undermine the best health-care system in the world in the name of fairness and equality.

They have no mandate to do this. Do you think that if the Clinton campaign had told the American people the truth in 1992 about its intentions for health care that Bill Clinton could have won the election? Imagine if they told us that Hillary was going to select a health-care task force of some 524 people that nobody will know, nobody will ever see, that no doctors or insurance people will be a part of the team, that meetings will be held in secret, and that the result could well be a payroll tax increase. How would that program have fared with the public? There is no way Clinton would have been elected. Instead, the Clinton campaign consistently denied that Hillary would have any special power or authority.

But let me be very clear about this: There was no health-care *crisis* in this country, at least not until Hillary got her mitts on health care. And the problems we have—like escalating costs—were caused primarily by the very kinds of liberal interventionist programs Hillary is now proposing. Like a true demagogue, she has whipped up hysteria and fear and scapegoated well-meaning businesses and the people who work for them.

It's all part of a well-calculated plan—a script the Clintons have followed before. More than a decade ago, Bill Clinton decided that reforming Arkansas's educational system would be the focal point of his gubernatorial administration. It would be his top priority. Naturally, he put his wife in charge of figuring out how to do it. She held hearings, spoke out on the subject, and chaired a commission that proposed sweeping changes in public-school standards, curricula, teacher incentives, even the length of the school day. Part of the formula for railroading the program through boiled down to this, according to *The Wall Street Journal*'s Gerald Seib: "Identify enemies everyone can see." Sound familiar?

The Clintons have returned to that strategy in their push for nationalized, socialized health care. Public enemy number one, according to Hillary and Bill, is the pharmaceuticals industry, which, they claim, has been responsible for massive rip-offs of the public and greedy profiteering. What this really means is that by the Hillary standard, the industry has been too successful. So she has made it a target. In fact, the U.S. pharmaceuticals industry has been responsible for developing all kinds of miracle drugs that have extended the lives of millions of people, not just in this country, but all over the world. Profits work, folks. They provide companies with the incentive to risk their earnings to develop solutions, such as cures for diseases. And far from ripping off poor consumers, several major U.S. pharmaceuticals companies have had long-standing programs that actually provide free prescription drugs to families that earn $35,000 a year or less. Have you ever heard Hillary mention that? *Nooooo.* Has she ever held up such a program as a positive example of caring and compassion by private industry? *Noooooo.*

The Clintons have also stirred up passions and fear by citing the misleading statistic that 37 million Americans are without health-insurance coverage. A CBO study, however, shows that 51 percent of those were uninsured for less than four months; and 72 percent for less than a year. A 1990 Census Bureau study found that the long-term uninsured amounted to fewer than 10 million. And don't forget that even the uninsured have access to health care through emergency rooms all over the country. Plus, many of those without coverage are unemployed. You would think our first priority would be to adopt policies that would lead to economic growth in order to put those people back to work as fast as possible so they wouldn't be dependent on the state. Many others choose not to be covered. Mostly young people, unmarried; they are employed but prefer to spend their money on other things— stereos, CDs, movies, etc.

So the situation is not nearly as critical as Ms. Rodham would lead us to believe. If you have any doubts about the status of American health care, just compare it with that in other industrial-ized nations. Ask anyone you know from a foreign country where they would most like to be treated if they had a medical emergency. Ask them which country is the envy of the world when it comes to health care.

All over the world, nations are moving away from centralized, socialized medicine toward private systems such as the ones we have in the United States. Russia, China, and several Eastern European nations are dismantling their nationalized programs and emulating the American model. And regardless of how we've all heard about the virtues of the Canadian system, most Canadian physicians who are themselves in need of surgery, for example, scurry across the border to get it done right: the American way. They have found, through experience, that state medical care is too expensive, too slow and inefficient, and, most important, it doesn't provide adequate care for most people.

By any standard you choose to apply, the health of the American people has never been better. We live longer than we ever have. Infant mortality is declining steadily. And medical care is available every day to most everyone who needs it. The American health-care system has sought after and achieved excellence rather than equality. And that's what bugs Hillary.

Before we go any further, dear friends, let me return to a principle that I think is very important to understand. You've heard me say frequently that no nation in the history of the world has ever taxed itself into prosperity. Here is a parallel truism for all of you to ponder: With the exception of the areas of national security and defense, never in the history of the world has government control ever lowered costs or improved efficiency. That applies to health care or any other industry.

In fact, government intervention—specifically the Medicaid and Medicare programs—is the biggest reason costs are escalating in health care today. When Medicare began in 1965, it cost taxpayers about $3 billion per year. It was projected back then that by 1990 the price would rise to $9 billion per year. The 1990 bill was actually $67 billion per year. The most conservative estimates today say that the program will cost $223 billion by 1997.

Once again, the pointy-headed theoreticians who devised this program made the mistake of assuming they were operating in a zero-sum game. They never imagined that the very creation of their program would increase demand for medical services. They have never figured this out. They still don't understand, or pretend not to understand, that if you tax something, it discourages that activity. Likewise, if you subsidize something or give it away, you encourage it. That's how the real world works, and that's just what has happened with Medicare and Medicaid.

It's human nature. Just think about the way you would behave. Suppose the government told you it would pay for all medical expenses, no matter how big or small. Naturally, you would be more likely to visit the doctor and seek treatments than you would if you were responsible for paying even part of the bill. That's the principle that makes socialized medicine fail every time. It is a fatal flaw. And there is no way it can be overcome. No matter how egregiously Hillary, her husband, and their crowd misapprehend human nature, it will remain constant. No matter how many times Hillary and her task force go back to the drawing board, we're looking at higher costs and lower standards of care.

Of course, what happens when the government pays for all medical care is that limits must be placed on the amount of care that can be offered. Thus, with Rodhamized medicine, you will always have rationing of care in one form or another. This is the case in Canada right now, which is another reason that so many Canadians visit the United States for medical treatment.

Government is not the solution, Ronald Reagan used to say. Government is the problem. This has never been more true than in the area of health care. Somebody please tell Hillary. Then, after administering the smelling salts, tell her again.

The issue facing the country is not the quality of health care, which is clearly the best in the world. It is simply a matter of cost and coverage. And the cost has been distorted by the intrusion of government into the marketplace. Further intrusion is not the answer. Competition is. Returning to a system that is market-oriented is. We need deregulation, not more government control.

Let me give you another way that medical costs are greater when the patient is not required to foot the bill for his treatment. Have you ever visited a dentist or doctor and been asked if you had insurance to cover some procedure or treatment? Depending on the answer, you may well be given two vastly different prices. Doctors may think twice about soaking a patient who is responsible for paying his bill, but if an insurance company or the government is responsible, they're most likely not going to think twice about it. Government policies and insurance coverage distort the factors affecting supply and demand and drive costs up. Third-party payers—either government or insurance—have insulated consumers from the true price of medical care and thereby removed any real incentive for cost control. You know how it works. Take auto insurance, for example. If you have a little fender-bender and sustain minor damage, you may consider paying the repairs out of your own pocket instead of turning it over to your insurance company; not because you're philanthropic, but because you understand that your rates may go up if your insurance carrier has to pay because of your negligence.

Government-imposed price controls don't work either. Medicare already operates under severe price-control regulations. Yet costs have continued to skyrocket because government undermines both the doctors' and the patients' awareness of the true cost of medical goods and services by propagating the fantasy that everything will be taken care of. This leads to endless demand and skyrocketing costs.

Let me give you some other reasons why Hillary's health-care plan won't work:

• By spending vast sums of taxpayer money on a new health-care bureaucracy, economic growth is sure to be hampered. Every study shows that as a nation's economy grows, its people get healthier. Likewise, when a nation's growth is stifled, health tends to suffer.

• You can be certain that whatever cost projections are made regarding Hillary's plan, they will be grossly underestimated. Just look at the history of Medicare or the history of Clinton promises and projections.

• Any plan for government-subsidized long-term health care is going to serve as a time bomb in the federal budget as the baby-boom generation moves closer to retirement age. Who's going to pay the tab? Our grandchildren? Such a tab will make our current deficit problems pale by comparison, because once you unleash this big-government monster, there will be no way to re-cage it.

• "Managed competition," in addition to being yet another Clinton oxymoron, is also a euphemism for government control. Increased regulation and more price controls will only make the system more bureaucratic and less responsive to the marketplace. They could also well result in rationed health services.

Maybe the most important thing to know about any socialized health-care plan is that it will result in lower-quality care and higher costs for most people. Even top Democratic policy wonks admit that.

"There will be all sorts of redistribution inherent in any major health-care reform," Robert Reischauer, director of the Congressional Budget Office, told *The Wall Street Journal.* "And those who right now have extremely generous benefits paid for by their employers will probably see either their costs rise, or their benefits shaved back, or a little bit of both." You know who he's talking about there? You. He's talking about most working people who have employer-subsidized health-care plans. As usual, you are the ones who are going to bear the burden.

But, as I have mentioned in a previous chapter, there's one group of people who won't be hurt by such a plan. You can bet on it. I have. The liberals in government who want to impose socialized medicine on the rest of us will not have to endure it themselves. And already there is a See-I-Told-You-So in the making here. Senator George Mitchell, Majority Leader, has introduced S. 1227, which includes a specific requirement that Congress and all federal employees be exempted from any nationalized health-care plan.

Isn't that liberal of them? Do you know what the politics of meaning really is? It's not a religious ethic, it's economic. The politics of meaning is really the same old politics of taxing and spending, of confiscation and redistribution. Some people have confused Bill Clinton with a moderate. Nobody has made that mistake with Hillary. And neither of them will be fooling anybody once their health-care plan takes effect.

I hate to say it, folks, SITYS.

13

ALGORE: TECHNOLOGY CZAR

I AM NOT BY NATURE AN ALARMIST. IN MY OPINION, HAND-WRINGING, apocalyptic thinking, and crying wolf are some of the distinguishing characteristics of liberalism. By contrast, I remain confident, steadfast, and of good cheer. I do not believe that our technological explosion is hastening the end of the world. But despite my generally optimistic outlook on life, I am by no means a Pollyanna. I never shy away from presenting the cold, hard realities of the world when they need to be articulated.

Folks, I have to tell you the truth. As you know, I am incapable of telling you anything but the truth. But, to some, the statement I am about to make may seem harsh. To others, it may seem rash. Trust me when I assert that it is neither. In fact, every word of this statement has been chosen with great care and precision. Are you ready? Are you sitting down? Are you comfy? Okay, get ready. Here's the statement that will serve as a theme for this chapter:

The only thing preventing the radical transformation of our great country from capitalism to abject socialism is the absolute incompetence of those now running it.

What do I mean by this? Well, there is a philosophy—statist,

158

anti-American, and anti-capitalist at its core—that has assumed the reins of political and cultural power in this country. Its adherents run both wings of the White House, both houses of Congress, the entire federal bureaucracy, the press, the entertainment industry, academia, the educational establishment, and just about every other important institution that frames the debate on the great issues of our age and are responsible for policy-making.

Yet, thankfully—and this is one of the reasons I remain optimistic—this radical philosophy, while certainly making important inroads in the shaping of public policy, has largely failed to be implemented. It will continue to fail because those responsible for its implementation simply don't get it. They just don't understand how the world really works. They are theoreticians, eggheads, pseudo-intellectuals, and policy wonks. They have, for the most part, never held real jobs outside of government in their lives. Therefore, count your blessings; they are ill-equipped to achieve their goals.

Perhaps nobody better personifies this point than Vice-President *Algore.* You may remember he wrote a book in which he claimed that the automobile is the gravest threat the Earth has ever faced. It won an award. On the other hand, my first book, though close to becoming the all-time best-selling nonfiction hardcover in history, has not and will not win any awards. Why? Because there's nothing liberal in it. Liberals are generally the ones who win awards. They give them to one another for important non-achievements, because, frankly, liberals are hardly ever rewarded by the public. Do you know who wins awards in television? People who produce documentaries that no one watches. Likewise, many of the authors who win awards are the ones who write books that no one reads. But, I digress.

The important fact to grasp about *Algore* is that this man, a mere brain wave away from the presidency, is the living, breathing definition of an environmentalist wacko. Why do I refer to him as *Algore?* When Bill Clinton was elected president, I aired a skit on my radio show called "Taxula." Clinton has more than lived up to his billing as the bloodsucking mad scientist Taxula. And Taxula's evil and bumbling assistant is *Algore.* For the proper imagery, think of *Algore* as being played by the late comic actor Marty Feldman.

Algore is a bona fide tree-hugging, spotted owl–loving, snail-darter–protecting, Gaia-worshipping, radical doomsday prophet who carries water for Greenpeace, the Sierra Club, and every other powerful environmental fringe lobby. According to *Algore,* the only thing standing between us and the destruction of the planet is his plan to "change the very foundation of our civilization." Heaven help us.

"But, Rush," you say, "I thought *Algore* was a moderate. The media say he is. He says he is. Why do you say he's a radical?"

Indulge me while I provide some important, well-documented, indisputable background details on our esteemed vice-president that will ultimately lead to a profound point about the direction of our nation. These are undeniable facts, my friends, that the establishment media would obviously prefer you did not know; otherwise, they would have reported them to you and I wouldn't be earning a living doing what they should be doing. Thank goodness I am here, once again, to serve the interests of humanity with the piercing light of truth.

Now, let's go back a few years and examine *Algore's* congressional voting records to see how he has "grown" in Washington from what appeared to be a pro-life moderate to an ultra-liberal crusader who can make Ted Kennedy look like a middle-of-the-roader.

Here are the facts: Even as a young member of the House of Representatives, *Algore* voted against both Reagan budget cuts and his tax cuts. In the Senate he has opposed the balanced-budget amendment, a line-item veto for the president, and a capital-gains tax cut. He voted for the huge tax-increase bill vetoed by President Bush in 1992. And this was no fluke. In 1990, he earned the National Taxpayers Union's rating as the biggest spender in the U.S. Senate.

But it's not just economic issues that make *Algore's* knee jerk. No, folks. He's even worse on crime. He voted in favor of the so-called "Racial Justice Act," which would have effectively ended capital punishment in the United States by imposing an unworkable racial quota system on every state. In 1991 he voted against an amendment to limit the ability of death-row prisoners to evade justice for years. He also opposed reforming the exclusionary rule that allows criminals to get off charges on technicalities when police seize evidence in violation of the Fourth and Fourteenth amendments, even while acting in good faith. He also voted with a small minority of his colleagues against a bill that required a minimum twenty-year prison term for drug-related homicides in the District of Columbia.

Algore takes a backseat to no one in catering to special-interest groups, even at the expense of public health and safety. For instance, in 1989 he was one of only four Senate members who opposed an amendment to require the notification of spouses of those infected with the HIV virus. The next year he opposed a bill making it a crime for individuals who know they have AIDS to donate or sell blood, semen, or other bodily fluids or tissues. In 1991 he was one of only eighteen senators who voted against a bill that called for a $10,000 fine and prison term for health-care providers who have the HIV virus and perform invasive medical procedures without notifying patients about their health situation. He also opposed a bill to allow health-care professionals to test patients for AIDS before non-emergency invasive medical procedures. In *Algore*'s world, the HIV virus appears to be entitled to more protection than human life itself.

Wherever there is a liberal battle to be fought, eventually *Algore* finds his way to the left side of the barricades. In 1987, he wrote in a letter to a pro-life constituent saying that his goal was to "reduce the outrageously large number of abortions which currently take place. In my opinion, it is wrong to spend federal funds for what is arguably the taking of a human life. Let me assure you that I share your belief that innocent human life must be protected and I am committed to furthering this goal." But, today, *Algore* stands before you as an enthusiastic supporter of the Freedom of Choice Act, designed specifically to prohibit states from placing any restrictions on abortion right up to the day of birth. So much for his commitment to the protection of innocent human life.

In 1990, the liberal Americans for Democratic Action rated him a stellar 78 percent—right up there with "Geriatric" Park's own Senator Howard Metzenbaum (D-Ohio). The National Tax Limitation Committee rated him at 15 percent—worse than California's retired senator Alan (the Cadaver) Cranston. The Competitive

Enterprise Institute rated him the worst enemy of the free market (this time tied with Cranston) in 1990.

To top things off, *Algore* earned a 100 percent rating from the most powerful and left-wing labor union in America, the National Education Association, by opposing educational choice. And in 1991, *Algore* really showed us what a change agent he is when he voted against a motion that would have required Congress to live under the same labor and civil-rights laws that it imposes on the rest of us. Agent for change—ha! That's what he wants you to have left in your pocket when he's done with you.

On cultural issues, *Algore* is also far from being a New Democrat. Eager to demonstrate his predictable liberalness, he supported spending more federal tax dollars on obscene art. Tipper, *Algore*'s better half (and I mean that literally), fought for proper labeling of records that contained obscene rock lyrics. To fully appreciate *Algore*'s timbre, one need only examine his behavior during a Senate committee hearing on record labeling when his wife's honor was being challenged by rocker Frank Zappa. *Algore,* far from defending his courageous wife, obsequiously and spinelessly told Zappa he had always admired his music. It took a freshman Republican senator to admonish Zappa for his disrespectful treatment of Mrs. Gore.

But to appreciate how radical, how out of the mainstream *Algore* truly is, you have to listen to what he says about the environment. Until now, that meant you had to read his book. Fortunately, I am going to save you some money, some time, and a good deal of boredom by highlighting it for you.

It's called *Earth in the Balance: Ecology and the Human Spirit. Algore*'s collaborator was Environmental Protection Agency chief Carol Browner. If *Earth in the Balance* accomplishes anything, it should be to discredit both of them from any serious participation in our nation's debate over the environment. It is nothing more than a hysterical, pseudo-scientific tract designed to cut off calm, reasoned discussion of environmental issues and simply push the nation toward irrational, irreversible, misguided (not to mention expensive) public policies.

Algore's book is full of calculated disinformation. For instance, he claims that 98 percent of scientists believe global warming is taking place. However, a Gallup poll of scientists involved in global climate research shows that 53 percent do not believe that global warming has occurred, 30 percent say they don't know, and only 17 percent are devotees of this dubious theory. During the summer of 1993 it was reported that *Algore* actually suggested that the record flooding that occurred along the Mississippi River in the Midwest might have resulted from global warming. Don't forget, folks: This guy's not really Taxula's lab assistant; he's the vice-president of the United States.

He claims that agriculture in America is threatened because of topsoil erosion. Yet, according to the Soil Conservation Service, thanks to technological breakthroughs, fewer acres have been suffering severe erosion in the United States.

He takes a gratuitous swipe at DDT, which he calls "a symbol of how carelessly our civilization could do harm to the world." Harm to the world? DDT has saved the lives of tens of millions of people! For instance, in 1951, 75 million people in India suffered from malaria. Thanks to DDT, that number was down to 50,000 in 1961. When India stopped using DDT, malaria came back strong, resulting in illness and deaths for millions. In 1977, the number of cases ranged between 30 million and 50 million.

In his book, obviously written before the budget deficit became his cause célèbre, *Algore* calls for America to embark on a "Global Marshall Plan," at a cost of $100 billion, to protect the environment. He has some ideas on how to raise that money: a tax on carbon, a virgin-materials tax, a higher tax on fossil fuels. This guy's got more taxes up his sleeve than Congress does. As part of this master plan, *Algore* would turn over authority for administering international environmental agreements to a U.N. Stewardship Council, modeled after the Security Council. This is no laughing matter, my friends. We're talking here about forfeiting U.S. sovereignty to a bunch of Third World America-bashers.

There is something intrinsically anti-American about the way *Algore* flagellates the U.S. over its environmental policies. He writes that cultures are like families and "our civilization must be considered in some way dysfunctional. . . . We consume the Earth and its resources as a way to distract ourselves from the pain. . . ." He draws comparisons to other dysfunctional families—like Nazi Germany and Mussolini's Italy. This, from a guy who gets lost hiking in a park with the Secret Service!

But the guiding theme throughout this master literary work is that solely because of our technological advances and our destruction of the environment, we are headed for the apocalypse. Doomsday is rapidly approaching. Environmental Armageddon is right around the corner. If you think I'm exaggerating, read his own words: "Now warnings of a different sort signal an environmental holocaust without precedent. . . . Today the evidence of an ecological Kristallnacht is as clear as the sound of glass shattering in Berlin." Hey, Al, maybe that was Tipper throwing out your crystals.

What's the answer? If you can't convince the electorate that government should be expanded for economic reasons, fabricate a crisis of another sort. But it's got to be grave enough to justify a massive augmentation of government. Over and over again, *Algore* makes it clear that he believes the threat to the environment is so severe that we need to resort to the kind of Draconian central planning that has failed so miserably in every place it has been tried: "Adopting a central organizing principle . . . means embarking on an all-out effort to use every policy and program, every law and institution . . . to halt the destruction of the environment." That is his solution. Let's consolidate all of our legal, political, and governmental resources (never mind the cost; never mind the proper purposes of these resources and the adverse consequences that would surely ensue from their diversion) to launch our assault on Western civilization, capitalism, and our very way of life. Let's give the federal government lots more money so it can solve our environmental problems just as it has solved so many other problems—poverty, illiteracy, homelessness, drug abuse, crime; you name it. What a track record big government has!

To listen to *Algore*, you would think that the reason we have environmental problems is that the federal government doesn't have enough money and enough authority to intervene in our lives. If only he were technology czar, he could make the right decisions for American businesses (such as paralyzing them) and we'd all be a lot better off.

Part of the problem, he says, is that our backward business community has placed too much emphasis on technologies "associated more with males than females . . . [and] ways to dominate nature receive more attention than ways to work with nature." If you can translate that non sequitur, you're a better man—uh, excuse me; person—than I. In typical psychobabble fashion, he suggests that "part of the solution for the environmental crisis may well lie in our ability to achieve a better balance between the sexes, leavening the dominant male perspective with a healthier respect for female ways of experiencing the world." Would someone please tell me what in the he—— this has to do with the environment?

Our paternalistic federal government knows best, of course, so *Algore* would hand out "tax incentives for the new technologies and disincentives for the old. Research and development funding for the new technologies and prospective bans on the old ones." (Pardon me, but I didn't think he believed in tax incentives and disincentives. Only trickle-down supply-siders believe that tax policy affects people's economic behavior.)

And this is the book that President Clinton called a "masterpiece." Do you see where this administration wants to take us? The federal government should pick the winners and the losers in business and set a strict industrial policy. It talks about "managed competition," but what it really means is "mismanaged noncompetition."

I say, Let the marketplace rule! These guys couldn't manage their way out of a recycled paper bag. Do they really think that the federal government doesn't have enough on its plate? Do they really believe they are capable of handling even more responsibility? Is the federal bureaucracy best suited to make decisions about which businesses have a future and which ones don't? According to this administration, it is. *The Wall Street Journal* reported last summer that prospects are brightening for legislation authorizing a national job-skills board that would prod industries to develop "voluntary" (Congress "prods," and industry "voluntarily" reacts?) national standards for work skills. Why do we need the federal government to educate employers as to the skills of potential employees? Where is their track record?

The federal government—whether it's headed by Clinton-*Algore* or Reagan-Bush—is simply not up to the job of micro-managing our economy, the marketplace, or the development of new technology. Don't buy into this malarkey. Central planning doesn't work. We don't have to spend our precious tax dollars on developing commercial technologies; that's what the free market does—free of charge. Let me give you an example.

HDTV, high definition television, is going to revolutionize the industry. Everyone acknowledges this. It will provide a much sharper picture, better resolution, and will bring to the home the CinemaScope movie experience. There are competing formats out there. The U.S. was involved in a digital system, and the Japanese are working on an analog system.

Zenith and General Instruments, two gigantic multinational corporations, went to the federal government a few years ago and asked for seed money for their research and development of this technology. They cried about how the U.S. was losing the home-electronics industry to Japan. They pleaded with then Secretary of Commerce Robert Mosbacher for a partnership with the federal government to develop HDTV and win back this huge business. Mosbacher and the Bush administration declined their request. It is not the U.S. government's place to go into business with you, said Mosbacher. If you don't have the resources to devote to this project, don't do it.

The companies were disappointed. But guess what? They went ahead and did it anyway—with their own money, not yours. Now there is a new alliance between three huge industry and research conglomerates: General Instruments–Massachusetts Institute of Technology, Zenith–AT&T, and NBC-Thomson-Philips–David Sarnoff Research Center–Compression Labs Inc.

It is expected that this merger of efforts will lead to a new digital broadcast standard that will lead the world in television technology. This would not have happened if the government had said yes. Instead, hundreds of millions of taxpayer dollars would probably have been squandered. The bureaucracy would have ensured this simply with paperwork, red tape, and government specs. This plan wouldn't be beyond the drawing board, the No. 2 pencils, and the T-square. The Japanese would be way ahead of us, but *Algore* and Bill Clinton would be congratulating themselves on the way they established a government-business partnership.

Was *Algore* involved in this coordination of efforts among the three conglomerates? No. Was Clinton involved? No. But with the current climate in Washington, if the same situation presented itself, you can bet that this administration would have jumped at the opportunity to get involved in a partnership with business. Remember, Clinton says we are falling behind other countries, such as Japan, where industrial planning by government is prevalent, precisely because we lack a national industrial strategy. He doesn't bother to mention that Japan's monumental public-works programs have not prevented its industrial output from falling 8 percent over the past year. There is a myriad of examples that expose the folly of Clinton's grand vision of a symbiotic relationship between government and business. Brink Lindsey, writing for *The Wall Street Journal*, argues that Europe's experience over the last twenty-five years shows a failure of government subsidies of business, e.g., the heavily subsidized computer industries in Europe and Japan are still way behind those in the U.S. The government-targeted companies that were supposed to help Europe regain technological parity have fallen short of the mark. It wasn't a government-backed concern that surpassed IBM, but entrepreneurial mavericks—Apple, Sun, and Dell. Clinton earlier proposed $187 million in additional funding for Amtrak, pointing to the experiences of both England and Japan. He must not realize that Japan's bullet train was a manifest failure, and that England is soon to privatize British Rail.

In the Spring 1993 issue of the Heritage Foundation's *Policy Review*, Karl Zinsmeister details the raging myths behind Japan's highly touted industrial policy. He shows that it is mere fable that Japan's spectacular economic rise is attributable to MITI—the Ministry of International Trade and Industry. He chronicles the manifold failures of MITI, which are seldom reported by our press. But forget the facts; ignore the evidence. *Algore*, Bill Clinton, Laura

D'Andrea Tyson, and Robert Reich*hhhh* think the proper role of the federal government is to pick and choose the winners and the losers in business and technology.

Government cannot and should not pick winners and losers in business or try to set industrial policy. If it were up to the "experts" in government, for instance, which of them would have selected my show for success? Which of them could have imagined how many jobs would have been created by the Rush Limbaugh program and its ancillary products in the publishing world? Government could not have done it. Even the experts in my own field said it would never work.

We don't need a technology czar in the United States—especially if it's *Algore*. This man is in way over his head right now. In 1991, Citizens Against Government Waste rated *Algore* as "unfriendly" to the group's goal of eliminating or reducing government waste and minimizing costs to the taxpayer. So what does Bill Clinton have him do in his administration? He is in charge of a "sweeping" review of federal agencies with an eye toward greater "efficiency and service." What expertise and experience did *Algore* have in quality-control management? Well, none exactly. But he did study how successful private companies like Saturn manage such efforts. May I ask a question here? Why not bring in the head of Saturn to run this effort? Why not turn to the private sector for help if it is the private sector that is the model? Hmmmmm? Why leave the task of re-inventing government to *Algore*, who has never managed anything bigger than his own taxpayer-supported offices?

You would think that if *Algore* and company believe so passionately in their environmental crusading that they would first put these ideas to work in their own lives, right? Well, just as with everything else, these hypocritical liberals exempt themselves from their own rules and regulations. *Algore* thinks the automobile is one of the greatest threats to the planet, but he sure as heck still travels in one of them—a gas-guzzler, too. He would also like to ban air conditioners that emit CFCs (chlorofluorocarbons), but he still uses them—even, he admits, in his limousine as he drives to venues to give speeches about why they should be banned!

Remember the way Bill Clinton left his 747 running on the tarmac at Los Angeles International Airport while he received a $200 haircut? Not only did that haircut cost the taxpayers tens of thousands of dollars, but think of the fuel that was burned and how the atmosphere was polluted. Well, it turns out that *Algore*, the environmental evangelist, isn't much more thoughtful when it comes to his own air-travel arrangements. "Ozone Man," as former President Bush once referred to him, uses a C-137 plane when there are much more cost-effective and lower-polluting models, like the C-20 and the C-9, readily available to him.

In a *USA Weekend* magazine interview, *Algore* said that he and Clinton were trying to "set an example" of environmental stewardship for the rest of the nation. Some example, huh?

Despite all their fear-mongering about the environment, I don't think this administration—*Algore* included—cares a whit about "saving the planet." I don't think it really believes there is any impending environmental holocaust. There are only two reasons these notions are being promoted: political expediency and personal empowerment. It simply boils down to this: Here's another way to panic people into ceding their own personal freedom and wealth and to allow the left to grab even more power and control over the lives of individuals. *Algore* himself provides a glimpse into the motivations behind his political makeover in his own book. He writes that he was worried at first about introducing his radical environmental themes into his 1988 presidential campaign. So what did he do? He stuck his finger up in the air to see which way the political winds were blowing. "I began to doubt my own political judgment, so I began to ask the pollsters and professional politicians what they thought I ought to talk about," he writes.

Nevertheless, we're all going to die, they say, unless we listen to *Algore* and Hillary. Life on Earth will cease to exist unless we give the federal government $100 billion more to be spent as it sees fit. Buy this plan or the world will eventually be destroyed. It's the worst kind of extortion and scare tactics imaginable.

And that's all it is, folks. There is little truth in any of the environmental doomsday scenarios—ozone depletion, pesticide contamination, global warming. There's an ozone hole, all right.

But it's a hole in the theory, not in the sky. And there are holes in every one of these theories. It's all a bunch of hot air.

In the next exciting and thrill-packed installment, I will cite chapter and verse on the latest scientific evidence that, once again, demonstrates that I, Rush Limbaugh, was right all along. *Algore* is going to have a lot of explaining to do.

14

THE O! ZONE—
AN ENVIRONMENTAL UPDATE

I HAVE BEEN PROVED RIGHT ABOUT SO MANY THINGS SINCE MY FIRST book was published that *See, I Told You So* could easily have filled several volumes by simply cataloging such validations. But on no issue has the evidence of my foresight and keen political instincts been more compelling than that of the environment.

What did I tell you? What have I been saying and writing that flies in the face of so-called "conventional wisdom"? How many times do I have the right to say "Nya-nya-nya-nya-nya-nya!" because of my uncanny calls on this subject? Come, let us count the ways:

• Despite the hysterics of a few pseudo-scientists, there is no reason to believe in global warming.

• Mankind is not responsible for depleting the ozone layer.

• The Earth's ecosystem is not fragile, and humans are not capable of destroying it.

• The real enemies of the radical environmental leadership are capitalism and the American way of life.

• There are more acres of forest land in America today than when Columbus discovered the continent in 1492.

• Less-developed cultures are not necessarily more pure or

171

kinder to nature than technologically sophisticated civilizations. In fact, the reverse more often is true.

• Big-government regulation is not the best way to protect the environment.

• Many environmental groups have adopted their cause with all of the fervor and enthusiasm of a religious crusade, abandoning reason and accepting many faulty premises on faith.

• Mankind is part of nature and not necessarily its enemy.

But, perhaps most important, what have I told you about the environmental movement? What have I said it's really about? What have I told you over and over and over again? If you have listened to my radio program, seen my television show, subscribed to my newsletter, or read my first book, you know how I have characterized this movement.

It's about panic. It's about fear. It's about instilling the American populace with terror, dread, and apprehension about the future. It's all about making you think that your way of life is "destroying the world." America is the root of all evil in the world, according to the environmentalist wackos. You, the citizens of the United States, are ruining everything. Unless the industrialized, civilized world is willing to make tremendous sacrifices with respect to people's personal lives, this planet is soon going to be uninhabitable, they say.

Now let's look at some recent developments. On May 30, 1993, *The New York Times Magazine* contained an article that proves so much of what I have been saying. Titled "Is Humanity Suicidal?," it was written by Edward O. Wilson, a professor of sociobiology at Harvard University.

The premise of the piece was laughable, but then you have to catch yourself, because, after all, it is being published by *The New York Times,* our nation's newspaper of record. The article asks us to imagine that there is a civilization far more intelligent than mankind, perhaps on Ganymede, the icy moon of Jupiter, waiting for us to destroy Earth. They are wise creatures, of course, and never interfere with inhabited planets. But when civilizations destroy their own world, this noble and highly advanced race moves in and takes over. They're waiting, Professor Wilson suggests, for what could be called "The Moment." That's the time when the forests shrink back to a certain point, carbon dioxide levels reach a critical stage, ozone holes open at the poles, and oil fires rage around the Persian Gulf.

These other beings, of course, are all-knowing and morally superior. However, to this Harvard professor, the rest of humanity is nothing more than a bunch of boobs bent on self-destruction.

"Darwin's dice may have rolled badly for Earth," Wilson writes. "It was a misfortune for the living world in particular, many scientists believe, that a carnivorous primate and not some more benign form of animal made the breakthrough. Our species retains hereditary traits that add greatly to our destructive impact. We are tribal and aggressively territorial, intent on private space beyond minimal requirements and oriented by selfish sexual and reproductive drives. Cooperation beyond the family and tribal levels comes hard." Sounds a bit like Michael Lerner, wouldn't you say?

Do you get this? It's just the worst luck for all living things that we humans are the ones who took dominion over the world. We eat meat. We destroy everything. We plunder the Earth. If only the dolphins had been the ones to make the leap, everything would be all right for planet Earth.

Humans, the good professor writes, are an environmental abnormality. Except for allusions to the Earth goddess Gaia, there is no mention of a supreme being or a Creator in this story. This, my friends, is what they're teaching your kid at Harvard. If you ever doubted me when I said that the militant environmentalists were anti-people New Age mystics, this article should prove my case.

It also illustrates the profound gulf between the people of theology and many in the scientific community. No allowances are made here at all for God. This is why modern, politicized science offends so many people. To take God's most perfect creation and debase it like this is insulting not only to humans, but to God. And this type of writing fits so well into the liberal political agenda. Liberal institutions love to fund this kind of wacky, anti-people theory. Liberal publishers love to support it. The liberal media love to publicize it.

Nevertheless, the truth continues to leak out. Even the liberal media cannot contain it any longer. Myths are being shattered. Real science is overshadowing pseudo-science. It turns out, after all, that advanced technology may not be the archenemy of nature. White males may not be the only ones in history who have used Earth's natural resources.

On March 30, 1993, *The New York Times* published a fascinating science-section story headlined: "An Eden in Ancient America? Not Really." Allow me to quote: "Contrary to widespread belief, evidence is mounting that pre-Columbian America was not a pristine wilderness inhabited by people who lived in such harmony with nature that they left it unmarked. Instead, many scientists now say, the original Americans powerfully transformed their landscape in ways both destructive and benign—just like modern people."

Oh, really? You mean the Indians were just like us, huh? They weren't perfect? This is about as startling a revelation as the discovery that males and females are indeed born with different traits. This, my friends, is why I tell you I am on the cutting edge of societal evolution. What have I been telling you? The environmental radicals have been holding up as a model for us to follow the agricultural techniques of the Native American people. Now we find out the truth. Their techniques were more abusive of the environment than our modern farming methods are. But do you think the radicals will revise their stories accordingly? Don't hold your breath.

The story goes on to explain that British researchers have analyzed soil samples in the highlands of central Mexico and discovered that ancient farming techniques caused a "staggeringly high" rate of erosion. What do you have to say about that, *Algore?*

"It is becoming abundantly clear to geographers, ecologists, and archaeologists that, whether for good or ill, ancient people had a heavy and widespread impact on their environment," the article by William K. Stevens continued. "Some scientists are convinced that a number of early civilizations were brought down by environmental degradation of the land. The brilliant cultural centers of ancient Mesopotamia, for instance, are widely thought to have collapsed because of over-irrigation, which forced water tables to rise and carry salt to the surface, where it made land unfit for farming. And some scientists suggest that erosion brought about by over-clearing of forests undermined the Maya of Central America."

But as corrupting as any civilization may be to the environment,

Earth is remarkably adept at healing itself. And this may come as a real shock to the eco-fanatics: Man can actually play a significant redemptive role in managing nature. Now, the real shocker: Human beings, operating freely in a capitalistic system, are better equipped to solve their own environmental problems, to clean up their own messes, than any other species operating under any other economic system. In other words, free markets and technology are not incompatible with, but essential to, environmental health.

Would it surprise you to learn, for instance, that America's forests are much healthier today in the 1990s than they were at the turn of the century? In fact, you could say that in the last seventy years America's forests have been reborn. There are 730 million acres of forest land in our country today, and the growth on those acres is denser than at any time, with about 230 billion trees—or 900 for every American.

According to a study by Jonathan Adler, an environmental policy analyst at the Competitive Enterprise Institute, New England has more forested acres than it did in the mid-1800s. Vermont is twice as forested as it was then. Almost half of the densely populated northeastern United States is covered by forest. Why? How could this be? If we are ravaging our land, as the environmentalists suggest, why are there more trees around—more forests?

There are several reasons that are important to our discussion. For one thing, technological breakthroughs have drastically reduced our need for timber. Wood preservatives, for instance, mean that timber products have a much longer life. The automobile, so cursed by *Algore,* has reduced the heavy need for timber required by the rail industry. Our agriculture industry, thanks to chemical fertilizers and pesticides, is more efficient and requires less land to grow even greater quantities of food. Most of the planting done— about 80 percent, in fact—is done on private land because there is a financial incentive to grow trees.

But there's an even bigger reason why we have larger, healthier forests today than 100 years ago. It's the simple fact that we know better how to put out forest fires today than was known at the turn of the century. Back then, 50 million acres of forest were destroyed by fire every year. That's an area representing the size of West Virginia, Virginia, or Maryland, for instance. In modern times, wildfires have consumed annually less than one-tenth of that amount of timberland.

"But wait!" you say. "How can that be? I thought man was evil and only destroyed the pristine wilderness. You mean, Rush, that humans have actually saved trees?"

Well, yes, until now, that is. Because if we leave forest-management policy up to Bill Clinton, *Algore,* and their environmentalist wacko friends, what's to prevent us from returning to the days of rapidly spreading wildfires that destroy 50 million acres or more a year? Remember back a few years ago when Yellowstone National Park was literally ablaze? Ultimately about 1.2 million acres were destroyed, $120 million of damage was done, and three people were killed. Why? Because, believe it or not, those managing the park made a conscious decision to let it burn.

The goal of the environmentalists—and this has been adopted by the current administration—is to create in our national parks and all land under federal and state control what they call "a vignette of primitive America." They want to set up "ecosystems" that are free of any contamination by man. You should understand that in their lexicon, "contamination by man" means "interaction with man other than those wearing Earth Shoes." In these systems, whatever happens naturally happens. Man, not being a part of nature, cannot interfere. If lightning strikes and causes a fire, it should be allowed to burn, no matter how much damage it does. This is the thinking behind our current forest-management techniques. It doesn't take a Rhodes scholar to figure out that it won't be long before we're right back where we were at the turn of the century—wondering why all the forest land is disappearing.

Conservationist Alston Chase calls this ecosystem philosophy a "quasi-mystical idea," and he's right. There is no logic behind it. There is no good reason for it. What the environmentalists are saying, in effect, is that some trees are better than others. Trees that have been planted by man are not as worthy or valuable as those that grow in "virgin" forests. What is a virgin forest anyway? Most trees live for only a couple of hundred years and then die. No tree lives forever. Nothing on Earth remains unchanged. So what are virgin forests? Are they made up of trees that have never had sex?

Nevertheless, the Clinton administration is determined to protect virgin forests. (Ironically, our government has little interest in promoting the virginity and innocence of our young people.) It is also establishing a policy to protect more ecosystems and has even signed the international biodiversity treaty that calls for setting them up around the world. This is just the latest technique to stop development and halt the timber industry. The trouble is, this time it's on a global level.

This policy is shortsighted, to say the least. To the environmentalists, it's a tragedy if a man drops a cigarette butt that starts a forest fire that destroys 100,000 acres. But if a lightning bolt does it, it's no problem. So, many environmentalists and the politicians they keep on a leash simply ignore reality and common sense. It reminds me of the researchers who recently ventured into the forests of California. Do you know what they found? No, not *Algore*. They found spotted owls. It seems the place is teeming with spotted owls—even though they're supposed to be an endangered species.

Once again, folks, all I can say is SITYS. But how many of you believed it when you were told that the spotted owl was one logger away from extinction? I was right yesterday, I am right today, and I will be right tomorrow. But you still won't hear about any of this from the major media.

There are other things I have warned you about. I mentioned earlier that widespread use of pesticides, along with chemical fertilizers, has—gasp—actually resulted in more trees being grown in the United States. Again, this flies in the face of conventional wisdom. Every day we're told how evil these things are—how we've got to reduce our reliance on them. Hogwash! Pesticides and chemical fertilizers have provided us with an unprecedented abundance of safer food than ever before. And, according to a recent report in *Investor's Business Daily*, the anti-pesticide, pro-organic campaign may actually be hazardous to the health of the nation.

Think about it. Everybody in America today can afford to buy fresh produce in his or her local market. Even the poorest Americans have access to healthy fruits and vegetables because of our ability to raise these crops economically. However, if America's farmers turned strictly to organic, pesticide-free techniques, you would see a dramatic drop in the amount and quality of produce available.

That's why it's laughable that the anti-pesticide, pro-organic lobby claims to be interested in improving America's health. Don't believe this baloney! Nothing would do more harm to the nation's health than to reduce the food supply, diminish its quality, and raise the prices of produce. Listen to the scientists—the experts in their field—not the crackpots who preach doom and gloom in furtherance of some far-out political agenda.

Perhaps the biggest environmental frauds perpetuated on us in recent years are the notions that Earth is heating up and that the ozone layer is disappearing because of man's abuse of the environment. I've been telling you for years that there is little scientific evidence behind either of these theories, and what I have been saying is being validated by virtually every new study being done, with the exception of those using solely computer models.

Let's just use our heads for a minute. Let's employ a little common sense. Scientists say a supernova 340,000 years ago disrupted 10 percent to 20 percent of the ozone layer, causing sunburn in prehistoric man. Wait a minute—I thought only man could destroy the ozone. I thought only modern technological innovation and the horrible products of human progress were lethal enough to damage the planet.

Has anything man has ever done even approximated the radiation and explosive force of a supernova? And if prehistoric man merely got a sunburn, how is it that we are going to destroy the ozone layer with our air conditioners and underarm deodorants and cause everybody to get cancer?

Obviously, we're not . . . and we can't . . . and it's a hoax. Evidence is mounting all the time that ozone depletion, if occurring at all, is not doing so at an alarming rate. Even *The Washington Post*—that haven of liberal mythology—published a front-page story on April 15, 1993, that dismissed most of the fears about the so-called ozone hole.

For years the media have been calling for immediate action and writing hysterical, alarmist editorials about the imminent threat that the ozone hole poses for humanity. Now, very quietly, they have begun whispering, Gilda Radner's "Saturday Night Live"–character Emily Latella–style, "Never mind." No apology, mind you. No *mea culpa*. Just "Never mind."

For example, here's what *The Washington Post* said in an editorial on February 5, 1992: "Once again, it turns out that the protective ozone layer in the sky is being destroyed faster than even the pessimists had expected. Until now, the disappearance of ozone had seemed to be limited to the polar regions. But the new data . . . warn that an ozone hole may open up later this winter over the temperate Northern Hemisphere with its dense population."

Then, on April 15, 1993, a front-page story had this to say: "In fact, researchers say the problem appears to be heading toward solution before they can find any solid evidence that serious harm was or is being done."

A few days later, the authoritative journal *Science* published a story headlined "Ozone Takes Nose Dive After the Eruption of Mt. Pinatubo." It pointed out that the ozone layer should show significant signs of recovery by 1994. But have you heard *Algore* or any other ozone alarmist step up and admit that he or she perpetuated a fraud on the American people? Have you even heard any of them admit they were dead wrong? No problem, I'll say it for them—and more articulately than they ever could.

That brings us to global warming. Even though quite a few scientists are now backtracking on their once-dire predictions of melting ice caps and worldwide flooding, *Algore* and a few hard-line doomsayers are sticking to their thermostats. *Algore* told the *Washington Times* on May 19, 1993: "That increased accumulations of greenhouse gases, particularly CO_2, cause global warming, there is no longer any serious debate. There are a few naysayers far outside the consensus who try to dispute that. They are not really taken seriously by the mainstream scientific community."

Yet we saw in the last chapter that there is nothing resembling a consensus on this issue among the scientists who have some expertise in this area. In fact, a majority clearly does not believe global warming has occurred. A fact you never hear the environmentalist wacko crowd acknowledge is that 96 percent of the so-called "greenhouse" gases are not created by man, but by nature.

Panic, fear, dread, doom and gloom—that's what the environmental movement is about. When the ozone-hole theory is discarded, the wacko environmentalists will come up with some new crisis—cellular phones cause brain cancer, power lines cause leukemia, irradiation of food will nuke us. There is never any shortage of techno-phobic scenarios. How many have we heard already? Do the following eco-hysterics sound familiar?

- In ten years, city dwellers will need gas masks to breathe.
- In a decade, America's mighty rivers will have reached the boiling point.
- In ten years all important animal life in the sea will be extinct. Large areas of coastline will have to be evacuated because of the stench of dead fish.
- Five years is all we have left if we are going to preserve any kind of quality in the world.

We hear wild claims like this every day from environmental wackos, right? Trouble is, these notable predictions weren't made last week or last month or even last year. All of them were made more than twenty years ago. Believe it or not, their author is not Ted Danson. In fact, each of these doomsday forecasts were made on or before the very first Earth Day in 1970!

It was *Life* magazine that claimed our air would be so polluted by 1980 that we would need to wear gas masks. It was commentator Edwin Newman who was predicting boiling rivers. And it was the godfather of the modern environmental movement himself, Paul Ehrlich, who was responsible for the last two false prophecies. It's amazing that this movement has any credibility left after nearly a quarter-century of forecasting an imminent apocalypse and having nothing to show for it.

But when you examine the track record closely, it gets even worse. For instance, back at the time of the first Earth Day, the big concern wasn't global warming, it was global cooling.

"If present trends continue, the world will be about four degrees colder for the global mean temperature in 1990, but eleven degrees colder by the year 2000," University of California professor

Kenneth E. F. Watt told the assembled multitudes. "This is about twice what it would take to put us in an ice age."

This comment reflected the view of most environmentalists for years afterward. The winter of 1976–77 was one of the coldest in a century, so environmentalists then were demanding immediate action to head off the coming ice age. We are now told that the exact same pollution they were blaming for the imminent ice age is about to cause the melting of the polar ice caps and a horrific global warming.

Yesterday it was an impending ice age, today it's the greenhouse effect. It doesn't really make any difference to the environmentalists as long as they have a crisis to push.

Former senator Tim Wirth, now undersecretary for global affairs and one of President Clinton's top advisers on environmental issues, explained it best to a newspaper reporter a few years ago when he said: "We've got to ride the global-warming issue. Even if the theory is wrong, we will be doing the right thing in terms of economic and environmental policy."

To Paul Ehrlich, even back in 1970, America was the problem. He called the American people "a cancer on the planet." Later, in 1990, he wrote an article published in the Environmental Media Association's newsletter, *EMA News*, titled simply: "Too Many Rich Folks." The problem with the environment worldwide, according to Ehrlich, is the Western way of life: capitalism, consumption, industry, and technology. If we would all just live like simple peasants, we might have a chance of restoring the Earth to its pristine state. Ehrlich's essay, which argues that the industrialized nations of the world—and particularly the United States—are destroying the Earth through exploitation and environmental degradation, is nothing short of a declaration of war on the rich.

"It is the rich who dump most of the carbon dioxide and chlorofluorocarbons into the atmosphere," he wrote. "It is the rich who generate acid rain. And the rich [who] are 'strip-mining' the seas and pushing the world toward a gigantic fisheries collapse. The oil staining the shores of Prince William Sound was intended for the gas-guzzling cars of North America. The agricultural technology of the rich is destroying soils and draining supplies of underground water around the globe. And the rich are wood-chipping many tropical forests in order to make cardboard to wrap around their electronic products."

Perhaps the most ironic part of this story is the fact that it appeared in the publication of an organization founded by Norman Lear to encourage the incorporation of anti-pollution themes in television programs and movies. For some reason, all this bashing of the rich goes over big with the folks in Beverly Hills and Bel Air. They don't take it personally in Hollywood. Hypocrisy has so totally enveloped the Hollywood culture that they unconsciously exempt themselves from self-scrutiny.

To Ehrlich, meanwhile, a man who prophesied more than twenty years ago that all important sea-animal life would be extinct in ten years, the way to save humanity from pollution and death is to force mankind to live in abject poverty.

"Poor people don't use much energy, so they don't contribute much to the damage caused by mobilizing it," he writes. "The average Bangladeshi is not surrounded by plastic gadgets, the average Bolivian doesn't fly in jet aircraft, the average Kenyan farmer doesn't have a tractor or a pickup, the average Chinese does not have air conditioning or central heating in his apartment."

Mind you, none of these notions has persuaded Ehrlich himself to move to Bangladesh, Bolivia, Kenya, or China. In fact, Ehrlich has not even adopted the lifestyle of an average Bangladeshi, Bolivian, Kenyan, or Chinese. By all accounts, he lives quite comfortably in a very large air-conditioned house in the United States. He still flies in jet aircraft, rides in automobiles, and feeds himself with the fruits and vegetables harvested by American tractors.

No, it's not Paul Ehrlich's lifestyle that needs changing, you see, but that of all the rest of us greedy Westerners. You and I are the problem. Get this, for instance: "Based upon per-capita commercial energy use, a baby born in the United States represents twice the disaster for Earth as one born in Sweden or the USSR, three times one born in Italy, thirteen times one born in Brazil, thirty-five times one in India, 140 times one in Bangladesh or Kenya, and 280 times one in Chad, Rwanda, Haiti, or Nepal . . ." So, what are we supposed to do? Pack up our babies and move to Haiti? The last time I checked, Haiti's entire population was manufacturing cheap boats from the roofs of their homes so they could get the heck out of Haiti. Maybe they don't know what a valiant contribution they are making to the salvation of the world by staying. Also note his phraseology: Babies, the epitome of innocence and harmlessness, represent disaster. And they tell us they are for family values.

But the silliness continues even further.

"There are more than three times as many Indians as Americans, so, as a rough estimate, the United States contributes about ten times as much to the deterioration of Earth's life-support systems as does India," explains Ehrlich. "By the same standard, the United States has 300 times the negative impact on the world's environment and resources as Bangladesh, and Sweden is twenty-five times more dangerous to our future than Kenya."

Ehrlich doesn't mention how all those environmentally correct Bangladeshis would survive without receiving care packages from the "dangerous" United States. But, then again, he probably doesn't care. People are the problem, as far as the environmental wackos are concerned. In their world, starvation, plagues, and death are blessings that simply buy more time for planet Earth. I've warned you before about the worldview of environmentalists. They are pantheistic; their God is an impersonal god, who resides passively in every fiber of the universe; to them, to destroy a plant is to destroy their god; to decimate the quality of human life, on the other hand, is of no concern, because humanity represents the greatest danger to the rest of creation.

How could so many people be fooled so badly? Only with the active complicity of a willing media or the stunning ignorance of a media blinded by political indoctrination and the scandalous misuse of our educational system. The environmentalists have even been allowed to set the terms of the debate by creating a new lexicon. They say "global" instead of "world." Why? Because "global" sounds smaller. You can visualize a globe in your hands. It's a much more finite term. They also prefer "planet" to "world." After all, we have all seen planets pictured in the pages of astronomy books. Again, it is a much more finite term. It's a little sphere. But "world" sounds much bigger. It's a tougher sell to convince people that the world is going to be destroyed. Plus, "planet" reduces Earth to the level of all other planets in this solar system and others. Earth is to be given no extra points for housing human life.

In the next chapter we'll explore some of the liberal follies in our public schools. Whether it's political disinformation or ineffective teaching techniques, from "Outcome-Based Education" to condom giveaways, the results are students who can't find America on a map, but hate it anyway.

15

THE DUMBING-DOWN OF AMERICA

I'M WILLING TO ACCEPT RESPONSIBILITY FOR THIS, BUT MY EXPERIENCE AS a student was not a happy one. For some reason, I always looked at school as if it were prison. To me, formal education was like purgatory. People said I had to go, so I went. I knew learning was important, but the process was total agony for me. Reflecting back on this, I sincerely wish that five years earlier something had clicked to make me actively want to acquire knowledge.

It wasn't until I had dropped out of college that I slapped myself in the face and said, "Rush, you've really blown it. You don't have a sheepskin that says you're educated and these other people do. Even though they may not be any smarter than you, they have a degree that says they are. So, Rush, you're going to have to be able to demonstrate what you know. You're going to have to show people." That's what finally motivated me to learn and to achieve.

My own experience leads me inexorably to the conclusion that kids need to be challenged. Kids need to be pushed. They need to be motivated to do their best work and learn. Like anything else in life, there needs to be an incentive.

I think back to the teachers in school who got the most out of me.

Who were they? Without exception, they were the teachers who pushed me the hardest. They drove me. It doesn't matter whether it was in a physical-education class, a typing class, or a government class. The teachers who had the highest expectations were the ones who got the best results. Even though I might have resented it at the time, I have to admit that the most effective teachers were the ones who were the most demanding.

This is why I believe our entire public-education establishment is going in exactly the wrong direction today if its goal is real academic achievement and excellence. For several reasons, however, I fear these are not the objectives of those running our schools. Rather, the trend seems to be toward reaching some kind of educational parity, to make sure no students feel badly about themselves. Student self-esteem is a higher goal than accomplishment. Competition is to be discouraged at all costs. No one should be permitted to fail. This stems from a warped notion that competition is harmful to personal development and, ultimately, to society. The pursuit of academic excellence, as is the case with the pursuit of excellence of any kind, is to be discouraged, because it results in some people achieving more than others. Even traditional educational goals, such as learning, must be subordinated to the greater liberal ideal of academic egalitarianism.

A couple of years ago, a seventeen-year-old high-school student from Wichita showed me the front page of her high-school newspaper. It contained a report that said teachers, administrators, and a school-board member in town believed that maintaining a C-minus grade-point average was too difficult for children. In some schools in the city, students were required to maintain only a D-minus to stay in school. It is undeniable that an educational system that invokes such a relaxation in standards is not interested in its students' learning, but in social engineering. It's all part of the paternalistic attitude of liberalism: We must take care of people, especially disadvantaged people, because they can't take care of themselves. But by taking care of them, what they really do is hold them down, discourage them from surmounting obstacles, and drag down everyone else in the process. In this way, the government-backed educational system fosters student dependency on its equalization authority, thereby justifying and perpetuating its existence. What responsible parent would tolerate such an encouragement of mediocrity?

And besides, since when is a C-minus average too tough to maintain? When I went to school, attaining a C was considered embarrassingly average. Therein lies the problem. We have allowed our perspective to be colored by those who preach that *competition, achievement,* and *success* are dirty words.

Today it's not uncommon to hear educators and others say, "We can't be too hard on our kids. Life is stressful enough. We must be sensitive to the trying circumstances under which they are growing up, which includes the horrors of AIDS and homelessness." With competitiveness having been stigmatized, it is no wonder American students have lost their drive.

My own instincts about the flaws inherent in this approach have been validated by the efforts of educators who have been successful despite the system. I think of California's Jaime (*Stand and Deliver*) Escalante, the mathematics teacher who taught underprivileged Hispanic kids advanced calculus over the strenuous and vociferous objections of naysayers who insisted they weren't capable. I think of Joe (*Lean on Me*) Clark, the former high-school principal who brought order and discipline to a crime-ridden inner-city school in New Jersey. And I think of John Taylor Gatto, who in 1991 was named New York State Teacher of the Year.

After being honored for his achievements, Mr. Gatto stunned his colleagues and New York State politicians with a stinging indictment of public-school education. He decried the dumbing-down of our population and the standardization and regimentation that depersonalize and dehumanize students, that emphasize equality and mediocrity and discourage excellence. His words really struck a chord with me.

"School," he said, "is a twelve-year jail sentence where bad habits are the only curriculum truly learned. I teach school and win awards doing it. I should know." Mr. Gatto vindicated me in more ways than one. I told you school was like jail for me. Just kidding. The lunacy had not yet infected our schools when I was attending.

And the problem is, as Mr. Gatto and an increasing number of other education critics are recognizing, that the current attempts at educational reform are in fact aggravating the problems rather than solving them.

One of the things liberals are famous for is manufacturing problems with their wacky theories, then proposing even wackier theories to solve the problems they have created. Our modern educational system is a perfect example.

The trend in education for years has been toward centralization of authority and moving away from local control. We've been moving toward value-free education and away from anything that smacks of religion. We've been moving toward dictatorship of the professional class (look at the power of the National Education Association) and away from parental involvement. And we've been moving toward someone's mischievous and misguided concept of promoting the student's self-esteem by discouraging his individual achievement and driving him away from anything that could be construed as competition. The results of these trends have been disastrous. The illiteracy and dropout rates are rising. And test scores have been nose-diving. But none of this should surprise you. This is a recurrent theme of liberalism. Remove personal responsibility and accountability, and in their place substitute the caretaker government.

So what's the prescription from the education doctors? You guessed it. Bigger doses of the same bad medicine. One of the worst ideas yet is the move toward something called "Outcome-Based Education."

An exasperated mother from Ohio called in to my radio show one day claiming that Outcome-Based Education—or "mastery learning," as it is sometimes called—was responsible for deteriorating standards in her child's school. She had called the principal looking for answers. The principal explained to her that kids are taught that there are no objective right and wrong answers—even in subjects like mathematics. The educational "process" is everything. Facts and "right" answers are secondary.

"Are you telling me, sir, that two plus two can equal five in your school?" she asked incredulously.

"Yes. What of it?" he replied, with the obvious disdain that the academic elite hold for the general public.

There are no D or F grades under this system. Some of these Outcome-Based Education systems have a new grade—L, which means the student is learning. What it is supposed to tell the parent is, "Your kid isn't doing so hot, but please don't beat him up. He's trying." Keep in mind, it is also the responsibility of the educators to superintend the parent-child relationship, it being implicitly understood in the liberal world that teachers are better able to secure the well-being of children than their parents are.

The educational theoreticians tell you that bad grades only serve to discourage underachievers. But that's not true. When I was in junior-high school, teachers graded with D's and F's, and, believe me, I got some. Now, just because I got an F did not cause me to withdraw from school. On the contrary, the poor grades served primarily to inform my parents, and me, that I was underachieving in those particular subjects. It was understood back then that parents were instrumental in educating their children. It was also believed that parents had a right to know just how well their kids were doing. The report card, reflecting my actual performance, rather than some diluted concept of performance, as is the case in certain schools today, was a red flag to my parents and allowed them to take corrective measures before real damage was done. The primary objective of Outcome-Based Education, it seems to me, is to avoid, at all costs, humiliating a student. The primary objective instead ought to be educating the student.

In the traditional system, if you failed a course, you had to take it over again. In some Outcome-Based Education programs, the student has the option. It makes failure acceptable. It makes an allowance for it. The school bends over backward to ensure that students who perform well academically do not get favorable treatment. The self-esteem of the underachiever is the highest concern. In short, it removes all incentives for achievement. Naturally, this breeds only failure and, worse yet, complacency about that failure. An integral part of education is being graded—being told by your teachers when you are doing well or when you are botching it. Being rewarded for your efforts is normal, desirable, consistent with human nature, and unquestionably healthy for human development. Conversely, punishment and discipline are fundamentally important tools for the unmotivated, capable, yet

189

underperforming student. They help students make adjustments so as to have a better chance at succeeding in school and, ultimately, in life. Even humiliation, when associated with self-induced failure, is part of growing up. It's a deterrent to future failures, and as such, it's one of the great motivators. Outcome-Based Education, in ignoring and denying these truths, does an unspeakable disservice to its experimental student victims. You can tell liberals are in charge of our public educational system because they are doing what liberals do whenever they take over an institution—lowering standards. Students are passing courses and graduating in larger proportions despite much lower levels of performance because of this new philosophical belief that no one should be held back. The ironic corollary result is that the achievers, being systematically reduced to the lowest common denominator under this coerced uniform mediocrity, are held back and taught at the levels of the slowest learners.

Even the most prestigious colleges and universities are finding out that a high-school diploma is meaningless in terms of real achievement. A recent University of Pennsylvania survey of more than 3,000 Ivy League students found that 35 percent could not identify the prime minister of Great Britain, John Major. Three of four could not identify Thomas Jefferson as the author of the opening words of the Declaration of Independence. Three of five could not name four Supreme Court justices. Half could not name their state's two U.S. senators. Forty-four percent could not identify Thomas Foley as the Speaker of the House of Representatives. Thirty-six percent did not know who follows the vice-president in the line of presidential succession.

In addition to lowering standards, the liberal school establishment ignores human nature and refuses to reward success and punish failure. Feel-good, standardless liberalism has taken the place of substance.

I am convinced that we're spending far too much time focusing on students' feelings. Remember the story from chapter 9, Dan's Bake Sale, about the third-grade teacher in St. Joseph, Missouri, who decided that her kids would conduct a bake sale to reduce the national deficit? You know how this kind of thing goes: Little kids can't bake, so parents do the work. The kids then sell the goods to a captive market. People buy anything if they think it's for kids.

So, the kids managed to raise $150 in this bake sale and sent it to President Clinton with a note explaining that it was intended to reduce the deficit. Incredibly, the president accepted the money and sent the teacher and kids a fax thanking them for their efforts and applauding them for their civic-mindedness and caring. The teacher and principal were heroes. The local newspaper wrote a story about them. And that's how I found out about all this, which, from the point of view of the teacher and principal, is probably the worst thing that could have happened.

People know that when they listen to my radio show or watch my TV show they are going to get pure, concentrated, undiluted piercing logic. Many can't deal with that because they construct walls around themselves so they can feel good. I'm all for the students feeling good, provided the wrong lesson isn't being learned. This little exercise in Missouri, however, resulted in the wrong lessons being taught to the students.

The teacher did exactly what liberals do when they say they care deeply about something. Without fail, they do something superficial and then act as if they have made a real contribution to society. What was the idea behind this bake sale? Was it to teach kids about the deficit? Was it to teach them about economics? Was it actually designed to do something substantive about the deficit?

No matter what the purpose was, this particular bake sale has to be characterized as a failure. Maybe, if it had been properly framed—by me, for instance—there could have been some real educational value in this idea. Unfortunately, now these kids have been taught that symbolism is on a par with substance. That's disinformation. That won't help them understand the problems our nation faces, and it certainly won't help them comprehend the potential solutions. It will help them to grow up as liberals, and this is good for no one, except liberals.

We ran the numbers. There are about 40,000 public schools (K–12) in the United States, according to former education secretary William Bennett. If each one conducted a bake sale a year and raised this same amount and applied it to the national debt, we would retire the debt in the year 2659 (and that's without factoring in interest that will accrue on the debt). And it certainly doesn't take into account the growth-stifling tax increases and runaway spending measures that President Clinton dreams of.

The other thing I don't like about this civics lesson with the deficit bake sale is that it conditions kids to the notion that the most important thing they can do with their money is to send it to the government. It lubricates them for the fiscal shellacking they're going to take all of their lives by the government. These poor kids didn't have anything to do with creating the deficit. It's a problem created by government, and it must be addressed by government. Wouldn't their $150 have been invested more prudently and meaningfully in their own community? There they could have seen the results of their work. The problem, after all, is not that the government doesn't have enough money to spend. But that's the message these kids were given. It's a lie. And it's damaging.

Unfortunately, though, it's not unusual for kids to be lied to in school today. Textbooks, though "politically correct," are often correct in no other way. Many are riddled with factual errors. According to an *Investor's Business Daily* story of June 1993, a recent Scott, Foresman text suggested that President Truman settled the Korean conflict by dropping an atomic bomb. A Macmillan/McGraw-Hill text claimed that both Martin Luther King, Jr., and Robert F. Kennedy were assassinated during the presidency of Richard Nixon. (Both were killed during the Lyndon Johnson administration, for those of you in public school.)

But, to me, the trend toward Outcome-Based Education is the most disturbing of all. It completely ignores the existing problems and will create a whole new set of dilemmas for America's young people. Why are we heading down this road?

This revolutionary concept in education was first developed in 1968 by educational theoretician Benjamin Bloom. (Isn't it interesting how so many of these wacky ideas go back to the 1960s?) Bloom called his approach "Learning for Mastery." Here's an excerpt from an article written by Carl D. Glickman that appeared in the November 1979 issue of *Educational Leadership*. You tell me if I am exaggerating when I say that the purpose of this approach is equality, not excellence.

"Mastery learning is built on the assumption that the majority of children can become equal in their ability to learn standard school tasks," he wrote. "As Bloom has written, 'To put it more strongly, each student may be helped to learn a particular subject to the same degree, level of competence, and even in approximately the same amount of time.' . . . What mastery learning does is replace 'page 55' with 'criterion-referenced materials' or 'learning modules.' As Bloom describes it, the more advanced students who finish the work quickly are busy with enrichment materials; the middle third use the full forty minutes to do the work; and the other third need extra time for reinforcing work, peer tutoring, and individual teacher consultations. Ideally, mastery learning works so that the previously faster, average, and slower students eventually reach the same levels of proficiency, and from that point on students can be taught together as a group, mastering the same materials at the same time."

How does this approach work in the real world? Not so well, I'm afraid. What are its consequences? The first real test came in the Chicago public schools in the 1970s. An article in *Learning* magazine in 1982 told the story: "Pupils, for their part, were becoming very astute at taking and passing subskill tests, but not at reading. A growing number of students, many teachers said, were entering high school having successfully completed the . . . program without ever having read a book and without being able to read one." It not only didn't help the lower-performing students, it affirmatively hurt everyone. It was classic liberalism: It spread the misery.

This was the forerunner of today's Outcome-Based Education programs. According to its proponents, our traditional approach to schooling should be completely scrapped and replaced with this radical new theory that has not been successfully implemented anywhere.

But it gets worse, folks. Ultimately, Outcome-Based Education seeks to abandon not only grades, but subjects as well. The view of the theoreticians behind this notion is that there should not be, for instance, a separate course called history that starts at some point and moves forward chronologically. The students, they say, should examine current problems and find out the history by asking about their origins. I'm convinced that so much of this tinkering is simply an attempt to reduce to such confusion what the schools are actually supposed to be teaching that there will be no way to measure success or failure.

There's also a social agenda behind Outcome-Based Education. Because the entire program is shrouded in education-establishment jargon and euphemisms, it's difficult to translate. But, for instance, when proponents talk about teaching "new basics," they don't mean readin', 'ritin', and 'rithmetic. They mean "attitudes" and "outcomes." Not only do they seek to bring everybody to the same level of underachievement, but they also have a social-engineering agenda. When they talk about "higher-order thinking skills" or "critical thinking," what they are referring to is a relative process of questioning traditional moral values. Don't "higher-order thinking skills" and "critical thinking" sound as innocuous as the "politics of meaning"?

Now that "equality" has surpassed "quality" as the number-one goal of our educational system, racial and gender quotas can't be too far behind. Some activists, for instance, were up in arms because boys made up 61 percent of the National Merit Scholarship semi-finalists in 1993. Naturally, it was assumed that this must be the result of discrimination, unfairness, and bias. Notice how the liberal mind works. Because somebody did better on a test, there must be discrimination. Do you know what the liberal solution for this is going to be? Let's make the test harder for the boys or easier for the girls so we have equality of outcome. Don't get me wrong. I'm not suggesting that there is a natural superiority of boys over girls. Far from it. In fact, I can remember when I was a kid, it seemed as if the girls always outperformed the boys academically. But I am suggesting that there might be reasons other than bias to explain why some kids do better on tests than others.

Whatever happened to the idea of rewarding achievement? Today, if someone performs at a higher level, the response is, We've got to do something about that. We've got to punish it. It's sick. This is where liberalism ultimately leads—to the abandonment of common sense.

Want another example? Picture this: A twelve-year-old seventh-grader stands before her class extolling the virtues of virginity and chastity and warning her classmates about the dangers of sex before marriage. "Do the right thing!" she says. "Wait for the ring." Her classmates repeat the pledge, and their teacher urges them on. The California public-school system has embraced a new curriculum called Sex Respect, a federally funded, ten-session course that stresses abstinence and the pitfalls of premarital sex. The teacher believes the approach is working with her students. The school is happy with the program. Parents are well pleased with the results. Unfortunately, the story does not end there.

The American Civil Liberties Union and its radically secular allies are challenging such programs on constitutional grounds. Their lawyers say that abstinence and marital fidelity are "religious concepts," and therefore it is inappropriate to teach them in a public-school setting. Planned Parenthood claimed in a Modesto, California, lawsuit last summer that teaching abstinence is tantamount to spreading fear. Can you imagine? Some liberals think it should be illegal and inappropriate to teach kids abstinence! What about the fact that on secular grounds, abstinence is preferable, as well? Taking the ACLU's line of reasoning to its logical conclusion, any code of behavior, any proverb, any concept, any practice that happens to be accepted according to any denomination, must be banned from the schools because it violates the Establishment Clause of the First Amendment. That just about includes anything, folks, except secular concepts, which, ironically, are touted by their humanistic adherents, with a zeal and a fervor that rival those of any churchgoer. This, my friends, is appalling.

But, yet, think of what the New York City school system was trying to teach to first-graders without any objection from the ACLU. The "Children of the Rainbow" curriculum sought to teach the virtues of homosexuality to six-year-olds! The only reason the program became a nationwide scandal was because one local elected school-board member in Queens, Irene Impellizzeri, persisted in her objections—even after being relieved of her duties by the New York City public-schools chancellor at that time, Joseph Fernandez.

One of the books recommended for first-grade readers, *Heather Has Two Mommies*, describes how two lesbians became mommies. (One of them was artificially inseminated by a "special doctor.") Another book was *Daddy's Roommate*, which pictures Daddy and his male roommate in bed together. A third was *Gloria Goes to Gay Pride*. In the first grade! Can anyone tell me with a straight face that such teaching is not for the express purpose of indoctrinating students with the false notion that homosexuality is as normal as heterosexuality? Surely no one can argue that it is healthy to encourage such a lifestyle. Even if you reject the moral objections to this lifestyle, you cannot honestly deny the overwhelming evidence that homosexual behavior statistically reduces one's life span.

And if kids are learning about homosexuality in first grade, what do you suppose they are learning in high school? Of course, we know many school districts are teaching kids about so-called "safe sex" techniques and distributing condoms. Here are some things excerpted directly from so-called "educational material" currently being distributed in the school system of New York:

• The Teenager's Bill of Rights: "I have the right to decide whether to have sex and who to have it with. I have the right to use protection when I have sex. I have the right to buy and use condoms."

• "Condoms can be sexy! They come in different colors, sizes, flavors, and styles, to be more fun for you and your partner. You can put them on together. Shop around till you find the type you like best. Be creative and be safe. . . . Guys can get used to the feel of condoms while masturbating." Don't these "helpful hints" just warm your hearts, folks? Don't they make you all want to move to New York, where your children can get a quality education?

I could have chosen as my examples more explicit material that actually encourages children—minors, mind you—to experiment promiscuously with oral and anal sex, but this is not a book by Madonna. Is this the proper role of public education? Is this a proper use of taxpayers' money? No wonder Bill and Hillary Clinton (even while hypocritically opposing school-choice measures) chose a private religious school for Chelsea.

Isn't it also ironic that the same crowd that supports handing out condoms to students is shocked that there is a rise in sexual harassment in the schools? What do you expect when you teach kids moral relativism and that premarital, and perverted, sex is to be encouraged? When the Ten Commandments are off limits, and it's against the law to teach abstinence, what kinds of messages are we sending these children? We give kids condoms, we tell them how to use them, and, when they do, we're shocked. With the confusing signals kids are being given today, the only surprise to me is that there isn't more mayhem and chaos in the schools.

If you ask the educational elite what's wrong with the schools today, you will get one easy answer every time: money. Do you really think the situation in the schools would turn around if we threw more money at them? What would they do with it? Buy condoms with even a greater variety of flavors and colors? We're spending enough money per classroom today to provide chauffeured limousines to the teachers and the kids. Unfortunately, the educational priorities of the schools are all messed up. And the money's not getting to the classrooms because of the huge educational bureaucracies we have established at the federal and state levels.

Let me give you an excellent example of how increased spending does not translate into better education. New York City recently spent $68 million on a project designed to reduce the dropout rate. So how much did it help? Did the dropout rate drop by 10 percent? No. Did it drop by 5 percent? No. Did the $68 million stop even one kid from dropping out? No. In fact, there was a 5 percent increase in the dropout rate after the $68 million program was launched.

According to *Investor's Business Daily,* most research into school funding shows little or no relationship between the amount of spending and student performance. Will you ever hear a liberal acknowledge those studies? Of course not. But who needs scholarly studies to discover the obvious? It is common knowledge that the government has been spending more and more on education with increasingly worse results.

Combined federal and state support for public elementary and secondary education rose from $64.6 billion in the 1982–83 school year to $240.9 billion in 1991–92. Average teacher salaries have risen, too, but not that dramatically—from $20,695 in 1982–83 to $34,413 in 1991–92, a 66.3 percent increase.

Spending more money is always touted as the solution to the problems afflicting inner-city schools. Why not? The liberals running those institutions see no logical relationship between rewards and performance. Give them more money even though they continue to fail. Don't you dare hurt their feelings, too. However, a Hartford, Connecticut, city school, once surrounded by crack houses and in an area of high unemployment, proved that the answer lies elsewhere.

James Parum went to the J. C. Clark School as principal in 1992 and was horrified to find a school with filthy walls and floors, and a playground filled with discarded furniture and crack vials. Of the 685 students at the school, 669 qualified for federal breakfast and lunch subsidies. This was a problem school in a tough neighborhood. But instead of giving up or pleading for more money, Parum assembled a team of volunteers who went around and asked residents to stop trashing the school, for the kids' sake. He then went to the men who congregated around the school, drinking and smoking crack, and asked them to stop. They did.

When some drug dealers operating across the street from the school refused to leave, Parum got the police involved. Then the volunteers cleaned up the inside of the school, and posted a sign that read WELCOME BACK—WE CARE ABOUT THE CHILDREN AT J.C. CLARK SCHOOL. When the kids returned, the school's teachers were amazed at the difference. One teacher said that for the first time she felt motivated to teach; kids used to swear at her, but now all she has to do is mention the principal's name and they behave.

Empower America released a report in 1993 that showed America's culture continued to decline over the past thirty years, despite massive increases in social spending. What America needs is more rugged individuals like this principal and more love, not more whining; not more scapegoating; and, most of all, not more money. Problems are best solved at the local level with individual initiative.

But the liberal solution for the schools is just the opposite—more centralization of authority and federally imposed standards. Bill Clinton's plan calls for a national curriculum and national testing. The way the president sees things, the federal government has done such a bang-up job with everything else, it only makes sense that it should take over the primary role of educating your children.

No, folks. That's not the solution. If we want to improve the American schools, we need to try some American solutions. We need to start teaching self-reliance and rugged individualism. We need to strive for excellence again, rather than the unachievable and counterproductive goal of equality. And, most of all, we need to introduce into our educational establishment some accountability. How? The way we have always done it in America with great success—through competition.

The fundamental problem we have with public schools today is the lack of incentives to give parents and local authorities more control. It's time to give parents some real choice—again, the same kind of choice Bill and Hillary Clinton made when they sent Chelsea to a private religious school rather than to a Washington, D.C., public school.

Is this realistic? The school-choice movement was virtually nonexistent ten years ago. As more and more parents realize they will never be satisfied with their government-controlled schools, the idea is becoming increasingly popular. Some states are already giving parents tax credits (vouchers) that can be applied to private-school tuition. Other jurisdictions are allowing open enrollment or choice within the public schools; that's a start, but it's not enough.

What we have in the case of America's public-school system is a failed monopoly. The way we have always dealt with failed monopolies in America is to break them up and foster competition. As in any market, when consumers have a choice, suppliers get very interested in quality. This is an idea whose time has come. Will it be a panacea to our educational problems? No. But it would represent a great start.

16

THE LATEST FROM
THE FEMINIST "FRONT"

FEW OF MY "THIRTY-FIVE UNDENIABLE TRUTHS OF LIFE" HAVE STIRRED as much controversy and outrage as Number Twenty-four: "Feminism was established so that unattractive women could have easier access to the mainstream of society."

Many have suggested that this statement is too rough, insensitive, cruel, and unnecessarily provocative. However, there is one absolute defense of this statement. It's called truth. Sometimes the truth hurts. Sometimes the truth is jarring. Sometimes the truth is the most provocative thing you can tell someone. But the truth is still the truth. And it needs to be heard.

Likewise, for years I've been telling you that the feminist leadership is basically anti-male. I've said this in many different ways on many different occasions. But no matter how many times I have said it and no matter how cleverly I have rephrased this message, skeptics abound.

"Oh, Rush," people say, "aren't you going a little too far? Aren't you overstating your case?"

Well, folks, once again, I have to say it. The evidence that I was right all along about feminism—as with so many other things—is now overwhelming. SITYS. It is now undeniable that feminism's brain trust, as it were, is completely and hopelessly out of touch with reality, not to mention with mainstream women. If for no other reason than to illustrate how right I have been about so many things, I'd like to take you on a brief literary tour of some recent feminist follies.

But brace yourselves, folks. What you are about to read may indeed prove shocking and offensive. Let this serve as a warning and disclaimer. If you are overly sensitive to vulgar terminology, I strongly advise that you skip the next few paragraphs. I don't want to be accused of resorting to shock value or crudity. But, in this case, I need to illustrate a point.

In a recent story distributed widely by the *Los Angeles Times–Washington Post* News Service, writer Elizabeth Hilts decried the fact that women—even politically successful ones—remain far too acquiescent. She is promoting a novel theory about what needs to be done to correct this.

To quote Ms. Hilts: "We've all heard of caring for our inner child. But it's the inner bitch that now needs to be nurtured. It's time to stop denying the inner bitch."

Interestingly (and, perhaps, appropriately), the name of the magazine that first published Ms. Hilts's thesis is *Hysteria*. Ms. Hilts says her use of this vulgarity should not be construed in a negative context. It's not a slur, she insists.

"I'm saying this is a part of us," she writes. And, apparently, this phrase has struck a chord in some quarters. Since the article appeared, she has been in demand on talk shows and is writing a how-to book on developing your "inner bitch."

Do you see what's happening here? Militant feminists are now trying to redefine a traditionally derogatory term for women. The idea is that a self-reliant, strong woman with resolve and character is, by definition, a bitch—or, at least she needs to be in order to compete in this man's world. Keep in mind, folks, this is not Rush Limbaugh—alleged hate-monger, bigot, misogynist, and homophobe—who is saying this. This is a radical-feminist theoretician. I personally consider use of this word in most circumstances a highly insulting characterization. In my opinion, by using this terminology, women are falling right into an old male-barroom stereotype. These women who think they're emancipating themselves are really doing nothing but fostering a degrading stereotype that has been perpetuated by true chauvinist pigs.

Intentionally or unintentionally, what these radical feminists are actually doing is strengthening and reinforcing a bigoted, sexist, and ugly stereotype. How ironic. Yet, doesn't it sound just like the liberals who want to fight racism with racism?

Please keep in mind, with everything I tell you in this chapter, nothing is made up. There are books being written about these screwball ideas. There are teachers teaching these theories and scholars writing doctoral theses about them. Lots of misguided people believe this kind of wackiness is part of a new wave of critical thinking. Actually, it is all part of the natural evolution of the feminist movement, which has always been led by a core of angry, bitter, anti-male women hell-bent on "Get-even-ism" (a term I coined to describe the mentality dominating the many classes of people in our society who think of themselves as victims: Correcting the problem is not enough; there must be retribution).

Another symptom of this trend is evidenced in the very way men and women interact with one another today. Do you think looking at someone is sexual harassment? Do you think all men are rapists? Do you think all sex is rape? If your answer to any or all of these questions is no, you are simply not, by definition, a feminist. Don't forget, you mainstream women out there who may think I am exaggerating: It is not you who defines feminism or sets the movement's agenda. You may prefer to think of the feminist movement as an innocuous, well-meaning organization committed to equality between the sexes. Wishing it so doesn't make it so. And I'm here to tell you, as painful or unpleasant as it may be to your ears, there is nothing innocuous about the feminist leadership in this country. And make no mistake, these women are the ones who set the agenda for the feminist movement.

The people who define modern feminism are saying that normal male deportment is harassment, near rape, abuse, and disrespect. These extremists, who make up the intellectual leadership of the modern feminist movement, are attempting to make the case that any expression of interest by a man in a woman is harassment. Inevitably, this is going to lead to several serious problems.

First among those is that men will become fearful about making any advances. This attitude will confuse men about what is right and what kind of behavior is acceptable. If no approach is welcome, then women will, by necessity, have to become the aggressors. Men will be afraid of crossing the line.

The second major problem with this trend is that it trivializes real sexual harassment, real rape. When people are labeling everyday, normal, male-female conduct as sexual harassment, we not only obliterate relations between the sexes, but we greatly trivialize true sexual harassment. Harassment is now being so broadly defined by some that it entails any behavior that offends or annoys or interrupts your life.

The fact of the matter is that women have far more power than most of them realize. It's a biological fact that males are the aggressors. We all know this is true. That means that the ultimate power—the power to say yes or no—lies with women.

If consent is denied and the aggressive male physically forces himself on the woman to the point of penetration, then you have rape—real rape. But this is the exception. Most men are not rapists. But militant feminists seek to blur the distinctions. Let's look at date rape, for example. I have a problem with feminists seeking to expand the concept of rape by adding such adjectives as *date* and *acquaintance*. Words mean things, a point I will expand upon in the following chapter. Especially in these times of hypersensitivity, it is very important that we are clear in our word usage. This is even more the case when the word in question represents criminal behavior, in some cases punishable by life imprisonment. This is dead-serious, folks. Rape means rape. It either is, or it isn't. It matters not whether it occurs on a date or on Mars. It is my belief that the date-rape concept has been promoted by those whose agenda it is to blur these distinctions. By calling it "date rape," the intent is to expand the scope of the very serious crime of rape, and to include within the category of "rape" behavior that certainly is not rape. Please don't misinterpret my meaning. As a firm believer that words have meaning, I'm very careful to use mine precisely. I condemn the act of rape as much as any other human being would.

It is inexcusable. Confusing its definition by trying to expand its scope deceitfully will only redound to the detriment of real rape victims. That is unconscionable.

Some militant feminists apparently harbor such animosity for the opposite sex that they want to criminalize the process of courtship —the old-fashioned "chase." I have news for these people: It's normal for boys to pursue girls. It's natural for men to pursue women. This normal and natural process, once called the fine art of seduction, is being confused with harassment. What was once considered an important part of the process of finding a mate is being mischaracterized as rape.

How should you channel normal masculinity and the aggressive nature of the male? Would these women prefer men as husbands, or leaders of marauding gangs? That is basically the choice. Because women can be—and need to be—a great civilizing influence over men.

Do you realize that in some cities today men can be arrested for making a wolf whistle at a comely woman? Now, I'm not suggesting that this is the kind of behavior we should encourage, but should it be criminalized? And what are the consequences of this sort of overreaction? The consequences are manifold. It's no wonder so many men and women have problems interacting. Rules and regulations like these are presumably meant to foster improved relations between men and women, but their effect is just the opposite. What is being fostered is an adversarial relationship between the sexes.

Take, for instance, the young star of "The Wonder Years," Fred Savage. The then sixteen-year-old was hit with a sexual-harassment suit by a former staffer of the show, Monique Long, who claimed that Savage repeatedly asked her to have an affair with him and—egads!—touched her by holding her hand. The lawsuit also charged that Jason Hervey, another actor on the show, harassed Long during her two years on the show as a costume designer, at one point touching her "in a sexual way." Long, thirty-two, claimed she was asked not to return to the show because of her complaints about the actors.

Have things gotten to the point where a man, or boy, can't ask a woman out? Can't flirt? Is it a crime to hold somebody's hand?

Wouldn't a more appropriate response to questionable behavior have been for this thirty-two-year-old woman to call the teenager's parents? Or even slap him in the face? Is our society so confused now about relations between men and women that a mature adult doesn't know how to deal with a flirtatious sixteen-year-old?

Today's feminists are confusing advances with harassment and confusing harassment with rape. To them, there is very little difference among the three things. Ironically, radical feminists suggest that women are little more than helpless victims, incapable of resistance to men's sexual advances. This point was brilliantly illustrated in a *New York Times Magazine* piece by Katie Roiphe, author of *The Morning After: Sex, Fear and Feminism on Campus.* Ms. Roiphe contends that "rape-crisis feminists" who constantly portray women as victims are perpetuating the very stereotypes that real feminism was supposed to shatter.

"Preoccupied with issues like date rape and sexual harassment, campus feminists produce endless images of women as victims—women offended by a professor's dirty joke, women pressured into sex by peers, women trying to say no but not managing to get it across," she writes. "This portrait of the delicate female bears a striking resemblance to that fifties ideal my mother and other women of her generation fought so hard to leave behind."

Now, Ms. Roiphe points out, it's the feminists who are characterizing women as helpless and resourceless in relationships with men. She questions frequently cited statistics like the one claiming that 25 percent of college women are victims of rape.

"We all agree that rape is a terrible thing," she writes, "but we no longer agree on what rape is. Today's definition has stretched beyond bruises and knives, threats of death or violence, to include emotional pressure and the influence of alcohol. The lines between rape and sex begin to blur."

Why is this happening? Ms. Roiphe suggests it is part of a political agenda. Feminists, she says, are using "rape as a red flag." They are turning an imaginary "crisis" into a powerful source of authority. Does that sound familiar? How many times have I told you how liberals invent crises solely to declare themselves—and government—as the problem-solvers?

Even some of the most respected feminist intellectuals are

defining down rape. In some cases, they say, even consensual sex is in fact rape.

"Many feminists would argue that so long as women are power-less relative to men, viewing a 'yes' as a sign of true consent is misguided," writes Susan Estrich, a professor of law at the University of Southern California. "Many women who say yes to men they know, whether on dates or on the job, would say no if they could. . . . Women's silence sometimes is the product not of passion and desire, but of pressure and fear." Susan Estrich, by the way, was one of Michael Dukakis's campaign chairmen—excuse me; chairwomen.

Feminists love to tell you that rape is an act of violence, not sex. But it's very clear in Estrich's remarks that no violence need be involved for some feminists to classify sex as rape.

Here's what Ms. Roiphe has to say to that: "The idea that only an explicit yes means yes proposes that, like children, women have trouble communicating what they want. . . . According to common definitions of date rape, even 'verbal coercion' or 'manipulation' constitutes rape. Verbal coercion is defined as 'a woman's consenting to unwanted sexual activity because of a man's verbal arguments not including verbal threats of force.' The belief that 'verbal coercion' is rape pervades workshops, counseling sessions, and student-opinion pieces. The suggestion lurking beneath this definition of rape is that men are not just physically but also intellectually and emotionally more powerful than women."

If you think Ms. Roiphe is exaggerating, listen to how Catharine MacKinnon, law professor at the University of Michigan, defines rape: "Politically, I call it rape whenever a woman has sex and feels violated." She goes even further, writing: "Compare victims' reports of rape with women's reports of sex. They look a lot alike. . . . In this light, the major distinction between intercourse [normal] and rape [abnormal] is that the normal happens so often that one cannot get anyone to see anything wrong with it."

MacKinnon is being taken seriously on campuses all over the country. At a University of Maryland arts fair, the Women's Coalition for Change posted the names of every male student at the university under the heading "These Men Are Potential Rapists."

The women claim they are only trying to highlight the problem of campus rape, but many male students are predictably outraged that they are being classified as potential rapists. Josephine Withers, the art professor who oversaw the project, isn't concerned about this because, as the *San Francisco Examiner* reports, "It's okay for people to be mad." What a scintillating revelation!

Here's the major point of Ms. Roiphe's *New York Times* piece, to which I shout a heartfelt "Amen!": Unless rape is defined as an assault involving physical violence or the threat of physical violence, then the term becomes virtually meaningless and indistinguishable from sexual harassment. And sexual harassment, in turn, becomes indistinguishable from normal sexual advances.

A widely ballyhooed survey of sexual harassment in the schools was conducted in 1993 by the American Association of University Women. Reported on the front pages of newspapers across America, the study found that a shocking 81 percent of students said they had been victims of sexual harassment. The news was jolting, until the discerning reader discovered how sexual harassment was defined by these people. Unwelcome comments, jokes, and looks served as sufficient litmus tests for victimization, let alone being touched or pinched. One is entitled to ask whether there might have been an agenda behind the sponsors of this survey.

Do you get the picture? If a kid today shows up in public school with a gun, the authorities become mired in confusion over what they can do about it. In some districts, they're actually debating whether they should kick kids out of school for showing up armed to the teeth. To do so, they profess, would retard the learning process, because jails don't provide a good educational atmosphere. In one California school district, students are taught how to duck under desks when gunfire breaks out! But if a boy brushes up against a girl, they literally want to make a federal case over it.

And here's another glaring example of liberals sending not only mixed, but diametrically opposed, signals: Why does it surprise anyone that kids are acting out their sexuality more overtly when the schools are giving out condoms and insisting that there's no way to discourage teens from having sex? In early grades, kids are getting in-classroom, coed instruction on how to put on a condom. In some districts, the homosexual lifestyle is explained by practitioners to primary grades including kindergarten. Kids are told there are no differences between boys and girls. They are told there is no such thing ultimately as right and wrong. Values are relative. Truth is relative. Morality is defined by individual choice. If that isn't a recipe for sexual harassment and other forms of sexual and physical abuse, I don't know what is.

And that's what the kids are taught in school. What are they learning by watching TV and today's movies? Our popular culture is inundated with vulgarity and sleaze—so much so that many of us have lost sight of the good, the wholesome, and the uplifting.

Don't doubt for a minute that there's a political agenda attached to this. It's called breaking down barriers. That's at the heart of feminism. Actor Michael Caine once said something that is perhaps the most succinct analysis of the primary problem with the feminist movement. Everything they're doing, he said, is oriented toward making themselves more like men. They want to join men's clubs. Now they even want to march into combat. This is why there's so much opposition to militant feminism. Men, as well as the overwhelming majority of women, don't want to blur the distinctions between the sexes.

The feminist movement no longer even makes pretenses toward old goals such as equality between the sexes. Instead, it seeks to reinvent completely the way men and women relate to one another. And don't believe it when feminists tell you they respect the choices of all women. They don't. On April 28, 1993, the Ms. Foundation for Women sponsored a day during which girls were encouraged to go to work with their father or mother. The idea was to show girls what the workplace is like and give them something to which they could aspire.

The event, however, clearly illustrated the bias of the feminist movement in favor of women entering the work force and against stay-at-home mothers. With all the media hoopla over this event, I didn't see one story about a stay-at-home mother keeping her daughter home from school. The Ms. Foundation would never consider that kind of exposure healthy for a daughter.

Remember the hubbub when Mills College, the all-women's institution in Oakland, California, decided it was time to admit men because of sagging enrollment? Do you recall the scene at Mills?

There were hysterical nervous breakdowns taking place all over campus. Women were in tears, sobbing uncontrollably. The reaction was so overwhelmingly negative on campus that the administration changed its mind and decided to continue to exclude men. That's okay with me. I think we ought to have those kinds of choices open to us. But contrast that reaction with the way feminists have targeted all-male institutions like the Virginia Military Institute and the Citadel (located in Charleston, South Carolina). Why is it all right to have all-women's colleges, but not all-men's? Hhmmmmm?

Please do not mistake this chapter, or anything in it, as a criticism of women. Feminists are framing the debate in a way that equates opposition to their views with being anti-female. In my case, nothing could be further from the truth. I revere women. I respect women. I think men need women. I believe that in terms of opportunity, we should forget what gender people are. We should forget what people's skin color is. I would prefer to see everyone encouraged to do his or her best. I would prefer to see excellence rewarded, so that people would have an incentive to achieve. I would much prefer to see people pursuing excellence than taking refuge in their gender and skin color.

But the radical feminists—that elite corps of abortion-on-demand zealots I call femi-Nazis—want to divide people. As I have illustrated, they do this largely through the victimization game. More often than not, however, their attempts at divisive propaganda—especially in the academic world—simply border on the absurd.

Take that bastion of political correctness, the University of Wisconsin, the institution where the former warden was the lovely and gracious Donna Shalala. The syllabus for a three-credit inter-session course in the philosophy department includes the following required readings: "Motherhood—the Annihilation of Women"; "Dyke Methods" (with this warning: Be prepared to discuss the methods in class); "Feminism and Vegetarianism"; "Eco-Feminism and the Eating of Animals"; "The SCUM (The Society for Cutting Up Men) Manifesto"; and "The Sexual Politics of Meat."

Geraldo calling. Sally Jessy Raphaël, where are you? Does this not sound like a promo for the "Donahue" show any day of the week? I'll bet some of you think I have to search far and wide for these oddball ideas and try to make something of them. You have me confused with someone else. I'm trying to tell you that this stuff is being taught to our future leaders under the guise of higher education. I've said again and again, I don't need to make things up. It's all here for you to see. You're welcome to check my data.

Again, I want to emphasize, as I have many times before, when I attack feminism, I am not opposing equal opportunities for women. I am totally in favor of equal pay for equal work. But I tell you most emphatically, this is not what the modern feminist movement is about. The NOW (National Organization for Women) gang, which certainly purports to represent the feminist movement, is about pushing an extreme left-wing political agenda with an emphasis on lesbianism and special rights for homosexuals. Some people may not like this description of feminism. If they don't, it is time they spoke up against the radical views and statements of those militant spokespersons. The trouble is, no one seems to be willing to distance themselves from these radicals. Until that happens publicly, isn't it fair to assume that these radicals do indeed speak for the feminist movement and have thereby transformed the original definition of the term "feminist"?

Am I the only one getting tired of this kind of insanity? Why is normal behavior in our society constantly labeled as sick and weird, while sick and weird behavior is consistently called normal? Perhaps the weirdest, most deviant behavior of all is the kind taking place in our universities under the guise of learned research. Some feminist scholars have come up with a new theory that should be excellent fodder for future "Donahue" shows. Have you heard about male lesbians?

The February issue of *Florida Trends* magazine reported on this new discovery, first offered in *Hypatia*, the self-proclaimed "journal of feminist philosophy," edited by Linda Lopez McAllister, a professor of women's studies and philosophy at the University of South Florida in Tampa. A *Florida Trends* columnist called McAllister to learn more about the "male lesbians" theory. McAllister said it had something to do with "post-structural thinking" and added, "I'm not sure I can articulate it." But, finally, this "scholar" came up with this: "There would be no reason why a lesbian would have to be a woman." According to post-structural thinking, "you could have a man make a claim he's a lesbian trapped in a male body, and except anatomically, he fits into the definition of what a lesbian might be." We have known for some time that liberals believe in moral relativism. It now appears that they believe in physical and gender relativism as well. Pretty soon we will probably be seeing university courses spring up whose purpose is to inquire into whether our existence is real or merely an extension of Freddy Krueger's dream.

See how the theoretical, academic mind works? Is a lesbian not simply a homosexual woman? Can we not even agree on that? Once again, folks, I want to remind you that you're paying hard-earned dollars to educate your kids in institutions that are promoting wacko theories like this.

This male-lesbian thing is good news for only one group—the lesbian movement. Recent surveys have shown their numbers are very scarce. But if they don't have enough female members, they can now broaden their ranks by accepting male lesbians as members, all thanks to post-structural thinking.

Now that we're past the inhibitions of "structure" in our thinking, all kinds of doors are opening up to the human race. Just ponder the possibilities with me:

• An Atlanta man has been charged with manslaughter in the death of a transsexual whose rear end he was injecting with liquid silicone to make his buttocks fuller. The man faces a maximum ten-year prison sentence for injecting the silicone, which came from an automobile-supply store. It's obvious to any observer that this procedure needs federal funding—if people want silicone in their butts, they should be able to go to licensed silicone-in-the-butt injection centers. It's a quick and easy way for people to feminize themselves. It's every transsexual's right to a safe and legal silicone-in-the-butt injection. We've got to get our backsides out of the back alleys. Only the most inhibited bigots could disagree.

• San Francisco chemist Merlin Starly has received a patent for suspenders that secure condoms in place so that they won't slip off during use. The condom suspenders are made of two plastic clips, which are attached to the wearer's legs by a "special adhesive." I wonder if these suspenders will work with the newly patented musical condoms.

• One of the hottest commodities on the talk-show circuit in 1993 was Sherrol Miller, a forty-four-year-old nurse from Louisville, Kentucky. She was on "Donahue" at least three times, "Sally Jessy Raphaël" twice, "Geraldo" once, "Joan Rivers" once, and "Montel Williams" once. What is her claim to fame? She explains it like this to The Wall Street Journal: "I was the tenth wife of a gay, con-man bigamist." But to simplify matters, let's just say that Ms. Miller (or is it Mr.?) claims to be a transsexual lesbian. Why not? If we can have male lesbians, there's no reason we can't have transsexual lesbians, right?

• According to several news reports in 1993, the next big push for special civil-rights protection will come from the "transgendered community." What the heck is that? It encompasses anyone who is a drag queen, transvestite, transsexual (lesbian or straight, presumably), hermaphrodite, and others (let me be careful here) whose gender identity does not correspond to their biology or expected social roles.

• The New York Times reports about how angry and distraught women have finally found a way to express themselves—by playing the drums. Penny Geneeson, one of the many leaders of this new movement, states the following: "Many of us are afraid—we somehow believe our own rhythms in drumming or dancing are not good enough. Drumming is about reclaiming and recapturing the feminine divine." The Times adds that Geneeson is one of many women "setting off on a complex journey of rhythm and consciousness" by expressing herself through drumming, which has become, for "growing ranks of women," a means of "spiritual transformation, stress relief, and personal growth." These drummers see themselves as "bearers for new traditions," and Geneeson has formed a "drumming circle" with other women. "Our culture does not allow women to make noise," claims Geneeson, and thus drumming is a valid means of female expression.

What does all this nonsense have in common? Radical feminism, male lesbians, transsexuals, musical condoms with suspenders, and lotsa drummers drumming are all manifestations of a political agenda with roots in the 1960s. This is all fruit we are reaping from the sexual revolution. We can laugh at it. It can make us cry. But we mustn't ignore it. If we do, it will consume our culture and become the accepted norm.

17

WORDS MEAN THINGS

My vast and astute radio audience has heard me say this over and over again. I even alluded to it in the last chapter: Words mean things. Maybe some of you have wondered, "Why the heck does Rush keep saying that? It's obvious that words mean things. What's the big deal? What is he really trying to say?"

"Words mean things" is one of those core assumptions—the kind of common-sense principle most people simply take for granted. Of course words mean things. Yet there is a significant segment of our society that apparently needs to be reminded constantly of this fact. These people are called liberals.

To many, saying the right words is enough. In fact, it is everything. Generally, that's all the left does. They pay lip service to their beliefs and convictions. Words are all you need. Saying the right thing is all that is required. Some liberals simply do not view language the way ordinary people do. They don't seem to realize that words have consequences. People, voters, even nations, rely on them. Think about it.

During the 1992 presidential campaign, Bill Clinton repeatedly called George Bush's policy toward the Haitian refugees "immoral." He promised that if elected, he would immediately enact a more humane approach and open America's doors to the Haitian immigrants. They were fine words. They made a nice sound bite on the evening news. They sounded compassionate, caring, and liberal.

But here's the important point: Clinton never considered the potential ramifications of these words actually being believed by desperate Haitians. After his election, thousands literally ripped the wooden roofs off their homes and began building ramshackle boats and rafts and setting off for the arms of a new promised land. About 400 drowned trying to make it to America's shores. The fortunate ones were immediately returned to an even more uncertain fate by the U.S. Coast Guard and Navy at the express orders of the new president, who reinstated the old "immoral" Bush policy.

But the most interesting aspect of this event was the new president's reaction. Clinton acted shocked that the Haitians would actually base a life-and-death decision on his rhetoric. After all, they were just words. Those were things Clinton said in a campaign to get elected. Why were these people taking them seriously? Obviously, the people of Haiti did not know the character of Bill Clinton the way the people of, say, Arkansas do.

To far too many people, words are everything and nothing at the same time. They manipulate words skillfully to convince the public that they are caring, compassionate, good, and wise, but ultimately they have no respect for those words. Words are often meaningless when they come out of the mouths of liberals. They will deny having uttered them the next day. When you prove to them that they actually said them, they will insist they were misunderstood. Thanks to the ethical gymnastics of liberalism, words can be both all-important and inconsequential at the same time.

Do you think I'm exaggerating? Am I, Rush Limbaugh, now guilty of stretching the truth to make a point? You decide. Listen to what New York State governor Mario Cuomo told a newspaper reporter a few days after President Clinton's inauguration: "What I wanted is what he has delivered," Cuomo said. "I wanted someone who could win, who believed essentially what I believe. The point is to make a body of beliefs president."

To make a body of beliefs president? First of all, Bill Clinton is many things, but he is hardly a "body of beliefs." I doubt very much if he has enough core beliefs and unshakable convictions to fill even the little finger on his left hand, let alone his entire body. But, more to the point, notice what is important to Cuomo. What is important about Clinton's presidency is what he says, what he promised, and what he stands for. It doesn't matter what he accomplishes as president. What matters to Cuomo is simply that he's there. Notice Cuomo's quote: "What I wanted is what he has delivered." That's present tense. In Cuomo's mind, and he is the quintessential liberal and thus representative of liberals in general, Clinton has delivered simply by winning the election. In reality, however, Clinton, as everyone now recognizes, did not campaign as a liberal, but as a New Democrat. Obviously, Cuomo knew something others would discover only later: that all the talk of being a New Democrat was just that—talk. Why else would Cuomo like what Clinton delivered?

The ultimate proof of my contention, however, can be found in the words of George Stephanopoulos, special policy adviser to Bill Clinton, who said the following in response to repeated questions about the president's lies: "We have become hostage to LEXIS/ NEXIS," referring to Mead Data Central's massive electronic database of newspaper and magazine articles, and the ease people thus have finding the president's contradictions. "The problem," he continued, "is an excess of literalism." Whoa! What does that mean? That we are taking the president too seriously? That we shouldn't attach too much meaning to his words? Exactly, my good friends. Point made.

The liberal New Age segment of the baby-boomer population delights in mischaracterizing the 1980s as mean, selfish, cold-hearted, and greedy. Why? Because they haven't yet read this book, wherein we've documented that the 1980s were a time of unprecedented prosperity and generosity. Liberals are content to characterize the eighties in pejorative terms because they believe the people in charge—personified by Ronald Reagan—were mean, nasty, and evil. Never mind what resulted from their policies. It's kind of the flip side of Lerner and Hillary's politics of meaning. Beneficial consequences flowing from conservative policies, despite how much prosperity is created, are entirely negated because of the allegedly greedy and mean-spirited attitude of Republicans.

Likewise, since those swept into power in the Clinton administration are nice people, all they need to do is be there and life will be happy and blessed for all. Nirvana will occur. Fairness and peace and equality will be the order of the day, even if their policies fail miserably. Why? Because they care. Or, more precisely, because they say they care.

The group of people running our country today, for example, believe they are morally superior just because they want everyone to have health insurance. Well, folks, I hate to point out the obvious, but just paying lip service to something does not qualify you as being compassionate. It never even occurs to these folks that everybody wants people to have access to health care. Everybody wants to end homelessness. Everybody wants to cure AIDS. Everybody wants to conserve our natural resources. Everybody wants to end child abuse. But just wanting these things does not get you there. Just talking about these things doesn't accomplish anything. Just complaining about things does nothing to solve the problem. Neither does enacting policies that have the superficial appearance of compassion, but do nothing to solve the problem, and often make it worse. The last three decades are replete with examples of "compassionate" liberal legislation that have brought harm to those segments of the population they were enacted to help—not to mention to the taxpayers in general.

Just a few examples are: forced busing, ultimately resulting in a mass exodus of the middle class from urban areas into the suburbs and doing nothing to "equalize" quality of education for minorities; the proliferation of the welfare state, creating an increasingly helpless and expanding dependency class; minimum-wage legislation, resulting in untold numbers of lower-income workers losing their jobs, all in the name of improving their lot as a class; the assumption by the federal government of the paternal role by pouring AFDC (Aid to Families with Dependent Children) monies into minority families, creating a disincentive for the maintenance of the nuclear family and ultimately substituting a poverty of values for economic poverty.

A well-documented editorial in *The Wall Street Journal* on July 13, 1993, by John Mueller of LBMC Inc., a forecasting firm in Arlington, Virginia, demonstrates the direct correlation between increases in social spending and unemployment. He raises the rhetorical question, "Should the U.S., like the European Community, accept an ever-higher rate of unemployment as the cost of expanding social programs?" Mueller then masterfully answers his own question: "Both theory and evidence clearly show that the main reason for the sharp rise in unemployment in the current EC countries over the past two decades has been the massive expansion of the region's social benefits and the minimum wage. President Clinton's proposals would accelerate the same process in the U.S." But the point is that for Lerner, Hillary, Teddy, Tom Foley, Senator Mitchell, and our president, it apparently makes no difference what harm flows from their policies. It matters only whether they are able to project an image of concern; that's what gets them elected, because they don't ever seem to be held accountable for their failed policies. The causality is simply too obvious for some to believe.

Their repeated answer for policy failures is that things would have been worse if they hadn't enacted their policies. That's what Tom Foley said during a radio interview about the 1990 budget deal. Mr. Foley was asked why Congress was going through this same charade again, i.e., promising to cut the deficit by half a trillion dollars in five years, while not committing to the spending cuts and increasing marginal tax rates on the "wealthy." How do you explain, Mr. Foley, that when you raised the top marginal rate on the upper class from 28 percent to 31 percent, you yielded for the Treasury a net **loss** of revenues to the tune of $6+ billion? His response: The deficit would have been much worse if we hadn't enacted the 1990 budget deal.

With that budget deal, just as with this one, the spending cuts are planned for the out years and will never happen, whereas the tax increases are immediate and growth-stifling. Foley is saying, in effect, that if we had cut spending as promised and left the tax rates alone, the deficit would have been worse. This is demonstrably false and utterly inconsistent with all of our historical data on the subject, and he knows it—and this gets me to my next point.

There is, I am sorry to say, a more sinister element within liberalism that is well aware of what it is doing. There is a percentage of liberals who are simply moral relativists. They simply have no respect for the truth. Thus, the manipulation of words and symbols is a tactical ploy—a calculated strategy to deceive. These folks don't care that President Clinton has broken dozens of promises. They don't care that he had to lie his way into office. In their eyes, Clinton simply did what he had to do to win and assume power. (I even heard CNBC talk-show hosts Phil Donahue and Vladimir Pozner justifying Clinton's lies to get elected. Knowing Vladimir's background, it shouldn't surprise us that he subscribes to the theory that the ends justify the means, but Donahue ought to be ashamed of himself.)

Why did Bill Clinton get elected? What did he say that made him palatable enough for even 43 percent of the American people to support? Is there any doubt that one of the principal reasons was his absolute, unconditional promise to cut middle-class taxes?

I submit to you that this was a cornerstone of his campaign. In his "Putting People First" campaign document, it states unequivocally: "We will lower the tax burden on middle-class Americans. Middle-class taxpayers will have a choice between a children's tax credit or a significant reduction in their income-tax rate."

So, my friends, which one did you choose this year—the children's tax credit or the tax cut? Oh, you mean you didn't get a choice? Well, my goodness, what happened?

Clinton made this promise in various forms throughout the entire course of his campaign. He started out in January 1992 by saying: "I want to make it very clear that this middle-class tax cut, in my view, is central to any attempt we're going to make to have a short-term economic strategy." His first campaign ad that same month stated: "I've offered a comprehensive plan to get our economy moving again. It starts with a tax cut for the middle class." In March 1992, he said: "We need to provide a tax credit of up to $800 per child to ease the burden on working families." Another campaign document published in September 1992 stated: "We should cut middle-class taxes immediately by 10 percent." In his first presidential debate with George Bush in October 1992, he said: "We want to

219

give modest middle-class tax relief to restore some fairness, especially to middle-class people with families with incomes of under $60,000 per year."

Plus, Clinton's tax-cutting and deficit-cutting promises became a focus of both the vice-presidential and presidential debates. He was challenged on his numbers; he was given an opportunity to retreat, to 'fess up. But he stood fast and with an air of moral superiority accused his challengers of demagoguery for exposing his fraud. Figure that one out: It's demagoguery to expose demagoguery.

I don't have to tell you again what happened to your tax cut after the election. (I shouldn't have to tell you because I told you all throughout the campaign that it was illusory. This is the ultimate "See, I Told You So.") Despite his rhetoric to the contrary, Clinton had a history of being a taxer and spender. He also had a history of disingenuousness. The man is bereft of character. So it was an easy call. But character doesn't matter, moron. It's the economy, stupid. So enough people either got fooled or were irreversibly angry with George Bush, and Clinton got elected. But let's examine, once again, what Bill Clinton said about that most important campaign promise once he was elected.

"From New Hampshire forward, for reasons that absolutely mystified me, the press thought the most important issue in the race was the middle-class tax cut," he said. "I never did meet any voter who thought that." Listen to that brazen, in-your-face disavowal. It reminds me of the scene in *Animal House* where Otter returned the car of the hapless pledge, Flounder, after borrowing it, totally wrecked. When Flounder cried that his older brother, who actually owned the car, would kill him, Otter smiled and in Clintonese quipped, "You ——ed up. You trusted me." So those of you who voted for this man, you screwed up; you trusted him.

Well, if he was really mystified by the way the press emphasized this issue during the campaign, why didn't he try to correct the misunderstanding then? Why did he wait until after the election? Words mean things. Character counts.

Unhappily, for all of us, Bill Clinton's duplicity didn't end with his election. His victory, tenuous as it was, reinforced—or, should we say "enabled"?—his subterfuge. Having realized that this kind of fraud and deceit was so successful during the campaign, he has institutionalized it as part of his administration. It has become the trademark of Clintonism. This is now the way he governs.

It started immediately after the election, even before he assumed office. It simply wasn't going to be possible to honor his commitment to cut the federal deficit in half in four years, he explained. Why not? Well, he was shocked to find out that the deficit was bigger than he realized.

Once again, folks, this was simply untrue. But he lies so casually, so glibly, so unctuously, so remorselessly. I don't know about you, but it frightens me. It is horrifying to realize that there is a pattern here, a consistency that one can attribute only to a genuine pathology, emanating from a dEarth of conscience.

Clinton knew months earlier what the deficit numbers were going to be. He was on record discussing them. But don't believe me, listen to the way *Newsweek* characterized this disingenuousness in its January 18, 1993, issue: "That's called spin control, early evidence that the Clinton folks have no intention of abandoning that practiced campaign technique once they're in office. On the contrary, Clinton's team plans to turn the White House into a mighty Wurlitzer of political propaganda. Clinton's use of symbols —the bus trips, the appearances on 'Donahue'—was critical to his winning campaign effort. Now Clinton veterans want to reimpose that kind of message control on the White House. After the inauguration, the inner circle will reincarnate the campaign's 'war room' in the West Wing as a nexus of the 'three Ps': press, policy, and politics. The notion is to create a 'perpetual campaign' to win Clinton's program and, not coincidentally, reelection in 1996."

Note the words *spin control* in the above quote. This is simply a fluffy way of describing a lie, or a series of lies. Also note that the majority of reporters more often than not characterize Washington lies as spin control, rather than as the falsehoods they really are, which only serves to illustrate the assertion that the press is often a willing accomplice to the deceit intended.

Liberals, but especially Bill Clinton, who has taken it to a new level, almost an art form, can say anything they want—no matter what the potential consequences—simply because they are liberals. There is no accountability. Let me give you some other examples:

• Remember how Bill Clinton attacked George Bush's policies in

Bosnia during the presidential campaign? Clinton said he had a plan to stop the violence. He was going to conduct limited air strikes. He was going to step up humanitarian aid. Most of all, he was going to do something—anything—to stop the slaughter. He was not merely planning to do it. He was *going* to do it; there was no equivocation. What happened when he got into office? Bosnia, he discovered, was a "crisis from hell," and it was back to the status quo. No apologies, no explanations offered.

• Senator Carol Moseley-Braun (D-Illinois) said during her campaign in 1992: "Women are better equipped to bring the economy back to health because they're better nurturers." I'm sure the feminists cringed at that. After all, what does it mean? When you're a liberal, you can just say these things without challenge—except by me, of course. It prompted me to ask: Where's the national nipple?

• Liberals tell kids in schools all over America that the best way to protect themselves from AIDS is to wear condoms while engaging in sexual intercourse. It's a lie. They are imposing a death sentence on kids. The failure rate for condoms is around 17 percent. They're teaching kids to play Russian roulette. Their rationale? They're going to do it anyway. Do what? Have sex, or use condoms? Does that excuse their promotion of condoms as "safe sex"? How can these people live with themselves? Easy, because they say they care. Well, I believe in making people live up to their words. To me, **words have meaning.** Since liberals care so much and since they believe kids "are going to do it anyway," maybe they would support me if I were to open up, around the city, a chain of Rush sex shops. Operating under the philosophy that they're going to do it anyway, I can provide the nurses, who can coach the little toddlers in the art of condom usage. I can provide adult beverages to enhance their foreplay, of course, recognizing that they are going to indulge in underage drinking anyway. I can provide sanitary beds for their even-safer sex. I can even provide cigarettes for their post-play smoke. And since we all know that they are also going to take guns to school, I can begin a mini-conglomerate where I sell them guns, too. At Rush's sex shop, you can have it all.

• General David Dinkins, the politically correct if inept mayor of

New York City, announced recently that he is committed to removing all cigarette advertisements from phone booths. "I am committed to protecting our young people and all the other city residents," Dinkins stated, "from the serious public-health implications of tobacco advertising." Remember, now, Dinkins is the same guy who wants to give away free needles and condoms, but he is finally "getting tough" by attacking tobacco advertising in city phone booths. The whole city is falling apart at the seams, violent crime is rampant, the schools are indoctrinating kids, and he's going to "protect" New York by taking ads out of phone booths. But this won't hurt the tobacco industry, because the cigarettes will be readily available at my sex shops.

• ABC-TV's "Good Morning America" recently covered the tabloid-like subject of "Bosses Who Get Murdered by Fired Employees." Why does such a crime happen? Is it because of the guy who pulled the trigger? Noooooo! With liberals, there are always deeper, root causes. The wrongdoer is never responsible, nor accountable, for his act. The guest expert on this show suggested that the crime might have been provoked by the boss's "insensitivity." In other words, some bosses deserve to die. The expert didn't actually say this, but that is the logical conclusion. While liberals don't usually approve of capital punishment for any crime, perhaps the "crime" of insensitivity might be an exception for them.

• And how about our president? Here's a man who based his entire campaign on class envy and class warfare. Then he gets into office and keeps *Air Force One* on the tarmac of Los Angeles International Airport for fifty-six minutes, backing up and delaying flights for his own convenience. This use of privilege is the classic hypocrisy you get from liberals.

The liberal media are as guilty as Clinton when it comes to saying one thing and doing another—of ignoring the fact that words mean things. Recall the Decade of Greed? That was the era when big corporations just did whatever they wanted in pursuit of profits, right? The media have drilled it into the American psyche that the 1980s represented a shameful epoch in our history because of the relentless and blind pursuit of profit.

But I thought that with the election of Clinton, we had put all that behind us. I thought we had moved on to a more progressive, sensitive, caring time. But yet, some of the very people who decried the Decade of Greed are displaying symptoms of greed themselves.

The New York Times, one of the nation's principal critics of the 1980s, spent $1.07 billion in 1993 to buy *The Boston Globe.* Where does that money come from? And why do the owners of *The New York Times* want another paper? Why can't they be satisfied with what they have? And guess where they're going to get the $1.07 billion: off the backs of their employees—the very journalists who chronicled the greed in the 1980s. These people are going to suffer. Why couldn't the owners of *The New York Times* give that $1 billion to a health-care fund for their employees? Think of the family-leave policy they could have created with that money. Think of the day-care facilities they could have built at the paper for Anna Quindlen and her friends.

Is there not a homeless problem in New York and Boston? Why couldn't *The New York Times* just have come in and handed these unfortunate folks some money? According to liberal theorems, they could have solved these terrible social problems that they write about every day, because throwing money at problems is all that is necessary. Why not send in that money to retire some of the federal deficit? Words mean things. Why do liberals exempt themselves from the socialistic gospel they preach? Why is it wrong for major corporations to strive for higher profits unless they are liberal corporations? You must look only at what they say, not at what they do—even if it is at variance with what they say. Because they simply don't realize that words mean things . . . or don't want to.

There's a related phrase I frequently invoke to explain the appeal of liberalism. You've heard me say this many times, too. Liberalism is "symbolism over substance." Symbolism over substance goes hand in glove with "words mean things."

Let me be very careful and very clear in what I am about to say in explaining symbolism over substance. This is a sensitive area, and I don't want to be misunderstood. Please read this with the utmost solicitude. (People in Rio Linda, this means "carefully.")

Let me begin with a sincere preface: AIDS is a dreadful disease. It's a tragedy of immense proportions. It's a human holocaust. I wouldn't wish the disease on my worst enemy. I feel genuinely sorry for anyone and everyone who contracts it—whether it be through heterosexual activities, homosexual relations, intravenous drug use, or blood transfusions. Like most rational people, I hope and pray that a cure can be found for AIDS and that the suffering it has inflicted can be brought to a speedy conclusion. If there was anything I could do to achieve that end, I would do it with great alacrity.

That having been said, however, may I pose a serious question? Why do people in Hollywood insist on wearing little red ribbons to the Academy Awards, the Golden Globes, the Emmys, the Grammys, and all their other major annual events? How does this gesture really contribute to the fight against AIDS?

Typically, at each of these spectacles, sometime during the course of the festivities, a very solemn and seemingly sincere actor or actress—somebody like Ron Silver or Susan Sarandon—will go to the podium and explain the red ribbon phenomenon to millions of television viewers. The explanation generally goes something like this: "You've probably noticed our red ribbons tonight. We wear them to help raise America's consciousness about the deadly disease AIDS, which can strike anyone. We wear them to illustrate our concern that we must stop AIDS now!" The plea is followed by pious applause and then it's on with the show.

Now, I hate to rain on anyone's parade, folks, but this little exercise—no matter how many times it is repeated—will not save even one person from AIDS. Even if everyone in the whole world decided one day to wear a red ribbon, it would not bring us a minute closer to a cure. And, sadly, when everyone at the Oscars wears them, it does not prevent even one person from contracting the disease. So, why do they do it?

Let's be honest. Hollywood stars wear red ribbons because it makes them feel good about themselves. It shows they care. It shows how compassionate they are. While wearing red ribbons, they're no longer rich, famous, self-indulgent, spoiled brats— they're transformed into kind, considerate, selfless souls who only want to make the world a better place in which to live.

This, my friends, is a perfect example of "symbolism over substance." That's what modern liberalism is all about. Appearing compassionate is more important than actually helping people.

Now, most of us live in the real world, and we understand that wearing ribbons doesn't cure AIDS or any other disease. But the Hollywood crowd has some explaining to do. If it really believes AIDS victims derive some benefit from people wearing red ribbons, why isn't it helping victims of other diseases? Answer: Even it knows wearing ribbons is a purely symbolic gesture and brings no substantive relief to anybody. Again, symbolism over substance.

But there's actually something a little sinister about this ribbon-wearing shtick. Are its practitioners not drawing hideous distinctions between deadly diseases? Are they not suggesting there is something morally superior—perhaps even heroic—in catching AIDS rather than, say, leukemia? Are we not moving in the direction of canonizing AIDS sufferers? And is that a step toward cure and prevention?

There's also something downright presumptuous about these little exhibitions. Hollywood's elite is not only demonstrating how compassionate it is, but it is also telling you—average Americans—just how stupid and callous you are. If you don't wear red ribbons, you don't care enough to find a cure for AIDS. Why, you don't even give your kids condoms.

Well, Americans aren't stupid. And they resent this kind of vacuous condescension. For this reason, I believe the red ribbons actually do a disservice to the very cause the Hollywood liberals are trying to promote. But that probably won't worry the red-ribbon brigade. Because in Hollywood, these people are more concerned with appearing to do the right thing than they are with attaining actual results. They're more concerned with saying the right things than with doing them. That's the essence of symbolism over substance. And that's why I will continue to remind liberals that **words mean things.**

18

POLITICAL CORRECTNESS AND THE COMING OF THE THOUGHT POLICE

WHAT HAVE I BEEN TELLING YOU PEOPLE ABOUT "POLITICAL CORRECT-ness"? Have I not told you about the threat this poses to free expression and the constitutional limits on government? Well, my friends, things just got a little bit worse.

In fact, for all intents and purposes, "political correctness," in my opinion, is now an obsolete term. It is far too polite and genteel a label to describe the brand of political oppression being imposed on certain kinds of thought in this country. From now on, let's call it what it is: thought control and "political cleansing."

Why do I call it "political cleansing"? When the Serbs launched a genocidal scorched-Earth policy against the Muslim population in Bosnia, it was characterized as "ethnic cleansing." Liberals are up to the same thing—only instead of wiping out a people, they are targeting certain ideas and viewpoints. Liberals so monopolize the marketplace of opinion because of their domination of the media, the arts, and the schools, that some of them have come to believe that their pet theories and beloved philosophical constructs have no legitimate intellectual competition, so they just declare other view-points off limits. That's what I mean by "political cleansing."

The hypocrisy of it is palpable. The left-wing thought police are forever paying lip service to the ideals of free expression, but they are the first ones in line to place restrictions on it for those with whom they disagree.

Take Texas governor Ann "Ma" Richards. She has two claims to fame. One is having told off George Bush at the Democratic National Convention in 1988. ("Pooooor Geooooorge," she drawled. "He cain't heppit, he was born with a silver foot in his mouth.") And the other is appointing Bob Krueger as U.S. senator to replace Lloyd Bentsen after his confirmation as treasury secretary. (Good choice, Ann. Years from now, long after Kay Bailey Hutchison's shellacking of him by more than 2 to 1 in a special election, Krueger's name will be little more than the answer to some political trivia question.)

Richards, on the other hand, may well be remembered years from now for something much more sinister. Recently, she signed into law a bill that enhances penalties for "bias-motivated crimes." Here's how it works: If you killed someone in Texas for the sheer sport of it, or because you wanted to steal the person's money, or because you got up on the wrong side of the bed that morning, you would be punished less severely than a murderer who killed because he was a bigot. In Texas, for instance, murderers who are motivated by bigotry and prejudice cannot be paroled, as can your normal, run-of-the-mill killer.

But it won't be just Texans who are subject to this kind of double standard of justice. A few days before "Ma" Richards signed her legislation, the U.S. Supreme Court opened the door for laws like it throughout the United States by holding that they pass constitutional muster.

Let's analyze this. Do you know what constitutes a "hate crime"? Put your thinking caps on. What tools do we need to determine whether a crime was motivated by hate or prejudice? Answer: We need thought police.

Through the power of a Supreme Court ruling, and the actions of "Ma" Richards and the Texas legislature, America has legitimized thought police. Our Anglo-American system of criminal law has always sanctioned the grading of offenses based on the actor's state of mind or criminal intent (referred to by the legal profession as *mens rea*). For example, negligent homicide constitutes involuntary manslaughter in most jurisdictions and is punishable far less severely than premeditated murder is. The criminal's state of mind, in terms of whether he intended to do it and planned it in advance, has always been deemed legally relevant in terms of grading the offense and the culpability of the criminal. But for the first time in our history of jurisprudence, with the full blessing of the Supreme Court, we are going to allow state legislatures to grade criminal offenses based on "why" a person committed the crime.

"But, Rush," some people will say, "it's wrong to be biased. It's bad to hate. It's not nice to be bigoted. Why not punish these people more?"

I agree that hating is wrong. Bigotry is bad. But until now, harboring these feelings has not been a crime. We've just made it a crime to express a bigoted thought. We've just made it a crime to hate. Quite literally, what we are doing is violating freedom of speech. The First Amendment of the Constitution of the United States has just been infringed.

Let's analyze this further. If burning a flag is protected speech, as opposed to conduct, then a bigoted state of mind accompanying a killing should be entitled to First Amendment protection as well (not the killing itself, but the inquiry into why).

Let's get to the real root of this. What we have at work here is vintage liberalism. Liberals refer to these crimes born of a bigoted mind-set as "hate crimes." The ostensible rationale for grading the offense more seriously is that a person is more culpable if he committed a crime out of hatred. But hold on. That's not it at all. Let's look beyond the impassioned liberal rhetoric for a moment. What about someone who, upon learning that his mother has been murdered, immediately kills her murderer? Is it not safe to assume that the murdering son's crime was motivated by hatred? Of course. But how does the law treat this man? How should it treat him? The answer is that if he committed the crime soon enough following the provocation, while still in the throes of passion and before having had time to cool off, his crime may be reduced from first- or second-degree murder to voluntary manslaughter and punished less severely. It is reduced because of his "adequate provocation."

How can a liberal explain the difference? Both the bigoted murder and the murder committed by the son are born of hatred, yet one may actually receive a *lesser* sentence. Now let's look at another equally interesting situation. Remember the lady who killed her child's alleged molester in cold blood in a public courtroom full of people who witnessed her act? Did she not commit her act of revenge based on her hatred of the man who had allegedly abused her child? Where were the outcries from liberals then, demanding that this woman not only be punished, but punished more harshly because of her "hate crime"? I don't remember any liberals clamoring for her head.

The plain and simple answer, folks, is that liberals couldn't care less whether a crime is committed with hatred—unless the hatred is of a politically incorrect variety. If a murderer commits a crime based on his hatred of African Americans, Native Americans, homosexuals, probably even pornographers, he is committing a hate crime that is deserving of more severe punishment than if he murders because he hates white males or right-wing evangelists, for example.

I am sorry if this is too blunt and direct for some, but I am speaking from the heart. I am trying to illustrate the danger in the codification of hate crimes. First-degree murder is first-degree murder. Assault is assault. And the full weight of the law should be brought to bear against the persons committing these offenses. It shouldn't matter whether the murderer kills someone because he's black or white or heterosexual or homosexual. Whether one does so because he hates something about the victim should be irrelevant in terms of grading the offense. By carving out a new type of crime called a "hate crime," we are delegating to the left, power over our *private thoughts*—as if they have the ability to get inside our heads and know precisely what we happen to be thinking at a given moment. Once we open this can of worms, it's going to be very difficult for us to put the lid back on it. Please don't misunderstand me. I am not going soft on crime. Just the opposite. In my opinion, we are not doing nearly enough to enforce the laws already on the books. But I am opposed to expanding the definition of crime in a way that encroaches on the freedom of expression and the freedom of thought.

If government can make it a crime to be a racist or a bigot, why not criminalize other viewpoints? Don't be fooled by the argument that this is not an infringement of free expression because the thought is coupled with a criminal act and it is the act that is being punished. Wrong. The thought itself that accompanies that act is what aggravates the penalty under these bizarre statutes. This is the insidious way the thought police can get their feet in the door to impose the tyranny of their views on the rest of society through the awesome enforcement authority of the criminal justice system. How long will it be before governments decide to make it illegal, let's say, to oppose abortion, or war, or homosexuality? These issues, just as with racism, prompt people to take political and moral positions. After all, what's unique about racist or bigoted viewpoints? Why should they be the only immoral positions to be criminalized? I fear the floodgates have been opened.

I have to disagree with Chief Justice William Rehnquist's opinion on this matter. He wrote that these laws are especially needed because bias crimes are "thought to inflict greater individual and societal harm. Its victims suffer distinct emotional harm more damaging than other victims." I beg to differ. Victims are victims. A murder victim is not less dead, nor more dead, because his killer murdered him in a state of bigoted passion. If I get mugged today by a guy who just wants my money, why should he get less of a sentence than a guy who mugged me because he doesn't like radio talk-show hosts? But that's the kind of thing that could happen with this new category of crime.

Just recently, this type of issue resurfaced when a psychopath in San Francisco murdered eight people allegedly because he was angry at lawyers for suing him. The president of the California Bar Association reportedly made a public statement denouncing this heinous crime, saying it was a result of the ceaseless lawyer-bashing in our society. That's ludicrous. The killer was a raving homicidal lunatic. It's that simple. So should we heed the lawyer's plea to create a new class of offense for lawyer-hate crimes? Do you begin to see the absurd, yet frightening extent to which this warped thinking can lead us?

Okay, maybe you're not worried about these laws because you're a law-abiding citizen and they're geared only toward punishing criminals. Fair enough. But these laws have implications for the way we all interact with one another. Hate-crime laws are merely the latest and most blatant manifestation of government creating a new category of thought crimes or infractions. But there are others that are victimizing perfectly innocent, law-abiding citizens.

Imagine, for instance, that you're a hard-working, mind-your-own-business, nose-to-the-grindstone student at the University of Pennsylvania. You have done nothing wrong, but you get a call to report to the judicial inquiry office. There you're told that the university wants to place in your permanent transcript a warning that you are a "racial harasser."

"There is no feeling worse than being completely, unjustly accused of racism," said Eden Jacobowitz, the victim of this witch-hunt. Believe me, Eden, I know.

This is a real-life story. This is not "theory." This is the way political cleansing and thought control affect innocent people in the real world. Listen to Jacobowitz's story. This is an excerpt from a letter he sent me after he was accused of racial harassment:

> On Wednesday night, January 13, 1993, members of a sorority were outside my window stomping their feet, and making a "woo-woo" noise, and shouting and singing at an extremely loud and noisy level. It was almost midnight and I was trying to study. I went to the window and shouted, "Shut up, you water buffalo!" And since they were singing something about a party, I said, "If you're looking for a party, there's a zoo a mile from here."
>
> Later, racial-harassment charges were brought against me because the sorority women were black. True, I knew the color of their skin, but it was a matter of absolute indifference to me. All I cared about was the fact that I was trying to study and my concentration was completely disrupted by extremely loud stomping and shouting.
>
> The next thing I knew, police came by the dormitory asking questions. Knowing I didn't do anything that actually should concern the police, I volunteered my information to them. Other people were shouting curses and racial slurs out their windows the same time I was shouting the things I was shouting, but all I shouted was "water buffalo." I thought this

would be the last I heard about this case, but I couldn't have been more wrong.

The police came by the next morning and I skipped class to talk to them. On that day I offered to speak to the women to explain my truly harmless intentions, but this was never granted to me, not by the police and not by the judicial inquiry office. The next day, January 15, I told President [Sheldon] Hackney about the entire incident, asking him to make sure that this case does not turn into one where the defendant is considered guilty from the second he's accused only because the case is under racial-harassment policy. . . .

I was notified by Robin Reed, an assistant judicial inquiry officer, that the case had been assigned to her, and she would conduct the investigation. . . . She decided that by my words I meant "big black animals that live in Africa." She decided that that's what water buffalo are—big black animals that live in Africa. Well, first of all, Mr. Limbaugh, water buffalo are indigenous to Asia. Second of all, that was the furthest meaning from my mind. "Water buffalo" described the noise they were making and is a direct English translation of the Hebrew word *behema*, which as slang simply means "fool." This word is used from Jew to Jew and has absolutely no racial connotations.

Of course, Sheldon Hackney, the man who presided over this fiasco of injustice, is not just the president of the University of Pennsylvania. He is also the husband of a friend of Hillary Clinton's and was, at the time, the president's nominee to head the National Endowment for the Humanities. That's why, I believe, confidentiality was critical to pushing the case against Jacobowitz. Perhaps the university tried to delay the student's hearing so as not to jeopardize Hackney's confirmation as head of the NEH. (He was confirmed in late July 1993.)

When that strategy failed, and syndicated columnists, *The Wall Street Journal* editorial page, and yours truly began crusading on behalf of Jacobowitz, the case was mysteriously dropped. The official story is that the "water buffalo" in question decided not to pursue the matter further. Why? Because, they said, the media attention would prevent them from having a fair hearing. Imagine that! I'm more than a bit skeptical. The only thing fair about this whole incident was the fact that the light of truth was able to shine on it. I can only speculate that perhaps Sheldon Hackney went to the "water buffalo" and said, "Listen, you can't win this thing. And I want that job at the National Endowment for the Humanities."

But look at all the media attention that was required before common sense prevailed at the university. And what would have happened had the president of the institution not been up for a high-profile government post? Eden Jacobowitz, a very decent young man, probably would have been shafted. And how many more Eden Jacobowitzes are there out there? And how many Sheldon Hackneys?

This was not Hackney's only contribution to the doctrine of political cleansing. While Eden Jacobowitz was being hung out to dry, 14,000 copies of the campus newspaper, the *Daily Pennsylvanian*, were taken and destroyed by a group of black students protesting what they saw as "blatant . . . perpetuation of institutional racism" by the paper and a conservative columnist.

What did Hackney do about it at the time? He issued a namby-pamby, feel-good statement that "two important university values, diversity and open expression, seem to be in conflict." I guess he thought "diversity" was being promoted by virtue of the "open expression" inherent in destroying 14,000 newspapers. And that was the end of it. Mind you, there was no talk about a hate crime. This works only in one direction. Because for the politically correct crowd, hatred of white males and/or conservatives cannot by definition be racist. It is a justifiable emotion based on centuries of discrimination and other evils perpetrated by white males. But, in the past, Hackney has adamantly defended free speech—or at least liberal free speech. When homosexual activists chalked sexually explicit and anti-religious graffiti on a campus sidewalk, Hackney ensured that maintenance workers were forbidden from washing it off in the interest of free expression. He stood up for a campus appearance by the racist Louis Farrakhan, minister, Nation of Islam. And he backed the National Endowment for the Arts in subsidizing sexually explicit and anti-religious artwork with federal taxpayer dollars. This is not a man trying to avoid controversy. This is a man with an ideological axe to grind. According to the Sheldon Hackneys of the world, we all have a right to open expression, but some have less rights than others.

Judith Kleinfeld, a professor at the University of Alaska at Fairbanks, knows what it's like to face the wrath of the political cleansers. She has specialized in teaching Alaska natives for more than twenty years. In September 1991, she told a committee of the Fairbanks Chamber of Commerce that, in the name of equity, the faculty was under pressure to graduate some native students who had not yet mastered the required skills.

Her remarks sparked widespread protests on campus. She was denounced as a racist. Threats were made against her life. The university launched a formal investigation of her. She was not permitted to teach classes in the education department. The federal Office of Civil Rights conducted a four-month probe on the basis of an anonymous complaint about Kleinfeld.

But the good news is that, like Eden Jacobowitz, Judith Kleinfeld refused to be intimidated. In the end, the OCR found that she had made no discriminatory remarks and closed the case. She fought back and she won. We don't hear much about the thousands of political correctness victims who roll over and lose. But their numbers must be legion.

PC is literally the law of the land on many campuses. And its theoreticians and top practitioners are bestowed with the highest honors and endowed with great authority. If, for instance, there was any stigma attached to the politically selective enforcement of speech codes in the universities, the lovely and gracious Donna Shalala could never have been confirmed as Secretary of Health and Human Services. Keep in mind what a powerful position this is. HHS has a budget larger than the budget of all other nations except Germany and Japan. And what was her claim to fame before landing a job overseeing a $590 billion agency?

She was a champion of multiculturalism as chancellor of the University of Wisconsin at Madison. She supported a rigid code limiting "hateful" speech, but it was so repressive that it was even struck down by the courts as a violation of the First Amendment. Some called her "the queen of political correctness"—and those were her admirers.

The Wall Street Journal editorialized recently that "the proliferation of speech codes at America's institutions of higher learning stands as one of the saddest chapters in this country's intellectual history." Such codes should be abolished. A few members of academia have seen the light.

"Offensive speech cannot be suppressed under open-ended standards without letting loose an engine of censorship that cannot be controlled," said former Yale president Benno Schmidt. "Vague and unpredictable possibilities of punishment for expression on campus . . . are antithetical to the idea of the university."

I'll go further. Limiting free speech in this manner is also antithetical to the idea of America. And, unfortunately, political cleansing has seeped out of the hallowed halls of academia and infected numerous other institutions, including, oddly enough, one that should have the very utmost respect for the First Amendment —the media.

One of the most important books written in 1992 (besides, of course, *The Way Things Ought to Be*) was David Brock's *The Real Anita Hill: The Untold Story*. Besides making the bestseller list, it single-handedly destroyed the credibility of Hill's "sexual harassment" allegations against Clarence Thomas.

Despite the book's popularity and its solid, original, well-documented, enterprising reporting, Brock found that many television shows canceled appearances by him, claiming that they couldn't find spokesmen from "the other side." Not surprisingly, few supporters of Anita Hill would dare go on the same show as Brock, so his dates were sometimes canceled.

Can you remember any other author, as a condition to being given a TV forum, being forced to share air time with members of the opposition? Do you ever see liberal authors matched up against conservative critics on TV? I'm so glad that I have my own highly rated radio and TV programs and don't have to subject myself to the filters and biases of the liberal media. However, the few conservative dissenters—like Brock—who break through the liberal media logjam face an amazing gauntlet of hypocrisy and double standards.

The man whom Brock defended with his book, Supreme Court Justice Clarence Thomas, has been particularly eloquent in attacking this country's new intolerant climate of political cleansing. When he spoke at Mercer University in Macon, Georgia, in 1993, he attacked the cultural elite for the "systematic character assassination of those who disagree with the latest ideological fad or accepted social norms." He gave as examples blacks who criticize welfare or women who criticize feminism.

"During the 1980s I watched with shock and dismay how friends of mine were treated for merely disagreeing with the new orthodoxy," he said. "Being the victim now is no more fun than it was twenty to thirty years ago." Clarence Thomas, like Eden Jacobowitz and David Brock, knows what political cleansing is all about.

Sometimes, the efforts by liberals to clamp down on all unpopular ideas and myths are downright ludicrous. One of their latest fads is applying pressure on sports teams to drop the use of Indian names and symbols. I continue to be puzzled over this for the simple reason that having a baseball team called the Braves or a high-school mascot named Redskin neither intends, nor does, harm to anyone. I am diametrically opposed to the politics of Ted Turner and Jane Fonda, but my political disagreements with them don't preclude me from defending their tomahawk chop. These symbols are not grounded in discrimination, abuse, or ill will toward Native Americans.

We have a professional football team called the Minnesota Vikings. In basketball, we have the Boston Celtics. No ethnic groups are offended by the use of these names and symbols and stereotypes. You don't hear steelworkers in Pittsburgh, or cowboys in Dallas, complaining about football teams being named after them.

Of course, many Native Americans sincerely want others to be respectful of their heritage. But does anyone truly believe these names were born of prejudice or racism? Does anyone really think that if the Atlanta Braves change their name it would in any way, shape, or form improve the lot of American Indians? It would not make one bit of difference. Once again, liberals are getting hung up on symbolism rather than substance. And they seek to censor certain forms of expression in the name of diversity and tolerance.

What makes liberals so intolerant of opposition? Why are liberals so reluctant to engage in open dialogue and debate? Why do they so often resort to *ad hominem* attacks and name-calling? Because they are unable to win the arguments on the merits. Demonizing and discrediting the reputations and backgrounds of their opponents is about the only ammunition remaining in their arsenal.

It was leftist Theodor Adorno, back in 1950 in his *The Authoritarian Personality*, who theorized that conservative characteristics—respect for authority, religious faith, and traditional values, to name a few—lend themselves to fascism. Well, I submit to you that if there's any fascism going on here, it's at the hands of the liberal compassion-fascists. Adorno's work provides the intellectual foundation for the kind of mean-spirited, unjustified labeling that is so prevalent in liberal circles today. This kind of intolerance, which is so typical of the left's political cleansing, is why we can't afford to ignore unfounded accusations of racism and bigotry, even when they're whispered by the president of the United States as part of a feeble joke. And that's something I will deal with in the next chapter.

19

CONSERVATISM AND RACE

IT'S ONE THING TO BE CALLED A TRAITOR BY THE PRESIDENT'S HALF-witted half-brother, as Roger Clinton referred to me in a recent magazine interview. (Why did he call me a traitor? Well, harrumph harrumph, because I *disagree* with the president, that's why!) It's another thing to be labeled a racist by the president himself.

To set the stage for what happened on that inauspicious evening in the spring of 1993, let me remind you of what prompted it. On my television show, I showed a two-minute video clip of Representative John Conyers (D-Michigan) grilling Attorney General Janet Reno over her decision to storm the Branch Davidian compound in Waco, Texas.

I thought the segment was interesting because there was a liberal Democrat taking on another liberal Democrat. Conyers was inexcusably rude, and Reno handled herself extremely well in a stressful situation. Never once, needless to say, did I make any reference to the fact that Representative Conyers is black or that Janet Reno is white. The man's race never even occurred to me. To me, this was an irrelevancy, to say the least.

"Put this woman in charge of the Bosnian operation now!" was my comment coming out of the clip. The point was that she was tough, decisive, and unflappable—characteristics wanting in some of the senior male staff members of the administration. Well, I guess I should have known better than to say something positive about a White House appointee. What happened next persuaded me that I would never make that mistake again.

The scene was the annual White House Correspondents' Dinner in Washington in the spring of 1993. The president customarily makes some remarks after the night's entertainment, which was provided that evening (in rather questionable taste, I might add) by comedienne Elayne Boosler.

". . . I've even been called fat by Rush Limbaugh," President Clinton began. (I have not called the president fat. What I said was that the reason the White House was having trouble raising private contributions to build the president's jogging track was that investors desire results, and though the president has been jogging for years, not many see any solid results. I also suggested that a fast-food "jog-through" be built along the jogging track since the president stops for such replenishment quite often. The sign above the jog-through should read BILLIONS AND BILLIONS OF WHOPPERS TOLD HERE.) After moderate laughter subsided, the president then asked, "Did you like the way Rush took up for Janet Reno the other night on his program? He only did it because she was attacked by a black guy." After a dissonant audience reaction, which I was present to witness, the president sheepishly trailed off, almost as if he regretted his utterance before it fully escaped his lips.

As I exited the ballroom at the end of the evening, several people approached me and asked why I thought the president had made the remark. Chris Matthews, Washington bureau chief of the San Francisco Examiner, even suggested I hold a press conference in front of as many as attended the dinner and demand a presidential apology. David Gergen, who at the time had not begun work in the Clinton administration, seemed perplexed and allowed that it was definitely a gaffe on the president's part.

For some time, one of the easiest and most effective ways to stigmatize someone—especially a conservative—has been to label the person a racist. Some suggested that Clinton might have been trying to smear me by "whispering" this accusation. If so, Clinton blew it. The joke sputtered, backfired, and missed the mark by an Arkansas country mile. The president was the one left there with egg on his face.

Why? Because, as I've said, for humor to work, it must be based in truth. Clinton's joke failed that test. I do not have a racist bone in my body. I despise racism. Racism has nothing to do with me. And to further exacerbate Clinton's predicament, it was clear that it was he who was noticing the color of people's skin.

Even the Inside-the-Beltway journalists present groaned (some even hissed) at the punch line. But, amazingly, even though it was all everyone was buzzing about at the dinner, the press failed to report anything about it the next day.

Remember the moral outrage that the press exhibited when Oliver North and others supposedly told some racist or homophobic jokes at a Republican dinner? I advised Ollie then that there is a double standard in the media that will permit that sort of thing by liberals, but not by conservatives. The fact that nobody publicly objected to Clinton's "joke" is a prime example of that. After all, this remark was insulting not only to me, but also to a fellow Democrat in Congress. Imagine what would have happened had I been speaking that night and made a similar comment. My statement would have been trumpeted as incredibly rude and disrespectful, and I would have been called to defend myself on every morning talk show. No one pressured the president to explain himself—at first. Only after I made an issue of the joke on my radio and TV shows the following Monday did the press—specifically *USA Today*—report it.

Following the *USA Today* front-page story, Dee Dee Myers, Clinton's press secretary, did issue this statement about the incident: "I think it was meant to be taken in good faith, certainly not intended to offend anyone." I'm still trying to figure out what "good faith" has to do with this. (Maybe I need to send Dee Dee an autographed copy of this book so she can read my chapter on how words mean things.)

But I didn't wait for an apology. I issued my own to the president: "Mr. President, I sincerely apologize to you, sir, for failing to realize that coming to the defense of a white Cabinet member of your administration would automatically qualify me as a racist. But given the way people such as you and your staff think about race relations in this country today, defending a white person in an argument with a black person automatically qualifies one as a racist. And so I plead guilty.

"And I promise, Mr. President, from this day forward, to never objectively examine the work of your Cabinet members and assess my honest opinion thus. I will automatically conclude that whenever they're involved in a confrontation with a black person they are wrong, simply because their adversary is black. So the days of defending your administration, when deserved, are over on this show. Thank you for teaching me a valuable lesson."

I was later criticized by *Chicago Tribune* columnist Clarence Page and others for not being able to take what I "routinely" dish out. I am perfectly capable of taking a joke, but this was not a joke. It is true that I often poke fun at political figures and vehemently criticize their policies. But Bill Clinton's attempted joke at my expense seemed to me to be a disguised effort on his part to plant an insidious seed that would begin to bear fruit; to suggest subtly that I was a racist in the hopes that it would eventually undermine my credibility as his most effective critic. The president wanted the label to stick. It was a cheap shot and it was malicious. But let's assume for the sake of argument that I'm being hypersensitive and misreading the president's "innocuous" intentions. I still could not afford to let such a statement by the president of the United States go unchallenged. In this case, silence would have been interpreted as acquiescence. I could not and will not ever stand silent in the face of a charge of racism, even when it is cloaked in jocularity. There is simply nothing funny about racism.

The president, as a Democrat and a liberal, is not alone in this. Even members of the press seem to be getting somewhat lazy and hysterical in their characterizations. For instance, Anna Quindlen, of *The New York Times*, writes: "If Rush Limbaugh had been on the air in 1863, how many listeners would have called in to applaud the Emancipation Proclamation?" In other words, you people and I would have been opposed to freeing the slaves. I would like to remind Ms. Quindlen and her liberal friends that it was a Republican, Abraham Lincoln, who authored the Emancipation Proclamation. And, as a matter of fact, had my show been on the air in 1863, there is no doubt in my mind that the overwhelming majority of my listeners would have agreed with me that slavery was an abomination and had to go. Her statement, insofar as it implies a racist bent to conservatives and conservatism (because notice that her indictment is primarily of my audience, rather than me), is utterly indefensible. It is tantamount to charging us all with racism—and not just some marginal racism, but extreme racism. It just doesn't get much more extreme than slavery. But you won't hear any criticism by the dominant media culture of Ms. Quindlen for her indiscretion because there is a blatant double standard that exempts liberals from scrutiny and accountability for such unfounded, categorical insults.

Ms. Quindlen, like most liberals, completely underestimates the American people. A program like mine could not have sustained such enormous growth and popularity for so long if I were a racist or a bigot. My audience consists largely of mainstream Americans who do not endorse, support, or want to listen to bigotry, racism, or fascism on the air. Oh, there may be a few hosts and programs with these characteristics scattered about, but they are few and inconsequential. A program based on those types of beliefs will not grow, prosper, and dominate the way mine has. Some liberals may prefer to think otherwise, but that is just further evidence of their arrogance and obliviousness to the nature and character of mainstream Americans.

It must be stated that all too often conservatives are considered racists, or at least less sympathetic to minorities than are liberals. In my opinion, this phenomenon is purely related to the conservatives' strong commitment to free enterprise and their concern with the expansion of government and the welfare state. Liberals and the Democratic Party long have been perceived to be the political allies of blacks and other minorities because they advocate massive wealth-redistribution programs. Conservatives have opposed affirmative action and quotas while liberals have generally supported them. Conservatives have been proponents, however, of civil rights (though they are often not given credit for this), but they draw the line with respect to affirmative action and quotas. For these reasons, not to mention their own racially charged propaganda, liberals have successfully convinced the overwhelming majority of blacks that they and the Democratic Party are their only homes.

Conservatives have always believed that blacks and other minorities would be better served in the long run by programs that foster independence, rather than those that foster dependency on government. As so many responsible black commentators have noted of late, "We are no longer living in the sixties. This is the nineties. We need to quit blaming other people and look to ourselves for self-improvement." That's right. Though we have not eradicated racism in this country, conservatives believe that the blacks' best avenue to success is through self-reliance. As long as the left and certain members of the black leadership continue to exploit blacks by encouraging them to dwell on the past instead of looking forward, it will be difficult for blacks to make significant further progress in this society.

Somehow, the vision that Dr. Martin Luther King, Jr., had for a color-blind society has been perverted by modern liberalism. It is axiomatic for liberals today that blacks can be represented only by black elected officials. This logic has so distorted the original intent of laws such as the Civil Rights Act that we are gerrymandering congressional districts to guarantee that blacks are elected.

It has been my great pleasure to get to know Dr. Thomas Sowell, the brilliant economist, author, and syndicated columnist. As a conservative black man, he says that the best thing that ever happened to him was being born in the 1930s so that he could become an adult before the unfolding of the civil-rights movement of the 1960s. As a result he has focused on individual achievement rather than becoming preoccupied and distracted by the defeatist victimization game and the kind of "Get-even-ism" the modern civil-rights movement so enjoys.

Another person from whom we can all learn, despite his controversial nature, is Phoenix Suns star Charles Barkley. There may be no harder-working man in all of professional sports. Here's a guy who is not gifted with great height or speed, but, because of his great work ethic, ebullient spirit, and relentless pursuit of excellence, he has become one of the true superstars of the National Basketball Association. He did it without the help of the civil-rights leadership. He didn't need any affirmative-action program. He was motivated by his singular drive to set himself apart and to excel.

Do you realize there are kids today who are ridiculed in school for high achievement? In some quarters it is simply not fashionable to succeed on your own merit and hard work. Some black people are still called "Uncle Toms" today for trying to make it in the system. Let me tell you, my friends: It's not conservatives who are afraid of what happens when blacks become entrepreneurs and successful businesspeople. It's not conservatives who label middle-class black achievers "Uncle Toms." We rejoice at every success of blacks, and there are far more than you might think.

Too many people who are living in desperate poverty today have been conditioned to depend on someone else for their prosperity. These people have not been trained to access the opportunities that still exist in America, but are instead depending on their leaders to do everything for them.

Conservatives believe that the great majority of people are capable. We have more faith in the individual human spirit than liberals do. Liberals provide excuses for people to fail, which is shameful, because America is not about failure and misery and mediocrity. There's room for everyone to make it here. One man's success is not another's failure. The American Dream still works. I know, because I've lived it. I am not a theoretician. I use my own life as an example. I'm nothing special. I practiced certain kinds of values. I worked hard. The worst thing you can do is believe that the deck is stacked against you and that success based on your own efforts is impossible.

Unfortunately, I believe that is largely the message being sent out by the civil-rights establishment. Too many young black people are getting the idea that they are going to get shafted, no matter what. The liberal establishment instills in blacks the idea that they are up against insurmountable odds.

I agree with Professor Walter Williams of George Mason University, who says: "We have things ass-backward in America. We lionize thieves and criminals as victims of society, while at the same time vilifying productivity embodied in the likes of Bill Gates [Microsoft Corporation chairman] and Henry Ford as the rich! We constantly hear calls to 'those who've been most blessed to give something back'—that's nonsense! It is the thief who should be giving something back because he's produced nothing, whereas Bill Gates and his ilk have already served their fellowman by making life easier for us all and providing jobs in the process!"

Professor Williams has long understood this concept. Now, even some liberals seem to be catching on. For a long time now I have criticized the Rev. Jesse Jackson for celebrating victimhood rather than championing excellence and personal responsibility. But in 1993 a new Jackson emerged—or maybe it was the old Jackson whom many of us had forgotten.

During the 1960s and 1970s, Jackson had a great message for young people. He emphasized self-esteem, hard work, pride in oneself, and self-reliance. But something happened to that message in the 1980s. Jackson retreated from his "up with hope, down with dope" theme, as he became a predictable ultra-liberal who mortgaged his soul to the Democratic Party.

The onetime pro-life clergyman became an outspoken advocate of abortion on demand. The message of self-reliance was drowned out by demands for more welfare and other government-dependency programs. Preaching personal responsibility took a backseat to extortionist demands of government and corporations.

In 1992, however, presidential candidate Bill Clinton made a calculated decision that he didn't need or want Jackson on his side. This was best illustrated when Clinton publicly rebuked rapper Sister Souljah at a speech to members of the National Rainbow Coalition. Clinton abandoned Jackson in an attempt to woo Southern white conservatives who had long ago defected from the Democratic Party.

With Clinton in power, Jackson faded from view. He made some futile efforts to capitalize on issues like the HIV-infected Haitian immigrants and statehood for the District of Columbia. But it was more difficult than ever for Jackson to regain popularity. Jackson also saw others eclipsing him within the black movement.

In 1993, Jackson found it was getting difficult to compete in this unfamiliar environment. Thus, he is giving signs—fleeting though they may be—of returning to his roots. This speech by Jackson in June 1993 didn't get much media attention (except for the Rush Limbaugh radio and television shows), yet it is a marked departure for him. He not only sounds like the old Jesse Jackson, he sounds like me! He's talking about the same conservative principles and values that I am always discussing—personal responsibility, self-reliance, pride, and true self-esteem based on achievement.

In his address, he compares the plight of black people today to what they faced thirty years ago:

> Can I get a word in this? When we went to church on Sunday morning, they didn't have to lock the church, nobody was there stealing no organ in no church. That's when we were in slavery! Now we've gotten free and foolish! And then everybody went around [saying], "What's wrong with those Negroes? What's wrong with those Hispanics? What's wrong?"
>
> I know what's wrong. We've gotten to Canaan, and we're free and foolish. Man, we've lost our . . . we know better. We know that you ought to raise the babies you make, we know better! You know you have to go to school, you know better! You know you ought to make your neighborhood safe, you know better! You know you shouldn't throw paper down on your street and walk away from it, you know better. You shouldn't curse in front of children, you know better! You shouldn't rape anybody, you know better! We know better!
>
> Thirty years ago we prayed to God . . . we prayed to God to be protected by law. . . . And here we are, thirty years later, no Bull Connor to stop us now, no George Wallace to stop us now. Thirty years later, no trenches being bombed, thirty years later, no Klan threatening us. We lost more lives through dope than we ever lost to the rope!
>
> Thirty years later, we're not threatened by someone wearing a white sheet and a hood. We're threatened by a brother, who is a hood living in the hood.

What's this? Has Jesse Jackson, too, become a ditto-head? Is this a case of another liberal icon realizing that I have been right all along? See, Reverend Jackson, I told you so. I sincerely hope this is a message you continue to preach. It is very valuable for all of us—no matter what race, color, or creed—to hear it over and over again.

Dr. Tom Sowell says much the same thing in a simpler way: "In many ways, blacks were more successful in overcoming the opposition of racists than in overcoming the effects of those who thought they were helping. Perhaps the most dangerous 'favor' done to blacks has been the making of excuses for all their problems. All human beings are so imperfect, no matter what color wrapping they come in, that to exempt any group from standards of performance and behavior is not a blessing but a curse." I can only add, Amen!

We all need to hear the message of personal responsibility, self-reliance, and honesty that you once preached, Reverend Jackson. This is a message for all Americans. Becoming the best we can be is the challenge. Let's stop exaggerating about the roadblocks to success in this country and start inculcating our citizens with confidence and the tools to succeed.

Liberals need to stop preaching class and racial hatred. They need to quit promoting the politics of hatred and alienation. We are all, first and foremost, Americans. We want to remove artificial barriers to anyone's improvement, many of which reside in the politics of class envy and government dependency. In this melting pot, all Americans can achieve if we can just overcome this nagging obsession with skin colors and religious denominations and be mindful of the truism that all human beings are equal in the eyes of God.

20

AMERICA IS STILL
WORTH FIGHTING FOR

SHORTLY AFTER THE 1992 ELECTION, AND BEFORE THE SWEARING-IN OF the Clinton regime, there was a poignant gathering of Republican big shots in Washington. The highlight of the evening, in which George Bush and Robert Dole were joined by many other senior party leaders, came when Bush and Dole made touching remarks about each other. Both men were actually moved to tears during the speeches.

I was fascinated not only by Dole's watery eyes, but by his words as well. He offered sentiments and tributes that were deeply rooted in love and respect for his old friend. Dole thanked Bush for the great service he had provided to his country. He cried when he talked about the enormous sacrifices that Bush had made. And after Dole was finished, Bush went to the microphone and reciprocated. He related that he had grave reservations about attending the event that evening. Why? Because, after all, he had been defeated in his bid for a second term as president. The election was over. He had lost. What was the point? But, he added, choking back the emotions, "I'm so happy I've come. It's one of the best nights of my life to come here and to be with Bob Dole and to hear these things."

What was interesting about this scene was the fact that these men had often been fractious rivals throughout their political careers. As members of Congress, as part of the Washington governing class, and as presidential candidates, George Bush and Bob Dole had competed fiercely with each other.

Throughout much of their public lives, Bush often seemed to have a leg up on Dole. First, there were skirmishes in Congress. Then it was Dole who was selected to run for vice-president on the ill-fated Gerald Ford 1976 Republican ticket. It was Bush, however, who was fortunate enough to be picked by Ronald Reagan in 1980. And later still, it was Bush who narrowly defeated Dole in the New Hampshire primary in 1988, when it looked as if Dole had a lock on it.

But on that night dedicated to honoring George Bush as he entered political retirement, all of the personal ambitions and competitiveness were behind them. You could clearly see that the lifetime rivalry had been built upon a foundation of mutual veneration and respect. Whatever jealousies and envy that once might have existed between them were long gone.

Why? Think about it. These guys—like all Americans of their generation—were defined by the intense life experiences they shared growing up in the late 1930s and early 1940s. Their formative years came during the Great Depression. So they understood firsthand the nature of a true economic malaise for this nation. Then came the trauma of World War II. Talk about the world being turned upside down! The World War II generation understands the reality of that expression.

George Bush entered the service as a member of a well-to-do Northeastern family. He served as the U.S. Navy's youngest flier, was shot out of the sky, and rescued. He was duly treated with the respect accorded a great war hero. Bob Dole also fought in World War II. But he came from less glamorous stock in Russell, Kansas. He was wounded severely in combat. He spent years recovering. His right arm is still practically useless as a result of his war injury, yet the term "war hero" is seldom associated with Bob Dole.

World War II had to be the defining experience in the lives of both Bush and Dole. It created an unbreakable bond between them, and among all other members of their generation. On that special, emotional evening, you can well imagine that they were beginning to come to grips with the fact that a new generation—one that didn't even begin to appreciate the kind of sacrifices they had made—was about to take over the reins of power and begin a new era of American leadership.

At this reflective testimonial, both Dole and Bush seemed to recognize that the torch was being passed. The tears shed that night, I am convinced, were not only the result of the realization that they had reached personal career twilights. Their generation— the one that had lived through, sacrificed in the cause against, and defeated the two great totalitarian threats of Nazism and communism—was letting go. Their day had come.

As it turns out, Dole has been renewed and rejuvenated by political events since the election of 1992. In some ways, he has never been better. Whatever he is eating and drinking, he should keep it up. It's amazing how vigorous and vital he is. Nevertheless, the people in charge at the White House represent a new generation —one that was shaped more by the values of the late 1960s than by the lessons of World War II and the Cold War.

That's why I think these two men were so moved that night. They were not shedding crocodile tears, my friends. This was not the kind of disingenuous emotionalism that you see emanating occasionally from the current occupant of the White House. These were honest, sincere, heartfelt tears. It wasn't simply the end of President Bush's illustrious political career (and what people assumed to be the end of Dole's). It was much more than that.

Not only had Bush and Dole and so many other young men of their generation risked their own lives, but they had faced down two nations that were literally attempting to put an end to the United States of America. Then, for more than forty years after that life-shaping experience, they engaged in another titanic battle—the Cold War that eventually resulted in the demise of the Soviet Union and the triumph of capitalism and freedom over communism.

What linked these two Republican leaders more than anything else was their experience in World War II—their shared sacrifice. That's real shared sacrifice; not the clichéd version that Clinton proposes as an anesthetic to the pain he intends to inflict on us with his arsenal of taxation weapons. Bush and Dole fought for something larger than themselves. They, and their peers, had to grow up and face awful truths, truths that carried devastating consequences and required profound character and responsibility early in their lives—when they were just seventeen- or eighteen-year-olds.

The characteristic that, more than anything else, distinguishes this new generation from the previous one is what I call the "crybaby effect." Many of the young leaders, typified by the cast of characters now running the White House, would like you to believe that things have never been worse in this country. They spend most of their time whining that ours is a nation in a perpetual apocalyptic crisis caused by our way of life! We are, in essence, a deteriorating nation whose decline will continue unless you and I confess our inferiority and culpability and cede control of our destiny to those in government who are wiser than we are. Frankly, they're nothing but a bunch of crybabies who have no idea how easy they have it compared to their parents and grandparents. The promises and dreams of America remain intact and have expanded for those who work to realize them. This should be the message of responsible, mature leaders, not the doom-and-gloom, pain-and-misery scenario that we hear articulated daily by the embarrassing group of mugwumps who run things at present, and who, if America is indeed threatened, must be considered the real culprits.

So why are these doomsday myths perpetuated? What causes this character flaw so typical of the baby-boom generation? Why have we become a nation of whiners? Clearly, one of the problems with some in my generation is that we never experienced the kind of threat the World War II generation faced. We were never required to make the kind of sacrifices that the World War II generation was asked to make. Things came too easy for us. To put it bluntly, many of the baby-boom generation are spoiled brats.

Does anyone really doubt my assertion that the problems we face today pale in comparison with the hurdles the World War II generation faced? In the late 1930s, America was looking at a 22 percent unemployment rate. There was no such concept as welfare. There was no minimum-wage guarantee. There was no "safety net," except for the one that family members provided. Grown men were selling apples on the street for a few pennies in an effort to support their families. People would accept any kind of work available.

The Great Depression—now, there was a *real* crisis. The kinds of economic setbacks we have experienced in recent years should not even be mentioned in the same breath as the hard times our parents and grandparents endured. Then, before the Depression had really even subsided, came World War II. Our nation was attacked by a foreign power for the first time since 1812. The American way of life—our very existence—was threatened by ruthless totalitarians in Japan and Germany.

Every able-bodied man was needed for military service. We were fighting in two major theaters—Europe and Asia. Casualties were very high in both. Fathers, sons, and husbands were being lost in untold numbers. Women were forced into primary roles in business and industry. Americans united and gave of themselves to save not only their country, but Europe as well. Young men lied about their age, ignored medical and physical disqualifications, and abandoned their livelihoods in order to join the services. They knew the library of their freedom was the United States of America. And they gave everything for it, including massive amounts of tax dollars to then wage and win the Cold War against the most murderous and threatening form of government in the history of civilization: communism.

And for what? Bill and Hillary Clinton, anti-war activists and America apologists extraordinaire, in the White House? Mikhail Gorbachev with his own "think tank" on the beautiful grounds of the Presidio army base in San Francisco? The United States military turned into a lab of social experimentation? The brave and courageous of the New Age shouting from the protest march that America is to blame for the troubles of the world and whose solutions include restructuring the American culture and dream to conform to the lowest common denominators among us?

Nothing was handed to the people of the World War II generation. They had to work hard and sacrifice for every opportunity, and in so doing they secured a life of relative ease and plenty for their descendants. So many people today have so much free time on their hands that all they can do is complain about their unhappiness.

The World War II generation doesn't get nearly enough credit for the way it rose to challenges, overcame obstacles, and contributed mightily to the advancement of mankind. I think it's time to renew our appreciation for this heroic generation. The time has come to incorporate the values and ideals that shaped those who gave us such a fine head start on our lives.

We can already witness the dangers that inhere in taking our liberties for granted. We seem to assume that because we have always been free, we always will be. As such, we forget the indispensable role of our military in preserving our freedoms. For America, this is nothing new. We have a history of letting our guard down.

Dick Cheney, George Bush's brilliant Secretary of Defense, warns that America has a history of becoming militarily complacent following each war in which it has engaged. He says that this attitude leading to the downscaling of our defense readiness stands as an invitation for potential foreign aggressors, such as Muammar Khaddafi and Saddam Hussein, to test our will. He reminds us of the infamous Carter years, when the military was emasculated to an unprecedented degree, culminating in an aborted hostage-rescue attempt with the malfunctioning of our helicopters in the Iranian desert. Cheney says that with the end of the Cold War and the pressures to cut spending because of the enormity of the federal debt, we are downsizing our military to an alarming level. He says that as a nation we have always paid a price for such irresponsible, unilateral disarmament.

As Cheney understands, the world, even without the Soviet empire, remains very unstable, volatile, and violent. We have a responsibility never to lose sight of that fact. But we are frightfully close today to having lost sight of it as the Democrats continue to hack away at one of the most legitimate functions of government: providing for the national defense. We are repeating our historical mistakes, not just with Clinton's economic policy, but with his military one as well—and as to the latter, no one even seems to notice.

But our problems don't end there. In addition to downsizing our military, we seem also, under the Clinton administration, to be rudderless in matters of foreign policy. Regardless of whether we are currently the world's only superpower, we cannot be without a coherent foreign policy that will define our relations with other nations and enable us to determine when, and under what circumstances, we should deploy our military.

How long is it going to take before some people learn you don't prevent or win wars with words, caring, and concern? We must maintain our military strength and preparedness as our best insurance against having to use force often in the future. The left, as you might expect, sees it differently. It actually seems to think you can achieve peace by talking tough while gutting your military.

I'm afraid that Mr. Clinton's strong suit is not foreign policy. Up to this point it appears that his foreign-policy credo is: Walk tall, speak loudly, and carry a little stick. He talked tough during the campaign, but after taking office, when it was time to follow through on his words, it became clear that his tough talk was little more than fiery campaign rhetoric. Ultimately, we huffed, and we puffed, and we stayed home. After all of the Clinton administration's threats, warnings, and gnashing of teeth, Secretary of State Warren Christopher (former foreign-policy guru to Jimmy Carter) announced that Bosnia was none of America's business and that the situation should be sorted out by the Bosnians. Christopher suddenly discovered what everyone else had known all along—that there was a "real" civil war going on, with Bosnian Serbs, Muslims, and Croats all committing atrocities.

Many people—including myself—breathed a sigh of relief when Clinton came to this decision (though don't count on this being the final word with this guy). It seemed to be the most reasonable course of action. But it's pure luck that the Clinton administration stumbled into this conclusion. It bore no resemblance to the administration's previous rhetoric.

It would have been more reassuring if Clinton had come to the conclusion that because we have no vital national interest at stake in Bosnia, such as we did in the Persian Gulf, there is no justification for risking American lives in a Vietnam-scale quagmire. Reasonable minds may disagree on whether, in fact, we do have a national interest at stake. In fact, foreign-policy experts Henry Kissinger and Jeane Kirkpatrick respectfully disagree on this point. But doubtless they agree on the proper criteria for deciding whether the U.S. should intervene militarily. First and foremost is the threshold issue of whether our national interest is involved. Mr. Clinton, paralyzed in the muck of his own inconsistent rhetoric, and again not realizing that words mean things, doesn't ever get to the point of engaging in such analysis. But what should we expect from a man who, in the past, at least, loathed the military—and whom we didn't require to reveal his foreign-policy philosophies during the campaign? What should we expect from a man who campaigned on the theme that President Bush had spent too much time on foreign affairs to the detriment of the economy? The sad truth is that our commander-in-chief has no sophistication in foreign affairs, and he has no cohesive principles to guide him.

To help us put into perspective the consequences of having a commander-in-chief who is well grounded in foreign policy, let's refresh our memories about how George Bush conducted himself in preparation for the war in the Persian Gulf. He identified the problem. He identified the solution. And he deliberately and coolly proceeded to implement his plan.

Yes, we had a clear objective: to drive Iraqi forces out of Kuwait and neutralize the war-making aggression of Saddam Hussein. Military commanders presented to the president a strategy that could be analyzed and successfully implemented, which permitted victory to be clearly defined, and thus a definite conclusion to the mission could be achieved, which would allow us to exit the region. The Persian Gulf war was thus won quickly and decisively, validating the U.S. military and its purpose. Liberals abhor the use of force, particularly when it is successful, for success confirms and advances the nobility of our military.

Military action in Bosnia, eagerly advocated by the left, presented nothing but a dead end. No objective, other than to make supporters feel good for having "done something." No strategy. No clearly defined victory. No culmination. No indication of when troops might leave. In other words, defeat. Yet, liberals couldn't wait to get involved. Why? Well, some suggest that deep in their cynical hearts, liberals rejoice in military failure because failure ensures timidity and reluctance in future considerations of the use of force. Failure also illustrates, in a convoluted sort of way, the inherent flaws that liberals claim exist in the American ideal, and it is these "flaws" that energize and propel their belief that America is iniquitous and villainous and therefore in need of liberal prescriptions.

But the point is that if you make the awesome decision to commit our troops, nothing short of total victory should be considered acceptable. And if you don't know how to define total victory, you have no business getting young Americans killed.

I'm not willing to ignore killing on a mass scale, but at the same time we can't lose sight of reality and allow our emotions to dictate our foreign policy. It takes guts to be a realist about Bosnia because it means making some very hard choices; liberals, though, often take a gutless approach by urging the U.S. to "do something, do anything" to stop the killing. They don't care if victory is possible or if there's a valid objective to be achieved; all they really want to do is make themselves feel better by projecting the appearance that they are trying.

Let's face it. There's a lot of evil in the world. There are a lot of bad guys out there. Americans must accept the fact that there's nothing they can do to rid the whole world of mean people and evil behavior. The U.S. has a big enough job simply watching out for its own national interests.

Now, if there's something we can do to make the world a better place that has a reasonable chance of success and the estimated sacrifice is not prohibitive, that's another story. However, all the good intentions in the world are not worth losing the lives of even one platoon of courageous American soldiers. You can't just send troops willy-nilly across the world without a clear end in sight, and right now real leadership is not being demonstrated. Just look at the way, for instance, American and United Nations forces pussyfooted around with one Somali warlord, General Mohammed Farrah Aidid. This guy was giving television interviews every day, while our forces were unable or unwilling to capture him. This is no way to run a war, or a humanitarian relief operation, for that matter.

But you can be sure that if the liberals got us into a war in Bosnia or anywhere else, it would be just this kind of campaign. The problem with the Bosnia hawks is that, at the first sign of real trouble, they would turn into chicken hawks. I would love to see liberals, who have ridiculed real patriotism over the years, raise the American flag in support of American jets flying over Bosnia or anywhere else. But, by their nature, liberals would celebrate victory after the first air raid because "the U.S. did something." Then they would begin to lose interest, or get distracted by some other crisis. Liberals are falling all over themselves to get us into a genuine civil war in which we have, at best, a debatable national interest. They are now preaching the domino theory—saying that this war could escalate into a worldwide war if we don't intervene. None of the warring factions involved has ever demonstrated any propensity, however, toward global expansionism.

Feast on the irony: These same liberals, or their philosophical predecessors: 1) characterized the Vietnam War as a civil war (when it was one communist nation attempting to consume another by force); 2) denied that the communists were expansion-oriented; 3) swore that there was no such thing as a domino effect; and thus 4) that we had no national interest at stake in Vietnam. These are the same people who are so unspeakably horrified at the atrocities in the former Yugoslavia, yet conspicuously failed to register their horror at the genocide that occurred in Cambodia by the "benevolent" communist regimes in the wake of the U.S. withdrawal; the same people who steadfastly refused assistance to the freedom fighters in Nicaragua. But to understand fully the liberal mind-set, it is essential that you understand that genocide is genocide only if it is perpetrated by a non-communist state.

Consistent with Clinton's aimlessness in foreign policy is his profound underappreciation for the military. Diplomacy is the art of maintaining relations with foreign nations. But in those situations in which diplomacy breaks down or is no longer accomplishing its purpose, the military is this country's chief instrument of last resort.

What have I told you over and over about the role of the military? What, have I explained countless times, is the whole purpose of the armed forces? It is designed to kill people and break things. That's what the military does. It destroys. The best army in the world is the one that kills the most enemy soldiers and razes the most strategic targets. It's that simple. This is important to remember if we want to continue to be a great nation—the world's only superpower.

We have to look at the military as a separate and unique institution with separate and unique requirements. It's different from all other institutions in our society, and our only standard must be excellence—no matter whose feelings get hurt, including heterosexual men who can't meet the physical or mental requirements. Our only concern should be that the military does what it is supposed to do. That way the rest of us can be assured that our freedoms will have the best possible chance of being preserved.

Let's analyze these types of issues from that pragmatic perspective. Would an all-female combat force provide our nation with the best possible defense? Clearly, the answer to that question is no. With an all-female combat force, would there be a need for men? Clearly, yes.

Now, with an all-male combat force, do we have the best fighting machine we can assemble? Clearly, yes. We've proved it time and time again. No one has ever suggested that women are vitally needed on the front line to improve our battlefield performance.

So, if there is no need for women in combat as it relates to our purpose and objective, why are we considering it? Obviously, the answer is, For political reasons. But do we want political considerations to interfere with our military preparedness and objectives? These same questions could be asked about the role of homosexuals in the military. But how can you employ logic against the kinds of arguments liberals make? Take columnist Ellen Goodman, for instance. She says the ban on homosexuals in the military should be lifted "so that straight men will learn what it's like to be sexually ogled." This flippant remark shouldn't be allowed to escape scrutiny. Ms. Goodman, perhaps unwittingly, has revealed (in addition to a toxic case of Get-even-ism) the fundamental misunderstanding that liberals have about the purpose of the military. It is not just another employer whose imposition of social experiments can be harmlessly effected. There will be consequences to a lifting of the ban in the form of harm to the military and thus, arguably, our national security. My logic is not tenuous, nor my analysis farfetched. Ms. Goodman's comment wholly fails to take into consideration, and even mocks, the potential effect that this would have on the military. If you don't want to accept my judgment in this matter, perhaps you should carefully weigh Ms. Goodman's opinion against the opinions of the Joint Chiefs of Staff, with more than 200 years of combined military experience among them.

I think I would prefer to listen to General Norman Schwarzkopf rather than Ellen Goodman. General Schwarzkopf echoed what I have been telling you for years: "The job of the military is to go to war and win, not to be instruments of social experimentation."

General Schwarzkopf says that although homosexuals have no doubt served honorably in the military, in every case he knows about, their units have become divided when others learn of their sexual orientation. *Every* case!

Did anyone notice Les Aspin's report, issued in his first months as defense secretary, that the military is not in a high state of preparedness? Recruitment is down, he complains, and the intelligence level of those enlisting is lower. Gee, I wonder what could be causing that? It must be that we are a bigoted society. It must be that young potential recruits are just a bunch of homophobes in need of re-education. Or, could it have anything to do with the fact that our young people see the U.S. radically cutting back on defense and no longer consider military service a worthy priority? Could it be that the best and the brightest of our young men have no desire to participate in the kinds of social experiments politicians are forcing on the military? Could it be that there is no way to foster esprit de corps when you treat the military like a social laboratory?

Unfortunately, there is a great naïveté throughout our citizenry when it comes to the importance of the military and the sacrifices it has made in the past and will be required to make in the future. For the Memorial Day version of my TV show in 1993, I sent my "man in the street" camera crew out onto the New York City streets to find out what people think of the holiday set aside to honor our war dead.

"It's just a day off from work and going out to the beach, or just maybe a great adventure," said one interviewee.

"The beach—barbecues, the beach, family," answered another.

I was glad to see the smiles on people's faces. They were obviously looking forward to enjoying their holiday. But Memorial

Day is far more than a good beach day or picnic. It's the one day of the year when we, collectively as a nation, remember those special individuals among us who made the ultimate sacrifice—those who gave their lives for their country and its freedom.

We don't need to come up with ways to ridicule and irritate our servicemen, as Ms. Goodman suggests with her inane and contemptuous ogling remark. Instead, we need to do far more to honor all our servicemen and servicewomen—those who have volunteered to serve America in times of peace, standing guard, at the ready, to defend us. The American military is in a class by itself, and no holiday could ever be enough to thank those who have served and are serving their country.

My friends, it would truly be an injustice for us to forget the literal pain and sorrow experienced by our troops. Most of us are so detached, so smug, and so far removed from the battlefields where our fathers fought and that claimed the lives of our honored dead that we cannot begin to empathize with them. Don't ever forget the magnitude and depth of the suffering that these soldiers endured. Don't ever forget the sacrifice of those generations that preceded us so that our country would remain inviolate and so that we could continue to live in freedom. Don't ever forget the World War II generation, nor abandon the cause for which it sacrificed.

21

THE CASE FOR LESS GOVERNMENT

"IT'S NO ACCIDENT THAT CAPITALISM HAS BROUGHT WITH IT PROGRESS, not merely in production but also in knowledge. Egoism and competition are, alas, stronger forces than public spirit and sense of duty. In Russia, they say, it is impossible to get a decent piece of bread. Perhaps I'm overpessimistic concerning state and other forms of communal enterprise, but I expect little good from them. Bureaucracy is the death of any achievement. I've seen and experienced too many dreadful warnings, even in comparatively model Switzerland. I'm inclined to view that the state can only be of use to industry as a limiting and regulative force."

No, folks, those are not my words. But they come from an equally great mind—Albert Einstein. Unlike some dreamers and wishful thinkers, Einstein was quite realistic in pointing out that self-interest and competition are stronger forces than sense of duty to the state. His letter is quite a contrast to the musings of those liberals who think they can achieve great things simply by caring more than anyone else, and that capitalism fosters "destructive" human traits such as competition, which are ruinous to our society. They believe that rugged individualism and self-improvement are evil—

only collectivism is good. It's amazing how anachronistic these liberals are. While they consider themselves the creators of "new ideas," the rest of the world has finally rejected these antiquated socialistic ideas based on their decades of miserable experience with them. To give you a flavor of this liberal mentality, I must "share" with you an excerpt from an article on Russia in *The New York Times Magazine,* July 18, 1993, by Andrew Solomon. The article, entitled "Young Russia's Defiant Decadence," chronicles the present corruption in Russia and implies how much worse off the country is since it discarded communism and became a free state. The concluding paragraph says it all: "The real source of the chaos of the new Russia is not the weakness of the police, the dominance of the mafia, the difficulty of constitutional reform, the undependability of Yeltsin, the spiraling inflation, the naïve policies of Western governments in their distribution of aid, the shortage of food, or the inefficiency of the state-run factories." Now, here's the clincher: "It is the ascendancy, in a society in which everyone was once asked to work for the common good, of a system of values whereby everyone has an eye only on his own progress, a country now run on the chance alignments and misalignments of hundreds of thousands of different, singular, individual agendas."

Could it be that Labor Secretary Robert Reich*hhhh* has begun writing under a pen name? He makes no secret of the fact that he believes that the United States needs to distance itself even further from the ideals of individual achievement and entrepreneurship. "To the extent that we continue to celebrate the traditional myth of the entrepreneurial hero, we will slow the progress of change essential to our economic success," he has written. "We must begin to celebrate collective entrepreneurship. We need to honor our teams more, our aggressive leaders and maverick geniuses less."

This is one of Bill Clinton's closest friends, going back to law school and Rhodes-scholar days in the 1960s. And he is typical of the utopian, social-engineering mind-set that dominates White House policy-making today. These ideas have never worked before, and they won't work for Bill Clinton, either.

For centuries, some people have tried to defy human nature. Jean-Jacques Rousseau, a philosopher whose ideas formed the basis for the French Revolution, believed that man, in his natural state, was good, but that civilization, society, materialism, and the trappings of modernity corrupted him. Karl Marx, too, believed that we could achieve "heaven on Earth," once the corruptive influences of capitalism could be dismantled.

This destructive myth was reconstituted in the revolutionary 1960s—that "if it feels good, do it" decade—and is still poisoning the minds and souls of Americans in the 1990s. Today's sixties-style idealists who are running the White House, as well as many of our most influential cultural institutions, think that a risk-free, problem-free society remains a goal worthy of striving for. Naturally, government is always the vehicle of choice on the road to this elusive utopia.

This futile paradise chase, consequently, enables government to do anything and everything necessary to address all human needs —real or imagined. Thus, the U.S. government's role in human affairs—which was once well defined and strictly limited by our Constitution—now extends to every conceivable facet of life. New "rights" are constantly being established in America today.

Now, let me be careful about what I am about to say. This is not intended as a criticism of government employees, nor is it an indictment of any hard-working, well-intentioned individuals. It is, however, intended as an indictment of the concept that government should continue to expand its scope, authority, and responsibilities into every avenue of our lives. I asked my radio-show audience not too long ago to think about what functions government actually performs well. Which government agencies do a good job? Which ones perform an important service well? There are a few. I don't think private enterprise could, for instance, do a better job of defending our country than the U.S. military services. But, even so, there are countless stories about inefficiency in the Defense Department. How many times have we heard about the $600 screwdriver or the $700 toilet seat?

I don't have any firsthand experience with it, but I am told that the U.S. Patent Office is fairly efficient and performs a function that is proper for government. I have always had a soft spot in my heart for NASA—the National Aeronautics and Space Administration. Back in its heyday in the 1960s, we got more bang for its buck than from anywhere else in terms of efficiency and value. Space exploration was responsible for much technological advancement that made life on this planet easier for all people. I'm not so sure it's true anymore, now that NASA has thrown its lot in with the politically correct crowd on global warming and ozone depletion.

But outside of a handful of departments, it's tough to think of any other government programs that are models of success and efficiency. How many are satisfied with the performance of the government's monopoly in education? And, more to the point, have any of the programs and bureaucracies devised since the 1960s to fight poverty proven successful? Let's face it, when you look at our vast federal system and the hundreds of billions of dollars it consumes, it's hard to find measurable success, but easy to find the harm that it's caused. There just aren't that many agencies that are really indispensable to the nation's security and well-being.

Let's just look at welfare as a case in point. The administrative costs on $1 of welfare in this country is 72 cents. That means if you want to give $1 of welfare to someone, by the time you pay the costs of salaries and other bureaucratic expenses of the welfare system, there is just 28 cents left for the recipient. That is disgracefully inefficient, and the last thing we need is another inefficient government agency.

That's just the practical argument against a growing, more intrusive, more powerful government taking over greater and greater areas of responsibility and consequently encroaching ever more on our personal liberties. But there are constitutional issues to consider as well. Supreme Court Justice Antonin Scalia observed recently that many Americans now believe in "an evolving Constitution" that can be used to remedy all societal wrongs.

"That attitude used to be confined just to law professors and judges," Scalia told a *Washington Post* reporter. "The Constitution is whatever we say it is . . . pass it on," he added, mimicking the attitude of the elitists who, in effect, used their legal arguments on the bench to legislate. Now, Scalia says, the "majority" of Americans see the Constitution that way. "The American people now feel that if there is anything that we feel dearly about, it must be in the Constitution. . . . We will squeeze it in somewhere. My view is that it contains a limited number of guarantees. The meaning does not expand or contract over time. It is not everything in the world. It is very little in the world, as a matter of fact. If you read the Bill of Rights, what does it contain? Certainly not everything that is good and true and beautiful."

Boy, if there was another brain I could use besides mine (and maybe Einstein's), it would be Scalia's.

The trouble with reading more rights into the Constitution is that jurists deprive the people of public debate. In addition, Scalia says, if you can read in rights, you can read them out as well. This, of course, is what we see happening today with the Second Amendment guarantee of the right to bear arms.

He is pointing out that the framers of our Constitution envisioned a very limited role for the federal government. Today, the utopians have distorted that vision and are expanding the bounds of the federal bureaucracy in the hopes of addressing every problem under the sun. Not only is this a perversion of the Constitution, it simply doesn't work.

It is utopian, and therefore unrealistic, to expect that every citizen will eat equally every day of the year. It is utopian to expect that every citizen will be provided the exact health care that citizens want every day of the year. It is utopian to believe that suffering of any kind can be eliminated through government intervention and action. As I have told you, there will always be poor people, however earnestly we try to eradicate poverty.

Certainly, it's honorable to attempt to reduce hunger, suffering, and poverty. But it is not realistic to expect that every citizen can be provided the same amounts of good food, comfortable housing, and fine health care. That is what communism and socialism tried to accomplish. Instead of producing utopia, instead of narrowing the gap between the haves and have-nots, the bourgeoisie and proletariat, they created a more rigid class structure. The ruling class arrogates all the power and riches to itself, while the rest of the people remain servants of the state. Just look around the world. Examine the societies that have attempted to make life more prosperous for people by relying on centralized authorities. You won't find much prosperity, and you won't find anything remotely resembling an equitable distribution of resources.

Equality of outcome or result is impossible because no two individuals are alike. We all have different abilities, talents, desires, ambitions, capabilities, and other characteristics. There is no way these differences can be equalized—even by force. Today, in the name of fairness and equality, the U.S. government is coercing greater and greater amounts of wealth transfers and redistribution. The utopians believe it is unfair that some have so much and others have so little. They see themselves as glorified Robin Hoods.

Once again, it doesn't work. If you penalize achievement and punish success, there is less wealth produced for everyone. This is the fatal flaw of utopianism. Also, the value to someone of something that is given to him is always less than the value of something he earned with his own blood, sweat, and tears. This is the lesson that countless socialist governments have learned in just the last five years. Why aren't we learning it here in the United States?

First, let's get one thing straight. I have often characterized President Clinton's economic rhetoric and programs as socialistic. I do not use that word lightly. I'll admit that America's gravitation toward socialism has been long-term and precedes the arrival of Bill and Hillary in the White House. Economist Milton Friedman recently observed that "in 1950, total government spending, federal, state, and local, amounted to less than 30 percent of national income; in 1992, to nearly 45. In addition, government-mandated expenditures by individuals and businesses have multiplied manifold. . . . The U.S. is today more than half socialist, compared to perhaps a third in 1950." And consider this: According to the Institute for Policy Innovation in Louisville, Texas, there are now more people working in government in America (19.2 million) than in the U.S. manufacturing industry (18.1 million).

Though Clinton didn't start the big-government bandwagon rolling, he obviously intends to accelerate it into hyper-speed. As I've pointed out, almost every program he proposes is based on the premise that government, rather than the individual, holds the solutions to society's problems. But it goes beyond that. According to the Clinton-Reich*hhhh* mentality, government mustn't just reactively solve problems. It must pro-actively manage society's productive and distributive resources to achieve the goals of the government, rather than of the individual.

Despite the compassionate rhetoric of the liberals, the reality is that they never really get around to fixing problems. Even when they have absolute control of every key policy-making institution in government, they find excuses for why nothing is working. For instance, according to Representative Pat Schroeder, the whole world is just in a grumpy mood, which explains why her party can't govern the United States.

"I wonder if the world is governable in any country," she says. "I haven't spoken to any leader in any country who's having fun." Trying to make decisions today is "like nailing Jell-O to the wall. We're like a planet with an attitude. Everyone's surly." Therefore, of course, we should give Clinton a break. "You can't fault [him] for not having an absolute road map to the future." Gee, I sure didn't hear this talk from her or any other Democrats a year earlier. I wonder what momentous events transpired in that time.

So, as long as liberals are in power, we can expect them to do what liberals do best—perform symbolic acts that make them feel better. Hardly anything substantive, however, is ever really accomplished, other than confiscating and spending more of our earnings. Let me give you an example. During the presidential campaign, Bill Clinton said he would raise the minimum wage when he was elected. Again, just a few days after Clinton was inaugurated, Robert Reich*hhhh* announced that hiking the minimum wage was a "very important" goal of the new administration. Why? Because, the liberals said, it is disgraceful that any American family might be forced to live on $170 a week, which is the full-time salary of someone working forty hours at the current minimum wage of $4.25.

Ladies and gentlemen, there are so many misconceptions and falsehoods attached to this policy goal that I scarcely know where to start dissecting it. But I shall, because this is important. Let's do this by shattering four myths about the minimum wage.

Myth No. 1: *The minimum wage helps poor people.*

Every credible study that has ever been conducted on the impact of the minimum wage shows that each and every time it is increased, a certain percentage of jobs is bound to be eliminated. A 1988 Congressional Budget Office study, for instance, projected that a proposed increase at that time would result in the loss of 500,000 jobs. Now, if your goal is to help the poor, why would you want to eliminate some of their jobs? Some studies, like one conducted by the Public Service Research Council in 1987, show that increasing the minimum wage actually increases poverty. But as long as the poor don't realize that it is bad for them, Clinton and Reich*hhhhh*, in the interest of appearing compassionate, rather than actually helping the poor, will go on advocating increases in the wage.

Myth No. 2: *Many heads of households are subsisting on minimum-wage salaries.*

Minimum-wage jobs are entry-level positions, most often filled by teenagers. More than 50 percent are between sixteen and twenty-four years old. Most of those jobs, 63 percent, are part-time. By eliminating even a percentage of these positions, we are cutting out the only way inexperienced young people can get their foot in the door of the job market. About 80 percent of minimum-wage employees live in non-poor households. About 20 percent come from households with annual incomes of more than $50,000.

Myth No. 3: *Minimum-wage employees are stuck in low-paying, dead-end jobs.*

The overwhelming majority of minimum-wage employees graduate from those jobs as their work skills increase. The percentage of Americans working for minimum wage decreased significantly through the Decade of Greed . . . er, the eighties. In 1981, 15 percent of the hourly work force worked at or near minimum wage. By 1992, this figure had dropped to 7.6 percent, according to the Employment Policies Institute. A Congressional Budget Office study found that within a year of beginning a minimum-wage job, 63 percent of employees had advanced.

Myth No. 4: *All minimum-wage employees actually receive only their minimum-wage salaries.*

In fact, many minimum-wage employees earn much more than

their salary. Waiters and waitresses, for instance, often receive far more money in gratuities than they do in salary. It is not uncommon for minimum-wage servers in fine restaurants to earn as much as $40,000 a year.

Once again, the liberal desire to raise the minimum wage is another example of symbolism over substance. Increasing it makes liberals feel good about themselves and they can say they did something to fight poverty. The reality, however, is that they have merely compounded the problem.

Now, I've been saying all this for years—as have many other conservative analysts and commentators. But, guess what? In a rare moment of candor, even Bill Clinton & Co. have acknowledged the potential destructiveness of a hike in the minimum wage. Just a few months after Robert Reich*hhhhh* made his impassioned plea for a higher minimum wage, the Clinton administration was, according to a *New York Times* report, backpedaling considerably.

The New York Times quoted sources in the administration as calling for a delay in any minimum-wage request because it feared an increase now would "undermine job growth." Well, no kidding. This is exactly what opponents of the minimum wage have always said. Is there a good time to lose jobs? Yes, according to liberal Democrats. They don't mind if the nation loses jobs during a Republican administration. Apparently, they just don't want any job losses on their watch. But in actuality, you can't convince me that Clinton just discovered the unemployment-generating aspects of increasing the minimum wage. In fact, *The Wall Street Journal* reported in an August 11, 1993, editorial that it had seen a copy of a July 20, 1993, memo from Labor Secretary Reich*hhhhh* in which he himself acknowledged the potential job-destroying effects of the minimum wage, yet urged another increase. Reich*hhhh*'s memo reads, ". . . most minimum-wage workers are not poor. And the potential effects of a minimum-wage increase on employment should, of course, be weighed." The editorial contains devastating statistics against the minimum-wage increase. Here are just a few of them:

- A 1978 survey conducted by the American Economic Association showed that 90 percent of economists believed that minimum-wage hikes cost low-skilled workers their jobs.

• In 1988, according to the *Fortune Encyclopedia of Economics*, only 8 percent of workers who received the minimum wage maintained families, and not all of those were poor. Editors of *The Wall Street Journal* add: "But by pricing such workers out of the labor market, Mr. Reich might very well make them poor."

Despite all these facts, and Reich*hhhh*'s awareness of them, he has urged an increase in the minimum wage to $4.50 an hour—and indexing it forever to inflation—as a "minimum prerequisite to reaching the goal of lifting families of four with full-time workers out of poverty."

Sooner or later, liberals are going to have to measure all of their wacky ideas and programs by some standard of accomplishment. If the rest of the media won't hold them accountable, I will. And when liberalism is forced to answer for what it has done, the madcap tax-and-spend party will be over.

In the meantime, even some liberals are beginning to question the results of their social experimentation. In a speech to the Association for a Better New York, Senator Daniel Patrick Moynihan (D-New York) offered some blistering criticism of the current leadership of the Big Apple. Moynihan's point was that the city was in better shape fifty years ago than it is today. He listed some illuminating statistics:

• In 1943, the population of New York City was 7,472,564, while today it is 7,322,564.

• In 1943, the number of welfare cases was 73,000, while today it is 1,200,000.

• In 1943, the number of gunshot homicides was forty-four, while in 1992 it was 1,499.

• In 1943, the illegitimacy rate was 3 percent; today it is 45 percent.

"New York was a much poorer city fifty years ago, but a much more stable one," said Moynihan. "I find myself wondering where so much went wrong." Well, I'll tell you, Senator. Which party has held a virtual monopoly on power in New York City for the last fifty years? Who is it that has promoted in New York the permissiveness, excessive tolerance, and basic cultural decay that are the hallmarks of liberalism? Yet, where's the accountability? Where is liberalism's intellectual integrity? Why are so few besides me pointing out the obvious?

New York City and most other urban centers are the bedrocks of liberalism. New York City and Washington, D.C., are cities that have been run by liberalism for more than a generation. If you want to know where liberalism leads, just visit these cities. The streets are filthy, crime is rampant, the infrastructure is deteriorating, and schools are failing. Is this what we want for all of America?

Oh, sure, the liberals who run these cities always have their excuses. They'll tell you they're not getting enough federal aid. The problem is in Washington, D.C., or in the individual state's capital. With liberalism, the problem is always somewhere else. But this ruse is beginning to wear thin. The recent election of wealthy Republican Richard Riordan in Los Angeles and the victory by an unapologetic conservative Republican, Bret Schundler, in the Jersey City mayoral race may be indications that even city dwellers are starting to wise up.

What are they beginning to see? That modern-day liberalism is repugnant to human nature. People respond to competition and being rewarded for their efforts. History has irrefutably proven that when you punish achievement and discourage self-improvement, you stifle economic growth. When you deter economic growth, you hurt those at all economic levels and, perhaps surprising to some, the hardest hit are the poor.

It is also axiomatic that the more intrusive government becomes, the fewer individual freedoms the people will have. Freedom should be the goal we strive for, not forced equality brought about by government redistribution.

Genuine compassion emanates from the heart of an individual. And individuals' hearts are likely to be much more compassionate and generous when they are given maximum freedom and latitude to operate and produce in society without fear that an excessive portion of their earnings will be confiscated.

Liberalism, socialism, and utopianism make empty promises to the world, but offer only a dead end. Capitalism, though not promising prosperity to all, greatly improves the lot of most and offers opportunity to all. Liberalism suggests that all answers lie in government intervention. More and more Americans (with the possible exception of Bill Clinton and a few others who have never worked in the private sector) are discovering how incompetent government is. So, doesn't it stand to reason that we should try to have less of it?

22

THE MANY PURPOSES OF CULTURE

"Culture?" Mario Cuomo once remarked. "What do you mean by culture? That's a word the Nazis used." No matter what the governor of New York thinks, *culture* is not a dirty word. *Webster's New World Dictionary* defines it as "the ideas, customs, skills, arts, etc., of a given people in a given period; civilization." Pretty scary stuff, huh, Mario?

However, killing a culture is something to be alarmed about. As much as I believe in supply-side economics, I also believe that if a nation irreversibly loses its culture, it cannot be salvaged, even by a great economy. Destroy a culture and you destroy a nation. And, believe me, folks, there are people today actively trying to obliterate all vestiges of the common American culture.

But what is "the American culture"? Is there such a thing? Can it be defined? After all, conservatives and liberals clearly have very different—perhaps, irreconcilable—ideas about America.

For starters, conservatives understand that America is, first and foremost, a country with a unique history and unique institutions. You may take this fact for granted, folks, but that's probably because you're grounded in reality, not idealism and fantasy. Liberals, however, tend to see America more as a grand social experiment—an evolutionary process, an ever-changing idea that perhaps someday will sweep over the entire world . . . er . . . planet, and lead to the creation of a new universal, utopian civilization. Ironically and tragically, some astute observers have noted, the nation that socialists and relativists reviled for so long may now provide their last great hope for the world.

Let's face it. American liberals no longer have any foreign models for their utopian dreams and ambitions. The Soviet Union is gone. China is embracing market reforms. Sweden is abandoning socialism. Cuba is simply a dictatorial police state. That makes it very tough to sell liberalism. The socialist nations of Western Europe—France, Germany, Norway—are all discovering that they simply cannot afford cradle-to-grave social benefits and are now taking steps to reduce the scope of their involvement in the lives of their citizens. There is no successful test case for these ideas anywhere. There never has been.

So liberalism/socialism today is re-inventing itself in the United States. All the other utopian models around the world have been discredited. Clintonianism, if you will, may be their last hurrah.

Conservatives understand—intuitively, in most cases—that what has made America a great nation is the commitment of its people to a set of fundamental, core values. Among them are belief in God, monogamy, devotion to family, law and order, self-reliance, rugged individualism, commitment to excellence, and rewarding achievement. Not coincidentally, these are the same concepts that constitute modern conservatism. As non-threatening and as non-controversial as these values appear to be to most, they cause liberals to have conniptions.

How often, for instance, do we see these elevating, positive, inspiring values assaulted on television shows, in books, in movies, and in other manifestations of the media and popular culture? Likewise, American conservatives, who dare to champion these uplifting and enduring tenets, are lampooned, ridiculed, reviled, impugned, despised, and demonized by the liberal establishment. Why? What is it about conservatism that so exercises the dominant media culture? What are the competing values that liberalism offers?

Liberalism propagates a very different vision of America. Among the ideas it celebrates are multiculturalism, humanism, secularism, feminism, racial quotas in hiring, political correctness in the university, special rights based on sexual behavior, sensitivity, fairness, and equality not of opportunity but of outcome.

What a stark contrast! And only one of these visions truly embodies the real historical American tradition. When liberals attack conservative core values, they are quite literally attacking what is—or was—the unique American culture.

One of the main vehicles used by liberals to attempt to de-legitimize "all that remains of a common national culture" for America is multiculturalism. By its very nature, multiculturalism holds that no civilization, no moral code, no way of living, is better than another. In general, it finds fault with little in most cultures—the exception being the actual nation of America, which is usually portrayed as an oppressive, racist, sexist, homophobic nation with few redeeming qualities. Therefore, it is the liberal American ideal, with all of its touchy-feely potential, that liberals seek to export as an ideology, not the real-life American culture.

But please understand, we are not intent on exporting our American culture as exclusively superior (even though we believe that the values upon which America was founded are second to none). No, we are not on an affirmative mission at all. We merely seek to defend for America its Judeo-Christian tradition against the onslaught that is taking place against it in our schools. We believe that although America is a melting pot, its citizens will blend together and live harmoniously only if they are willing, not to discard their heritage, but to recognize that they are first and foremost Americans. They must realize and appreciate the fact that they are citizens of the greatest nation in the history of the world, not just for white males, but for people of all races, genders, and religions. You may challenge my statement that they must appreciate the greatness of this country. If so, I say to you that national allegiance and patriotism are absolute minimum requirements a nation must demand of those who want to enjoy its citizenship. And patriotism is a part of America's unique culture.

Our nation provides its citizens with more political and economic freedom than any other country in the history of the world. It has been able to do that through the years only because of the dedication and commitment of our forebears, who understood these freedoms were worth fighting for. They understood that the preservation of our freedoms was dependent upon the geographical, political, social, economic, and cultural integrity of America as a nation; not as some amorphous landmass that enforces no territorial or moral boundaries. For any nation to survive as a cohesive national unit—and this is especially true of America because it has so freely opened itself up to all peoples, cultures, and influences— its citizens must be imbued with a strong sense of *nationalism* and *patriotism*. That's right. Those are not dirty words. For America to remain the beacon of light it has been to the rest of the world, that "shining city on a hill," its citizens must honor their social compact with one another and, above all, with the United States of America. For America to remain the melting pot, it must encourage its citizens truly to melt in and not segregate themselves to the point of Balkanizing the nation.

"For the liberal, America is not a nation but a civil religion ('an idea'), and loyalty to it is not a matter of sentiment but of ideological commitment," writes John Gray, author of "The Left's Last Utopia," in the *National Review*. "But, of course, America is also—and first and foremost—a nation existing in history, with an unavoidable legacy of particular traditions, institutions, common ways of thinking and speaking."

One's patriotism, therefore, can be identified by his ideology. If you have ever wondered why liberals got so panicked by exercises of American strength during the Reagan and Bush administrations, it was because the wrong America was winning.

Contrast the liberals' trepidation about, and opposition to, the use of force during the Persian Gulf war with their generally interventionist fervor over Bosnia, as I mentioned in an earlier chapter.

Think back to the Clinton inauguration ceremonies, when liberals were talking about how they had been freed from their chains of bondage. Why were they singing songs of freedom as if they had just been released from the gulag? And do you remember actor Ron Silver at the inauguration relating how at first he felt uncomfortable as the air force jet formation whisked by overhead? Then he immediately felt a sense of relief when it dawned on him that "Hey, now we're in power. Those are our jets."

Now, let me digress here for a moment to address those liberals reading this. You may not recognize yourselves. But the important thing to remember is that—like any other group—liberals have leaders and followers. For most people, liberalism, as I've said before, is the most gutless choice anyone can make. Liberals just want to be thought of as good people, and the easiest way for them to accomplish that is to call themselves liberals. Being a liberal, to those folks, means being more caring, compassionate, and sensitive. The leaders of this movement are the people I am writing about. Others should not take offense. Just swallow hard and use this as an opportunity to learn more about the way conservatives think.

When liberals look at America, they see two things: a country that scares them, and a potential launching pad for their idealistic, utopian dreams. This helps explain why they have such an "us *vs.* them" mentality—why the presidency is so important to them, psychologically and otherwise. This explains why they felt so jubilant at Clinton's inauguration ceremony. This is the dynamic that John Gray characterizes as the clash between the actual nation of America and the civil religion invented by liberals.

"Given the tendency of American culture . . . to veer between idealistic optimism and anger when the idealism is thwarted, it was only to be expected that attachment to America as a civil religion should come to express itself as hatred of the values and institutions that are most definitive of America as a historic nationality," writes Gray.

In other words, when liberal idealists are confronted with America's sometimes conflicting historical values, they get angry at the institution of America. They blame the nation. Think of what motivates the homosexual movement in this country. Homosexuals are upset with the way traditional institutions have dealt with their lifestyle. So they set out to radically change or even destroy these institutions. This is an example of a skirmish in the ongoing Culture War.

Let me give you another example. Let's discuss that bane of

modern liberalism, *discrimination*. Frankly, I'm getting tired of the word—at least the way it is used most of the time today. The fact of the matter is that I've been discriminating a lot lately. Sometimes discrimination is a good thing.

For instance, I have been searching for a new place to live. Ever since I moved to New York City, I have lived in my fashionable Upper West Side apartment. Now I'm looking for a new place. So I have done what you do in New York City when you want a new apartment—hire somebody to officially fleece you.

Under the guise of helping you find an apartment, this person takes 15 percent of whatever you settle upon. And what does he do? He opens the door for you. But you must pay him for this service because you can't see any apartment without an appointment—and this fellow is the only one who can make an appointment. It's just the cost of doing business in that bastion of compassionate liberalism known as New York City.

I have looked at a number of places. I have loved some and I have found others to be lacking. In other words, I have discriminated. I have been really mean and insensitive to some of these apartments. You should hear some of the thoughts that go through my mind when I look at different places. Some of these apartments are nothing but rat holes! I'm not even going to tell you how much they cost. But I am being discriminating. And I am offending rat-hole apartments. Therefore, discrimination is not always bad, is it? Most of us do it all the time to determine what we like. In fact, it wasn't that long ago that when someone said, "He's got discriminating taste," it was a compliment.

Liberals have now come up with the idea that discriminating among people, places, and things anytime for any reason is wrong. Do you want to know how absurd this has become? Liberals now contend that we should not even discriminate among people with respect to actual achievement! To see how far liberal insanity can go, you have to look at New York as an example. New York's Department of State now informs all those taking tests for certification as real-estate salespeople (those aforementioned door openers) of the following: "Your examination application slip will be marked either 'passed' or 'failed' and returned to you by mail. Numerical scores are not given to prevent possible discriminatory employment practices based on achievement levels." Discriminating based on achievement? So now we are saying that institutionally we'll try to prevent employers from hiring the best people for the job—never mind what harm this may do to overall productivity.

Here's another wacky example of how the liberals' obsession with discrimination clouds their reasoning powers. In 1992, the Orlando, Florida, Orange County Expressway Authority made hiring the homeless a condition for contractors to bid on an $80,000 highway landscaping job. Homeless people, the requirement said, would have to account for 10 percent of the laborers. Expressway Executive Director Howell Worrell said the idea was to get homeless people working at dead-end temporary jobs into a business in which they had an opportunity to work their way up.

He was quoted in the *Orlando Sentinel* as saying: "I can see this becoming an on-the-job training program where they start out doing basic landscape work and move into equipment, operating, maintenance work—who knows?" The paper reported that it might be the first program of its kind anywhere. It should be the last. What about the poor guy who is legitimately unemployed but not homeless? This is where Clintonianism is leading us: Maybe Clinton should have reserved a position in his Cabinet for a homeless person. Or maybe only homeless people should be able to build his jogging track. This is what passes for compassion among liberals. They no longer discriminate between good ideas and bad ones.

But even the liberals' obsession with discrimination is phony. I am here to tell you that liberals don't give a rat's tail about ending discrimination. Do you know what liberals really mean by "fighting discrimination"? Getting even. Liberals don't fight discrimination with non-discrimination. They use proof of past discrimination to foster reverse discrimination. It's another idea that pits class against class, and is counterproductive and anti-social in every way except for the fact that it promotes liberalism.

"You find out what it's like for a while, pal!" That's the way liberals fight discrimination. Do you think I'm exaggerating? Ask the rich—the latest scapegoats for every evil in our society.

Here's what John Adams, one of our Founding Fathers and second president of the United States, had to say about the kind of class warfare being perpetrated by the current administration: "It is agreed that the end of government is the good and ease of the people in the secure enjoyment of their rights without oppression. But it must be remembered that the rich are people as well as the poor, that they have rights as well as others, that they have as clear and as sacred a right to their large property as others have to their's which is smaller, that oppression to them is as possible and as wicked as to others."

Do you think Bill Clinton has ever read John Adams? Do you suppose he cares what the framers thought about issues as critical to our self-governance as property rights? Do you realize that if wealthy people are not secure in the enjoyment of their property rights, no one is? If big government can confiscate the wealth of a rich person, what is there to prevent it from taking yours?

If you declare a phony war on discrimination of all kinds (as opposed to genuine instances of discrimination, such as those based on race, ethnicity, religion, etc.), as liberals have done, you effectively declare war on thinking, on weighting alternatives, on decision-making of all kinds. It's clear why liberals want to do this. Very few people could possibly make a rational choice to follow their agenda. People have to be coerced into liberalism, tricked into it, or bullied into it.

Let's take a look at the way these conflicting worldviews—conservatism and liberalism—deal with a specific and real problem. One of the many myths of liberalism is that crime is inextricably linked with poverty.

This argument is used to justify (or at least rationalize) 1992's Los Angeles riots by pointing out how blighted much of South Central L.A. was even before the arson and looting spree. Liberals ask: What would you expect people living in such conditions to do?

The everyday violence and mayhem we see in other U.S. urban settings is also blamed on economics by most liberals. If only we could provide more good jobs and more affordable housing in our cities, they say, the crime rate would nose-dive.

After seventy-five years of witnessing disastrous socialistic programs around the world and thirty years of seeing the results of failed welfare programs here at home, you would think the utopians would begin to lose faith in the god of materialism.

Let me posit two facts that prove conclusively that there is no direct causal connection between poverty and crime: 1) Most poor people never resort to crime; and 2) even some wealthy people commit evil acts to enrich themselves further.

Even a liberal should be able to comprehend these truisms. This alone ought to dispel the notion that poverty is the root cause of crime. Nevertheless, let's not stop there. Let's probe even more deeply into this poverty-equals-crime myth. Where, do you suppose, is the poorest community in the United States? Harlem? East Los Angeles? The South Side of Chicago?

Surprise, surprise. None of these famous "bad neighborhoods" is even on the top-ten list. In fact, the most financially strapped areas in the United States are not even urban areas. According to the latest U.S. Bureau of the Census report, the poorest community in the United States is Shannon County, South Dakota, followed by Starr, Texas, and Tunica, Mississippi. When was the last time you heard that the residents of one of these communities rioted to protest their living conditions?

Since we have more crime in the United States today than at any time in history, it should follow that these must be the worst of times economically, right? Wrong. During the Great Depression, even people fortunate enough to be employed often earned far less by any standard than today's welfare recipients, but the crime rates were low compared to those of today.

But how can we explain this? What was different about the 1930s that permitted a dramatic increase in poverty without a skyrocketing crime rate? And why is it that, even today, many poor people are able to rise above their economic disadvantages, while others cannot? I suggest to you that the answer has to do with attitude, values, a common culture.

Times were very tough in the 1930s. There was a lot of misery. But most people had not yet been conditioned to the idea that they deserved to have a better life handed to them by the government. People were willing and eager to work for one. They were just grateful that the government didn't get in their way. And they would cheerfully accept any job that came along, no matter how menial it might have seemed.

Can we honestly say this is still true today? And given the choice between working for a relatively low wage and collecting unemployment or welfare benefits, is there any doubt that in the 1990s some are more inclined to choose the easy way out? Isn't it the case today that we are more likely to blame our misfortunes on others and look to the government for help, rather than relying on our own initiative? Do you see how successful liberalism has been in infecting our culture with its new religion?

Let me illustrate. A sixteen-year-old kid recently *stole* a New York City A-train subway and took it for a forty-five-mile, three-hour ride. What was the reaction of the liberal establishment? Former Mayor Ed Koch (by comparison, one of the more sensible liberals in town) said he hopes the city would be "very careful" not to ruin the kid's life, especially since it seems the lad is a "good kid" who simply had an obsession with driving subway trains.

Koch suggested that perhaps the teen should be given an "internship" at the Metropolitan Transit Authority and then be allowed to take the civil-service exam for subway conductor when he reaches the legal age.

How did other liberals view this incident? "They should give him an 'A' for effort and let him go," chimed in William Kunstler, the left-wing attorney who defended the Chicago Seven in 1968. "He's a black kid in New York who loves the subway system, who did a very daring thing which came to no harm. I can see the dangers of his action, but it ended nicely, nobody was hurt. To make this a criminal case in our already crowded court system . . ."

Now, why would Mr. Kunstler consider it critical to mention that the kid was black? Would he view the crime differently if he were white? And isn't that an example of "discrimination"? I wonder if he would be willing to give me an "A" for effort if I went out and took a 747 for a spin. Would I be able to get an internship with a major airline if I safely flew a 747 for three hours? After all, this youth was driving a subway train with hundreds of members of the general public on board.

The Rev. Herbert Daughtry, pastor of the House of the Lord Church in Brooklyn, even said, "If he can pick a train and drive it up and down the tracks, he doesn't need to be in jail, he needs a mentor who will influence him to develop his extraordinary talent. It would be a mistake to send him to jail."

There you have it—the reactions of three different liberals who are fairly representative of the knee-jerk liberal approach. Steal a train, get a job. There was a time not too long ago when Americans all agreed that crime deserved punishment. This was part of the common American culture before the religion of liberalism began to conflict with traditional values and common sense. Today liberals imply that there is a vast victim class that cannot help itself without government help. These victims cannot escape poverty—and even a life of crime—without some form of affirmative-action program and massive transfer payments.

The reality is that there are plenty of self-reliant souls today who are managing to pull themselves up by their own bootstraps. What makes them different is that they believe in themselves (not the government) and in the efficacy of hard work. Unfortunately, we are not doing enough to cultivate that old-fashioned work ethic. This is the essence of conservatism—self-reliance, rugged individualism, the work ethic.

Do you hear, for instance, how our cultural elite is demeaning traditionally entry-level jobs? Ask a liberal why there are so many drugs being sold in our cities and he or she will probably tell you that teenagers look at the job prospects facing them and decide that it makes more sense to sell crack for $100 an hour than to flip hamburgers at McDonald's for minimum wage.

The truth of the matter is that such a choice makes sense only if you have no fundamental moral values—no sense of right and wrong. If you have no conscience and don't mind poisoning people, sure it makes sense to sell crack. Using the same faulty, materialistic, liberal illogic, however, wouldn't it make more sense for the average middle-class worker to rob banks rather than work a forty-hour week?

We've got to stop making excuses for ourselves and for others. America was conceived as a land of opportunity, not because it offered the best government handouts, but because it was the only country in the world where you could create your own job. But while re-invigorating America with an entrepreneurial capitalist spirit would be a step in the right direction, it is not enough. Free-market economics alone will not solve the problems of our inner cities. Not even enterprise zones—as promising as they are—can effectively address poverty, hopelessness, despair, and crime in a moral vacuum.

No, we must also return to our American roots. We must resurrect our traditional family values. We must discourage the government from substituting itself for the father as the head of the household in our inner cities. The reason most people—rich and poor—do not commit crimes is simply because they know it is wrong to do so. Without a sense of right and wrong, all the material goods in the world won't deter one person from doing evil to another.

23

LIES ARE FACTS; FACTS ARE LIES

WITHOUT QUESTION, PRESENTATION, PACKAGING, IMAGING, AND SU-perficiality are all extremely relevant in the political world. As a person whose livelihood is dependent not only upon the message, but its critical delivery, I will readily admit that in the real world, form, though not as much as substance, does indeed matter. I've told you countless times that I attribute my success both to my political views and my "reportedly" entertaining way of presenting them. With my background I am uniquely qualified to address the interrelationship between substance and form, am I not?

As an expert in both form and content—in both delivery and substance, in both entertainment and profundity—I must tell you that the two should never clash. One's message, for example, should never be contradicted by his manner of communicating it. Before you jump to any conclusions, I'm not talking about such things as a conservative message being heralded by the Pretenders' bumper music. I'm not referring to my show at all, except as a paradigmatic contrast to what I'm going to tell you. Because my show, though it contains various styles, never—let me repeat this—*never* betrays the truth. What drives my show is truth—truth in both form and substance. And my audience consists of those who have the courage to believe and live the truth. That brings me to a matter that concerns me in the most profound way.

Before, at least during my adult lifetime and even during my precocious childhood, the great debate in this country was ongoing and vibrant. My father's subscription to the Great Books of the Western World always included an annual edition that featured a section on the Great Debate. In the early 1960s, Barry Goldwater authored the conservative side of one particular year's version of the Great Debate. The essays, which I read, were extremely instructive and informative. But in re-reading them, I notice something much more profound in them other than their applicability to the "then current events." I am stricken by the fact that the debate was genuine; it was based on facts and the interpretation of those facts by those who possessed different worldviews. Nowhere in my reading, however, did I detect the most minute hint of intellectual disingenuousness; of perversion of form over substance; of propaganda; of the subordination of truth in support of one's political cause. That, I think, is what differentiates that period from the one in which we are currently living.

For, you see, folks, as a conservative, it's no longer enough to out-argue your opponent, to demonstrate the superior reasoning underlying your ideas. As an advocate of political conservatism, you must also first demonstrate your moral timbre as a human being. You must overcome the presumption that you're insensitive and don't give a damn about anybody who makes less money than you.

Today liberalism, because of its utter philosophical bankruptcy, has had to resort to magic tricks, to illusions, to distortions. We are no longer engaged in the Great Debate. The forensic playing field is no longer level, for those responsible for enforcing the rules of the game have long since discarded their objectivity and "fairness." They've abandoned all but a tenuous pretense to the pursuit of truth, of investigation and fact-finding. With experiential truth and empirical evidence refuting their credo at every imaginable turn, they're reduced to faith: faith in a set of beliefs long since discredited; faith in a lifestyle long since proven to be harmful; faith in a valueless value system; faith in a secular nihilistic world devoid of answers but full of trendiness, chic-ness, Hollywood glitter, pseudo-elitism, and arts-and-croissants self-adulation.

My friends, we must come to grips with the fact that in this society, conservatives face an uphill battle. Whereas before we began on a level playing field as we entered the Great Debate, today we've got to counteract or counterattack the propaganda just to get *into* the Great Debate. I've already discussed the methods that the left is using to censor the conservative message in other chapters. It just keeps getting worse.

Whatever you glean from this book, remember this: Today there is no longer a fair dialogue occurring. Those who boast about their allegiance to the First Amendment are violating it as a matter of gross political survival. We've got them on substance; that's why in today's distorted debate, *Lies have become facts; Lies are facts.*

In our culture, the liberal view and liberalism are vigorously fueled by the press. The press spews the lazy, clichéd liberal compassion-mongering lines, such as, 37 million people in the U.S. are without health care. Never mind that this number is hotly disputed; never mind that many of the uninsured choose not to be; never mind that they all have access to health care. What matters is that there is a potentially flammable issue to work up people, and to hell with the facts. The president says that we've got a health-care crisis, and we've got to fix it, and the press echoes his pronounce-ments. Thus, they become the accepted facts. Let's blame the Republicans, even though the Democrats have controlled Congress for eons. It's just this simple with the pseudo-intellectual liberal elite: Republicans have been in the White House for twelve years; health-care costs are too high; therefore, Republicans don't care about people. Is that underlying, absurd premise ever challenged by the major media? Of course not! And why not? Because they have no compassion; they're hateful. *Period. Exclamation point!*

If you question my assertion of the press's liberal bias, consider its uniform concern about Clinton being overworked. When Ronald Reagan and George Bush took a vacation, they were immediately cast in an unfavorable light. With Reagan, it was further proof of the press's conviction that he was "senile and needed to convalesce"; with Bush, he was "insensitive, out of touch, elite, and outrageous" for vacationing while ordering the troops to the Persian Gulf.

Contrast this with the press's sycophantic characterization of Bill Clinton's sojourn with the real elite at Martha's Vineyard as "long-overdue relaxation."

Let's face it, folks. In today's LEXIS/NEXIS-fearing, Stephanopolous-Clinton world, facts are lies. And lies are facts. And, by the way, that's not redundant! Truths are being distorted. And distortions are being treated as truths. And that's not redundant, either. You need examples? I'm glad to accommodate you:

• **The prosperous Reagan years.** Why, they're a failure now—an utter and abject failure in every way imaginable. Bill Clinton says it, and the press, without challenging him on it, repeats it. For proof, re-read my chapter on the eighties. Better yet, commit it to memory.

• **The deficit.** The deficit is the fault of Republicans. The president pronounces it, and the press reports it. The Democrats' domination of Congress (which controls this nation's purse strings) for half a century is wholly disregarded.

• **Housing starts.** A recent *New York Times* article blamed the Reagan-Bush years for the slump in housing starts. And do you know why? Because too much building occurred. We have a glut of buildings because too much construction occurred. The 1980s featured phony prosperity, guided by incorrectly applied tax relief. So, the economic problems of today are not the fault of people who've been running things for more than four years since Reagan, and by all means they are not Clinton's fault; they are *Reagan's* fault. Bill Clinton says it, and the press reports it. So now that the fear of Clinton's economic plan is beginning to sink in and further retard certain areas of the economy already faltering from the effects of the 1990 budget deal, Democrats and the media have concocted yet another creative use for the eighties. Don't just blame them for bad things that *didn't* occur during that decade; blame the eighties for every bad thing that's happened since, and for Clinton's current and future failures.

• **The markets' response to Clinton's plan.** Bill Clinton says that the markets are enthused over his policies, and the press reports it. The fact of the matter is, the markets are not enthused by Bill Clinton's policies, and, in fact, are somewhat frightened. Some in the press admit it. But for the Washington and White House press corps, whatever the president says, that's what is. The Lie becomes the accepted truth because perception—in this case, *mis*perception—becomes reality.

• **The triumph of Clinton in Tokyo.** Bill Clinton went. The White House put on a big public-relations show. The press said it was a rousing success. Why? What was accomplished? He went there and temporarily stopped his Japan-bashing, he smiled real big, and he hobnobbed with a bunch of world leaders—all of whom have one foot in their political graves. It would have been impossible for Clinton not to have appeared more popular than any of the world leaders he was with. And because the press portrays Clinton as the undisputed, charismatic leader of the free world, that distortion becomes reality.

By now, most objective people have come to expect lies from Bill Clinton. Seeing is believing. But the press is another story. I don't think mainstream media journalists are evil. I don't think they're stupid—and I know they're not employed by pre-Yeltsin *Pravda.* So why, then, do they blindly parrot the Clinton line? Their families are not being held hostage. They're under no threat to report the party line. Yet, they do. Why?

Could it be laziness? Some would say that it's lazy journalism. There is some of that, perhaps. But I think another dynamic is at work here. There truly does exist an inside-the-Beltway mentality in D.C., and it envelops more than just the politicians and the bureaucrats. The press is also part of that Washington, D.C., culture—a culture that is devoid of reality, and ignorant of how lives in America are really lived and how people are getting by. Members of the Washington elite become more insulated the longer they remain there. Bill Bennett says the best advice he ever received while serving as secretary of education was given by his wife, who told him to get out of Washington and into the cities of America to see what's really going on and how people actually live.

The press, as part of the D.C. insider culture, tends to get caught up in its own involvement. During the administration of this Democratic president, they appear to feel as though they belong, as though they are part of the team. They are so enamored of Clinton that they sometimes gush in their reports. You can see it in their stories about his sojourn in Martha's Vineyard. The press seemed to be collectively intoxicated about how Clinton was treated there. My gosh, you'd have thought it was the Beatles coming to town. Or Elvis.

Martha's Vineyard is the summer citadel of this country's elite, which is exactly who Bill Clinton's friends are. So what is the big deal about his receiving royal treatment? But the press itself seems to be caught up in it. Everyone associated with the press is running around trying to make sure they're invited to the right occasions, or that they're seen in the right places. Whether they deny it or not, they are insiders whose objectivity has become a casualty.

Now, I know some of you are saying, "Rush, how can you say this? You know that *Time* magazine placed a diminutive picture of Clinton on its cover and the entire press corps was very hard on him at the outset." My answer to you, folks, is that members of the press were trying to establish their credibility. As part of that process they had to administer their obligatory hits on him. And maybe there was the added factor that they were a bit perturbed with him for so masterfully and so quickly demonstrating his fallibility. But the Clinton-bashing was guaranteed to be only temporary. During the height of the media's criticism of Clinton, I predicted that later they would launch a massive campaign to resuscitate him. I said there would be—and there has certainly been—a symphony of support.

I'm not alleging a sweeping media conspiracy here. I don't contend that they confer, cavort, and conspire to elevate Clinton's image. They don't need to. They all just happen to believe the same way. They are as predictable and unthinking as the Hollywood elite. They are part of the same culture as Bill Clinton. They are cloaked in idealism. Many of them truly believed that Clinton was going to change the world. They were convinced that he would finally actualize all of the lofty ideals that journalists originally went to school to help accomplish. They would all change the world together, make it a better place. Then their bubble burst and reality set in. It became clear that Clinton was not, in fact, the Messiah. But once its initial shock and disappointment wore off, the press realized that Clinton, despite his abundant flaws, was still the best friend it had—the closest thing to an idealist. So the press began—grudgingly, in some cases—to build him back up. *SITYS.*

There is a major difference between me and the dominant media culture. I freely, openly, and proudly admit my bias, my conservative predisposition. All of my listeners know that I editorialize and analyze from a decidedly conservative worldview. But the major media—at least the overwhelming majority of them—will not admit their bias. They simply cannot bring themselves to confess their liberalism. Rather, they'll say something along these lines: "We are journalists; we are professionals. We're objective; we're not liberal; we're not Democrats. We are above all that. We answer to a higher authority: the First Amendment and the pursuit of objective truth. We don't editorialize—we merely report the facts and let the chips fall where they may." If they would just admit their bias, it would be another story. But they don't. They may be fooling themselves, but they are not fooling us.

So, on balance, the Clintons have in the press an ally that immeasurably enhances the likelihood that their programs will be enacted by Congress. You've got a bunch of willing participants in the press, helping Clintonmania sweep across the country with no scrutiny.

All you have to do to verify my analysis is look at the facts. Correction. That's all you would have had to do before. But today, an examination of their "facts" may not enlighten you. Why? Because, again, facts are lies today. And lies are the new facts.

There is no better evidence of this than Clinton's 1993 budget debacle. As I detail for you in the next chapter, the passage of the 1993 Budget Reconciliation Act was possible only because lies are now facts. Only because the real facts about the 1990 Budget Reconciliation Act were distorted and suppressed could Congress have gotten away with the 1993 act.

Despite all of this, however, I remain undaunted and undeterred. I stand ready, willing, and abundantly able to provide you with the truth. On my shows, in my newsletters, and in my books, facts are not lies and lies are not facts. In the EIB venue, the truth rings loudly and clearly, cogently and passionately. For I am most passionate about the truth and want to ensure its dissemination to the public.

As evidence that the awesome and profound power of the truth is beginning to be heard in this country, I cite to you a call to my radio

show on August 30, 1993, from Melvin, a young black gentleman
from Sacramento, California. Melvin told a moving story.

He said that until recently he had been a very bitter person, angry
at the plight of the blacks in this country and their treatment by
whites. He said that his views were very liberal and in sync with
today's black leadership. Nobody, he said, could tell him anything.
He led protests while serving in the marines in the Desert Storm
operation. Even the rigid discipline of the military couldn't break
him; the military couldn't thaw him out, because he didn't care.

Melvin then said that someone turned him on to my radio
program and he began listening. He stated that he began to be
attracted to the message because it was based on *facts* and on *truth*.
He said that he began to see that the bitter and hate-filled message
of the black leadership was doing *nothing* for him, his family, or
other black people. He said that upon listening to my show he
discovered that his own negative attitude had been holding him
back personally and in business. He admittedly was not nice to
people with whom he worked and had a poor attitude toward his
job. This was all due to his bitterness about and preoccupation with
race.

He said that when he listened to my show he learned that the
conservative message is not anti-black. It is race-neutral. He said
that it really impressed him that I was advocating that all people,
irrespective of the color of their skin or their gender, should be the
best they can be. The ideals of self-worth, self-reliance, and rugged
individualism greatly appealed to him. He said that he would have
preferred not to have identified himself as a black man because we
should strive toward color-blindness. Precisely. But to tell his story
properly, he felt, he had to state that he was black.

Melvin said that these ideas not only appealed to him, but that he
had incorporated them into his life. He said he has adopted a totally
new outlook on life: He is now positive, optimistic, and happy. He
has begun to treat his co-workers with more respect and his
customers with kindness. As a direct result, he says, he has already
received a promotion. He says that his family are still Democrats
because they believe that only the Democrats have helped blacks
over the years. He now knows that this lie is not a fact. He now

strongly believes in the conservative and American ideal that all Americans should be the best that they can be and should not rely on government for their support. He has told his family and friends that it's not fair for him and them to be working hard to pay taxes so that those who refuse to work, because of their bitterness or whatever, will be able to eat. He said that he is on a mission to spread the word and turn more people on to EIB.

Now, I want you to understand, I am not out there recruiting evangelists for this show, and that is not my goal. I am immensely gratified, though, that this young man has taken away something positive from my show and that he is willing to share it with his friends. That, my friends, makes it all worthwhile.

But don't forget Melvin's main point. He was moved from his formerly stolid, inflexible position by facts, by truth, and by knowledge. As you know, Melvin, I, too, am driven by facts and the truth and will continue to press forward in the pursuit of truth, regardless of the effort of some to muzzle me and others. So, thank you, Melvin. Your call has meant more to me than you will ever know. Be persistent in your efforts and eventually we'll overcome this current malignancy pervading our political landscape that is characterized by falsehoods, distortions, and deceptions.

24

THERE THEY GO AGAIN

Bill Clinton was elected primarily because he convinced enough American people that this country was in dire economic straits and that he would remedy our problems by implementing "change." I told you in an earlier chapter that George Bush departed so radically from the policies of Ronald Reagan that history books would eventually treat the Reagan and Bush eras as totally different periods. I told you that a more logical pairing, which history will ultimately reflect, would be the Bush/Clinton period. But what I haven't yet told you is that this confusion—about the domestic-policy differences between Bush and Reagan and the domestic-policy similarities between Bush and Clinton—is the result of a calculated strategy of the Clinton campaign.

Besides using class warfare in his campaign, Clinton masterfully confused the Bush era with the Reagan era in order to blame the recession caused by the Bush/Democratic Congress 1990 budget deal on Reagan and, ultimately, Reaganomics. Clinton shamelessly characterized the entire twelve-year period, including the Reagan and Bush administrations, as trickle-down, supply-side, and Reaganomics. But we all know that Bush's reign had nothing to do with supply-side. He began to distance himself actively from it immediately upon taking office. As I will document for you in this chapter, the 1990 budget deal, which Bush and Congress agreed to, and Clinton's 1993 budget plan are strikingly similar.

Clinton's scheme was as brilliant as it was duplicitous. It employed age-old strategy whereby you blame something other than that which is responsible for causing the problems. That which is blamed is the straw dog. In this case, Reaganomics became the straw dog. It went something like this: Clinton first successfully engineered a wholesale history rewrite of the 1980s in order to demonize Reaganomics (which process I described in detail in my earlier chapter about the 1980s); then he disingenuously accused George Bush of continuing the policies of Reaganomics, when he hadn't. Having set up Reaganomics as the straw dog, he was then able to argue, once elected, that he had a mandate to change course from the path of Reaganomics—even though this country *hadn't been* on that prudent course since the 1990 budget deal. This is how Clinton has proceeded to implement a sequel to the 1990 plan under the rubric of change.

With that background, you might be interested in what Bill Clinton himself has said on the subject of someone who keeps trying the same failed policies: "My wife, Hillary, gave me a book about a year ago in which the author defined insanity as just doing the same thing over and over again and expecting a different result." Clinton offered this statement in one of the presidential debates in October 1992. Interesting, huh?

Clinton has touted his 1993 budget plan as the bill that will correct the mistakes of the last twelve years by reducing the deficit by $500 billion over the next five years. This was exactly the goal of Bush and the Democratic Congress in 1990. Here is how President Bush explained it on September 30, 1990: "The bipartisan leaders and I have reached agreement on the federal budget. Over five years it would reduce the projected deficit by $500 billion; that is half a trillion dollars." With these words began the unraveling of George Bush's presidency.

Bush would still be president had he never uttered those words, had he never agreed to forge a bipartisan coalition with the Democrats. Once the budget deal was signed, the Democrats backed away from it, denied all responsibility for it, and, in fact, attacked Bush for breaking his "no new taxes" pledge. Worst of all, they got away with completely escaping accountability for it by scapegoating George Bush. In a word, they Bushwhacked Bush.

This should anger the average American, because the Democrats who engineered the 1990 budget deal are the same architects of Clinton's plan today. At that time, they also promised a $500 billion reduction in the budget deficit, claiming that the largest tax increase in history (at that time, at least) would bring the deficit down to $60 billion by 1995. Now, barely three years later, the Democrats have done it all over again, passing the largest tax increase in history, a hike dwarfing that of 1990. Believe me, I would not harp on this but for the fact that no one else in the major media is calling your attention to it.

The dirty little secret of Clinton's "deficit reduction" scheme is this: Though it has been billed as the first meaningful effort at deficit reduction, it's not deficit reduction at all. The administration's own projections show that under the plan the total debt will increase more in four years than it did in any four-year period in the 1980s. Does this seem possible based on what you have heard Clinton and most media analysts say? Yet, it's undeniably true. The deficit inherited by Bill Clinton from George Bush was somewhere around $240 billion. Under Clinton's plan it's going to exceed $300 billion—yet it is called "deficit reduction."

The real problem is not the budget deficit, but rampant federal spending. The deficit is the result of that spending. In the fiscal year 1993, federal spending was $332 billion greater, for instance, than it was the year George Bush was sworn into office. That means that we spent 29 percent more in 1993 than we did in 1989. Consumer prices, by comparison, rose during that period at a rate of 16 percent. However, the economy for that period grew by only 6.6 percent. By 2003, according to *The New York Times*, the federal budget deficit will be nearly $700 billion—including all of the optimistic projections of the Clinton plan. If you believe the Clinton rhetoric, you would think the Democrats are somehow addressing the issue of out-of-control spending. They are not. Rather, Clinton and the congressional leadership are brazenly using the deficit as an excuse to raise taxes and increase spending even more.

The maddening thing is that in a few years, when it becomes clear that Clinton's plan has not reduced the deficit, he and his congressional conspirators will simply say that if they hadn't done something, the deficit would have been worse (as if there is some supernatural force driving the deficit inexorably out of control). This is exactly the line that Tom Foley used to blame the failure of their 1990 plan to reduce the deficit. In other words, they're trying to set up a plan that can't fail. Whatever happens with the deficit—no matter how much it grows—they will say their plan was successful because the deficit would have grown even more had they not enacted it.

You must understand that when the Democrats use the term "cuts," they do not mean real reductions. (See the discussion of baseline budgeting in Chapter 11: The Decade of Fraud and Deceit.) When Congress claims that it has cut the budget, it is never talking about actually spending less than in the previous year. What it means by a budget cut is *a reduction in the projected increase*. In other words, the government is still spending more money—just less than it had planned to. So, if Congress plans to increase the budget by 10 percent, but then increases it by "only" 5 percent, it congratulates itself for having "cut" the budget by 5 percent.

Am I engaging in hyperbole when I say that the 1990 and 1993 acts are virtually identical in substance? As discriminating readers, you are certainly bound to wonder. Well, let's take a peek. The 1990 budget deal had the official name of "1990 Budget Deficit Reduction Act," and it imposed tax increases on the "rich," raising the top marginal rate from 28 percent to 31 percent so the "rich" would have to "pay their fair share." Supposedly, only those making $200,000 or more would be taxed more heavily. Déjà vu! The 1993 plan calls for even steeper marginal income-tax rate increases on the "wealthy" by raising the top rates from 31 percent to 36 percent for all those married couples earning more than $140,000; and a punitive 10 percent surtax on income above $250,000, which effectively raises the marginal rate to 39.6 percent. The top corporate income-tax rate will increase from 34 percent to 35 percent.

The 1990 budget deal also increased the beer tax from $9 to $18 a barrel, and this tax is going even higher in 1993. Taxes on table wine, which were increased 629 percent in 1990, went from 17 cents to $1.07 per gallon. The gasoline tax was raised 5 cents per gallon in 1990, and now it is being raised at least another 4.3 cents; and the tax on cigarettes was raised in 1990 by 4 cents a pack in 1991. Admittedly, the 1993 budget deal does not raise taxes on alcohol and tobacco, but I will wager any one of you that Clinton will try to increase either or both of these taxes again to help subsidize the national health-care plan, which, we have been assured, will contain no new taxes despite the projected $100 billion to $150 billion price tag. Any takers?

In terms of the spending cuts, the 1990 and 1993 deals are also similar in that most of the "promised" cuts are scheduled for the "out" years—the period that begins after the incumbent president's term has expired.

So in terms of the basic numbers, the Democrats are repeating the 1990 budget deal, policy for policy, idea for idea, and approach for approach; it's almost the same plan that was implemented to fix the last twelve years. Even *The New York Times* (another opinion-leading publication for the liberal media) has admitted this. The only differences in the plans is that Clinton's 1993 plan is even worse, in terms of higher and more progressive taxes, and it has spending cuts that are even more illusory. Congress has also managed to sneak other confiscatory measures into the 1993 bill, such as an increase in the estate tax rates, more-restrictive limitations on deductions for personal retirement plans (which will deter savings and thrift, promote dependency on Social Security for retirement, and give Congress even more of our money to spend—all of which expands and escalates the dependency cycle), and the elimination of any ceiling (formerly $135,000 per year) on income subject to the 2.9 percent Medicare payroll tax, effectively raising the top marginal rate to 42.5 percent.

On my radio and TV shows, I played portions of statements made by the central players in 1990, then juxtaposed those with their statements in 1993. The statements speak for themselves.

Leon Panetta, Clinton's director of the Office of Management and Budget (OMB), was a ranking member of the House of Representatives in October 1990. Today, he conveniently forgets about his key role in the passage of the 1990 budget deal. He has adopted the class-warfare rhetoric of the Clinton administration and claims no one did anything about the deficit for the twelve years before his team took over the White House. But let's go back and listen to what he was saying in pushing through the deficit plan signed by President Bush in 1990.

"Is there sacrifice involved?" he asked in a fiery speech on the Hill. "You bet there is! You can't develop a deficit-reduction package that doesn't involve sacrifice on the part of everyone. The economy is in desperate straits, and the question we have to ask tonight is 'What happens if we fail?' That's the question you have to ask. What happens to this economy if we fail to adopt a serious deficit-reduction package for this country?! The answer to that is that if we fail, it is almost comparable to an act of irresponsibility because we know if we fail we doom our economy to a deep recession." (At least he was right in forecasting a recession. Too bad he forgot to place the blame where it truly belongs: the 1990 budget deal.) Mr. Panetta's rhetoric in 1993, this time as a member of the administration, was the same.

Representative Richard Gephardt (D-Missouri), Majority Leader in the House of Representatives, was one of the impassioned proponents of the 1990 budget deal. Here's what he said on September 30, 1990: "What we can produce [is] a reconciliation bill in ten days or two weeks that we can bring out here, and get 218 votes, half of this side and half of this side, so we can address this deficit problem that everybody in this room knows has to be solved for the future of this country, and I would even say for the future of the world."

On October 27, 1990, Thomas Foley, Speaker of the House then and Speaker of the House now, said: "We said at the beginning of the process that we are going to be concerned that any of the burdens we are asking the American people to bear to bring down the deficit would be borne fairly and equitably, and based on the ability to pay. That's exactly what happened in the final product. What the Senate adopted tonight, what the House adopted at seven A.M. this morning, reflects a very strong and progressive proposal in terms of ability to pay. Those who earn less than $20,000 actually have their tax burden reduced. Those in the middle-income areas carry only the responsibility for increased levies on beer and wine and cigarettes which are largely voluntary taxes in a sense, plus a five-cent gasoline tax. The income-tax effects are totally on those with higher income levels, mostly areas over $200,000 a year. So the *progressivity* of this package has been achieved. There are savings in the proposals as well—two times the amount of tax revenues are achieved in savings, domestic entitlement savings, and defense discretionary savings." In 1993, Foley and Senate Majority Leader Mitchell stood together after passage of the 1993 bill and proclaimed it as the most *progressive* bill in years.

Senator Jim Sasser (D-Tennessee, and chairman of the Senate Finance Committee) was downright boastful about his role in the 1990 budget deal at the time and now seems to have plumb forgotten about that plan to reduce what he calls *"the daficit."* Here's Sasser in September 1990: "At the risk of sounding immodest, we are on the verge of getting the largest *daficit*-reduction package in the history of this republic, putting that *daficit*-reduction package into law."

Now here's Sasser in June 1993: "Now let's bear in mind, while we're being critical of this administration and this president, he didn't create these *daficits*. These *daficits* are the result of twelve years of the most irresponsible fiscal policy in the history of the United States." (Note that Sasser conveniently omits the fact that 1990 was in that twelve-year period he vilifies.)

In trashing the 1980s, Clinton has focused on the increase in the deficit, which he says was caused by unconscionable tax breaks for the rich. The reason Clinton singles out the deficit is that there is virtually nothing else that happened during the eighties that can be attacked on economic grounds. But Clinton and the press have obscured the truth about the deficit in the 1980s. From 1985 to 1989, the deficit was being *reduced* via an expanding economy, growing taxpayer base, and lower taxes. The chart on page 303, from the March 19, 1993, issue of *The New York Times* shows that after the Reagan tax cuts really kicked in (1985–89), the deficit began to decrease dramatically, despite unchecked, spiraling Democrat congressional spending. This occurred precisely because the tax-rate reductions—as I pointed out in the 1980s chapter—caused almost a doubling of revenue, a fact you'll never hear from the major media.

In addition, the chart compares the Congressional Budget Office projections for the years 1994 through 1998 with the revenue and deficit figures for both the Reagan and Bush periods. In the chart, the projections used by the Clinton administration are those of the Congressional Budget Office, just as he promised he would do during his State of the Union address on February 17, 1993. (You may remember that he drew loud cheers from the Democrats when he proclaimed the CBO numbers to be more accurate and realistic than the OMB numbers used by the Bush administration in 1990. Using the CBO numbers is also one way the Clintonites justify their assertion that the problem is being tackled seriously for the first time since 1981. Bush, you see, didn't really mean to support deficit reduction in the 1990 deal because he refused to use the projections of the CBO. Neat little trick, isn't it?)

Clinton's deficit projections for the years 1994 through 1998, which are optimistic and Clinton-favoring to say the least, are mind-blowing when compared to Reagan's. Notice how Reagan's deficit shrank from $221 billion in 1986 to $152 billion in 1989, when gross-revenue receipts were $991 billion. Now, let's take a gander at the part of the chart showing Clinton's own projections about his plan. For 1998 he projects revenues of $1,481 billion— that's almost $1.5 trillion—and his projected deficit is nevertheless $361 billion—almost 2.5 times the $152 billion deficit of 1989, despite 50 percent more revenues (from $991 billion to $1,481 billion). And, even worse, his projected deficit will be 19.6 percent of total spending, compared to Reagan's 13.3 percent in 1989.

I simply cannot emphasize enough that these CBO numbers are Clinton's own figures. This is how he plans to "reduce" the deficit by raising taxes. And also keep in mind that his optimistic projections assume that his promised spending cuts in the out years come to fruition and that the tax increases don't shut down the economy and reduce the tax base. This stuff is amazing, folks! Clinton's deficit reductions are going to be increases, even compared to this year's figures. The budget deficit will be less than $300 billion in 1994, and up to $361 billion in 1998. But in Clintonspeak,

Rise, and Fall, of the Deficit

Federal spending, in billions of dollars

		TOTAL SPENDING		Deficit as a Percentage of Total Spending
		RECEIPTS	DEFICIT	
	'80	$ 517	$ 74	12.5%
	'81	599	79	11.7%
	'82	618	128	17.2%
	'83	600	208	25.7%
	'84	666	185	21.7%
	'85	734	212	22.4%
	'86	769	221	22.3%
	'87	854	150	14.9%
	'88	909	155	14.6%
	'89	991	152	13.3%
	'90	1,031	221	17.7%
	'91	1,054	270	20.4%
	'92	1,092	290	21.0%
	'93 EST.	1,148	327	22.2%

CONGRESSIONAL BUDGET OFFICE estimates for 1994–98, which allow for growth at the rate of inflation but reflect estimates of the Bush administration cuts in military spending

	'94	1,214	296	19.6%
	'95	1,290	302	19.0%
	'96	1,355	301	18.2%
	'97	1,413	327	18.8%
	'98	1,481	361	19.6%

Sources: Office of Management and Budget

this is the first meaningful deficit-reduction package in recent history. Yeah, just as night is day. Welcome to the "politics of meaning."

Furthermore, the "spending cuts" that were a part of the 1990 budget deal proved to be just as elusive as the higher tax revenues. The first "out" year after the 1990 deal was 1993, and the spending cuts that were part of the program never materialized. According to the 1990 budget deal, total spending for 1993 would be $1.381 trillion. However, Clinton's 1993 budget is $1.466 trillion, or about $85 billion more. This illustrates that these "budget deals" and compromises are meaningless when it comes to actual budget projections. The tax increases are always put into effect, but the reductions in spending never are.

Similarly, the 1990 budget deal projected that total expenditures for 1994 would be $1.343 trillion, but President Clinton's own budget shows that the government will spend $1.513 trillion in 1994. Thus, about $170 billion more will be spent in 1994 than what was promised in 1990. The government is—surprise, surprise—spending far more than what the Democrats promised back in 1990. Why should these people be trusted again? Why should they be believed?

But even if we could believe them, is there any real likelihood that Clinton's program can work? I must tell you that I am confident that the plan will not work, for a number of reasons. As I said, tax increases retard economic growth and, other things being equal, accentuate the deficit problem. No country has ever taxed itself out of a deficit or into prosperity. But also, I know the history of Democratic Congresses. As I have told you, they do not follow through on their promises to cut spending.

Now, here is my point. In 1990, George Bush was president and was enjoying a 90 percent-plus approval rating on the strength of our victories in the Persian Gulf war and Cold War. The Democrats had every reason to sabotage George Bush by orchestrating the budget deal, then distancing themselves from it when the economy began to falter. They knew the president, rather than Congress, would be held accountable. Thus, they had no incentive to fulfill their promises to cut spending. George Bush took the full heat for that budget fiasco, even though it was the Democrats who initiated it and were principally responsible for its passage.

The difference this time, and the reason my well-publicized bet against the plan is arguably quite risky, is that the Democrats now have a vested interest in making this plan work. They control both the Executive and Legislative branches of the federal government. So, is it not reasonable to conclude that this time, in order to save their own political skins, they will follow through on the promised spending cuts? Otherwise, the deficit will continue to soar off the charts. Not to worry. A little-known fact is that the Democrats summarily rejected a Republican proposal to enact legislation that would have made these cuts mandatory. They didn't want to hem themselves in. Why should they? Spending cuts are against their religion, and term-limit proposals that would apply to most of them have not yet been passed into law. So they can continue to use the power of incumbency to confiscate our wealth and use it to buy votes to perpetuate their terms in office.

But aside from the promised spending cuts, what about the revenue side? Will their tax increases dramatically raise revenues, as promised? Better yet, will more revenues be generated from the rich? And less from the poor? Let's look at what happened in 1990, when the top income-tax rate was raised from 28 percent to 31 percent. The total income-tax receipts in 1991, the first year after the 1990 budget deal was signed, fell—the first decline since 1983, because the wealthy found tax shelters, stopped investing, decided not to put their money at risk, and curtailed other activities that would increase their tax burden.

U.S. Treasury figures on income-tax receipts in 1991 show that the wealthy (defined as the 850,000 people who earn $200,000 a year or more) paid substantially less in actual tax dollars than they did the year before. In 1990, the rich paid $106.1 billion in income taxes, but in 1991, after the tax increase, they paid $99.6 billion. Did you get that? Though their tax rate went up, from 28 percent to 31 percent, the "rich" paid $6 billion-plus *less* in revenues. And it wasn't because of a weak economy. In fact, total income for 1991 rose 3.3 percent.

But following the 1990 budget deal, non-rich Americans paid

$3.3 billion more in taxes, a 1 percent increase, even though their tax rates stayed the same. The bottom line is this—the Clintonomic approach to tax rates doesn't hurt the rich nearly as much as it hurts those trying to *become* rich.

So why are Clinton and Congress pushing through a plan that won't work? Why are they intent on raising your taxes? To reiterate, it is because Clinton's political party, which controls both houses of Congress and the White House and, therefore, all federal expenditures, wants to drive a wedge between the middle and upper classes in this country, pitting the lower classes against the upper classes. As the spending mounts, so does the dependency of those receiving it, which the Democrats hope will translate into more and more appreciation of them by more and more voters. Do you get the drift? Simply put, what is going on here is an attempt by the Democratic Party to transfer to the left as much as it can of the wealth, power, and culture of America.

It's bad enough that Clinton's tax plan won't work in economic terms. But what may be even worse is that it is an assault on the American Dream. This tax bill constitutes a breach by the federal government of its compact with the American people to ensure them maximum freedoms and to protect their private-property rights. This plan is antithetical to capitalism in that it punishes competition, productivity, and success. This is a critically important point that I very much want you to understand. Clinton talks about raising the rates on the rich, when in fact he is raising rates on the high-income producers. Though there is some overlap, there is a world of difference. I think of the rich as those who have already accumulated or amassed a great amount of wealth. Those people have their funds invested in various things, many of which are tax-exempt, such as municipal bonds. Thus, much of the earnings on their already-amassed wealth will escape all taxation and certainly won't be affected by the increase in marginal tax rates. Many high-income producers have not yet amassed substantial estates, but, for the first time in their lives, they have reached their maximum earning potential. Many of them doubtlessly planned for years that they would use their increased earnings in their peak years to retire debt from leaner years (when their living expenses were higher, such as the cost of their children's education), and to begin to build a nest egg for their eventual retirement. The primary onus of these marginal tax increases, therefore, is going to fall unfairly on those who have busted their tails all of their lives to finally arrive at their most productive level. Their reward for working hard, for savings and thrift, for believing in the American Dream, in America's promise to them, and in the full faith and credit of the United States government to honor its social contract with them, is punitive taxation. Their reward is outright theft from a president who has always fed from the government trough, and outright theft from an arrogant body of lawmakers who raise their salaries by legislative fiat; who write checks out of thin air and vacation at the expense of lobbyists who represent anyone but the congressmen's constituents; who exempt themselves from their own laws; whose self-legislated retirement funds are at an unconscionable level relative to the private sector; and who obviously don't give a damn about the will of the people. But they transparently seek to pacify us by their insistence that the tax hikes and the retroactivity fall only on the top 1 or 1.5 percent. Americans know better and will make that abundantly clear the next opportunity they have to vote for term limits, or for their particular congressman.

The naysayers claim that the country can't grow itself out of its economic problems. Why not? I agree that we mustn't ignore the spending side of the equation and that we must curb discretionary and mandatory spending. I've never advocated the myopic approach that focuses solely on the growth side. But, what's wrong with growth? The only thing wrong with a growing and expanding economy is that it empowers individuals and weans them from the nipples of a pervasive and all-encompassing government. The point is that we need to tackle our fiscal problems with a sensible, balanced, two-pronged approach, which focuses on cutting spending.

An equally important step toward deficit reduction and a growing economy would be to scrap the capital-gains tax, or, at the very least, to index it to inflation. This would release a massive tidal wave of funds that would sweep across the country and revitalize the economy. Larry Kudlow, chief economist at Bear Stearns in New York City, estimates that a federal spending freeze coupled with indexing of capital gains to inflation would reduce the deficit to $60 billion in five years. Who needs tax increases? Only those who want to have control over more of our private lives.

I sincerely don't want Bill Clinton to fail, unless failure is defined as the defeat of his current economic policies. But this is not about Bill Clinton. It is about America and Americans. I want America to remain the freest nation on Earth—and I want everyone to prosper, including Bill Clinton. So let's look forward to 1994 and 1996, when we can elect people who believe in the American Dream and will do everything in their power to promote it, so that all Americans, including Bill Clinton and his family, can prosper.

25

THE POLITICALLY CORRECT
LIBERAL LEXICON

My friends, it's sometimes difficult to understand those of the left. Because they think differently from normal people, they speak differently. Euphemism and exaggeration are the staples of their propaganda smorgasbord. But now, thanks to me, you will be able to make sense of their gibberish and jabberwocky. Without the benefit of an expensive translator, you will be able to comprehend the blatherings of academicians and multiculturalists. As kind of an intermission from the erudite thoughts and profound musings you are being asked to consume in this tome, I offer you this guide to the esoteric jargon of liberalism. Understand that these are not my definitions. This information is brought to you only with the desire to provide insight into the liberal mind. Bits and pieces of this information had to be smuggled out of the secret archives of the Institute for Policy Studies and other left-wing think tanks, often at great personal risk to members of the Limbaugh Institute for Advanced Conservative Studies.

———

A (archaic): a grade indicating excellence during the less-enlightened, competitive era of education

aardvark: endangered species

abalone: endangered species

abandon: what conservatives do with their social responsibilities

abase: what should be done with standards of all kinds

aberrant: conservative

aberration: the popularity of Ronald Reagan

abhorrent: the popularity of Ronald Reagan

abnormal (archaic): in less enlightened times, not normal

A-bomb: weapon used by United States to destroy peaceful people of Hiroshima and Nagasaki

Abominable Snowman: endangered species

abomination: Reaganomics

abortion: women's most important civil right; the sacrament of radical feminism

abracadabra: what liberals say when creating new government programs

absentee: the way rich Republicans vote; should be made illegal

abstain (archaic): the way sex education used to be taught

abstract: the way liberals think

absurd: trickle-down economics

academia: a place where great ideas flourish

academic freedom: freedom of student or teacher to hold or express views without fear of arbitrary interference, except when such ideas are deemed racist, bigoted, homophobic, insensitive, chauvinistic, jingoistic, imperialistic, religious, conservative, or politically incorrect

Academy Award: recipients get to make great political speeches and wear red ribbons

accomplishment: what the government allows you to do

acculturation: a term used by arch-conservative Bill Buckley; thus, off limits

acetone: hazardous waste

achievement: what the government allows you to do

acid: what liberals ingested frequently in the 1960s

ACLU: official guarantor of all constitutional rights

acquittal: what ACLU tries to get in all criminal cases

ad hominem: an attack against a liberal

adolescence: best time to give away condoms

aerosol: destroyer of the ozone layer

Afghanistan: The Soviets' Vietnam

agitprop: news

AIDS: virus that occurred because of Ronald Reagan and George Bush

AIDS epidemic: what Reagan and Bush caused

AIDS research: what Reagan and Bush refused to fund

air conditioning: destroyer of the ozone layer

Algore: environmental expert and spiritual guru.

all-American: exclusionary

alligator: endangered species

America: nation in decline

American Dream: what Reagan and Bush destroyed

Americans: those who profited unfairly in the 1980s

Americans for Democratic Action: non-partisan group that evaluates politicians fairly

androgynous: describes a group deserving special civil-rights protection

animals: a collection of endangered species

anteater: endangered species

antelope: endangered species

apathy: why more liberals don't vote

arch-conservative: all conservatives

archenemy: Rush Limbaugh

arch-liberal: communist

art: something government needs to subsidize without regard to standards

asbestos: the most dangerous substance known to man

assimilation: opposite of multiculturalism; should be discouraged

atheism: our official religion

automobile: according to *Algore,* the greatest threat to the planet (besides people)

B: the kind of motion pictures Ronald Reagan made

baboon: endangered species

back alley: where all abortions took place before *Roe* v. *Wade*

balanced news story: opportunity to quote two liberals and give one personal opinion

Bible: a dangerous book that should be removed from school libraries

bicycle: the preferred method of travel, besides walking

bigot: someone winning an argument with a liberal

bisexual: lifestyle deserving special civil-rights protection

blasphemy: saying anything critical about Mother Earth

Boy Scouts of America: subversive paramilitary organization

budget cuts: what cause homelessness and poverty

budget deficit: the result of Reaganomics and the reason for tax increases and higher spending

Cabinet: panel of top presidential advisers that should "look like America"

Caldicott, Helen: expert on nuclear weapons and the environment

campaign promises: lies told to get elected

capital punishment: cruel, unusual, and barbaric practice

cataclysm: what the planet is headed for unless people listen to *Algore*

censorship: 1. when parents try to influence which books are used in schools; 2. when the government refuses grants to artists because their work is obscene

centrists: liberal Democrats

change: something to work toward whenever Republicans are in office

choice: something good when it comes to abortion, something bad when it comes to education

Clinton, Bill: co-president

Clinton, Hillary: health-care and education expert; co-president

cohabit: same as marriage

collective bargaining: negotiation between organized workers and their oppressor

Colorado: hate state

Columbus, Christopher: originator of genocide, racism, sexism, and homophobia against Native American peoples

Columbus Day: indigenous people's day

communist: idealist

conspiracy: what happens whenever two or more right-wingers gather together

Constitution: outmoded document written by dead, white, male, homophobic slave owners

contributions: confiscating the American people's hard-earned income, by force if necessary, so there can be increased government spending

cop: armed mercenary in constant need of supervision by civilian review boards

crazy: rationally challenged

crime: something caused by a combination of economic inequities, societal alienation, and too many guns

crocodile: endangered species

Cub Scout: junior member of subversive, homophobic, paramilitary organization

death: cessation of life caused mostly by cars, refrigerators, air conditioning, greed, overpopulation, capitalism, big business, and Republicans

debauchery: a style of art particularly deserving of federal funding

Declaration of Independence: a historical document that should not be read or displayed in public schools because of its overt religious nature

defendant: an innocent victim of America's injustice system

defense: the only area of the federal budget that can always be cut

deficit: caused by tax cuts and overspending on the military

deficit reduction: increased taxation and spending on social programs

Dellums, Ron: expert on the military

dementia: people who suffer from this illness represent a solid voting bloc for liberalism

Democratic Party: captive of liberalism since 1972

deodorant: destroyer of the ozone layer

dependency: what liberals foster for their own empowerment; a social condition caused by Republican lack of compassion

depravity: a popular art form deserving of federal subsidy

discrimination: the worst sin any human could commit

diversity: when liberals of all ethnic persuasions get together

dolphin: the most intelligent and noble of all nature's creatures

Dykes on Bikes: a nonprofit public-interest group

eagle: endangered species

Eagle Scouts: if the Boy Scouts are a dangerous, homophobic, sexist, paramilitary organization, these are their Green Berets

Earth: the source of life

ecology: one of the great religions

education: indoctrination

elephant: endangered species

Emmy Award: an opportunity for making great political speeches and wearing red ribbons

English: one of several languages spoken in America

enigma: why aren't liberals more popular?

entitlement: a glorious part of the federal budget you can never cut

environment: our first and highest duty is to protect it

environmentalists: clergy socialists who care about the planet

equality: primary goal of education; is achieved by fostering mediocrity and sameness

esteem: very important, especially the "self" variety

ethics: the way liberals behave

euthanasia: everybody's right

evangelicals: dangerous right-wing zealots

evolution: the way we got here

exclusion: Republicans' byword. Is the party of it.

extinction: what we're all facing if we don't listen to *Algore*

extremists: Republicans

F: a grade that no one should ever get under any circumstances

fairness: spreading pain and misery equally

faith: something you need lots of to be a liberal

family: any group of people living together

family income: everything you earn, plus money you could earn by renting out your house

family planning: abortion on demand

family values: code words for male chauvinism and homophobia

fascist: synonym for "conservative"

father: non-vital member of the family

federal government: vital member of the family, primary bread-winner; the best place to make most decisions

feminist: spokesperson for all women

fetus: unviable tissue mass

First Lady: co-president

freedom: hedonism. Eliminating it is the goal of conservatives.

fundamentalists: they want to impose their morality on us all

gangs: organizations of disadvantaged inner-city youths

Gergen, David Rodham: responsible Republican

giraffe: endangered species

global cooling: excuse for higher taxes, more spending, and bigger government

global warming: see *global cooling,* a synonym; excuse for higher taxes, more spending, and bigger government

God: a construct of primitive Americans to justify their bigotry and homophobia; the only thing you can't talk about in schools

Good Book: *Heather Has Two Mommies*

googolplex: goal for federal budget

Gorbachev, Mikhail: savior of the world

government: panacea. Has the answers for most problems

gridlock: checks and balances in government; Republican tool to impede progress

growth: 1. what accounts for liberalization of the views of office-holders who spend enough time in Washington; 2. when related to the economy, something created only in the public sector

hate: what motivates conservatives

hate speech: any speech that defends the values of mainstream America

health care: latest civil right; more to come

health-care reform: rationing health care to cause long lines, poor quality of care, and increased government spending

heir: someone who inherits your tax bill

help: what the government is there to do for you

hero or **heroine:** anyone who attacks conservatives, e.g., Anita Hill

heterosexual: the only lifestyle not deserving of special rights

Hill, Anita: expert on sexual harassment

hocus-pocus: words uttered to make new jobs programs work

Hollywood: where our dreams come true

homophobia: mental illness

homosexual: alternative lifestyle deserving special civil protections

humanism: one of the world's great religions

idealists: visionaries

inclusion: everybody but white males and conservatives

Internal Revenue Service: the compassion police

internationalism: the way all global disputes should be settled

intolerance: something we must do away with, except as it pertains to conservative ideas

investment: increased government spending

jobs program: increased government spending

Johnson, Magic: expert on how to avoid getting the HIV virus

jungle: always use "rain forest"

justice: a concept incomprehensible to politically incorrect juries; something juries don't always understand

King, Rodney: expert on nonviolence and getting along with one another

L: the only grade necessary in public schools; indicates learning is taking place

labels: what conservatives try to stick liberals with

left: center

legerdemain: the way liberals stay in power

Lerner, Michael: the spiritual leader of liberalism

lesbian: member of discriminated-against minority group in need of special civil-rights protection

liberal: centrist visionary radical

liberal arts: what they teach you in college

lie: strategic deception, spin

Limbaugh, Rush: the most dangerous man in America

litmus test: something liberal presidents, but not conservative presidents, should use in choosing Supreme Court justices

marriage: domestic partnership

Marxism: foundation for liberal economics

middle class: rich

military: 1. federal jobs program; 2. good place to conduct social experiments

morality: 1. something only liberals can be trusted to impose; 2. defined by individual choice

NAACP: National Association for the Advancement of (Liberal) Colored People

Nazis: conservatives

neo-conservatives: traitors

news story: opportunity to give personal opinion

1980s: Decade of Greed

1960s: era of optimism

nonpartisan group: Democratic special interest

NOW: National Organization for (Liberal) Women

nuclear weapons: Republican instruments of death

omniscient: the federal government

patriot: a person who will fight to the death to defend his fellow flag-burner

patriots: liberals

peace: achieved through better understanding among peoples

people: creatures that imperil the world

personal responsibility: code words for racism and homophobia

Phillips, Kevin: responsible conservative

planet: what liberals call the world

pluralism: two or more liberal views

politics of meaning: politics of taxation

poverty: root cause of crime and urban despair

prayer: the only kind of speech the First Amendment doesn't protect

press: our best friend

private sector: vicious, greedy, lust-ridden segment of our economy that competes with government for people's revenues

progressives: socialists

quotas: the way we equalize things

racists: conservatives

Reagan, Ronald: personification of evil; created greed and despair in the 1980s

red ribbons: the way to cure AIDS

Republicans: party of the rich

revenue enhancement: taxes

rhinoceros: endangered species

rich: anyone with a job in the private sector

rich Republicans: redundant; they're all rich

right: wrong

right wing: conservatives

rugged individualism: code words for greed and selfishness

school: indoctrination center

school choice: code words for dismantling public schools

secularism: one of the world's great religions

self-esteem: the most important lesson we can teach in schools (besides how to put on a condom)

share: steal

Sisters of Perpetual Indulgence: a non-profit, tax-exempt public-interest corporation

socialism: economic democracy

Soviet Union: a place where socialism failed because the right people weren't in charge

special interests: people who disagree with liberals

spending cut: what you promise gullible conservatives to justify higher taxes

spotted owls: excuse for turning loggers into herb gardeners

suburbs: dangerous bastions of racism, exclusion, gun ownership; should be dismantled

taxes: lifeblood of liberalism

tax incentives: tax breaks for the liberal rich

taxpayer: rich person

Thanksgiving: the day we give thanks to the indigenous people of America for saving the Pilgrims

topsoil: capitalism is destroying it all

town meeting: taxpayer-subsidized public-relations campaign

undocumented worker: potential Democratic voter

unicorn: endangered species

utopia: our goal

war: obsolete way of settling disputes

Washington, D.C.: where most problems are solved; should be fifty-first state

water buffalo: 1. endangered species; 2. racist epithet

women: feminists

workers: what liberals, socialists, and communists call employees

26

"THE HUSH RUSH LAW"

To the consternation of many liberals, I am subject to no government authority in writing this book. Though this volume will be mailed via the U.S. Post Office, though it will be delivered to bookstores over public highways, and though it has already been transmitted over electronic networks, no federal, state, or local agency has the slightest control over what I might say. (Heh-heh-heh.)

The reason is simple—though I have to keep reminding my opponents what it is. The First Amendment to the U.S. Constitution states: "Congress shall make no law . . . abridging freedom of speech, or of the press." Newspapers, magazines, books, pamphlets—the "old" media—have an absolute right (barring obscenity or libel) to publish whatever they want.

Because our Founding Fathers were keenly aware of the tremendous struggles waged throughout history against press censorship, Americans gained the constitutionally guaranteed legal right to publish free of government control. The American model of democracy was firmly grounded on the *imperative* of free speech—and an absolute rejection of licensing or regulating the press. As a direct result of this cherished right, the final decisions on the fairness, accuracy, and value of what I write here are left entirely to the marketplace. I am free to write, others are free to disagree . . . and the rest of you are free to have the courage to believe the truth.

But absurd as it may seem, my friends—and many Americans simply do not realize this—these bedrock rights and freedoms do not necessarily apply to broadcasting. The United States has freedom of the press . . . until we get to the *electronic* press. The American Revolution has not yet spread to the nation's airwaves. Radio and television broadcasters must be licensed by the federal government—and there lies a slippery slope.

To beg any government's permission to speak is to ask for trouble. Can you imagine asking *this* government—Bill and Hillary Clinton, George Mitchell, Tom Foley, Donna Shalala, Ted Kennedy —for consent to broadcast critical opinion of (not to mention poking fun at) their politics, their policies, their mistakes? Hmmm? Remember, folks: There is no true liberty when the government parcels it out to you in pieces.

But that kind of government shackling of freedom of speech—in defiance of the U.S. Constitution—is precisely what we will have in store if the Fairness Doctrine is re-enacted. If that happens, I, Rush Limbaugh, the poster boy of free speech, will be gang-muzzled.

As we go to press, "fairness" legislation is popping up all over Washington, D.C. There's S. 3, a rider to the campaign reform bill that passed the Senate in June 1993. There's S. 333, the "Fairness in Broadcasting Act of 1993," sponsored by Senator Ernest "Fritz" Hollings (D-South Carolina), slithering its way through committee. In the House of Representatives lurks H.R. 1985, also called the "Fairness in Broadcasting Act of 1993," sponsored by Representative Bill Hefner (D-North Carolina). Representative John Dingell (D-Michigan) and Representative Ed Markey (D-Massachusetts) are brewing yet another "fairness" bill.

Let me quote from a July 15, 1993, memo—on official congressional letterhead—by Representative Hefner, pushing for his bill:

Dear Colleague:
Over the course of the last several months we have all

324

experienced the impact of misleading information about the contents of the stimulus package, the budget-reconciliation bill, and other issues of public interest. Our offices are bombarded with calls and letters that are prompted by TV and radio talk shows that often give totally false and misleading information or even make inflammatory and derogatory remarks about our public officials. THE FAIRNESS DOCTRINE IS URGENTLY NEEDED.

Derogatory remarks about our public officials! Excuse me, Mr. Congressman, but the last time I looked, that was protected speech—unless this is no longer the United States of America.

Now, folks, is there any doubt at whom this legislation is aimed? Every member of Congress will deny that the desire to re-impose the Fairness Doctrine has anything whatsoever to do with my show, or with the rise of conservative talk radio. But don't be fooled. It is true that the urge to regulate comes naturally to government officials, and the wish to muzzle the press certainly pre-dates me. But Representative Hefner's memo unwittingly reveals the inspiration for this particular piece of legislation.

What's Wrong with Fairness?

"Every responsible broadcaster I know likes the Fairness Doctrine," wrote my esteemed fellow broadcaster Larry King in a September 1993 *USA Today* column, "because fairness is what the U.S.A. is all about."

Wait a minute. Before we get to the issue of who likes the Fairness Doctrine, let's examine the premise here. *Fairness* is what America is all about? Would somebody please find "fairness" for me in the Constitution? Would somebody research *The Federalist Papers* and locate "fairness" as the legal or philosophical basis for the structure of the American political system?

You can't. Yet somehow we have gotten this notion that fairness is the guiding principle of the country. And it is dangerous indeed when we say it is, and when we assign government the power to adjudicate "fairness" in the marketplace of ideas.

325

"But, Rush," you say, "who could possibly be against fairness?"

Indeed, let me quote from S. 333, the "Fairness in Broadcasting Act of 1993": "A broadcast licensee shall afford reasonable opportunity for the discussion of conflicting views on issues of public importance." It sounds totally harmless, doesn't it? Who could be against the idea that radio and television broadcasters, influencing millions of people over the people's airwaves, should take care to provide balanced presentations of controversial issues? Who could be against the idea of mandating good journalism?

Only spoilsports like Madison, Jefferson, and Hamilton. My friends, the Founding Fathers were not naïve. They did not insist on an unregulated market of ideas because of some pie-in-the-sky belief in the "fairness" of free speech. They knew very well that public debate has never *been* fair. When the First Amendment was being conceived, the press was highly partisan. Only a handful of daily newspapers served the entire nation, and most of those publications made no pretense to "objectivity." Yet the writers of the Bill of Rights still insisted that the government steer clear of any "corrective" action. "Congress shall make no law . . ." looks pretty plain to me.

And it has been pretty plain to the Supreme Court—for printed materials. Licensing of printers has been explicitly unconstitutional since 1825. Laws to regulate newspapers to promote "fairness" or "equal time" are out of the question. In *Tornillo* v. *The Miami Herald* (1974), the prevailing legal precedent, the Supreme Court voted 9–0 to *overrule* a Florida statute that gave political candidates a right to reply when attacked by newspapers. The Court held that the statute usurped editorial discretion, which must be free of government control.

But while freedom of the press was ensured by the Founding Fathers, who expressly protected eighteenth-century communication, newer forms of speech have not been so fortunate. Just as the printing press was seen as a threat to governments in the Middle Ages, so the electronic media have been seen as *dangerously* influential. "Ooooh, no!" the thinking goes. "You can't trust the public to know what to do with information it gets from radio and TV."

With broadcasting, huge numbers of people can be informed cheaply and instantaneously. That efficiency—in the hands of private, unregulated speakers—is powerful, and it has made the government very nervous. So, rather than extend First Amendment protection to the new technologies, the approach of the Congress, the courts, and the Federal Communications Commission (FCC) has been to go backward.

Thanks to the Radio Act of 1927, anyone wishing to communicate with the public over the airwaves has had to apply for a government permit. In one fell swoop, the electronic press was placed under *political* control, and politics has had a field day with this scheme ever since. Politicians have two interests: They want their backers to win valuable broadcasting licenses, and they want as little negative publicity as possible.

A Short History of the Fairness Doctrine

The Fairness Doctrine was formally initiated in 1949 by an FCC ruling on radio, and it soon applied to television stations as well. The FCC later summarized the policy:

> The Fairness Doctrine, as developed by the commission, imposes upon broadcasters a two-pronged obligation. Broadcast licensees are required to provide coverage of vitally important controversial issues of interest in the community served by the licensee and to provide a reasonable opportunity for the presentation of contrasting viewpoints on such issues.

My friends, **no one has any idea what this means.** Who decides what issues are "vitally important"? Who decides what is "controversial"? How many "contrasting viewpoints" are required? In 1979 the FCC itself admitted that it had never even defined what "the community served by the licensee" referred to. Was it a neighborhood? A city? A region? Could it be, in the case of national programming, the whole country? In truth, the Fairness Doctrine means what three of five FCC members says it means: three government officials, appointed by the president, confirmed by the Senate, and given annual operating budgets by the Congress. Sound a little risky to you?

It has indeed been risky . . . to freedom of speech. Bill Ruder, assistant secretary of commerce during the Kennedy administration, admitted: "Our strategy was to use the Fairness Doctrine to challenge and harass right-wing broadcasters and hope that the challenges would be so costly to them that they would be inhibited and decide it was too expensive to continue." The Nixon administration harassed left-leaning stations. Significantly, when Nixon was irate over what he perceived as slanted coverage in *The Washington Post*, he ordered his operatives to look into making renewals more difficult for the *broadcast licenses* that the *Post*'s parent company owned.

None of this would have surprised the Founding Fathers, who knew well that any government allowed to encroach on press freedom would do so.

And, in fact, no one—except, apparently, for Larry King's friends—claims that the Fairness Doctrine ever made radio or television better. When it was in effect, in essence it assured mediocrity, guaranteeing less controversy, less risky programming, and less editorial outspokenness. Stations whose licenses were challenged at renewal time on Fairness Doctrine charges were forced to mount expensive defenses. They learned to avoid the expense by avoiding the provocation. "The Fairness Doctrine was in the back of everyone's mind each time they thought about covering a controversial issue or taking an editorial stand," says David Bartlett, president of the Radio–Television News Directors Association.

The situation was offensive to many broadcast journalists, including Bill Munroe, former host and executive producer of NBC's "Meet the Press." Munroe objected to the fact that broadcasters did not have the same free-speech rights that publishers did: "As a young man I worked for a newspaper," he told the FCC. "I was impressed with the spirit of independence on the part of the editors. They didn't care if something they put in the paper offended a major political figure. Later I went to a television station and discovered the managers were a little afraid. . . . They were timid, conscious of government looking over their shoulder in a way that the newspaper publisher and editor for whom I had worked had not been. I began to feel I was a little bit less than free."

And how did the government monitor "fairness"? Not very well, Larry. They responded to complaints from people offended by a station's coverage, or investigated stations when their licenses were challenged at renewal time. This was haphazard at best, and many scholars researching this issue—and, eventually, the FCC itself— were appalled by the results.

James McKinney, former chief of the Mass Media Bureau (the FCC branch that regulates radio and TV broadcasters), described the embarrassing way the commission's enforcement process actually worked: "We . . . sit down with tape recordings, videotapes of . . . what has been broadcast on a specific station. We compare that to newspapers [and] other public statements that are made in the community. We try to make a decision as to whether it is of public importance in that community, which may be two thousand miles away [from Washington, D.C.]. . . . When it comes down to the final analysis, we take out stopwatches and we start counting the seconds and minutes that are devoted to one [side of the] issue compared to the seconds and minutes that are devoted to the other side of the issue."

This is the government of a free society?! Paying bureaucrats to monitor the speech of American citizens with stopwatches? Good grief!

Supporters of the Fairness Doctrine say, "Well, maybe there were a few excesses, but really, hardly any complaints resulted in formal FCC actions. Most of them were dismissed or settled. Only one station ever saw its license actually revoked under the Fairness Doctrine." That, my friends, is no evidence that the Fairness Doctrine wasn't a burden on broadcasters.

Scholars, in fact, have called the Fairness Doctrine a tax on controversy. The tax was not imposed directly. It involved problems at renewal time, requests for additional information, and possible hearings in front of the commission. Lawyers' fees. Uncertainty about renewal, which could freeze credit lines or halt an impending sale of the station. Lots of administrative time. And a huge headache. Those who say the Fairness Doctrine didn't really hurt broadcasters because few stations ever lost a license are completely ignorant of how the threat of non-renewal under the Fairness Doctrine actually worked. Indeed, radio and television stations were so afraid of the government that to avoid Fairness Doctrine challenges, they in effect censored themselves.

The Incredible Case of *Red Lion* v. *FCC*

If you think the courts can be counted on to stop any political shenanigans under the Fairness Doctrine, think again. In the 1969 Red Lion case, one of the most disturbing in First Amendment law, the Supreme Court failed to overturn a blatant attempt at censorship by the Kennedy-Johnson administration.

First, the facts. Red Lion Broadcasting owned WGCB, a tiny religious station in Red Lion, Pennsylvania. On November 25, 1964, as part of a daily fifteen-minute program, right-wing preacher Billy James Hargis criticized Fred Cook, who had written *Goldwater: Extremist on the Right.* Hargis, a Goldwater supporter, called Cook a "professional mudslinger" and cited a *Newsweek* report that Cook had been fired from *The New York Times* for ethical violations. Hargis called *The Nation,* which Cook wrote for, a "scurrilous magazine which has championed many communist causes." Hargis's broadside lasted two minutes; the entire fifteen minutes of airtime on WGCB had cost the Rev. Hargis's organization $7.50.

Fred Cook wrote to the station demanding the right to reply. WGCB responded with a rate card, offering Cook airtime at its usual price. Cook held out for free equal time, and the case went to the FCC.

When the commission sided with Cook, Red Lion challenged the decision all the way to the Supreme Court. The question was whether the FCC's "right of reply" rules, sister regulations to the Fairness Doctrine, were a violation of the First Amendment. In a unanimous 8–0 decision (Justice William O. Douglas was ill), the Court ruled that due to the "scarcity" of radio-station frequencies, broadcasters did not have the same First Amendment protections that applied to newspapers.

The Court's reasoning regarding scarcity has been savaged by experts. In fact, there were twenty competing AM stations and twelve FM stations in the Red Lion market. (The scarcity-of-the-airwaves argument, which is *still* used by Congress, has been rendered even more absurd by the technology explosion.) But more shocking was the Court's 1969 finding that the Fairness Doctrine regulation did not create any "chilling effect."

Unbeknownst to the Supreme Court, the whole case was a setup.

It was later revealed that Fred Cook had not even heard the WGCB broadcast. After discovering that the Fairness Doctrine could be used against its political opponents, the Democratic Party had created a front group called The National Council for Civic Responsibility to monitor conservative radio. The letter Fred Cook had signed demanding equal time was crafted by Democratic National Committee (DNC) lawyers!

No "chilling effect" on free speech posed by the Fairness Doctrine? The Democratic Party was spending thousands of its own dollars—behind the scenes—in a brazen attempt to silence its political opposition. As Wayne Phillips, who headed up the DNC campaign against the right-wing broadcasters, later said: "Even more important than the free radio time was the effectiveness of this operation in inhibiting the political activity of these right-wing broadcasts. . . ."

Phillips's assistant, former FCC attorney Martin E. Firestone, concluded: "The right-wingers operate on a strictly cash basis, and it is for this reason that they are carried by so many small stations. Were our efforts to be continued on a year-round basis, we would find that many of these stations would consider the broadcast of these programs bothersome and burdensome (especially if they are ultimately required to give us free time) and would start dropping the programs from their broadcast schedule."

The Supreme Court opinion in the Red Lion case unknowingly aided the Democratic National Committee in its blatant attempt to crush critics. It sided with the dirty-tricksters.

Legal precedent is not on our side, my friends. I fear that the courts may not protect us from the Fairness Doctrine.

The Public Interest

In 1984–85 the FCC conducted an extensive public proceeding to determine if the Fairness Doctrine was "promoting public discussion of controversial issues from balanced perspectives"—which was supposed to be its goal. A huge amount of evidence was presented, including testimony from actual broadcast journalists such as Bill Munroe and Dan Rather, showing that the Fairness Doctrine was, in fact, sabotaging free speech.

In the words of the FCC:

> On the basis of the voluminous factual record compiled in this proceeding, our experience in administering the doctrine and our general expertise in broadcast regulation, we no longer believe that the fairness doctrine, as a matter of policy, serves the public interest.
>
> . . . We believe that the interest of the public in viewpoint diversity is fully served by the multiplicity of voices in the marketplace today and that the intrusion by government into the content of programming occasioned by the enforcement of the doctrine unnecessarily restricts the journalistic freedom of broadcasters.
>
> Furthermore, we find that the fairness doctrine, in operation, actually inhibits the presentation of controversial issues of public importance to the detriment of the public and in degradation of the editorial prerogatives of broadcast journalists.

Listen up, Larry. Here we have the very agency charged with responsibility for the Fairness Doctrine examining its own record and saying, "Hey, it's not working." On August 4, 1987, the Federal Communications Commission demonstrated the courage to change —it abolished the Fairness Doctrine.

Congress was outraged. Senator Ernest Hollings cried, "You've got a bunch of children over there" at the FCC. In every legislative session since, members have introduced bills to re-impose the doctrine. Reagan vetoed the legislation; Bush was able to stop it by threatening to veto it. Now there's a Democratic president in power who has given every indication he'll sign on.

In the meantime, let's take a look, my friends, at what has happened under deregulation.

The Limbaugh Effect

When the FCC concocted the Fairness Doctrine in 1949, it believed that radio stations did too much "entertainment"—music—and not enough "informational programming." In those days, public-affairs or news shows were actually labeled "non-entertainment programming." That's because stations routinely complied with Fairness Doctrine–type licensing requirements by presenting boring public-affairs programs about municipal sewage or the history of debentures. And the public, as demonstrated by its refusal to *tune in*, expressed little or no interest. What kind of "public interest" was served by forcing stations to present programs that audiences didn't care about? This is the logic of the government regulation, in which the symbolic goal of promoting "a diversity of viewpoints" ends up wasting everybody's time.

And then, ladies and gentlemen, I arrived. My show—three hours a day of event-driven discussion, covering every front-burner political, social, and cultural issue imaginable, with callers of all ideological persuasions phoning in to agree or disagree—is precisely what the regulators *said* they were trying to promote. My success has spawned dozens of imitators. It has touched off a frantic scramble to cash in. Even among *public* radio stations, the Limbaugh Effect has been profound. In 1989 there were only eleven non-commercial stations in the entire country devoted to all-news programming; in 1993 there were 184. Isn't it rich? I have helped to revitalize even the boring pseudo-intellectuals of public radio.

Talk radio has been so invigorated that it has jumped right off the airwaves and onto magazine covers and newspaper front pages—everyone is talking about talk radio. Now it is overtaking all the other formats, and hundreds of radio stations are programming more news, and more talk, than ever before.

It would be a joke today for the FCC to refer to informational programming as "non-entertainment programming." On radio, on broadcast television, and on cable television, there is an explosion in the amount of news and information available. It's attracting huge audiences and, therefore, eager entrepreneurs. Now, all-news/all-talk cable-television networks are popping up everywhere: both NBC ("NBC Talks!") and CBS are developing channels of their own, while informational programming already dominates CNN, CNBC, Court-TV, Headline News, The Learning Channel, The Discovery Channel, C-SPAN-1, and C-SPAN-2.

This huge transformation, bringing news and talk out of the non-entertainment backwater and into the mainstream—where Americans actually tune in—has been made possible by deregulation. When the FCC removed rules prohibiting cable operators from bringing in satellite programming, finally allowing competition in the marketplace, television was turned upside down. Today, 62 percent of U.S. households subscribe to cable, and the range of choices on cable systems is the primary reason why. The great opportunities to watch new cable programming are entirely a product of marketplace competition.

The same effect may be noted in radio. The relaxation of federal controls has led to a vast expansion in choice for consumers. Where the old policies of regulation under the Fairness Doctrine failed miserably, a competitive marketplace has responded to consumer desires better than any bureaucrat could have dreamed. For the year 1980, the *Broadcasting Yearbook* listed 110 all-news stations in the United States. By 1992, this number had mushroomed to 530 (see Table 1, on page 136). No kidding: an increase of 381.8 percent.

But that's not all; stations with talk-radio formats increased from 244 to 349 (up 43 percent)—and news/talk, which was not even a category in 1980, grew to 530 in 1992. If we include "public affairs," another whole new category, there was a phenomenal increase in informational program formats: 355 in 1980 to 1,459 in 1992. Driving this success was an increase in FCC-licensed radio stations of exactly 50 percent during the dreaded "twelve years of Reagan-Bush."

Spoiled by Success?

The media's coverage of news, politics, and controversial issues—diverse viewpoints in the marketplace—has skyrocketed under the FCC's deregulatory initiatives. Folks, deregulation is what gives you diversity. Deregulation is what gives you more points of view. Deregulation is what provides the opportunity for even more opinion. When the Fairness Doctrine was in place, designed to assure the discussion of controversial issues, to assure and promote diversity on the air, **there wasn't any!**

Congress should be overjoyed now. Instead, it is hopping mad about "irresponsible viewpoints" being expressed in the press, and particularly over talk radio. Now that the public is able to choose among truly diverse sources, the powers that be don't like what they're seeing and hearing.

All talk radio is not conservative, of course—every kind of viewpoint is coming out of the deregulated communications marketplace. But due to increased competition—and, especially, to *me*—conservatives are no longer excluded. The market is catering to those millions of Americans who feel that the rest of the media isn't telling them the whole story, or has a political and philosophical view at odds with theirs, or holds nothing but contempt for their beliefs. By shining the light of truth, and by not making fun of the cherished values and beliefs of most Americans, I have become, in the words of *The Wall Street Journal*, "the Godzilla of Talk Radio." Nobody put me in that position—no network, no government program, no producer. You in the audience who have voluntarily tuned the dial to my voice—you alone—have caused my success.

Liberals talk about being "pro-choice," but when millions of people make choices they don't like, watch out! With my show and other conservative talk shows out-competing liberals in the market, suddenly "something must be done" to regulate this terrible slant in the broadcasting market. *Talk radio is ruining America! Talk radio is a threat to democracy!*

Of course, the onslaught of Dan Quayle jokes, or the constant vilification of Ronald Reagan—those were no cause for alarm. Limbaugh telling the truth about President Clinton's 1993 budget—warmed over from the failed 1990 budget—now *there's* a crisis.

TABLE 1

RADIO STATION FORMATS: 1980–92			
Radio Station Format	**1980**	**1992**	**% change**
News	110	530	+381.8%
Talk	244	349	+43.0%
News/Talk	0	530	–
Public Affairs	0	50	–
Total	355	1,459	+311.0%

Sources: *Broadcasting Yearbook 1980,* pp. D-74 to D-94; *Broadcasting & Cable Yearbook 1992,* p. A-486.

TABLE 2

RADIO AND TV STATIONS: 1979–92			
Broadcast Station Category	**Jan. 1, 1979**	**Jan. 1, 1992**	**% change**
AM Radio	4,549	4,988	9.7%
FM Radio	4,089	6,036	47.6%
Radio—total	8,638	11,024	27.6%
Commercial TV—VHF	516	n.a.	–
Commercial TV—UHF	216	n.a.	–
Noncommercial TV—VHF	102	n.a.	–
Noncommercial TV—UHF	158	n.a.	–

Sources: *Broadcasting Yearbook 1980,* p. A-7; *Broadcasting & Cable Yearbook 1992,* pp. E-15, E-110.

Exposing the daily absurdities of "the Raw Deal"—that's a national emergency. The fact that you finally have a real choice—call Congress! There oughta be a law! A choice between an entire media industry of liberals on one side, and Rush Limbaugh on the other, is not considered "fair."

Well, I agree: Even with half my brain tied behind my back, they're no match for me.

I Am Equal Time

A liberal's idea of balance was seen in the political sparring on the "MacNeil/Lehrer Newshour": liberal Mark Shields "debating" so-called conservative David Gergen. They always agreed with each other. And now you can see just how conservative Gergen is, as Bill Clinton's chief spin-doctor. To liberals, the genuine conservative view is so absurd and so without merit that it doesn't even register on their radar screens. The dominant liberal culture ignores the conservative perspective because it is so alien to them that it literally doesn't exist.

Flip on the nightly news. It doesn't make a whole lot of difference which network you watch; they're all the same—liberal. That's why I'm so popular, why I've defied the experts, why I've astounded the media elite with the size of my audience. They don't even see the offensiveness of a press corps marching in lockstep, asking the same questions, making the same assumptions, accepting the same analyses.

But when I come along and give people a choice, and millions and millions grab at the chance, liberals react with vehemence against my "one-sidedness." What it means is that now the public is able to get the one side of the news that liberals didn't want to let you have.

The Fairness Doctrine is supposed to stimulate coverage of controversial topics from balanced perspectives. That is exactly what my show helps to do . . . in a real, substantive way—not in some sterile, bureaucratic never-never land of lawyers, "public-interest obligations," and pre-dawn "community programming." "The Rush Limbaugh Show" promotes vigorous debate on news items that would be totally ignored if I didn't bring them up, and infuses the marketplace of ideas with a new energy. And I can prove it.

Just look at how my shows have finally provoked public debate on . . . the Fairness Doctrine. Think about it. Had you even *heard* of the Fairness Doctrine before I started talking about it? Never before has the doctrine been the subject of public discussion. And now everyone is talking about it. Who do you think caused that? Hmmm?

When the Fairness Doctrine was abolished in 1987, who noticed? Yet, since I brought it up on the air, there have been dozens of news articles and opinion pieces all across the fruited plain, all along the political spectrum. The subject has been the focus of an entire show on CNN's "Reliable Sources," has been a front-page story in *Investor's Business Daily,* and has been the subject of lead editorials in *The Wall Street Journal* and *The Washington Post.* The *Los Angeles Times* ran one op-ed in favor of the doctrine, and one opposed. And virtually every television show and published piece discussing the Fairness Doctrine have put my name in the lead.

When the Fairness Doctrine was dropped in 1987, there was no Great Public Debate on its merits. It was, instead, a quiet, almost behind-closed-doors battle fought out among the courts, the Reagan-administration FCC, and the Congress. According to Representative Ed Markey (D-Massachusetts), the chairman of the House Subcommittee on Finance and Telecommunications: "The commission, sensing a window of opportunity, acted on August 4, 1987. First, the commission issued the report required by Congress. . . . The commission then dispatched couriers to the Hill to deliver the report. While those couriers were still waiting for cabs . . . the commission voted to repeal the Fairness Doctrine, an act that many of us will be hard-pressed to forgive or forget. Technically, members of the commission could argue that they complied. . . . They adhered to the letter of the law, but they clearly acted in contravention of the spirit of the congressional command."

Markey was dissed by the FCC—ignoring "the congressional command"! The real issue, Mr. Markey, is not whether you and your Capitol Hill buddies got a chance to debate the issue. The real issue, in a democracy, is whether the citizens had such an opportunity. They did not. Until deregulation, and the explosion of free speech thanks to courageous talk-show hosts such as myself, "the Godzilla of Talk Radio," nobody even knew about it.

Representative Markey, you should be overjoyed that the American people finally have a chance to debate openly this "Fairness in Broadcasting" measure that you're pushing. Instead, you and your colleagues warn that public debate is dangerously unregulated. But I will admit this: If I were in your shoes, I wouldn't want the public to discuss freely what "the congressional command" was up to, either.

And you shouldn't be surprised, my friends, that Senator Ernest Hollings is leading the charge for the Fairness Doctrine in the Senate. This is the same Senator Hollings who crafted an amendment as a favor to Senator Kennedy to punish a conservative newspaper. The amendment would have forced media magnate Rupert Murdoch to divest either Boston TV station WXFT or the *Boston Herald*. Kennedy detested the paper, which continuously editorialized against him, and hoped the measure would deal it a deathblow.

In March 1988, a U.S. Court of Appeals pointedly ruled Hollings's amendment unconstitutional. Hollings, entirely unrepentant, griped that the court "has arrested the policeman on the beat, while the culprit has gone free." That Ernest Hollings thinks of himself as a cop, and of disagreeable speakers as criminals, gives you a perfect window into the mind of a censor.

I say: Let a thousand flowers bloom. If people are willing to read a newspaper, if people are willing to tune in to a TV or radio show, if someone wants to state a view, radical or moderate, let free speech reign. And let the public decide who succeeds.

No one forced me on the public; in fact, I had to form my own network to go national. And the only thing that made that happen was you—the listeners, the viewers, the audience. You were free to choose, and millions of you chose to listen to—or to watch—me. Anyone in America should have just the same right to speak or to listen. And if Congress doesn't like the outcome? Well, as some wise thinkers wrote two centuries ago: "Congress shall make no law . . . abridging freedom of speech, or of the press."

Whether you encounter them in a book, on television, or on the radio, those are among the sweetest—and most American—words you will ever find.

27

A SUMMARY AND PRESCRIPTION FOR THE FUTURE

I TOLD YOU THAT IN THE LATE 1960S THE EXTREME LEFT CAPTURED THE Democratic Party and has been controlling it ever since. Many conservative Democrats have been so frustrated over the years that they have broken party ranks and become Republicans. Others remained true to the party, but became known as Boll Weevil Democrats (conservative Democrats from the South). Many of them, by voting with the Republicans during the early 1980s, made possible the passage of President Reagan's tax-cut package.

The liberal wing of the party has been struggling against increasing pressure from more-moderate elements to stay in control of the party. The Democratic Leadership Council was formed by a group of ostensibly centrist Democrats to nudge the party back toward the center. Bill Clinton, as you know, was very involved with the council. For that reason, among others, many voters were fooled into thinking he was a moderate, a New Democrat.

We have established irrefutably that Bill Clinton is not a moderate and that he is aggressively pursuing a leftist agenda, from his social policy to domestic and foreign policies. Let's admit it. Even many of us who knew that Clinton's self-portrayal as a moderate during the campaign was a ruse still believed he would be pragmatic enough to govern closer to the middle on some issues. Some of us thought, for example, that he would be liberal on social issues and perhaps more moderate on economic ones, if for no other reason than to secure his re-election. But as it has turned out, Mr. Clinton's deceitfulness in campaigning as a moderate has been more than equaled by his unabashed arrogance in governing as a full-fledged liberal. Sure, there are certain anomalous exceptions, such as his support for NAFTA (North American Free Trade Agreement). But for the most part he has been calling plays right out of the liberal handbook.

Let's just review some of the things he's done and others that he's tried. Many of his nominations for the courts and his appointments to various executive positions have been so far to the left that he's actually had to deny knowledge of the nominee's philosophy when the public outcry ensued (to wit: Lani Guinier). But Clinton has been persistent. He has basically worn down his opposition by continuing to offer up for appointment one radical after another. Now, most of them have been confirmed.

In addition to his appointments, Clinton, at some political expense, has veered left on other social issues, such as executive orders on abortion and gays in the military. In domestic policy, as we've said, he's governing to the extreme left by recommending and presiding over the largest tax increase in history. In foreign affairs, he is governing aimlessly enough to be considered a liberal there as well, not to mention his emasculation of the military during the budget proceedings. Make no mistake about it: Despite all of his gaffes, upsets, disappointments, and false starts, Bill Clinton is succeeding in the implementation of his policy agenda. It matters not that his economic bill passed by only two votes in an over-whelmingly Democratic House, and that his vice-president, *Algore*, had to break the tie in a Democratic Senate. The bill passed and it is every bit as legally enforceable as if it had passed unanimously. And, believe me, Bill Clinton is treating it as if he has a clear mandate. You've got to give the guy credit for brazenness.

Having said all that, I'm going to ask your indulgence for a moment. Try to divorce yourself for an instant from your awareness that Bill Clinton is in office and is getting his way on most of his liberal policy proposals. Try to forget for a second that the Democrats have monopolized Congress for the last two generations and that their control seems as solid as ever, notwithstanding recent public scandals that have tainted that body.

What I am going to ask you to focus on, instead, are many of the issues I've been discussing throughout the pages of this book. What do the political-correctness movement, the Fairness Doctrine, the Democrat-controlled Senate Judiciary Committee's character assassination of highly qualified Republican nominees in utter disregard of their constitutional authority, the multiculturalist movement, the environmentalist movement, the anti-American educational establishment, the assault on family values, the frantic effort to rewrite the history of the eighties, the politics of meaning, the radical-feminist agenda, the assault against the Judeo-Christian tradition, and even Bill Clinton's tax bill have in common?

I know what you're thinking: They're all subjects treated in this book; or, they're all being sponsored by the left; or, they are the undoing of this great nation. But those are not the correct answers. The answer, in a word, is *desperation.* The common thread underlying all of these pernicious movements is a mentality of hysteria, panic, chaos, frenzy, and abject desperation. No, my friends, these movements or trends are not the undoing of this great nation. Paradoxically, they are going to lead to its salvation and restoration to sanity.

What we are witnessing are the last desperate gasps of a dying philosophy—a political and social philosophy so adored by the left that it has been adopted by many of them as their religion; their spiritual connection; their politics of meaning. Do not consider the prevalence of liberalism in our cultural, social, and governmental institutions as evidence of the demise of the United States of America. Consider these institutions as liberalism's temporarily occupied zones. (Admittedly, they may have a firmer domination of the major media, with the exception of yours truly: the personification of equal time.)

You can't help but recognize the imminent implosion of liberalism in our society as you behold their last-ditch efforts to impose

343

their views by coercion. It's doubtful whether many of the leading liberals in this nation truly believe in liberalism anymore. As I've told you, many of them cling to it as their only access to power. If they truly believed in their stated cause, they would have no fear of allowing it to stand or fail on its own; in a word, of allowing it to *compete* in the marketplace of ideas. In our educational system, from our kindergartens to our prestigious universities, liberalism has bullied its way into the curriculum, and actively seeks to suppress opposing ideas. From the prohibition of the teaching of abstinence in our grade schools to the suppression of "politically incorrect" speech on our campuses, liberalism is rearing its ugly head in our educational establishment.

If liberals were not themselves running scared, because they are worried sick about the intellectual validity of their orthodoxy, would they tolerate the greatest threat to the First Amendment in our history (political correctness)? As self-styled champions of free speech, would they not vigorously oppose the censorial, Rush Limbaugh–silencing Fairness Doctrine or "The Hush Rush Law," as *The Wall Street Journal* called it in the lead editorial of September 1, 1993? If they thought that they could get their ideas adopted through conventional democratic means, would they resort to such unfair tactics as character assassinations and the destruction of reputations to ensure that liberal judicial activists secure appointments to the land's highest court? (Carter State Department spokesman Hodding Carter, in an appearance on "This Week with David Brinkley," admitted that liberals and Democrats have had to resort to the judicial branch to "legislate" policy that they've not been able to enact democratically.) If they were confident in their ideas, would they totally distort historical facts in order to paint the successes of conservatism as failures and the failures of liberalism as successes? If they believed in the efficacy of their doctrine, would they have to invent such vague constructs as "the politics of meaning" to shamelessly divert our attention from their policy failures? If they truly believed in the scientific validity of their apocalyptic theories on the environment, would they be willing to distort facts to promote their agenda? If they were truly trying to raise revenues from the rich, would they have enacted policies virtually guaranteed to accomplish the opposite result? If they were seriously trying to reduce the deficit, would they not attack the one major culprit, profligate spending, rather than attacking the major-income producers?

No, my friends, for most in that dying breed known as "the left," this is no longer about principle. **IT IS ABOUT POWER AND CONTROL.** And power is a more corruptive influence than money. That's why they are willing to stop at nothing as they experience the worldwide rejection of their ideas.

Instead of losing heart and becoming defeatist about the "apparent" domination of our institutions by liberalism and liberals, focus on what is in their hearts and souls. There you will find their recognition and awareness that they are on their philosophical deathbeds.

Let me put it in perspective for you. Try to be sensitive to your liberal friends. Put yourselves in their shoes as you try to empathize with how they must feel. At the dawning of the sixties, with President Kennedy's inauguration, liberals were anxiously sizing up this nation as their most exciting new laboratory. Now, a third of a century later, most of them know what three-plus decades of liberalism have wrought. Trillions of dollars and thousands of government-expanding, freedom-constricting, and life-controlling laws later, this country is in a total mess. Not by any means an irreversible mess, mind you, but a colossal mess—one that *would* be irreversible, however, if liberal prescriptions could only be used. And what's more, these desperate souls know it. Everything they have ever believed in is shattering and disintegrating before their very eyes. Wouldn't you be devastated as well if one day you awoke to discover that every ideal, every principle, that energized your passions and guided your life was a hoax? Wouldn't you, too, at least for a while, fiercely and stubbornly cling to your lifelong beliefs? Believe me, friends, that's what many of them have been going through. So have mercy on them; be compassionate toward them; hell, be liberal toward them.

Now, back to business. With the disintegration of liberalism around the corner, the Republican Party finds itself at a major crossroads in its history. But at the very time when an ideologically cohesive party could pick up the pieces and forge a sustaining majority, the Republican Party is in total disarray. There are as many factions and movements in this contentious and fractious party right now as there have ever been. As of yet, no leadership has emerged. The infighting and name-calling abound. Add to this the ubiquitous irritant and competitor for the Republican voter, Ross Perot.

Too many people in the Republican Party are busy pointing fingers of blame, rather than trying to re-pitch Ronald Reagan's big tent. Many people have suggested that with our victory over communism and the demise of the Soviet Union, Republicans no longer have an enemy around which they can rally. I disagree. We have plenty of enemies, many of whom I have described for you in this book. But the very framing of that statement betrays a mind-set that I passionately caution against. We Republicans must get out of this negative mode. We are not a party of people cemented together by bonds of negativity. We are a party of ideas—positive ideas; American ideas; ideas that have made this nation the longest-enduring free nation in the history of the world.

We must not view ourselves as the grand opponents or enemies of certain ideas. Maybe that's how we acquired the label "reactionaries." We must not simply react and respond. We must boldly, and actively, take charge. We have ideas to sell and we need to get out there and sell them. Happily and thankfully, we come armed with the knowledge that we are in the mainstream; we are in the majority. Why else do you think my programs are ringing such a harmonious chord among so many in this nation—other than my unique talent, wit, wisdom, insight, incredible humor, cheerfulness, and integrity? . . . All on loan from God, of course.

We must perceive and sell ourselves:

> *Not as the party that opposes government, but that which champions individual freedoms!;*
> *Not as the party that opposes higher taxes, but that which champions entrepreneurship!;*
> *Not as the party that opposes abortion, but that which champions every form of human life as the most sacred of God's creations!;*
> *Not as the party that opposes the expansion of the welfare state, but that which champions rugged individualism!;*
> *Not as the party that hates sinners, but as the party that denounces immorality but forgives indiscretions!;*

See, I Told You So

Not as the party that is mean-spirited, but the party that truly cares about people and their self-worth.

Is the Republican Party the proper vehicle with which to carry conservatism into the twenty-first century? Many Republicans are questioning whether it is. I want to remind you that this same phenomenon occurred during the seventies, when some wanted to defect because of differences within the party. Some conservatives believed the party was no longer capable of articulating the conservative message. Well, we all know what happened in 1980 — Ronald Reagan brought this party together in an unprecedented manner, using conservative themes in the process. Contrary to the beliefs of many country-club Republicans, conservatism is not what scares people off. Indecision, acrimony, and failure to adhere to stated principles are the real culprits.

Though Ronald Reagan is certainly unique and was the best possible leader for the conservative movement and the Republican Party, there is absolutely no reason that either the movement or the party has to be retired with him. And I am sure he would agree. He did not invent the ideas that he popularized. His ideas were grounded in the American tradition; in our unique American culture. Conservatives believe in America and we can re-unite under conservative themes.

So we should neither reject nor abandon the Republican Party. The Republican Party is resilient. It is just sorely in need of leadership. Plus, abandoning it would create a void that literally would catapult Ross Perot's United We Stand movement into even greater prominence. Don't misunderstand me. We must not ignore the Perot voters. They are a very sincere, genuinely concerned, and patriotic lot. They feel they no longer have a political home; and, frankly, you can't blame them. They want candidates who will address the issues about which they are concerned. It is not difficult to identify those issues. Quite simply, they are the federal deficit, the federal debt, and political and governmental corruption.

It is my belief that the Perot coalition itself, however, is fragile in that the "volunteers" may not be in accord on the proposed solutions to those issues. I would imagine that many of them would not be supportive of Perot's economic plan, as it calls for even more burdensome taxes than Clinton's. These Perot people were "volunteers" long before Perot had even written his plan. And regardless of what you've heard, they did not participate in its formulation. Thus, it would be only pure coincidence if they all happened to be in favor of it. They united around their common disgust with government and their feelings of disenfranchisement. In a nutshell, as a group, they are mad as hell and they're not going to take it anymore. Again, this is not a criticism or mockery. I respect their sentiment and, in many cases, share it. I just believe that the Republicans ought to recognize that although Perot's supporters are loyal and united in their frustration, they also are receptive to considering solutions other than those offered by Perot. If the Republicans can just provide the leadership for them to rally around, they will probably be eager to respond.

What, then, should the Republican Party do to solidify its forces and encourage people to come back into the fold? First, we must not interpret the defeat of George Bush or the narrow passage of Clinton's tax bill in the summer of 1993 as a rejection of the conservative ideal. Conservatism is alive and well; indeed, it is thriving on a global level. We must quit making excuses, and admit that we temporarily lost our imagination and spirit. We permitted ourselves to be outmaneuvered in the political debate. It was not slickness or campaign proficiency on the part of our opponents that did us in. We did ourselves in. To rebuild the Republican Party and the conservative coalition, we should unapologetically trumpet the conservative themes of less government, and expanded political and economic freedoms. We must rekindle our pride in those ideas and resist efforts of liberals in both parties, the media and the cultural elite, to paint those ideas as minority, fringe, or extreme. We must forever put to bed the myth that capitalism is based on greed. In the words of Jack Kemp, "it is based on faith"—faith in the individual. Conservatism is the home of the individual, and it is time that we invited the American people back home as we prepare to lead this nation into the twenty-first century.

All of this sounds good, but what, specifically, can we do? First, we need to resolve our intramural conflicts. We can't begin to sell ourselves to the public until we sell ourselves to one another. We need to bring together the neo-cons, the paleo-cons, the religious right, the plain conservatives, and even the moderate Republicans. We must recognize that we need one another if we are to survive as a political force. We must avoid stridency and rancor. As such, we should stress our commonality and de-emphasize our differences. Caveat: This does not mean that we should water down, dilute, or compromise our message. That would be playing right into the hands of liberals and Democrats. Our message should be as clear and consistent as ever. The platform must not be moderate, but unequivocally conservative. But in articulating it, we must do a much better job of presenting our case. We must not allow ourselves to be mischaracterized as cold-hearted, uncompassionate, elitist snobs.

Clinton, Stephanopoulos, and the boys are always saying that they just need to do a better job of explaining their message to the people. They've got it backward. The people understand their message, and they don't like it. That's why Clinton and his boys lie about it every chance they get. But the Republican and conservative message truly does need to be explained, because there is an ongoing, active campaign to distort it.

Here is my blueprint for reuniting the conservative movement and the Republican Party, some of which appeared in *The Limbaugh Letter:*

The Educational System

We need to publicize the message that federal intervention has contributed to the deterioration of our schools. People need to understand the lunacy that abounds in our public schools, from the encouragement of "safe sex" by distributing free condoms, to suppressing freedom of religion. Not all public schools are bad, but overall, the system is bankrupt. It is estimated that three-fifths of our high-school students either drop out or graduate with no more than the equivalent of a seventh-grade education. Why should we continue to prop up this manifestly failed system? The left is obviously more interested in protecting the educational system from much-needed reform than in the welfare of our children and improving their education. We should vigorously promote educational choice and the voucher system to instill competition in our failing schools. By doing so, we will be giving lower- and middle-class families the same mobility as the wealthy by providing them the means to choose the best schools for their children, rather than imprisoning many of them in inferior public schools that are all too often urban war zones. The teachers' unions, the education bureaucrats, and many Democratic politicians believe they should have the prerogative to tell middle-class Americans where their children should attend school. How often, for example, have you heard government officials discuss the possibility of "giving parents the right" to choose the school their children will attend? Give parents the right?! Good grief, this is the United States of America! Who do these people think they are, that they can *grant* (or deny) parents that right? As Bill Bennett says in response to this idiocy, "Let my people go."

Family Values

We must become a people who believe in something—a people of conviction. Despite the constant sermonizing by the media, Republicans did not lose the presidency because they were "co-opted by the right wing" on values. The case on values was simply not made effectively and persuasively. Few Americans would disagree that some of the most serious problems facing America today—crime, drug abuse, AIDS, teenage pregnancy, child abuse, and so on—all result from a breakdown of values. But don't get hung up on labels here. Call it family values, traditional values, or whatever you want; what is important is that conservatives capitalize on this opportunity for them to explain that traditional functional values are what make a society work—what hold it together.

The Environment

Environmental issues will be a fertile battleground during the years to come. If V.P. Gore does nothing else in the administration, he will bring these issues to the forefront in the coming days. All we can reasonably ask for is a thorough public discussion guided by facts and reason rather than hysteria. We need to do our part to expose the true anti-people, anti-business, anti-capitalist agenda of the environmentalists as this dialogue continues. Once people are made to see that the environmental movement is the new home for socialism and that there is an enormous cost to the environmentalist agenda, both economic and political, they will reject its excesses. Flushing out the environmentalist leadership and exposing its real agenda will be difficult, but will be much easier with anxious *Algore* in office.

Local and State Government

We must focus on local and state government. Some of us have forgotten that our movement is not dependent on the presidency alone. Let's not forget the concept of federalism. We say we believe in the governing unit closest to the people, but some of us have become, as grass-roots conservative organizer and Free Congress Foundation founder Paul Weyrich says, "monarchists at heart." The real energy of ideas occurs at the local level. Liberalism survived the Reagan revolution because liberals were so well entrenched in Congress, the state legislatures, the city councils, and the school boards. That is from where the power flows, and that is where conservatism needs to flourish.

Foreign Policy

In redefining their platform, Republicans must not ignore the critical issue of foreign policy, just because the Cold War is over and the Soviet Union has disintegrated. In fact, some would argue that our world, even including Russia, is much less stable today than before because there is no balance of power to preserve the peace. As Third World nations develop weapons of mass destruction and delivery systems for them, it is imperative that we construct a cohesive and consistent foreign policy. As guiding principles in this area, I suggest that Republicans advocate the promotion of the national interest as our highest priority. We can vigorously support democratic movements throughout the world and promote human rights, but we must always be guided by military and diplomatic realities and our national interest. With such guiding principles it will be easy to justify our intervention in some areas, e.g., the Persian Gulf; and not others, e.g., the Balkan states.

The Economy

Any discussion about building political coalitions must ultimately

351

deal with the economy. As economic issues are always paramount in politics, especially during peacetime, we need to direct our heaviest artillery to this area. Supply-side economic policy should be our rallying point. All people abhor taxes. Cutting marginal tax rates and capital-gains taxes to stimulate productivity is a populist theme that conservatives and Republicans have exclusively owned. As long as we can convince the people that: a). cutting tax rates did work in practice during the 1980s and b). tax cuts are not responsible for the exploding federal debt (spending is), we can again make this a winning issue. By talking about growth and opportunity we can cut across cultural, economic, social, and racial lines to reach all people. If we approach this with optimism and confidence, we can rebuild the conservative tent to include not only Reagan Democrats, but Perot's volunteers and minorities as well.

The Party of Growth, Hope, and the American Dream

I can't state strongly enough that the Republican Party must be the party of growth. It is not acceptable for House or Senate Republicans merely to respond to Bill Clinton and the Democratic Congress that they want to cut spending first. *This vagueness and vacillation about their willingness to raise taxes have got to go.* Either they are Republicans or they are not. And if they are going to sit there and go along with tax increases when taxes are as high as they are, they have no business calling themselves Republicans; they have no right to expect people to vote for them instead of the Democrats, and they do not deserve to be re-elected. The Republican Party is and must always be the party of growth, of private enterprise and entrepreneurship, of rugged individualism; of hope; of the American Dream.

Optimism

Most of all, it's important that we don't get depressed and become defeatists. We just can't be naysayers and cynics anymore. On the contrary, we should be of good cheer and a positive mien. Ronald Reagan would not have won his elections in 1980 and 1984 without his upbeat demeanor—without that smile on his face. And the most significant goal Reagan accomplished—even more impressive than ninety-six months of uninterrupted economic growth without inflation—was to restore the confidence of the American people, the sense that this is indeed a great country. There's a lesson in that. Sourpusses, people who are constantly bitter and angry at the world—the Outraged—don't prosper in America, no matter how right they may be on the issues. That's why we've all got to keep our spirits up.

Political conservatism is the logical home for the great majority of Americans, because it champions the principles upon which this nation was founded. As we work together to rebuild our party, we should always remember that our cause is quite noble: The Republican Party is the primary vehicle to ensure that the United States of America adheres to the political and economic principles that have made it the greatest nation in the history of the world.

INDEX

Achievement, 9, 20, 33, 245, 263
    academic, 186, 188, 189, 194
    discrimination based on, 280
    negative attitudes toward, 12–13,
        24–25
    punishing, 29, 53–65, 125, 272
    rewarding, 7, 275
Acton, Lord John, 136
Adams, John, 73, 280–81
Adler, Jonathan, 175
Adorno, Theodor, 238
Affirmative action, 25, 151, 243, 245,
    284
Aid to Families with Dependent
    Children, 217
Aidid, Mohammed Farrah, 257
AIDS, 23–24, 161, 217, 222,
    224–26
Ailes, Roger, 28
Ainge, Danny, 11–12
America, 16, 23–33, 174, 245
    confidence in, 16–17, 352–53
    dumbing-down of, 185–99
    greatness of, 8, 276–77
    mischaracterized as rotten, corrupt,
        unjust, 25, 66, 129, 172, 184, 253,
        276
    myth of decline of, 252
    worth fighting for, 249–61

American Civil Liberties Union, 38,
    195
American culture, 274–75, 276, 278,
    284, 285, 347
American Dream, 12, 15, 16, 54,
    107–08, 123, 245, 308
    Clinton's attack on, 306–07
    Rush Limbaugh and, 32–33
    Republican Party and, 352
American Indians, 68, 69, 70, 174,
    183, 237
Anti-Americanism, 129, 130, 159,
    163–64
Anti-capitalism, 28, 159
Aspin, Les, 260
Audience (Rush Limbaugh), 1, 17,
    18–22, 103–04, 214, 243, 287,
    337, 339

Baby-boom generation, 253–54
Bake sales, 102–03, 108, 190–92
Barkley, Charles, 244–45
Bartlett, David, 328
Bartlett, Robert, 113
Bennett, William, 84, 95, 191, 290,
    350
Bias crimes, 231–35
Bible, 70, 73
Bill of Rights, 72, 137, 266, 326

INDEX

Black family(ies), 91, 95–96
Blacks, 69, 91, 114
  conservatives and, 243–45, 247–48,
    293–94
Bloom, Benjamin, 192–93
Body of Liberties (Mass.), 72
Bosnia, 222, 227, 255–58, 277
Bradford, William, 70–72
Brett, George, 23, 61
Broadcast licenses, 324, 328, 330, 333,
    334
Broadcast television, 334
Broadcasting deregulation, 333–34,
    334, 339
Brock, David, 236–37
Brown, Hank, 104
Browner, Carol, 40, 162
Budget deal (1990), 296–97, 298–99,
    300–01, 304
Budget deficit, 44, 115, 163, 289
  rise and fall of, 303f
  see also Deficit reduction
Budget process, 139–40
Budget Reconciliation Act, 292
Budget Reform Act of 1979, 139
Burke, Edmund, 73–74
Bush, George, 35, 36, 42, 43–44, 117,
    121, 123–25, 160, 219, 220, 228,
    233
  Bosnia policy, 220–21
  cabinet, 140
  defeat of, 348
  departure from Reagan policies,
    295, 296–97
  and Dole, 249–52
  foreign policy, 256
  Haitian policy, 214–15
  1990 budget deal, 300, 302,
    304–05
  press treatment of, 288, 289
Bush administration, 84, 166, 277

Caine, Michael, 208
Capital-gains tax, 308–09, 352
Capitalism, 54–55, 58, 87, 107, 149,
    272–73, 348
  see also Free market; Market
    economics
Carter, Hodding, 344

Carter, Jimmy, 35, 38, 112, 114, 124,
    147, 254
Carville, James, 146
Censorship, 73, 237, 323, 330–31
Central planning, 58, 164, 166
Chancellor, John, 20
Charitable giving, 114, 121–22
Chase, Alston, 176
Cheney, Dick, 254
Chicago public schools, 193
Children, 25, 40, 92, 95, 217
  challenging, 28–29, 185–86
  crimes by, 100
  family structure and, 97–98
"Children of the Rainbow"
  curriculum, 195–96
Children's Defense Fund, 40
Christopher, Warren, 255
Citizens Against Government Waste,
    168
Civil disobedience, 86
Civil religion, 277, 278
Civil rights, 76, 243
Civil Rights Act, 135–36, 244
Civil rights movement, 244–45
Clark, Joe, 187
Class envy, politics of, 15, 53, 54
Class warfare, 64–65, 118, 248,
    280–81, 295
  Clinton theme, 9, 54–55, 58–59,
    64, 300
Clintonmania, 292
Clinton, Chelsea, 36, 196, 199
Clinton, Hillary Rodham, 36–37,
    40–41, 129–30, 169, 216, 218,
    233, 253, 324
  and health-care reform, 141, 142–57
Clinton, Roger, 239
Clinton, William, xiv, 13, 16, 32, 72,
    106–07, 110–11, 112, 114, 122,
    165, 191, 192, 246, 273, 324
  advisers, 24, 40
  cabinet, 140–41
  campaign, 25, 53, 152
  class warfare theme, 9, 54–55,
    58–59, 64, 300
  domestic policy, 342
  economic policy, 118, 123, 124–25,
    138–39, 289–90, 295–308, 335

educational policy, 198–99
foreign policy, 255–56, 258
inauguration, 277–78
industrial policy, 167–68
leftist agenda, 36–37, 341–42, 343
lies, 43–44, 46–52, 220–21, 349
and meaning of words, 214–16
and minimum wage, 270
as New Democrat, 25, 34–36, 37,
    38–39, 41–44, 124, 150, 216, 341
presidency, xv, 86, 159, 253, 263
press treatment of, 288–91, 292
and Rush Limbaugh "joke," 240–42
socialism of, 267–68
State of the Union Address, 127–28
tax policy, 61, 343
values of, 128–30
Clinton administration, xiv, 12, 29,
    108, 217
Clintonianism, 275, 280
Cold War, 6, 87, 251, 253, 304, 351
Collier, Peter, 146
Columbus, Christopher, 67–68, 69
Communism, 253, 263, 266, 346
Compassion, 6, 63, 272
liberals and, 80, 149, 150, 217
Competition, 12–13, 28, 55, 155, 262,
    272
in education, 186, 187, 188, 199
Condom distribution, 196, 197, 207,
    223, 348
Congress, 115, 159, 340
budget process, 139–40
deficit reduction, 115, 117
Democratic control of, xv, 343
exempt from laws, 134–36, 157,
    162
Congressional Budget Office, 44, 114,
    268–69, 302
Conservative movement, 88, 349–53
Conservative worldview, 281–85,
    292
Conservatives, 125, 274–75, 288
Conservatism, xiv–xv, 20, 73, 107,
    287, 347, 348
benefits of, 216–17
blacks and, 243–45, 247–48,
    293–94
in Clinton campaign, 35–36

and race, 239–48
values in, 284
Constitution, 7, 55, 72, 73, 76, 96,
    137, 264, 324, 325
evolving, 265–66
Conyers, John, 239
Cook, Fred, 330–31
Cranston, Alan, 161, 162
Crime, 131–33, 160–61, 223
bias-motivated, 228–29
by children, 100
poverty and, 83, 281–84, 285
Criminal law, 86, 228–29, 231–32
Cultural institutions, 86–87, 88, 264
Culture, 96, 162, 198, 274–85
Culture War, 78–79, 87–88, 91
Cuomo, Mario, 119, 215–16, 274

Dan's Bake Sale, xiv, 101–09, 190–91
Daughtry, Herbert, 283
Decade of Greed (1980s), 9, 67,
    110–26, 128, 223, 224, 269
Declaration of Independence, 75, 190
Deficit reduction, 41–42, 115–17, 139,
    218, 307–08, 345
bake sales in, 102–03, 108, 190–92
Clinton plan, 220, 221, 296,
    297–99, 301–04
Defining deviancy down, 97, 99
Dellums, Ronald V., 24
Democratic Leadership Council,
    38–39, 124, 341
Democratic National Convention,
    37–38, 86, 228
Democratic Party, 15, 35, 37–38, 243,
    244, 246
and deficit reduction, 304–05
liberal wing of, 96, 341
and 1990 budget deal, 297
Dependency, 4, 5–6, 37, 64–65, 124,
    134, 138, 217, 244
breaking cycle of, 7–8
educational system and, 186–87
liberalism empowered by, 63
Desert Storm, 15
Dingell, John, 324
Dinkins, David, 222–23
Discipline, 97, 189–90
Discrimination, 194, 279–81, 283

Dole, Robert, 249–52
Donaldson, Sam, 117
Douglas, William O., 330
Downey, Morton, 31, 32
Dukakis, Michael, 35, 38, 206
Dumbing-down, 185–99

Earth in the Balance (Gore), 162–63
Economic democracy, 39
Economic growth, 54, 153, 272, 297
    1980s, 112–13
    tax increases and, 304, 305–08
Economic policy, 42–43, 111–12, 118,
    123, 124–25, 138–39, 160,
    289–90, 295–308, 335
Economy
    conservative blueprint for, 351–52
Education, 75–76, 84, 265, 343
    funding for, 197–98
Educational system, 13, 75–76, 183,
    344
    liberal follies in, 184, 186–99
    conservative blueprint for, 349–50
Egalitarianism, 28, 55, 186
Ehrlich, Paul, 180, 181–82
Einstein, Albert, 262, 266
Electronic media, 324, 326–27
Empowerment, 63, 82, 92, 134
Entitlements, 102, 137–38
Entrepreneurs, 5, 29, 57, 117, 245
Entrepreneurship, 65, 107, 263
Environment, 350–51
Environmentalism, 151, 168–69,
    171–84, 343
    Gore and, 159, 160, 162–65, 168,
    169, 174, 176, 179
Envy, politics of, 64–65
Equal time, 337–40
Equality, 15, 33, 272
    goal in education, 191–93, 194
Equality of opportunity, 137
    vs. equality of outcomes, 7, 55, 276
Equality of outcomes, 7, 13, 55, 194,
    266–67
Escalante, Jaime, 23, 29, 187
Estrich, Susan, 206
Excellence, 2, 7, 10, 20, 33, 275
    academic, 186, 187, 199
    in military, 259

pursuit of, 4, 14–15, 28, 29, 125
Excellence in Broadcasting (EIB)
    Network, 12, 17–18, 27, 146,
    292

Fairness, 15, 23, 54, 58, 64, 122, 267,
    276
    in broadcasting, 325–27
Fairness Doctrine, 324–25, 330–31,
    334, 335, 337–40, 343, 344
    history of, 327–30
    and public interest, 332–33
Fairness legislation, 324–25
Family(ies), 40, 99, 149
    nuclear, 84, 96, 98, 99, 217
    single-parent, 94–95, 99
    two-parent, 92, 94–95, 97, 98
Family values, 93–94, 96, 146, 183,
    285, 343, 350
Feder, Don, 146
Federal Communications Commission
    (FCC), 327–28, 329, 330–31, 332,
    334, 335, 338–39
    Mass Media Bureau, 329
Federalism, 351
Federalist Papers, The, 136, 325
Feminism, 200–13, 237, 276, 343
Fernandez, Joseph, 195
Firestone, Martin E., 331
First Amendment, 195, 229, 236, 288,
    323, 326, 327, 344
First Amendment law, 330–31
Flowers, Gennifer, 144
Foley, Thomas, 190, 218, 298,
    300–01, 324
Ford, Gerald, 38, 250
Foreign policy, 255–58, 351
Forests, 171, 175–77
Founding Fathers, 7, 73, 74, 76, 136
    and press freedom, 328
Frank, Barney, 136
Fraud
    decade of, 127–41
    in environmentalism, 178–79
Free enterprise, 25, 57, 71–72, 73,
    102, 107, 243
Free market, 7, 60, 175
Free-market economy, 57–58, 62,
    284–85

INDEX

Free speech/expression, 230–31, 234, 236, 344
  political correctness and, 227, 228, 231
Freedom(s), 74–75, 76, 77, 97, 254, 272, 276–77
Freedom of Choice Act, 161
Freedom of speech, 323–25, 340
  Fairness Doctrine and, 328–29, 332–33
Freedom of the press, 323–25, 326, 340
Freedom without responsibility, 84, 94, 129
Friedman, Milton, 125, 267
Fund, John, 120–21
Fundamental Orders of Connecticut, 72

Gatto, John Taylor, 187–88
Geneeson, Penny, 212
General Instruments (co.), 166
Gephardt, Richard, 300
Gergen, David, 35, 240, 337
Get-even-ism, 202, 244, 259
Ginsburg, Ruth Bader, 135
Glickman, Carl D., 192–93
Global warming, 163, 169, 171, 179–81, 265
Goldwater (Cook), 330
Goldwater, Barry, 85, 287
Goldway, Ruth, 39
Goodman, Ellen, 259–60, 261
Goodman, Paul, 129
Gore, Al, 34, 53, 67–68, 106–07, 158–70, 174, 342
  environmentalism, 175, 176, 179, 350, 351
Gore, Tipper, 162, 164
Government, 79, 134
  and economic performance, 123–24
  limited, 72, 73, 76, 262–73
  role of, 2, 5, 8, 25–26, 74, 122, 147, 150, 168, 264, 266, 267–68
  and social problems, 7, 64, 76
  and unemployment, 26–27
Government intervention
  in economy, 55, 58
  in health care, 154–57

Government regulation, 172, 333
Government spending, 118, 122, 298, 304, 307
  cuts in, 138–39, 140, 298–99, 304, 305, 307, 352
Gramsci, Antonio, 87–88
Gray, John, 277, 278
Great Depression, 83, 131, 250, 253, 282
Greenberg, Stanley, 124
Guinier, Lani, 35, 36, 342
Gun control, 132–33

Hackney, Sheldon, 233–34, 235
Haiti, 182–83
Haitian refugees, 42, 214–15, 246
Hargis, Billy James, 330
Hatch, Orrin, 135
Hate crimes, 228–31, 232–35
HDTV, 166–67
Health care, 61, 155, 266, 288
Health-care reform, 41, 44, 217, 299
  Hillary Clinton and, 141, 151–57
Hedonism, 83–84, 97
Hefner, Bill, 324–25
Hill, Anita, 236–37
Hilts, Elizabeth, 201
Hinckley, David, 17
Higher education, 83, 210, 235–36
History, teaching of, 66–77
Hollings, Ernest, 324, 332, 339
Hollywood, 182, 225–26
Homosexuality, 196, 207, 278
Homosexuals, 95, 210
  in military, 24, 36, 259–60, 342
Hooker, Thomas, 72
Horowitz, David, 146
Housing starts, 289
Humanism, 130, 276
Humphrey, Hubert H., 37, 96
Hussein, Saddam, 254, 256
Hutchison, Kay Bailey, 228

IBM, 57–58, 167
Ice T, 81
Impellizzeri, Irene, 195
Individualism, 8, 9, 55, 64, 77, 199, 262–63, 275, 284, 293, 352
Industrial policy, 167–68

Invisible hand, 24, 27, 117

Jackson, Jesse, 55, 80, 246–47, 248
Jacobowitz, Eden, 232–34, 235, 237
Japan, 166, 167, 290
Jefferson, Thomas, 147, 190
Jeffries, Leonard, 82–83
Job creation, 27, 36, 117, 123
   1980s, 112, 114, 121
Job skills, 25–26, 165–66
Johnson, Lyndon, 36, 37, 95, 192, 330
Judeo-Christian tradition, 76, 93, 276,
   343

Kansas City Royals, 30, 61, 112
Karp, Walter, 75
Kay, Dan, 101–02, 103
Kemp, Jack, 60, 113, 348
Kemp-Roth tax cut, 113, 121
Kennedy, John F., 125, 330, 345
Kennedy, Robert F., 192
Kennedy, Ted, 136, 160, 324, 339
King, Larry, 325, 328
King, Martin Luther, Jr., 69, 192, 244
Kirkpatrick, Jeane, 256
Kleinfeld, Judith, 235
Koch, Ed, 283
Koppel, Ted, 85
Krauthammer, Charles, 147
Krueger, Bob, 228
Kudlow, Lawrence, 140, 307–08
Kunstler, William, 283

Lear, Norman, 182
"Learning for Mastery," 192–93
Left (the), 96, 214, 256–57, 341
   cultural warfare, 87–88
Lerner, Michael, 146–47, 148–50,
   151, 173, 216, 218
Lesbians, 212
   male, 210–11, 213
Lewis, Anthony, 9
Liberal mind-set, analysis of, 126,
   127–41
Liberal worldview, 281–85
Liberalism, xiv, 6, 8, 15, 21, 29, 67,
   76, 77, 101, 102, 110
   and big government, 73
   as dying philosophy, xv, 343–45

empowered by dependency, 63
facts and lies, 287–94
failure of, 147–48, 344
faith in government, 273
fundamental fallacy of, 150
of Gore, 161–62
hallmarks of, 272
jargon of, 309–22
new-age, 130–31
and obsolescence of values, 78–89
poisons the soul, 78–81
values in, 275
view of America, 276
Liberals, 8, 20, 79, 188, 278
   ideas about America, 274–75, 278
   intolerant of opposition, 237–38
   knee-jerk, 79–80
   and meaning of words, 214–15,
      219–22
   and role of government, 2–3,
      262–73
Lies/facts relationship, 286–94
Limbaugh Effect, 333–34
Limbaugh Letter, The, xiii, 46, 102, 104,
   349
Lincoln, Abraham, 242–43
Lindsey, Brink, 167
Local government, 351
Long, Monique, 204–05
Los Angeles riots, 5, 79, 80–81,
   84–85, 91, 281
Luxury tax, 59–60

McAllister, Linda Lopez, 210–11
McGovern, George, 37, 38
McKenzie, Richard B., 121
McKinney, James, 329
MacKinnon, Catharine, 206
Madison, James, 73, 136
Magaziner, Ira, 39
Managed competition, 61, 156
Market economics, 54, 61–62, 131
Marketplace, 123, 125, 148–49
   broadcasting in, 334, 335
   and job skills, 165–66
Marketplace of ideas, 325–27, 338
Markey, Ed, 324, 338–39
Marx, Karl, 71, 145, 264
Materialism, 281, 284, 285

INDEX

Matthews, Chris, 240
Mayflower Compact, 70
Media, 88, 125, 183, 275, 335–37
  Hillary Clinton and, 144, 145
  liberal, 142–43, 173, 223–24,
    292
  and political correctness, 236–37
  and Quayle, 90, 91
  see also Press
Media culture, 29, 291–92
Media establishment, 5, 80
Medicaid, 154
Medicare, 154, 155–56
Mediocrity, 28, 33, 187
Memorial Day, 260–61
Metzenbaum, Howard, 161
Military (the), 6, 15, 24, 113, 253, 261,
  264
  downsizing, 254, 255
  gays in, 24, 36, 259–60, 342
  role of, 258–61
Miller, Sherrol, 212
Mills College, 208–09
Minimum wage, 25, 63, 217, 268–71
Minorities, 243–44
  see also Blacks
Mitchell, George, 56, 80, 157, 218,
  301, 324
Mondale, Walter, 35, 38
Moral absolutes, 81, 93
Moral relativism, 77, 129, 196, 211,
  219
Morality, 7, 81–82, 83, 84–85
  Hillary Clinton and, 143–45, 151
  legislating, 85–86
  as matter of choice, 208
Morning After, The (Roiphe), 205
Mosbacher, Robert, 166
Moseley-Braun, Carol, 222
Moynihan, Daniel Patrick, 56, 95–97,
  271–72
Mueller, John, 218
Multiculturalism, 66–67, 69, 235, 276,
  343
Munroe, Bill, 328, 332
Murdoch, Rupert, 339
"Murphy Brown" speech, 90–91,
  93–94, 96
Myers, Dee Dee, 241

NASA, 264–65
National Basketball Association, 11,
  13–14
National Council for Civic
  Responsibility, 331
National Education Association, 162,
  188
National Endowment for the
  Humanities, 233–34
National Football League, 13
National Rifle Association, 132–33
New Age, 34, 151, 173, 216, 253
New Deal, 131
New Democrats, 20, 34–45
  Clinton as, 25, 34–36, 37, 38–39,
    41–44, 124, 150, 216, 341
New World Foundation, 41
New York City, 271–72, 279
  school system, 195–96, 197
New York Times, The, 9, 12–13, 174,
  212, 224, 270, 289, 297, 299, 301,
  330
New York Times Magazine, The, 143,
  144, 145, 172–73, 205, 263
Newman, Edwin, 180
Newsletter (Rush Limbaugh), 3, 88,
  107
  see also Limbaugh Letter, The
1960s, 128–30, 143, 149, 192, 251,
  264, 341, 345
1960s generation, 86–87
1980s, 53–54, 87–88, 109
  Decade of Greed, 110–29, 216, 269
  economic record of, 289, 301
  history of, 67, 296, 343
1990s, 127–41
Nixon, Richard, 38, 62–63, 192, 328
North, Oliver, 241
NOW (National Organization for
  Women), 210

Omnibus Deficit Reduction Act of
  1993, 111
Optimism, 7, 15–16
  Republican Party and, 352–53
Ordinary people, greatness of, 18–22
Out-of-wedlock births, 95–96, 98
Outcome-Based Education, 28,
  188–90, 192–94

INDEX

Outcome-Based Education *(cont.)*
  social agenda of, 194–95
Ozone depletion, 169, 171, 173,
  178–79, 180, 265

Page, Clarence, 242
Panetta, Leon, 299–300
Parents, 28, 98–99
  and education, 188, 189, 199
Parum, James, 198
Paternalism, 25, 165, 186–87, 217,
  285
Patriotism, 276, 277
Perot, H. Ross, 35–36, 37, 346,
  347–48, 352
Persian Gulf war, 255, 256, 277, 288,
  304, 351
Personal responsibility, 7, 24, 108–09,
  188, 246, 247, 248
Pharmaceuticals industry, 60–61, 143,
  152–53
Phillips, Wayne, 331
Phillips Curve, 113
Pilgrims, 69–72
Planned Parenthood, 195
Political cleansing, 227–28, 232–34,
  235, 236, 237, 238
Political correctness, 40, 67, 209,
  227–38, 276, 343, 344
  lexicon of, 309–22
  in textbooks, 192
Politics of meaning, 142–57, 194, 216,
  304, 343, 344
Popular culture, 99, 208, 275
Poverty, 84, 91–92, 114, 245
  and crime, 83, 281–84, 285
Poverty programs, 115, 265
Powell, Colin, 24
Premarital sex, 194–95, 196
Press (the), 326
  liberal bias of, 288–91, 292
Price controls, 62–63, 155–56
Profits, 53, 54–55, 57–58, 152
Property rights, 71, 281, 306
Public interest
  Fairness Doctrine and, 332–33
Punishment, grades of, 97
"Putting People First" plan, 36–37,
  43, 219

Quayle, Dan, 43, 44, 90–100, 335
Quindlen, Anna, 224, 242–43

Race, 239–48
"Racial Justice Act," 160
Racial quotas, 194, 276
Racism, 68, 69, 135, 231, 234–35,
  238, 241–44, 248
  political correctness and, 232–35
Radio, 324, 334
  see also Talk radio
Radio Act of 1927, 327
Radio program (Rush Limbaugh),
  56–57, 88, 102, 127–28, 159,
  172, 191, 292–94, 299
  and Limbaugh Effect, 333–34
  success of, xiii, 2, 3, 18–20
Radio stations, 333–34, 336t
Rape, 202, 203–04, 205–07
Reagan, Ronald, 16, 109, 110–26,
  143, 146, 155, 160, 216, 250,
  333, 346
  cabinet, 140
  deficit, 302
  economic policy, 295
  leadership, 106, 347
  optimism, 352
  press treatment of, 288, 289, 335
  record of, 54
  tax cuts, 301, 341
Reagan administration, 84, 277
Reagan-Bush period, 121, 295–96
Reagan coalition, 35–36
Reaganomics, 111, 120, 123, 125,
  295–96
Real Anita Hill, The (Brock), 236–37
Real income, 112, 113–14, 115
Red Lion v. *FCC*, 330–31
Rehnquist, William, 231
Reich, Robert B., 4, 24, 25–27, 39, 58,
  168, 263, 267
  and minimum wage legislation,
  268, 269, 270, 271
Reischauer, Robert, 156
Relativism, 86–87
Religion, 151
  and schools, 84, 85, 188, 195, 349
  in U.S. history, 69–73, 76
Reno, Janet, 239–40

INDEX

Republican Party, 36, 345–46
    agenda for, 346–53
Reverse discrimination, 280
Richards, Ann, 228–29
"Right of reply" rules, 330–31
Rights, 76, 95, 137, 266, 276
    new, 264
Riordan, Richard, 272
Risk, risk-taking, 25, 26, 57, 125
Roiphe, Katie, 205, 206, 207
Roosevelt, Franklin Delano, 36, 37, 138
Rousseau, Jean-Jacques, 145, 263–64
Rowan, Carl, 133
Ruder, Bill, 328
Russia, 87, 153, 262, 263
    see also Soviet Union

St. Valentine's Day Massacre, 96–97
Santayana, George, 74
Sasser, Jim, 301
Savage, Fred, 204–05
Say's Law, 117–18
Scalia, Antonin, 265–66
Schmidt, Benno, 236
School-choice movement, 199, 349–50
Schroeder, Pat, 24, 268
Schundler, Bret, 272
Schwarzkopf, Norman, 15, 260
Second Amendment, 266
Secular humanism, 77
Seib, Gerald, 152
Self-esteem, 28, 247
    goal in education, 186, 188, 189
Self-reliance, 7, 8, 9, 25, 33, 63–64, 100, 102, 199, 275, 293
    for blacks, 244, 246, 247, 248
    ethic of, 5
    among poor, 284
Sexual harassment, 196, 202–05, 207, 208, 236–37
Sexual revolution, 213
Sexuality, 207–08
Shalala, Donna, 4, 23, 40, 209, 235, 324
Shearer, Derek, 39
Silver, Ron, 277–78

Smith, Adam, 24, 27, 117, 145
Social engineering, 186, 194, 263
Social experimentation, 271
    in the military, 259, 260
Social policies, liberal, 131–33
Social problems
    government and, 6, 267–68
Social spending, 218
Socialism, 39, 67, 87, 121, 131, 149, 158, 266, 281, 351
    Clinton and, 122, 128, 130
    in early U.S., 71–72
    flaw in, 55–56
    U.S. gravitation toward, 267–68, 275
Socialized medicine, 153, 154, 157
Soil erosion, 163, 174
Solomon, Andrew, 263
Somalia, 257
Soviet Union, 58, 254, 275, 346, 351
Sowell, Thomas, 244, 247–48
Speech codes, 235–36
Spirituality, 150–51
State government, 351
Statism, 87, 128, 130, 137, 158–59
Stephanopoulos, George, 216, 349
Stevens, William K., 174
Success, 4, 7, 54, 187, 190
Success (Rush Limbaugh), 1–3, 16, 18–19, 24, 27, 29–33, 57
Supply and demand, 62, 117–18
Supply-side economics, 59–60, 72, 113, 117–18, 119, 165, 352
Supreme Court, 85, 190, 228, 229
    and Fairness Doctrine, 326, 330–31
Symbolism over substance, 63, 150, 191, 224–26, 237, 270

Talk radio, 3, 18, 26–27, 30–32, 325, 333–34, 335
Tax cuts, 120, 352
    middle-class, 42–43, 219–20
Tax increases, 117, 297, 298–99, 302, 308, 342
    and economic growth, 304, 305–08
Tax rates, 116*t*, 117–18, 122, 136, 218, 298, 301–02, 305–06, 352
Taxes, taxation, 4–5, 59–60, 79, 114, 115, 151

Taxes *(cont.)*
   under Clinton, 36, 44
   and economic performance, 120
   and prosperity, 131, 154
Technology, 164–65, 166–67, 174,
   175
Television show (Rush Limbaugh),
   88, 172, 191, 239–40, 260–61,
   299
   success of, xiii, 2, 3, 18–20
Television stations, 336*t*
Ten Commandments, 84, 85, 196
Tenbrock, Christian, 120
"Thirty-five Undeniable Truths of
   Life, The," 78, 81, 200
Thomas, Clarence, 236–37
Thought police, 227–38
Tocqueville, Alexis de, 64, 75–76
Tornillo v. *The Miami Herald*, 326
Trickle-down economics, 53, 60, 117,
   118–20
Truth, xv–xvi, 200, 208, 219, 241
   in Rush Limbaugh programs,
   286–87, 292–93, 335
2 Live Crew, 82
Tyson, Laura D'Andrea, 24, 40, 120,
   167–68

Underclass, 64, 92
Unemployment, 26–27, 38, 91, 112,
   114, 153, 218, 252, 270
Unemployment benefits, 25–26
United We Stand, 347–48
University of Wisconsin, 209–10
Unwed motherhood, 91, 99
   see also Out-of-wedlock births
Upward mobility, 9, 123
Utopianism, 58, 264, 266–67, 272,
   275, 279

Values, 7–8, 21, 76, 78–89
   American, 275, 279
   liberals' use of, 145–46, 147, 148,
   275–76
   poverty of, 90–100, 217
   relative, 208
Van Cliburn Competition, 12

Victimization, 209, 244
Victims, 64, 80, 81, 205, 284
Vietnam War, 37, 86, 258
Virginia Military Institute, 209

Wall Street Journal, The, 120, 124–25,
   148, 152, 157, 165, 202, 218, 233,
   236, 270, 271, 335, 338, 344
Wanniski, Jude, 113
Washington, D.C., 153, 161, 272
Washington, George, 73
Washington Post, The, 43, 144–45, 178,
   179, 328, 338
Waters, Maxine, 55, 80
Watt, Kenneth E. F., 181
Way Things Ought to Be, The
   (Limbaugh), xiii, xiv, 2, 110, 120,
   236
Wealth creation, 55–56, 60, 123
Wealth redistribution, 29, 54, 93, 122,
   131, 150, 151, 243, 267
Welfare, 92, 102, 265
Welfare programs, 41, 124
Welfare state, 6, 64, 121, 217, 243
Weyrich, Paul, 351
WGCB, 330–31
White House Correspondents' Dinner,
   240–42
Whitehead, Barbara Dafoe, 95
Will, George, 117
Williams, Walter, 245–46
Wilson, Edward O., 172–73
Wirth, Tim, 181
Withers, Josephine, 207
Women, 203–04, 206, 259–60
Words mean things, 214–26, 256
Work ethic, 63–64, 284
World War II, 131, 250–52, 253–54
World War II generation, 253–54, 261
Worrell, Howell, 280

Yellowstone National Park, 176

Zappa, Frank, 162
Zenith (co.), 166
Zero-sum game, 55–56, 60, 120, 154